International Development Management for Public and Nonprofit Organizations

T0270980

Managing international development and aid programs often relies on trial and error and flexibility. Practitioners need a mix of management theory and field practice to prepare them for work in other countries—transitional, developing, wealthier, and poorer alike. Filling an important gap in the literature for graduate students and practitioners in the public sector, private firms, contractors, and nonprofit organizations that manage development assistance projects, this is a guide to dealing with core issues likely to be faced in doing field work.

International Development Management for Public and Nonprofit Organizations offers an accessible primer on the basics of managing and motivating people, teams, and organizations. It focuses on challenges and opportunities to managing in difficult cultures and contexts, including hostile political regimes. The book takes a deeper look at management in four sectors: public finance, urban transport, K–12 education, and natural resources and the environment. Presented throughout the book are 28 cases, designed to stimulate critical discussions, as well as five technical exercises to allow integration of theory and practice. This textbook is supplemented by slides for teaching along with a sample syllabus. It is addressed to current and future international aid managers, including those enrolled in international management and international development courses at the university level. Professional development organizations, such as contractors, nonprofits, and donors, will also find the book a useful addition to their training materials.

George M. Guess is an Adjunct Professor in the Schar School of Policy and Government at George Mason University, USA. He is the author of *Building Democracy and International Governance* (Routledge, 2018) and co-author, with Thomas Husted, of *International Public Policy Analysis* (Routledge, 2016).

"*International Development Management*'s practical, core-issue contributions will be of considerable value to current and aspiring professionals in public and non-governmental positions. The detailed and engaging case studies and experiential exercises provide outstanding practical learning opportunities. Professor Guess' extensive experience in the field and as a public administration professor richly informs his treatment."

Peter Koehn, *Professor Emeritus in Political Science, University of Montana, USA*

"International development projects, however carefully researched and elegantly designed, often fail at the implementation stage because of the unanticipated challenges facing project managers. George Guess' important new book offers operational remedies to these challenges. It is a must read for aspiring development professionals."

Andrew S. Natsios, *Executive Professor, George H.W. Bush School of Government and Public Service; Director, Scowcroft Institute of International Affairs, Texas A&M University, USA*

"Guess' book offers insight into, and skills to navigate, the most difficult managerial challenges of international development, from weak institutions to corruption to under-resourced budgets. The light-hearted approach is chock-full of examples and deceptively effective to equip the next generation of international aid managers."

Christine R. Martell, *University of Colorado Denver, USA*

International Development Management for Public and Nonprofit Organizations

George M. Guess

Routledge
Taylor & Francis Group

NEW YORK AND LONDON

Designed cover image: © Getty Images

Cover should be viewed while listening to "Stranded in the Jungle" by the Cadets (1956).

First published 2024
by Routledge
605 Third Avenue, New York, NY 10158

and by Routledge
4 Park Square, Milton Park, Abingdon, Oxon, OX14 4RN

Routledge is an imprint of the Taylor & Francis Group, an informa business

© 2024 George M. Guess

Library of Congress Cataloging-in-Publication Data
Names: Guess, George M., author.
Title: International development management for public and nonprofit organizations / George M. Guess.
Description: New York, NY : Routledge, 2024. | Includes bibliographical references and index.
Identifiers: LCCN 2023055583 (print) | LCCN 2023055584 (ebook) | ISBN 9781032670928 (hardback) | ISBN 9781032670881 (paperback) | ISBN 9781032670959 (ebook)
Subjects: LCSH: Economic development projects--Management. | Nonprofit organizations--Management.
Classification: LCC HD75.8 .G77 2024 (print) | LCC HD75.8 (ebook) | DDC 658/.049--dc23/eng/20240309
LC record available at https://lccn.loc.gov/2023055583
LC ebook record available at https://lccn.loc.gov/2023055584

ISBN: 978-1-032-67092-8 (hbk)
ISBN: 978-1-032-67088-1 (pbk)
ISBN: 978-1-032-67095-9 (ebk)

DOI: 10.4324/9781032670959

Typeset in Sabon
by KnowledgeWorks Global Ltd.

Access the Support Material: www.routledge.com/9781032670881

Table of Contents

Detailed Table of Contents

Preface

Managing international development programs and projects is a work in progress. Much of it is trial and error and being flexible enough to try new approaches. This practice-heavy and theory-light approach is widely used despite the extensive academic background, linguistic skills, and overseas experience of many aid managers and staff. Needed for graduate students and practitioners in the public sector, private firms, contractors, and nonprofit organizations that manage development assistance projects, this is a guide to dealing with core issues likely to be faced in doing field work.

International development assistance consists of projects/programs funded by grants and loans that are designed and executed by donors or private contractors and NGOs whose purposes are to stimulate income and employment opportunities in transitional and developing countries. Management of these efforts requires skills in adapting to novel political cultures, performing fiscal, revenue and budget systems and talents to move processes in sectors such as education, transport, and environmental protection. University programs in public policy, nonprofit management, and public administration include courses in international development and international or comparative public administration which focus on the sources, uses, and impacts of aid. The traditional division of subject area is international business, nonprofits (NPOs/NGOs), and public sector work. The work boils down to managing public assistance to achieve overseas development, which is roughly like managing domestic public assistance to build personal resilience and institutional capacity. The work of most international aid managers requires stringing together all three markets, such as a private contractor executing a bilateral and multilateral donor contract using local staff as well as expats from multiple countries. Or an aid manager might work with NPOs executing donor contracts or on a host government contract with local country funding. International managers must manage and navigate these spheres and types of employees.

This book is addressed to current and future international aid managers. Such practitioners need a mix of management theory and field practice to give them an idea of what work in other countries, transitional, developing, wealthier, and poorer is like. The approach is what is called "experiential learning", where readers and students in training and technical assistance on the job share their professional needs with instructors, professors, or expat trainers. The context is a field setting where the purpose is to get the task or job done well. It is experience-based with a high premium on sharing experiences to derive practical lessons. In this sense, the "experiences" are scenarios, hypothetical sets of facts, some of which are derived from real cases and situations, others that are derived from relevant films and literary observations.

Professional development organizations, such as contractors, nonprofits, and donors, should find the cases and materials of this book as a useful addition to their training materials: International City Management Association (ICMA) in Washington DC, Government Finance Officers Association of Canada and the US (GFOA) in Chicago, IMF and World Bank Institutes also in Washington, DC. The topics of this book also parallel those given for IDM executive education certificates by the Center for Strategic and International Studies (CSIS) in Washington, D.C. The chapter topics are called modules and delivered as short courses over the course of 1-1/2 days.

The origin of this book is principally from my graduate MPA course in *International Management* offered at George Mason University's Schar School of Policy and Government and which I have taught for the past ten years. The GMU structure is similar to that of about 40 public policy, administration, and international affairs schools in North America and the UK. Such schools are subdivided into multiple degree offerings. The Schar School, for example, offers the MPA and MPP degrees with concentrations in international management and international development as well as the MA in Political Science and International Affairs degrees. International development, public, and nonprofit management courses can be taken by graduate students who are accepted into the Schar School. Many of these schools also offer undergraduate degrees in public policy, administration, political science, political economy, and international development that might well use this textbook in upper division courses. Nevertheless, the Schar School structure, course availability, and degree offerings are common to universities across North America.

International Development Management for Public and Nonprofit Organizations or IDM is divided into four parts. First, we discuss the basics of management: what it is and is not. This includes guru advice on managing people, teams, and organizations. We examine the results of current trends as digital trends to monitor and evaluate management and the tendencies to micromanage staff outputs with digital reporting and oversight systems. Many of these efforts have turned into mechanical exercises at the cost of substantive results. We discuss generic management issues in national (often recognized as public administration or public sector management) and international organizations, as well as private firms, and NGOs that work in overseas international development. Many excellent works are available on international development and this book will not attempt to replicate them.[1]

This book presents 28 often provocative cases that it is hoped will stimulate critical discussions, and five technical exercises to allow integration of theory and practice.

Second, we cover the larger context of management, including such topics as how to deal with the problems of motivating teams and individuals in puzzling political cultures that have often been weaponized by hostile regimes. What are some effective adaption methods? How can conflict be minimized? Here we present cases of common problems faced by managers in transitional and developing countries. The cases point to ways that conflicts and issues might or might not be favorably resolved. The book focuses on management as opposed to policy-making and implementation at the strategic level. It is an international management book not one on policy-making or analysis.

Third, managers routinely spend most of their time trying to sort out and resolve problems. Managing is problem-solving! Some are routine and actionable others are ill-structured and messy. They are harder to define and resolve. To resolve them managers must first identify them and their associated sub-issues. Managers typically focus their limited resources at the operational or technical level. Efforts at the strategic level are the remit of higher level policy managers as distinguished from those who deal with the daily routine problems of systems maintenance. When defining problems, managers must also identify and anticipate obstacles to successful implementation of programs and projects and minimize them. Often the obstacles are routine and could be identified beforehand by comparative analysis of similar projects to reveal lessons that could have been absorbed from their project planning phases.

Finally, international development managers or IDMs typically work in sectoral areas at the technical level. The book will focus on management of four sectors: the public finances, urban transport, operating and reforming K–12 education, and natural resources and the environment. It is important that international managers gain experience in one or more sectors as aid projects are typically aimed at particular sectors that can be critical to country development, such as preventive health or water management.

Those with practical interests and problem-solving skills applied to international development may be employed initially by one of the many development aid firms or NGOs that exist in such places as London, Berlin, or the US. Such organizations survive on winning aid donor contracts to execute overseas projects and on donations from a variety of sources to deliver specific services, such as meals for the hungry and homeless. NGOs work at home and abroad to deal with such universal problems. In the overseas aid industry, your colleagues will include a variety of types. For example, home office administrative support staff, home office managers, and supervisors attached to your group and its project portfolio. Others passing through your firm or NGO will be short-term consultants working on a specific project task, such as training in Ghana. STTA will work overseas on short-term assignments according to project timelines that can be two to five years. Others are long-term project personnel, such as chiefs of party and resident advisors. They serve for several years then may move on after project completion to another firm and project consistent with their skills. You will discover that some long-term people can spend most of their 20–25 year careers doing this, rotating from one country to another, and that they have no physical homes in their countries of origin. I met two such people in Pakistan in the early 1990s while working on an ADB project. Because of threatening geopolitical tensions with India and local anti-Western activities, ADB ordered us to evacuate the country. Two New Zealand judicial reform experts plead with ADB to let them stay because they had no homes or families to go back to! ADB sent them to London until the dust settled!

Preface Note

1 On economic and social development see for example: Albert O. Hirschman (1964) *The Strategy of Economic Development* (New Haven, CT: Yale University Press); and Hirschman *op.cit.* (1971) *A Bias for Hope: Essays on Development and Latin America* (New Haven, CT: Yale University Press); Gerald Meier and James E. Rauch (eds) (2005) *Leading Issues in Economic Development (8ᵗʰ ed.)* (New York: Oxford University Press); Brian Levy (2014) *Working with the Grain, Integrating Governance and Growth in Development Strategies* (New York: Oxford university Press).

Acknowledgments

The author wishes to thank the invaluable assistance of Shannon Wellens in the technical formatting and editing of this manuscript for Routledge. I would like to thank: Laura Varley, Alexandra McGregor, and Elizabeth Hart at Routledge for their patience and support in framing my thoughts for this book. I also want to thank my aid pals for their friendship, insights, pointers, and criticisms over the years. Many have been guest lecturers in my GMU *International Management* graduate course at the Schar School of Policy and Government over the past ten years. Some are no longer with us. Aid pals include Bill Allan (IMF), Malcolm Holmes (WB), John Crotty (IMF), Jack Diamond (IMF), Dennis DeSantis (DAI), Steve Rozner (DAI), Eric Nelson (DAI), Graham Scott (New Zealand DOF), Sandy Mackenzie (IMF), Elnar Dervishi (DOF Shkoder, Albania), Darian Diachok (USAID), Paul Guenette (DAI), Don Mickelwaite (DAI), Jorge Irisity (COP, Nicaragua, Dominican Republic), Bob Klitgaard and Ken Koford (301st Civil Affairs Group alums), Rob Grosse (U. Miami), Bob Saunders (COP, Kyrgyzstan), Charles Denton (my friend and mentor, CID/Gallup Costa Rica), Jim Wesberry (ICGFM), Bobbie Mircheva (my friend and DAI colleague from the Bulgaria local government project), Jorge Sanguinetty (Dev-Tech), Malcolm Greene (Bannock Ltd), Ivan Kostov (MOF Bulgaria), Vesselka Shertreva (Bulgaria DAI local government project), Juan Bautista Schroeder (my friend and mentor at OAS Costa Rica), Janine Manns (Nathan Associates), Jim Budds (DAI public administration reform project in Albania), Jim Rowles (my longtime friend), John Blomquist (Abt Associates, Kyrgyzstan), and Bob Ebel (WB). My colleague Paul Posner came up with the term "pracademic" to describe university professors who during their careers traveled back and forth between teaching on campus and overseas technical assistance, training, and applied research. That list includes Ron Chilcote (my UCR thesis advisor), Mel Gurtov (my longtime friend and UCR committee-member), Paul Farnham (my GSU co-author and now CDC staffer), Alberto Guerierro-Ramos (my professor and friend at USC), David O.

Porter (my professor and friend at UCR), Stephen Peterson (PFM pracademic), Christine Martell (my friend, aid colleague, and co-author at University of Colorado, Denver), Brian Levy (my friend and neighbor: WB and SAIS), Jorge Martinez Vazquez (my friend and mentor at GSU), Roy Bahl (my friend and mentor at GSU), Ted Poister (my best "frenemie" at GSU), Don Axelrod (my almost colleague at SUNY Albany), Bill Dunn (my colleague and mentor at U Pittsburgh), Tihana Bartulac-Blanc (my friend and CDEM Deputy Director at AU), Bernard Dafflon (my colleague at U Fribourg in CH), John Petersen (my colleague at GMU and in Pakistani aid work), Stepan Toepler (my colleague at GMU), and Jeff Straussman ("pracademic" first class at SUNY, Albany). Of course, none of the above people are responsible for any mistakes of fact, omission, or exaggeration found in this text. They are all mine!

Over the years, the author was team leader for various projects, including the budget and tax reform in Romania; budget specialist on multiple Bulgarian projects; director of research for the Local Government Initiative of the Open Society Institute in Budapest; budget specialist for the public administration and local government reform projects in Macedonia and Albania, respectively; budget specialist for the World Bank budget reform and internal audit project in Nicaragua, and chief of party for the Pakistan fiscal decentralization project funded by Asian Development Bank (ADB).

He graduated from UC Berkeley (BA) and Riverside (PhD) in political science and holds an MPA from USC in Los Angeles.

In addition, he was director of the master's in public policy program at Central European University (CEU) in Budapest; and co-director with pracademic Robert Pastor of the Center for Democracy and Election Management (CDEM) at American University in Washington, DC. He was a Fulbright Professor to Uruguay at Universidad de la Republica in Montevideo and later to Costa Rica, Honduras, and Belize in the Fulbright Central American Research Program to continue studies on forestry policy. He was an Organization of American States fellow (OAS) to Costa Rica for dissertation field work for two years.

The author wishes to thank his family: wife Regula, his two sons Andy and Marty, and grandson Kian for their patience, encouragement, and understanding. As always, their continued support has made all things happen.

1 Dimensions of Management

Learning Outcomes

These are guides for students and faculty on what to expect in each chapter and what one should reasonably be able to do after reading and discussing the cases and contents of the chapter.

1 To distinguish the meaning of management as a noun vs. verb.
2 To develop criteria for identification of the most important person in an organization, group, or team.
3 To explain the ingredients of effective management.
4 To distinguish Theory X from Y managing styles in *Discussion Case #1: Incident in the Oriente* by Paul Theroux.
5 To explore your experiences of putting together teams, managing them in different tasks toward different objectives, such as finding useful decision-making information, winning a game, and beating contract competitors.
6 To engage in role-playing exercises in which team leaders must deal tactfully with sensitive situations. *Exercise #1.1* focuses on Moses and his team in *Oriente* which performing their construction tasks poorly and of which he has lost authority and control. *Exercise #1.2* focuses on Warburton and his assistant at the *Borneo outstation*. Both are class exercises in which feedback is solicited from the class and me.
7 To discuss whether Moses was an ineffective leader but an effective manager. Or was he an effective leader but an inefficient manager?
8 To identify the likely theoretical and practical problems of motivating and managing groups. What kinds of theories are most useful in guiding managers to be efficient and effective? (e.g., economic, sociological, anthropological, political?)
9 To explore ways Warburton could resolve the interpersonal conflict with Cooper in the context of the Borneo outstation in *Discussion Case #2* by Somerset Maugham.

DOI: 10.4324/9781032670959-1

10 To suggest techniques to avoid people just getting on your nerves. How can managers prevent that from happening and maintain objective distance from team members?

11 To explore why people do what they do? Institutionalized role behavior? Having a bad day...? Class snobbishness and conceit? Class resentment? Simple bad manners? Inability to control impulses such as resentment and anger? Racism? Reverse racism? Control by social media? How can managers respond with professional self-control, "boldly and humbly" in each instance?

12 To explore strategies of trust-building within and between organizations.

13 To apply the bullying criteria of offensiveness and intimidation to aid project managers, such as Cooper and Moses, to distinguish driven and task-motivated managers from those unreasonably and persistently aggressive.

14 To explain the problems of recruiting, promoting, sacking, and laying off staff.

15 To detail the main determinants of managerial effectiveness, e.g., understated competence, team management, communicative with all sorts of people, emotionally mature, boringly dependable, and confidently aggressive.

16 To explain the strengths and weaknesses of methods to stimulate productivity and strengthen organizational culture.

17 To review effective methods for establishing team collaboration and avoiding bullying for large, complex, and novel multi-objective projects.

Preface to Development Management

First, some basics.... What is management? And what is good or effective management? Management is considered an "intangible asset" which also includes human capital, intellectual property, and software. Like physical assets, such as equipment, property, and inventory, intangibles such as management contribute to economic growth and development. But unlike physical assets intangible assets are not included in commercial enterprise book value. A common foreign assistance goal (both for host countries and aid projects as well) is to increase "management capacity" and "logistical knowhow"[1] which means a combination of greater investment and targeting funds to what can achieve this best. Given the fluffiness of the management concept, the capacity-building goal is somewhat tautological: allocating more funds and know-how to identifying the best methods of increasing management capacity in the first place! "International management" is even more elusive in that its effectiveness is constrained by political culture and institutional factors in other countries. Small- and medium-sized commercial firms, city management of municipal services such as refuse collection and disposal and public transport, and NGOs have to not only manage their finances to deliver basic needs such as meals for the homeless and aid to citizens infected by viruses but also negotiate their effectiveness space between unsupportive states and civil societies. These provide some of the clearest examples of challenges faced by international managers.

In general, governments and businesses consist of organizations that are structured to carry out functions by assigning roles to distribute funds and dispense rewards and sanctions. Commercial, public sector, and non-profit organizations deliver medical services, provide education, prepare to fight wars, and fight them, and mine for ore, oil, and gas. Structures can be centralized or decentralized and report to voters, shareholders, or city councils or quasi-public boards. Governmental institutions perform societal functions such as judicial, rule of law, electoral, environmental, foreign affairs, security, financial, and fiscal. The institutions that perform these are strong or weak, effective, or ineffective and responsive to public needs or insular and self-serving.

Organizations must be managed within the frameworks of protocols and routines geared to outputs of their particular services or products. A rough guide to purposes can be gleaned from the formal organizational chart. Managers perform tasks according to their roles to achieve short- and long-term goals. Tensions often arise between roles, tasks, available resources, reporting burdens, and managerial capacity to direct staff to achieve objectives. Frictions between individuals generate petty squabbles and conflicts. This is especially true for overseas projects with personnel from different cultures and levels of experience. Instabilities are caused by sudden redefinitions of roles and reassigned responsibilities. Funds may be added or cut, objectives can be changed in mid-project, and of course managers can be easily replaced. Unlike structures that are fixed, these items such as tasks, resources, and personnel are variable making for an unstable and challenging tenure in organizational employment. An important managerial task is to maintain control while minimizing internal frictions, tensions, and threats to smooth operations.

This chapter introduces the concept of "management" as both a hierarchical position (noun) and a set of skills applied to activities or tasks (verb). The ingredients of effective management as a position consist of adequate authority and defined responsibilities. The four structural necessities or core ingredients of effective management are as follows: First, an appropriate hierarchical role and job description. One needs to know the scope of their job tasks and responsibilities which will likely be some of the metrics on which you will be evaluated. Second, one needs adequate authority for such changes as transfers of budget funds between line-items and for personnel decisions such as hiring a chief of staff and removing teachers. Third, managers need to receive receipt of timely personnel and financial performance information from other departments in the organization. Fourth, one needs clear accountability and reporting lines and the preferred team or unit performance criteria and responsibilities. Without these core ingredients, the "manager" is just a position on the organizational chart—like a toy steering wheel on a dashboard that doesn't control the wheels of the real car.

The core skills for effective management are leadership, goal-setting, motivation, and mentoring. A common paradox is that the manager must motivate teams to achieve goals and objectives. The manager must also motivate remaining staff to keep working after layoffs. Here the manager must demonstrate fairness, assurance to remaining staff, and allocate remaining workloads fairly in the eyes of his/her teams. Core management tasks include personnel, budgeting, and paperwork/process. That means a capacity to tell staff what they are expected to do and why they are doing it. Most skills and tasks depend on the ability to write disciplined memos and reports that are brief, clearly themed, and well-structured. It is said that successful leaders often create the right conditions so that others can achieve ambitious goals. Challenges arise such as how can a leader-manager avoid destructive internal competition and conflict between employees? The manager will have to identify whether roles have been defined and differentiated to avoid endemic personnel conflict. In worse cases, situations of low-level chronic dislike are endemic, and everyone appears to dislike everyone else. The unit still functions, but people are unhappy. The manager must also explore strategies to be more sensitive to small group dynamics and role definition and differentiation to achieve more successful results.

Managers must perform four tasks. First, they must lead and inspire staffs and teams of personnel, dealing with such tasks as recruitment, motivation, monitoring, and evaluation. A distinction is often made between *management* and leadership. It is said that leaders are skilled in motivating and inspiring staff to do what they otherwise might not do. But managerial candidates should also have *leadership* skills in order to motivate and inspire their staff to perform tasks and take on additional challenges. So, despite the oft-noted observation that leaders may not be adept at detailed and inspirational management, and technical or operations managers may not be effective leaders, the distinction may lack a real substantive difference. As discussed below, leadership may be harder to achieve when managing and attempting to inspire high-performance actions from staff in different political cultures. Second, they must direct staff through processes, from project management and specification development through procurement to implementation all according to regulatory and licensing systems. The more unique part of the overseas management job is that processes must be led and managed through a contextual filter of sociocultural and political forces that affect organizational and project efficiency and effectiveness. An example of this would be a manager of local operations for an international forestry firm, or of a donor-funded forestry project to improve sustainability consistent with international forestry standards.

Third, managers must prepare and deliver budgets consistent with annual calendar schedules. Most importantly, they must control budgets: defending cash flows and maintaining incomes and operations in response to the data in regularly reported cash flow and income statements. Fourth and finally, aid technical assistance and training often zero in on sectors, such as urban transit, education, and the environment. Other sectors not covered in this book are health care, energy, elections, sanitation, and water and sewerage. Sector management, such as urban transit, requires specific skills related to procuring equipment such as rolling stock or logistical systems such as signaling. Such operations management skills can be transferable to defense and postal service sectors, but less so to others such as social assistance services.

The contextual challenges to performing these four tasks in unstable poor countries are treacherous. International development management (IDM) is a unique talent or set of skills and experiences that equip one for almost any challenge in any sector. After working for a few years in a quasi-war zone for a failed state, one feels as a survivor in combat, complete with life-long regimental solidarity with one's project team!

Managers in public sector, NGOs, commercial firms, and city-state enterprises will perform the four types of tasks in varying degrees depending on their status. Employees in these organizations may have line or staff roles, meaning they function at a technical-operational role, often in sectors such as urban transport or environmental regulation. Their status may also depend on background, such as engineering or science personnel who often begin in operational roles and may "graduate" to senior staff members. Many line personnel prefer to stay in operational field-level roles to avoid the paperwork of what they view as desk-type jobs. Employees may rotate within large international development firms and organizations: from HQ to overseas project chief of party (COP), to field work, and finally to individual plumbing-type assignments, common in public financial budgeting, accounting, auditing, and evaluation work. Organizations may rotate personnel as a matter of course to provide them with experiences at staff-line levels, performing tasks in multiple sectors such as education, environment, and finance.

The Quest for Development

For more than a century, development has been variously defined and used as rationale for aid spending to help poor people. "Development...". What then is development? To define "it" as sustained generation of income and employment opportunities or growth with equity is excessively mechanical, narrow, and utilitarian. To really "develop" countries and upgrade their human development on the broader UN Human Development Index (HDI) scale, a definition must include broader quality of life and socioeconomic measures. As an in-country specialist, you work on projects to fix slices of the development pie, to respond to basic needs. The basic needs consistent with your project terms of reference (TOR) might be effective health care systems for patients, a very large piece of the pie that encompasses narrower needs to get back to work and earn income to improve the quality of people's life and that of their families.

Or, you might be charged with planning, financing, procuring, and implementing a road or school construction project. To do this you conduct appraisals for projects and local contractors as well as train project workers on how to do these tasks when your job is over. The road project is a narrower slice of the pie with wide benefits to road users and school system students. You learn quickly from trying to purchase supplies that the institutions and systems for procurement are weak and that the relevant laws and regulations for transparency of prices and quality are not enforced. The bidding and procurement systems are also like many places you have worked, including rich countries, riddled with financial leakages and corrupt practices. You gradually learn of your team worker's family hardship stories when invited to their homes or socialize with them after work. For instance, banks are directed to loan to the friends of the often-illiberal political regime and other insiders, some of whom you report to in the respective ministries of public works and education for your project. As noted by North et.al,[2] poor countries exhibit outward forms of modern public institutions but are in fact functionally merged with private sector profitability interests in a "neopatrimonial" relationship. Real institutional functions are opaque in what Riggs (1964) called poor and "prismatic societies". Transparency and neutral decisions are belied by such local corrupt practices as "limited access orders" to extract rents and resources from the state (Fukuyama, 20, 26). Such mechanisms limit fair competition and access to rents by all but a few insider monopoly interests. The "way things are done around here" benefits extractive mining interests seeking concessions beneficial to them but not to country development. Institutional purposes are distorted by the draw of vast financial gains and profits. You also find that the civil service is inward directed (not a public serving operation at all!) and largely filled with ghost workers, paid no-shows that have other jobs to do when they should be delivering and maintaining service operations. No assistance or support usually can be counted on from any local public institutions. Your project is "host country" so as far as the donor, other than producing useless reports to them you are on your own! Banks mostly do not lend to your workers or their families for personal or commercial loans, and this stymies savings and investment needed for growth and wider development.

Thus, the red flags are there even in the narrow slice of the pie for which you are responsible. Institutional incentives are misaligned, rule of law is weak and unenforced, and land tenure is insecure affecting the productive use of both urban and agricultural land as collateral and collection of fees and taxes. Land titles can rarely be used as collateral for bank loans obstructing savings needed for wider development. Growth and development are blocked by such multiple obstacles as obtaining bureaucratic approvals for any action large or small—such as spending approved money or transferring funds between budget items as managerial needs shift during project implementation. All these are constraints to your project goal of creating "feasible entry points".[3] These are where "modest changes in one part of the system can evoke adaptations in other parts, in a cumulative process". You would like to get the sector and its systems on their way to effective production of public services and construction of capital assets. To you, looking at the big picture, that would be development progress.

But you realize that the actual "way things are done around here" persists and will be hard to change in the short term. You recognize how such obstacles and problems constrain development progress of almost any kind and why underdevelopment persists in poor countries. Some development projects achieve spectacular successes. Others do and then are blocked by wars, coups, pandemics, and natural disasters. Such experiences can move expat aid workers to despair of real country curses blocking their paths! You had even hoped that your project might contribute to liberal democracy since ultimately you would like to convince the illiberal regime to allow rule of law, political accountability, and individual if not comprehensive human rights. How naïve! But you don't want your trainees and co-workers treated as immature children after you leave.[4] You pursue this backdoor path to changing regime incentives for benign development. You are confident that a common pattern of open markets and open societies leads to real institutional and socioeconomic development. All that is required is to institutionalize political accountability and rule of law and create a well-functioning state. Your project can help by overcoming local obstacles and implanting modern norms and practices, at least in the procurement area. This would be an important access point to stimulate: fiscal discipline and program accountability in the state.[5]

During your management work and observing personal and institutional reactions, you learn more about the larger context of constraints and opportunities as well as their theoretical bases and discover that the UN has narrowed "development" down to 17 "sustainable development goals" or social development goals (SDG), such as clean water and poverty reduction, for which it tracks progress each year. Whatever "it" is, external financial and technical assistance is necessary if not sufficient to move these indicators. How to create income and employment opportunities for the poor....? By providing basic and effective health care and educational systems.... By providing budgeting and financial management systems to ensure national and municipal services receive funds and are able to generate and mobilize their own sources of revenue.... By providing basic environmental protections and resilience against floods, fires, and other natural disasters.... By providing basic local transportation options for people who cannot afford to buy cars but need good roads to at least ride their bikes on.... Development assistance targets such sectors in its projects and can assist countries in providing income and employment opportunities through improving as a means to that end.

For such reasons, smarter aid (DA or overseas development assistance, ODA) design and management is necessary. Aid systems reforms to this end will be covered in **Chapter 8**. Operationally, development is the creation of income and employment opportunities which as they grow in number lead to national growth. Development is growth with equity. Development and well-being require a supportive state that provides safety nets, roads, energy, health, safety, and security. Because poor country states are often weak and serve as transmission belts for corrupt rent-seeking that drain treasuries for often socioeconomically useless public investments, they fail to support sustained growth or even growth spurts, choking off national development. In short, the relationship between growth and development is non-linear, largely a function of the backward and forward linkages provided to suppliers and secondary finishing industries that are generated by such linkages. Those opportunities are maximized by good managers and leaders.

In short, it can be said that growth is a necessary but not sufficient condition for development. Poorer countries can still have higher human development indices (HDIs) if the distribution of wealth is relatively egalitarian.[6] Economic growth ((gross domestic product (GDP)) is a function of demand and expectation of demand for products from car and truck manufacturing, chemicals, semiconductor, and food industries which all invest, train, and absorb labor, which in turn generates more investment and growth. Growth then requires capital expenditures or new orders for investment goods. In principle such orders and investments can be made by private firms or public (i.e., China) to increase their GDP and growth. More importantly, capital investment decisions require stability or reduction of economic and political uncertainties. For growth to turn into socioeconomic development investments, trade and aid are all required in different mixes depending on the country's context.

From Trade and Investment to Development Assistance

The lines between aid, trade, and investment are increasingly blurred today. International trade began hundreds of years ago with initiatives sponsored by states in order to obtain raw materials and natural resources abroad. Sponsoring states sought geopolitical and defense outposts abroad. Dutch, Belgians, British, Germans, Ottomans, Russians, French, and US efforts were competitive. All discovered that stable states were essential and that core investments were required such as ports, roads, electricity, water, sewerage systems, and thus most worked in their own ways to build these in order to at least protect their investments and country nationals that worked there. And the Chinese, with an aggressive commercial culture, learned how to fuse aid, trade, and investment together from observing then copying the examples of Western cultures in action on their own turf. More importantly, the need for overseas management capacity in donor country programs and host country states in supporting areas of municipal services and infrastructure investments and maintenance was evident to all countries engaged in early trade for their respective national interests and "empires". Aid to enhance local development was mostly a byproduct but essential to these undertakings. The inevitable result is that Chinese trade, aid, and investment activities today are fused together.

China just signed up 21 more Latin American/Caribbean countries to its massive Belt and Road Initiative (BRI), an effort to string together geopolitical, investment, trade, and development initiatives. Apologists for Western aid efforts see this as a threat to existing bilateral and multilateral development institutions. As I told my Chinese ministry of finance (MOF) classes ten years ago in Washington, no one has a monopoly on development, and all must follow roughly the same paths to achieve success in the well-known core sectors such as education, health, transportation, security, environmental protection, and agriculture. Those who deviate or try shortcuts with crash investment projects often lose money, fail, and end up with embarrassing "white elephants". Badly appraised BRI projects have ended up increasing debt burdens of countries such as Pakistan to unsustainable levels. Nevertheless, the BRI example is instructive for development planners and managers. Between the years 2005 and 2021, China invested billions of dollars in the region mostly in mining and energy. Last year, the yuan surpassed the euro as the second most important foreign currency for Brazil's central bank. Further, a Chinese state-owned power company purchased a Peruvian power supplier to give the Chinese a near monopoly over their electricity grid. Among other major transport infrastructure projects, the Chinese are constructing a megaport at Chancay near Lima. Thus, geopolitical ties have followed economic trade and investment ties in an almost classical sequence of growing influence.

The final link is Chinese provision of economic aid and technical assistance. China has engaged local law enforcement agencies in Latin America. They have trained police in Argentina and Brazil, donated cars and investigative equipment to Nicaragua and Costa Rica, and sold surveillance equipment to Ecuador.[7] Security and law enforcement is an area where technical assistance and training and equipment are needed. In many countries of the region, security and law enforcement is the top issues for locals often besieged by criminal gangs and lawlessness. The local security issue will be examined further in **Discussion Case #12** on Brazilian police budgeting. But since the late 1960s, law enforcement has been an area that the US has barred itself from providing technical assistance and training. In that era, the US provided torture equipment to the Uruguayan military police and security services to be used against the Tupamaros. The outcry from the US public over revelations from the "Dan Mitrione affair" after the kidnapped CIA official posing as a us agency for international development (USAID) traffic specialist became a famous Costa-Gavras film "State of Siege" (1972). The exposure resulted in a Congressional ban on DA aid to local police forces that still prevent any assistance to those institutions. The Chinese have effectively and usefully filled this vacuum.

Another example of how growth from foreign investment and trade can lead to sectoral development is provided by the Scott Paper Company pulp and paper mill in Costa Rica, the first to serve the Central American market. In the late 1970s, USAID supported a small farmer pulpwood supplier scheme. Selected farmers around Turrialba were given fast growing exotic pine saplings and provided extension to learn how to care for them—planting, pruning, and harvesting. The farmers were growers providing primary inputs to the growing pulp and paper-making industry. The time needed for mature pulpwood in the Turrialba region was only about five years. In the interim period, the farmers could earn other income from sales of pruning and fencepost. The pulp and paper factory had received tax credits from the Government of Costa Rica (GOCR) for initial construction of the mill conditioned on buying pulpwood from designated suppliers to provide them steady incomes, technical skills, and employment. The project developed a secondary manufacturing base for pulp and paper to substitute imports and generate export revenues. That dynamic contributed to national growth and wider forward and backward industrial development linkages to the furniture manufacturing and construction materials sub-sectors. The GOCR scheme also provided tax credits, apprenticeships, and vouchers for participants to learn trades in the forest sector in newly established forestry management programs at several state vocational institutes in Costa Rica.

Private vs. Public Sector Management

Good managers are needed in both public and private sectors to stimulate and sustain growth and development. Most enterprise managers are charged with satisfying shareholder values and maximizing profits. Nevertheless, modern public sector managers must know what commercial investment means and why it is critical to development. They work constantly with private firms and capital markets to raise funds, for instance, on municipal bond markets to finance infrastructure. To work effectively with private firms, hire private consultants, and manage private contractors, they must have the skills to negotiate contracts and concessions that if handled badly can disadvantage the governments and especially their budgets and treasuries. An enormous power, skill, and pay gap (asymmetry) exists between private and public sector employees—such as lawyers and financial experts—to purchase assets such as buses and railway rolling stock and to negotiate concessions and contracts for the sale or lease of mining, oil, and gas commodities. This skill and expertise gap has been a critical factor historically and presently for maintaining poor country "underdevelopment" (exploited and cheated of natural and labor resource potential).

Your deeper responsibility as a public sector manager is to try and save your organization money by acute financial management, creative capital financing methods, and exercise of deft contracting skills. Such savings can accrue by avoiding expensive consultants, by spotting hidden but costly downstream financial liabilities, or through tighter private public partnership (PPP) contracts. How you manage your budget and utilize it for programmatic needs depends on your management skill as well as your discretion and budget authority. If such matters are overlooked or simply unknown to you, the private side will exploit weaknesses to their advantage. For these reasons, basic purposes and techniques of financial management will be covered in *Chapter 5*. More of these issues will become clearer in *Discussion Case #6* on Guyana's efforts to utilize and not to waste or lose its newly discovered oil resources. For as is known, countries with well-paid, skilled, and clever public sector financial management professionals, such as Botswana, with low debts and prudent fiscal managers, have grown and developed on the heels of their valuable natural resources (i.e., diamonds).

Fictional literary narratives often provide some of the clearest insights into the causes and consequences of modern international management dilemmas, such as how to prevent underdevelopment or negative development from loss of natural resource potential. In Joseph Conrad's

Nostromo, mine owner Charles Gould put it to the latest dictator about to overthrow the *Costaguana* government that without the San Tome mine and the concession held firmly in the experienced hands of his family, no investor would touch the "ill-omened corpse".[8] His point was that a clumsy nationalization would scare off other investors.[9] He emphasized that *Costaguana* had been and always would be dependent on foreign capital and expertise.[10] What he didn't say is that because of its technical inability, fear, or corrupt government officials, *Costaguana* has been consistently unable to negotiate its fair shares of concessions, loan agreements, or contracts. It underplays its hand. "We underestimate or overestimate our strength always. We refuse to wound and thereby throw away our hand. We create problems for the future" said V.S. Naipaul in *The Mimic Men.*[11] That is, if you have resources like those of Guyana (*Discussion Case #6*) or *Costaguana*, sink the knife and "wound": drive a hard bargain, don't "throw away your hand"!

Diamond-endowed countries like Botswana have been driving hard bargains for many decades, with highly trained and paid civil servants, to maximize the development potential and profitability of its resource. The lesson of places like Botswana is that it is hard to manage natural resource endowments without the right policies in place. Without them, the bounty from resources is often squandered or stolen by plundering elites, and the result is underdevelopment. The result is blamed on the "cursed" resource rather than the rapacious elites and their short-sighted get rich quick decisions. The right policies are stable tax regimes, land tenure and contractual rights, stabilization funds to prevent boom and bust currency changes from the Dutch disease and to invest development proceeds in basic needs and infrastructure for growth and development.[12] Needed to execute such policies are "tough purchasing agents"[13] or skilled public sector managers and policy-makers that know how to negotiate maximum royalties and dividends from mining and oil concessions. Botswana was once a very poor South African country until 1967 when the mining giant De Beers discovered diamonds there and the country's elite began to defend itself from predators through promulgation of the right policies and acquisition of skilled public sector management. Botswana wisely built on its existing resource strengths to diversify ahead by investing in secondary manufacturing sector skills to cut and polish diamonds and keep the new jobs at home.

In the Conrad tale, *Costaguana* is a composite Central American/ Caribbean country. It was first exploited by British mercantilist policies of resource extraction and later endured plundering by multilateral mining, drilling, and forestry firms (multinational corporations, MNCs) that controlled governments and engineered coups and bribed their way to self-serving policies in the areas of taxation, subsidies, concessions, protection and security for their operations, and appropriate market to port roads. *Costaguana* could be a bit of Honduras Guatemala, Haiti, and El Salvador. With its silver ore it took the opposite development policy path from that taken by Botswana! Like many poor countries, *Costaguana* was doomed to underdevelopment by profiteers and plunderers, accompanied and encouraged by local elites bribed and purchased by foreign capital. Its silver resources were called vapidly a "resource curse" which could have been turned into real development resources by better "governance", diplomatic negotiating skills, and managerial capacities. An operational definition of governance is the will and capacity of government regimes and institutions to anticipate, plan, and prepare for the future. Governance is hard to come by in poor, underdeveloped countries endowed with valuable resources. State institutions are fragile and beset by ethno-nationalist and populist groups led by regional warlords that compete for power and the spoils of wealth. Unfortunately, national development, stability, or security is rarely even a secondary objective of this competition for control of state power.[14]

On the other side of the table, sit private sector managers who need to know that investment means the transfer of needed capital, skills, and systems in a profit-making enterprise. Profit-maximizing at the expense of locals should not be the primary objective! The host country's government needs to remind the firm that foreign investment there should be a shared project that ultimately serves and benefits public needs and those of the firm for profit. The host country provides a platform for development— not a private treasury for purposes of plunder and profiteering.[15] Within organizations, public sector managers often manage cost centers for accountability to demonstrate their financial as well as service value to that organization. Cost center success can help them avoid budget cuts in succeeding years when revenues are short. State enterprise managers have even more financial accountability, as well as more discretion to manage their budgets, personnel, and costs. Similarly, NGO managers have to come up with ways to raise additional funds to finance operations and meet budgets. They are like private sector managers in having to focus on the main management tasks of defending margins (measured by income or operating statements) and cash flow (measured by cash flow statements). NGO managers and commercial managers usually have the authority and discretion to vary inputs like labor, transport, and commodity supplies in order to maintain output targets (e.g., meals for the poor, as discussed in *Chapter 4*). Public sector managers are often unable to vary inputs because they lack authority and discretion. Management is constrained by the structural problems inherent in unstable and poor contexts ("poverty and uncertainty" to use Caiden and Wildavsky's terminology[16]). Transitional and developing countries need to support management with reliable governance and legal systems. They should be open to foreign expertise and collaboration. But often they lack these basic preconditions.

In short, public and private sectors are different but alike only in "trivial ways" as Sayre quipped in his 1958 essay.[17] His point was that the requirements and contexts of each are different. Financing and managing a payroll for survival in a brutal market are largely different tasks from managing in a largely cost-free environment subject only to spending the money and being audited for it. Nevertheless, the development sector and its technical work overseas require some caveats. These caveats make the study of private financing and accounting vital to strengthening overseas governments and stimulating development. They are also critical for survival of NGOs. First, the development firm (or NGO) must be managed as a firm in a competitive market where no contract wins or wins and bad in-country performances mean going bust. For this reason, firms avoid uneconomic contracts from donors who fail to pay up to a firm's break-even point. More on this will be explained in the Pakistan case (*Discussion Case #9*) and the private aid firm Practical Concepts in Development (PCD). Second, country financial officials and policy-makers face substantial asymmetries of power and expertise when dealing with legal, financial, and accounting officials from large multinational mining and investment firms. They must understand the intricacies of finance as well as the meaning of legal terms in concession contracts for mineral and forestry resources. They must be matched by expertise from donors, firms, or organizations such as extractive industry transparency initiative (EITI) (described further in the Guyana *Discussion Case #6*).

Third, public capital investment projects are or should be financed by pay-as-you use financing techniques, often bonds or contracts with PPPs that define the rights and liabilities of parties for such events as default, debt, and impossibility of performance. They also use sale and leaseback and other creative capital financing techniques that leverage market advantages. This requires close partnerships with country governments and even changes of laws or regulations to accommodate such financing. Failure to know capital market finance for a country can be fatal. Such gaps in knowledge can lead to further exploitation of host countries and more despair of "resource curses". Fourth, sectoral development projects targeting local government are especially important for strengthening budget and tax systems for general fund agencies as well as city and state enterprises that deliver fee-financed services such as sanitation. Regulated public utilities such as heat and electricity organizations, water and sewer authorities, health care agencies, and city transit agencies all employ cost accounting and budgeting based on accrued expenses, rather than cash expenditures in order to set prices properly and calculate needed levels of public subsidies. This applies as well to the financial skills needed to contract out service and employ NGOs to deliver services such as social assistance and meals for the poor. Officials need to be familiar with these as the management of these services and sectors is not trivial and not like general government public sector management at all! With scarce budget resourced and worldwide aversion to taxation, modern government, private sector cash management, and financing skills are critically critical.

In an international arena, where serving multiple masters in puzzling cultural contexts is the norm, management of people, processes, and finances becomes chaotic and there are no easy blueprints to follow. (US city managers would say this precisely describes the contexts in which they often have to function and explains their high turnover rates, which average about two years!) Increasingly, both commercial and public managers have to serve multiple masters, trying to please both shareholders as well as a range of societal stakeholders representing environmental, governance, and justice issues. Overseas managers must act on incomplete information and inadequate resources often with unforgiving time pressures—and do all this in novel cultures. Managers in home offices often forget these field constraints in the rush to apply simple performance metrics. Tough decisions are complex and gray, not cut and dried to be guided by simple how-to management books. As in baseball, the real world of management decision-making requires a mix of strategy, statistical analysis, psychology, and mystery. Tolerance for ambiguity and responding properly to stress are two core qualities. Especially now, that means empathy and receptivity to employee personal and mental health issues as they affect job performance. It also means clear acceptance of responsibility, and of personal accountability for mistakes. High-quality managers know how to mix all of these parts effectively. To succeed, managers must have a workable management approach and a set of successful and easily adaptable management and communication tools. And if these don't work, he or she must start over with some new ones! High-quality organizations focus on culture as the determinant of their success which means managers who connect with their teams empathetically as well as intellectually to achieve objectives.[18]

Issues and Cases

Management: Noun vs. Verb

When one interviews for a management job, she or he needs to know if the organization is treating their particular position as a noun, that is, simply a position on the organization chart, a potential box-checker or form-filler. Or might they treat it as a position that also expects verb-type actions, meaning an exercise of skills and action decisions on which one would be judged and evaluated? Very often the noun-verb distinction comes up in the question of who is the most important person in an organization? The answer often boils down to identifying the "influencer", the "go —to" guy who knows where and how to get things done. It could be the formal CEO position, a noun. It could be that the CEO is also the chief influencer, combining position and using formal and informal authority to act and get things done. Or it might be that the roles of formal CEO and informal influencer, the "verb" who gets things done (a Mr. Johnson, discussed later in Discussion Case #7), are entirely separate.

How can you determine the real job structure or description vs. the nominal or advertised position? By asking questions during the interview.... Remember, they don't hold all the cards. If they consider your questions impertinent, you don't want to work there anyway! You really don't want to accept a bad job full of nasty surprises. By then it's too late! For example, ask how much authority you would have, over personnel, over the budget to move funds around from item to item? What responsibilities will you have on which you will be evaluated? To whom do you report and how often? Is there a senior manager point person to whom you are accountable? How many? These kinds of questions will help you assess whether you would want to work there or not.

Remember that as a manager in the overseas aid business, you will be responsible for taking actions. It is not a desk job focused on box-checking (if it is—look for a new job!). You should be supervising the running of organizations efficiently, productively, and reliably. In other words, you are or will be a verb more than a noun! "Organization", for your small world, may be a project, a unit, or subunit of an organization, or just a team. You will be exercising your skills in overseeing administrative processes, especially human resources, and budgeting and financial management, often for a specific sector like health where your supervisors and point people in country may be in the ministry of health and on up to the prime minister's office. Your job is likely to be a combination of staff and line roles, such as head of maintenance where you supervise and lead and continue to perform technical tasks. Where did you get these skills? Your management experience in holding similar positions is a big advantage. If this is your first job with this kind of job description, you likely gained your skills from role-playing, simulations, and case analysis exercises in graduate management courses. Management institutes and university graduate programs have existed since the early 1900s. In the UK, management and administration schools began to appear in the 1920s when Oxford developed a degree in "political economy" which might or might not have had much to do with actually running an organization. Otherwise, in the UK, business and public administration schools did not appear until the 1960s.

Only recently has it been a field of study, like economics or biology. Management was something you did and learned on the job! Not any more.... As a sign of urgency and spur to action, the annual *World Management Survey* of management practices among firms has repeatedly found that productivity is strongly correlated with better management. More rigorous research efforts to pin down relationships between adoption of innovative public and private governance and politics have been more difficult. That is because unlike more applied theory-driven disciplines, such as economics, in-depth causal connections in management must proceed from small samples generating qualitative information from which inferences must be made on organizational cultures, governance, and productivity results. Management is an intangible asset that strongly affects tangible asset production. The puzzle is to rigorously describe which factors under which conditions work and do not work in generating monetary outputs. The economics of markets, supply, and demand for resources can be directly monetized. The non-monetary intangible cultural and overt management techniques and systems that affect business and government results are qualitative and must be inferred. This explains the frustration of economics to provide its monetary explanations to public management and private business. Disciplines like economics can measure overseas development results in HDI indices and GDP data. But for achieving them, softer intervening variables that generate growth and development again have to be inferred from small sample qualitative data.[19]

Even more challenging for rigorous academic studies of the effects of management techniques and culture on public service results and market outputs is the fact that they depend on even fluffier concepts such as leadership and team motivation. Realistically, almost all your actions as a manager will be part of a team, some horizontal decisions by your unit, others imposed vertically from above, and still others you may impose online workers below you within the organization. Your managerial actions will likely include setting targets, developing a management plan with results milestones, building solidarity, motivating with financial and nonfinancial incentives, and evaluating. What authority do you have to take all these actions? What types of actions might you be able to take, for say providing incentives and building team consensus? Remember the classical management writers, such as Luther Gulick and his seven functions: POSDCORB (1937): planning, organizing, staffing including hiring/firing, directing or leading, coordinating, reporting for physical as well as fiscal results, and budgeting, including your management transfer authority. Which of these functions can you perform? Find out what management tools the organization already uses, such as MBO, ABC, CSR, TQM, and see if you can gauge the breakdown of Theory X and Y personality and style types during your interviews (which include two-way one-on-one meetings, reactions to your presentations, and even lunchtime behavior).

For example, if the organization for which you are interviewing uses a management by objectives (MBO) system, first established by Peter Drucker in 1954, find out how that is working.[20] Does it effectively measure staff performance output and productivity? Other public and private organizations find that it creates better communication between management and employees. On the other hand, there is evidence that a time and metric-driven organization of planned goals and objectives increases stress. It can generate frenetic activity and performative work at the expense of real results. There is also evidence that management can become obsessed with established objectives at the expense of other responsibilities and dynamics such as the culture of conduct and the work ethos.

Be on the lookout for hints of organizational or individual pathologies, such as stove-piping and internal silos, managerialism or obsessions with measurable results, and Taylorism (1911) with his famous time management system as the optimal way to get results. His ideas and systems were so famous worldwide that it was even distorted and misapplied by none other than Joseph Stalin in the 1920s to drive Soviet industrialization with slogans ("Long Live the Numbers!"), and the prodding by the state police (Cheka, KGB), all of which measured results by the physical norm and through the Marxist net material product system! The black satirical and dystopian novel by Yevgeny Zamiatin, *We* (1921), was based on a society in which Taylorist mechanical principles governed all human and organizational relations under penalty of death or imprisonment! Mao's frightened and fanatical followers during the ten-year Cultural Revolution behaved like Zamiatin's Taylorist characters, reduced to "Maoist algorithms": inputs, rules, outputs....

Modern management gurus echoing earlier and foundational prescriptions such as Taylor include Franklin Covey's Leadership Great Results Program and the Seven Habits of Highly Successful People, such as executive coaching and leadership confidence-building: films such as *Little Miss Sunshine* and the star consultant's "Nine-Point Pyramid" which featured maxims on the way to the top as "refuse to lose", "success theatre". Others include George Gallup's "Entrepreneurial Acceleration System" which stresses performance management, which is one of the many self-motivational writers and systems developers out there. The Silicon Valley venture capitalist Ben Horowitz's motivational maxim is also notable, with such tidbits as "If you are going to eat shit, don't nibble!". All these writers, systems promoters, and acronyms are important to have tucked away in your interview toolkit in case you are asked about them.

Aid firms are strong on high-energy participatory management tailored to results evaluation since their superiors have to report results regularly to such overseers as USAID and Congress (known confusingly as "clients"!). Thus, those involved in project planning, proposal-writing, monitoring, and evaluating, such as you, must become familiar with multiple oversight systems and protocols. The firms will also have their own in-house systems. My firm Development Alternatives Incorporated (DAI) had the computerized TAMIS or technical assistance management information system on which we entered data on projects and personnel actions. You might ask how and whether you will have responsibilities for all or part of this cycle since the fiscal lifeblood of the firm depends on winning project contracts? Will you, for instance, or your group's project assistants do the data entering? Remember also that modern management fads and jargon terms such as "reengineering systems", streamlining systems", and "reinventing structures" are usually based on simple expansions of POSDCORB functions, now called: "spans of control", "hands-off management", "participatory management", "delayering", and so on. This is also a good time to ask the firm's turnover rate, which is a good indicator of how stable the place is and how likely you could be terminated and for what reasons. Can you, for instance, be let go without stated cause? Can you be sacked without notice...? On such common problems, see the classic film "Up in the Air" with George Clooney for tips on how brutal hiring and firing can be and how to cope with them.

Effective Management

If managers are to direct and motivate teams, they must be effective at this. Writers have distinguished distinct types and styles of management. The preferred style is often a function of context and personality. Macgregor's Theory X and Y types are often useful for a quick snapshot of what employees face and prefer. The Theory X manager can fit the context of truculent employees who face difficult existential issues in an unstable organizational context, such as Twitter where narcissistic managers such as Elon Musk to issue the "my way or the highway" edicts. This normally backfires if the staff revolts. But in the Twitter case the expectation is that he wants to make major staff cuts and is not concerned about fairness, remaining workload burdens, or assuring survivors that they will keep their jobs. The Theory X hardline approach is fast and aggressive and should be used only in herding up operations where time is limited. By definition X type managers fail to motivate beyond fear and instilling passive obedience.

An example of Theory X in action can be readily seen in films and team managers. In *Star Trek: The Next Generation*: "Chain of Command" (S6, E10–E11), Captain Picard is captured by the *Cardassians* on mission and temporarily replaced as Enterprise commander by the humorless appointee Captain Jellico. Jellico believes in aggressive action to instill fear and respect in both his own crew and the *Cardassians* to show that he meant business. Jellico was a man who compensated for his insecurities with calculated displays of decisiveness. But his aggressive, unpredictable outbursts lead inevitably to increased conflict and to the brink of war. In organizations, such as the national health service (NHS), authoritarian sticklers for rules impart fear of blame if things go wrong. This produces a conservative atmosphere of risk-aversion and keeping the head down behavior that allow mistakes to fester and crises to suddenly emerge. It leads to excessive respect for rules and hierarchies. Productivity suffers. Similarly, in soccer team management, the antics of hard-boiled manager Roberto Mancini of the Italian team were famous. He would gather his team and engage in long periods of shouting and ranting at them for their stupidity. Team members called the sessions "hairdryer" tirades since the wind from his mouth actually made their longish hair flutter. Such outbursts are comic at first but then humiliating and then dysfunctional since they can lead only to permanent disrespect by the staff. No one has any incentive to improve or fight for victory.

The blatant Theory X type of the Italian soccer team manager and his "hairdryer" tirades against his own players were famous. Oddly enough, by treating his players as fools and knaves, they often came together and won! The image of a coach shouting so loud at his players that their flamboyant crops of hair fluttered in the torrents of wind is the stuff of comic books. But it actually happened! I was once on the receiving end of such a tirade by the Minister of Planning in Santo Domingo. He shouted long and loud at my two team members and I sitting around a table in his office for being incompetent idiots. Sitting next to me, my Colombian colleague's lengthy hair actually fluttered as if in a violent storm. In that case, his antics didn't have any effect on our productivity except to cause our chief of party to resign and take a similar job in the middle of an Indonesian warzone. "At least I know what I'm up against there!" he huffed on his way out of the country. How can a tormented staff deal with such autocratic and abusive leaders? Christopher Boehm (2007) viewed workplaces as animal herded into hierarchical and tribal relationships and man as the "political primate in all this". He spoke of the use of "leveling mechanisms" ranging from assassination, and flight, to peaceful confrontation. Our COP chose flight. But for the others, the thought of violence through an agent (always cheap in poor countries) and easily getting away with it inevitably crosses the minds of many teams working on overseas aid projects.

On the other hand, cultures, institutions, personnel needs, and your expectations of them vary. IDMs with "transnational competence" (TC) (Koehn and Rosenau, 2010) must mix together people who might be the same with these variables to get the best results. As suggested by Grosse

(2023), people are the same and need to be treated with the same empathy and respect everywhere. They should be managed "boldly and humbly" (Klitgaard, 2023) with clearly stated expectations and criteria for rewards and punishments. But institutional support, cultural nuances, and legal and regulatory rule enforcement vary widely across rich and poor countries. Western managers are perplexed by "mirroring" and "way round" reactions and adjust. Managers must mix context, languages, and styles together to obtain best individual and team results. Managers come to recognize that employee loyalties are often not to organizations, but to their mates, team members, groups, tribes, sects, and/or leaders which compete for these loyalties with task performance in many contexts. To sort all this out and meet project objectives on time takes patience and understanding. More than one IDM whom I have known begins to ask themselves the questions: "Have I been set up in this leadership role?" "Have I been dealt a band hand?" or "Should I just drop back 10 yards and punt on this job?".

Thus, to lead and manage the organization or team for the long term, more Theory Y type characters and behavior are often needed. This is the modern manager: the low-ego compassionate boss who gives people incentives and autonomy. The empathetic manager who "manages by walking around" with a personal touch is much preferred by most staffs and is needed to keep both turnover at a minimum and shareholders in commercial or state enterprises happy. Theory Y types work with staff to build trust, break down silos, and push them to coordinate and work together with peers and managers. The prototypical Y manager must be bold and clearly communicate job expectations but avoid micromanaging the details of the job. Klitgaard (2020) identifies these ideal qualities as being "bold and humble". His ideal type of manager would encourage risk-taking and bridge-building rather than the silo-defensiveness and "we-they" relationships. The Theory X manager relies on edicts and commands and tight monitoring and micro-control; the Y type manager is low ego, compassionate, and relies on trust, consensus, and inherent staff capacity and authority and autonomy to do the job right with only periodic management intrusion to keep the team and employee on course.

To lead and manage an organization or team overseas for development work also requires "TC" according to Koehn and Rosenau.[21] Such people are adept in nurturing "transboundary relationships", connecting with people, and establishing networks, alliances, and partnerships (2010:15). The quality of transnational competence (TC) is missing from many foreign advisors and technical personnel sent abroad to manage development aid projects. According to a Canadian survey by Canadian international development agency (CIDA) in 18 countries, foreign advisors lacked social skills, were unable to establish social contacts with locals, and failed to acknowledge counterpart skills or abilities. The findings applied to Canadian and World Bank experts who were termed "visiting firemen" with "sharp elbows" by "indigenous management" (2010:91). The authors noted that in many cases the experts were unable to span functional or national boundaries in their operational work and were unable to establish trust between locals and themselves (2010:92). In short, IDMs must have intercultural communication skills (2010:13), including interpersonal rapport and emotional self-confidence (2010:15). The point is IDM recruiters should screen for these qualities to staff aid projects, along with flexibility and high tolerance for ambiguity.

It is important to recognize as a development manager the nuances and constraints imposed on aid recipients as individuals by race, class, and degrees of poverty. These are essential parts of the political culture. And they affect how one manages them as an outsider, and even one from that region returning to do aid management. For such micro insights, literature, film, and arts can be an important resource to understanding the ground-level context beforehand and while working in country. V.S. Naipaul for instance provides an analytic guide into the behavior of class relations and politics in Isabella in his novel *The Mimic Men* (Naipaul, 1967) that could be usefully applied in other LA/C countries. It is for these reasons that we draw upon fictional insights in the cases and to stress that the writers were there first, not as aid workers but as neutral observers trying to figure things out.

Managing Intragroup Dynamics and Interpersonal Conflict

What types of managerial talents are needed to direct, motivate, and control isolated teams on missions for long periods of time? Researchers have examined what keeps groups working together coherently in contexts such as rural development projects, medical rescue missions, submarines, air squadrons in wartime, and commercial flight crews, where the teams are isolated for long periods of time. They find that in addition to a good team leader, different roles or personality types are needed such as (1) clowns to break the ice and bridge groups, (2) peacemakers-bystanders to reduce conflict, (3) storytellers to encourage reflection, (4) social secretaries to schedule recreational events, (5) team leaders to direct operations, and (6) a mixture of introvert and extrovert personality types. They suggest that, for example, a clown or a "room guy" is needed to lighten the mood and may be the most important role of all—someone like a Gerardo Parra or "Baby Shark" on the team to loosen up the Washington Nationals clubhouse during the unlikely 2019 World Series in which they went from wild card hopeful to be the series victor![22] Casual chafing between married couples and team members is a useful social lubricant. Without it, slights and resentments can accumulate to breaking points. The dynamics of group work require having someone to constantly "chirp" at you, foster chemistry, and keep the project in line. This could be the team leader but often can be inconsistent with their character.

Guidance on Writing Evidence-Based Management Memos

This case is especially amenable to writing an evidence-based memo which could be addressed to your superior or a committee. Clear and forceful memo-writing is an essential management skill. The memo should contain crisp descriptions and persuasive arguments for each point. IMF missions sometimes ask for clear thesis statements at the beginning of each paragraph with each statement in the paragraph supporting the thesis statements. For *Oral Briefings* and *Discussion Case* (e.g., #13 on Colombian tax reform) assignments, the memo should be limited to three to four pages and cover the following topics: (1) background on problem (see *Chapter 3* on actionable problem identification), supporting data and information and demonstration of contextual similarities for comparisons, and (2) the quantitative and qualitative information should support the case for dealing with this as an actionable public problem. The data can be both primary (recent surveys) and secondary (recent articles), (3) options that have been tried in the past and results, and (4) preferred option in the case of this problem and why you think it is more workable in the short term.

Consider the cases as opportunities to develop and present management or policy memos either to your superiors or to a group meeting at which senior management will be present. You need to hold your audience. Be forceful: make the problem your problem, the most important on earth! Make your claims and facts vital and startling to your audience.

Discussion Case #1: Incident in the Oriente

Note: The case issues and questions should be answerable from the materials in this textbook. The full reference materials for each case are cited in the notes. Based on these materials, it can be expected that attentive and curious students are likely to proffer the best options, answers, and practical management lessons.

Managers make decisions typically on limited information and for which they are held accountable anyway. It's what managers must do. More importantly, the issues are not straight-forward yes/no actions but involve paradoxes, trade-offs, and opportunity costs no matter what the manager does or does not decide. Non-decision making has consequences. Often managers must make decisions urgently under pressure from conflicting stakeholders. In this case and the following ones, decisions must be made, and you need to advise team leaders and other managers on what to do. Here, team leader Moses faced a paradox of at least three contradictory forces: contract deadlines affecting project completion, the threat to his firm's reputation for completing projects on time and within given budgets, and the fact that he had lost control and his team's respect. He believed (correctly or incorrectly) that he needed to take dramatic action in order to regain authority and control.

In Paul Theroux's "Incident in the Oriente" (from **Harper's** 2011), Max Moses was the COP or leader of a project team that was building an oil depot in the Amazonas region of Ecuadorian jungle. They were a private contractor paid for by the Government of Ecuador. Doing the specified construction work for least cost using local labor and materials enabled the firm to make more profits. Having a motivated team enabled them to complete their work on time and under budget. Moses prided himself on creating a loyal, cooperative team in order to successfully complete jobs, which in his view was really as important as creating and leaving monuments, which lead to more contracts in order to move from one job to another as part of the "traveling circus" of the overseas aid business. Unlike some contractors, Moses paid his labor in dollars every two weeks.

The core project team in Oriente consisted of five men and one dog, Silsbee's Labrador retriever. The project also included hundreds of local day workers for particular tasks. For instance, hundreds of Malay fishermen were signed on for barging cement for an offshore fuel dock in that country. The Ecuadorian core team lived in separate refurbished steel shipping containers with one separate for mess. This arrangement was part of Moses' frugality effort of "find it, fix it up" and save funds that might be needed later in the project if not gained outright as profits. Moses wanted a loyal, cooperative work team. But "harmony", in the sense of friendliness and humor, was not his way since it wasted time, affected deadlines, and relaxed the locals who worked as short-term labor. Silsbee and Tafel became friends or workmates as often happens on teams that work closely together for long periods of time. Tafel was in charge of organizing and supplying work teams to do specific tasks such as building steel frames. As well as operating the backhoe, he drew up the plans according to Moses' directions but did the payments accounting and paperwork. The increasingly friendly relations between Tafel and Silsbee, evident from their constant chattering and joking, Moses viewed as insolence and implied disloyalty to both his leadership and the rest of the team. The narrator knew this because he was in charge of "staging", meaning scaffolding and skeletal towers of frames and ladders, and was thus a close confident of Moses. But Moses questioned Silsbee's need for a dog and later blamed them when some locals stole a few propane tanks and the dog "didn't even bark!". Did Moses' concept of cooperation and loyalty contradict his dislike of inter-team friendship and loyalty? Should Silsbee and Tafel pick up on that from his glances and expressions and modify their behavior?

The job was behind schedule, and one of Silsbee's welders negligently set fire to a scaffold. Moses told Tafel to reprimand Silsbee which he did but was later seen laughing it up with him. Then Silsbee's dog killed several chickens which meant they couldn't eat them. Moses, who had a jaw-twisting lisp and slipping tongue, had likely frustrated him when complaining to Silsbee about "his wab". Work inefficiency problems continued, 200 gallons of diesel oil leaked out of a drum because a tap was left running, and there were more thefts of equipment. The project was running behind schedule to meet the deadline with the oil drillers. It was also on a tight financial margin as Moses had invested all the money he had been advanced by his firm. Added to these problems, he felt he was losing control, yet he knew he couldn't sack Silsbee and Tafel. He needed Tafel's loyalty back and for Silsbee to take orders. Chivers told the narrator that he might flog both of them. But that was not how he operated. He might have read them the riot act. Whatever he did to them, they would both still be friends and the loyalty problem would recur. What would you have done?

Moses summoned Tafel to his container and gave him an order to shoot Silsbee's dog with his rifle which he did. At dinner, Moses said grace and announced that they were ahead of schedule, and if they kept at it and took orders more quickly, they would likely get bonuses.

Questions

Was Moses' order to Tafel a "bold and or humble" motivational strategy? Was Moses a Theory X or Y type of manager, or a combination of both types? Did Moses manage his team efficiently, in the sense of completing task results at least cost? Did he do so effectively, in the sense of longer term outcomes and team morale? Was he an effective leader? Were fear and cruelty more effective motivators than empathy here? By shooting Silsbee's dog Moses was shifting blame for his mistake-prone group from his crude and humorless management style to two staffers who were trying to combine enjoying themselves while working long hours. What other methods could Moses have employed that would incentivize his team to work more carefully? How about a team meeting at which Moses pointed out the mistakes that were made, pointed to loose protocols as the probable causes, accepted personal responsibility, and asked for suggestions on how to improve? Might that have been preferable in the long term to shooting Silsbee's dog? Think of such Stanley Kubrick films as "The Shining" and "2001 Space Odyssey". The message there was that if three or more people are stuck in a confined space in the middle of nowhere, such as a lockdown, one of them will go mad and try to murder the others. Could that have happened here? How can addition or elimination of roles to a team beforehand prevent this from happening? What roles were missing from this team?

Role-Playing Exercise #1.1: Dealing Tactfully with a Sensitive Situation

The case presents a delicate situation for Moses. His authority is challenged by sub-par and careless work from his team of Silsbee, Tafel, and Chivers. He wants them back on track and under control. Play the role of Moses having an individual exchange with Silsbee over his performance. Remember, in playing a role effectively, you are talking to someone while pretending to be someone else. Role-playing is actually a form of deception. So, how would you deal tactfully with Silsbee and the rest of the team in a group meeting? In your role, act it out, deceive us, convince us that you would be diplomatic but firm with Tafel and the rest of the team. The rest of the class and the instructor will provide feedback following the role-playing.

Role-Playing Exercise #1.2: "The South Seas Freighter Hostage Decision" ("Those Who Work")

As should be evident from Moses' actions, international managers often make split-second tough and often outrageous choices for which they must take the heat later. A 2018 French film *"Those Who Work"* (*Ceux Qui Travaillent*) (by Swiss director Antoine Russbach) covers the life, work, crisis decision, and eventual sacking of Frank, an international shipping manager and man of action. Frank has worked his way up from uneducated truck driver to logistics expert, responsible from Geneva HQ for guiding massive freighters all over the world. Terrorists in the South Seas off Africa capture one of the ships under his control.[23] He suddenly has to deal with (1) the transport of valuable cargo on time, (2) terrorist monetary demands in exchange for their hostages consisting of the kidnapped crew and ship, (3) fears and risks that extortionate deals made with terrorists often fail and end up in more killings and loss of property. He thus knew that the provision of a negotiating team and money was high risk. The crew might be killed anyway, and valuable time would be lost for the perishable cargo. Frank made a brutal decision and decided to use force to retake ship and to avoid dealing with dicey security officials off Africa gave his team permission to toss a captured remaining terrorist overboard.

For this decision, after a brief hearing, his firm fires him. He is thrown into deep depression, loses his home, and his family leaves him. He works with sympathetic training and recruitment firms and has to make choices that would compromise his moral principles but will pay high salaries. What would you have done and how would you deal with dealt with the consequences?

Discussion Case #2: Borneo Outstation

The action takes place in a Borneo colonial outstation in the 1890s. British "Crown Colonies" like Borneo were divided into districts run by district officers (DOs) and assistant DOs (ADOs). Colonial outstations were the deconcentrated units of the British colonial service and served to control and administer affairs depending on the needs and topography. In this case there is a sectoral "afforestation" officer to deal with technical forestry issues. There could be projects like roads, prison, and forestry management which would be the responsibility of the district Resident.

Outstations often were located near trading posts for such commodities as furs, pelts, and hardwoods that could be traded locally and exported. The British model was "mercantilist", meaning mostly extraction for export. State trading firms, such as the East India Company, invested and stimulated one-way trade with England. Tropical hardwoods in such Crown Colonies as British Honduras (now Belize) were exported to England with few benefits for local economic or forest sector development. Trading posts from these investment ventures (variously called colonialism and imperialism) rarely evolved into permanent settlements and cities in the expected economic development sequence. The British colonial model differed from the Spanish or French in that Common Law property and administrative law and state institutions were implanted locally. The British implanted a semblance of a devolved governance structure, while the French and Spanish colonies were more unitary and tightly controlled from Paris and Madrid via Civil Law. Local civil society institutions between the state and citizens developed in several British colonies. In addition to games such as tennis, polo, and cricket, norms such as fair play and being a "gentleman", the British also exported the epidemics which wiped out natives in the South Seas and Latin America.

The characters here are the Resident Warburton and his new assistant Cooper.[24] The British colonial officials stationed in Borneo in the Federated Malay States (FMS) are served by Malay "boys" who cook, clean, and service them. After independence in the 1960s, FMS became Malaysia and united with several other states, including Singapore (but in 1965, Singapore left the FMS and became independent). The Resident assistant's boy appointed by the Resident is Abas. Warburton is a stiff, elaborately courteous, formal-by-the-book, upper class Brit. He graduated from Eton and Oxford as his family had for several hundred years. For evening dinner, he dressed every evening in a tie and white dinner jacket. Cooper is a working-class "colonial" from Barbados, born and educated there. They worked in hot, humid mosquito-ridden conditions in which cases of malaria were frequent. In these turgid conditions, dining mostly alone, Warburton made a concession and wore his white dinner jackets rather than formal evening wear. But he still wore his high collar and boiled white short, silk stockings, and patent leather shoes. He dressed as formally as he would in his London club in Pall Mall. Cooper showed up from his bungalow near the compound in a ragged jacket and khaki shorts, the same ones in which he worked. Warburton noted this and asked him to dress when dining with him at least to dress more formally. The white men, in his view, needed to wear their usual costumes of civilized society in order to maintain their dignity and to avoid losing the respect of the natives.

The Resident invited Cooper occasionally to dine with him, and every day at six after work finished, they shared a gin and bitters at his compound at the "Fort" where Warburton lived to recap the day's progress. Warburton soon learned from Cooper that he had been in the Boer War and had been passed up for commission because he was a "colonial", meaning "non-white". Cooper had never lived in England and in fact resented the British. Warburton was a hot-tempered, red-faced man with pugnacious features. His blue eyes were cold and could flash with a sudden wrath. He viewed himself as a man of the world hoping for a just one that would do his best to get along with Cooper. He sized Cooper up as an envious, ill-bred, vain, and self-assertive fellow. Cooper by that juncture viewed Warburton as a common snob who dearly loved a lord, touchy and quick-tempered. The fact was that Warburton despite his aura of an unadulterated snob had inherited his wealth from a father who was a Liverpool industrialist and had never done a day's work in his life. Like many entitled Oxford and public school grads of the day, after they ran through their money gambling, betting in horses, and cavorting in London, they accepted posts in the colonies. In this routine, they maintained their class respect as hearty "good fellows".

As Resident, Warburton no longer had to be a sycophant craving the smiles of the great, as he was now the master whose word was the law. Now he worked to resolve local conflicts and keep the peace between rival chiefs and head-hunters. He became a skillful administrator and was known as strict, just, and honest. He got on well with the Malays, admired their customs, courtesy, manners, gentleness, but also their sudden passions. He felt he was able to adapt British colonial rules and customs to Malay values and behavior. He spoke fluent Malay and with Malays he mixed condescension and kindliness to keep them at ease.[25] He knew in their minds he took the place of a native Sultan while also occupying the role of the foreign colonial power. Warburton had no patience with white men who simply yielded to native customs.

In their chats, Cooper often watched him with supercilious eyes and a mocking smile on his lips. Cooper writhed at the snobbery of Warburton's tales of social life among the royal lords, princes, and earls. When Cooper spoke about his work supervising his teams, Warburton gently advised Cooper several times during their chats to treat Malays politely, patiently, and kindly. He did this because Cooper commonly referred to the Malays as "niggers" and scoundrels. When told by Warburton not to do this, as Malays were not people of color, Warburton informed him that he thought they were the same thing. At that point, Warburton simply said, "you are a very ignorant man", and left it at that. But Cooper's bad manners, conceit in his own judgment, and intolerance were getting on his nerves.

A few months after Cooper's arrival at the station, an incident happened that turned the Resident's dislike into bitter hatred. Warburton had to leave the station in his hands and go up-country on an inspection tour. He had concluded that Cooper was a capable fellow. The only thing he did not like was that he had no indulgence. He was just, honest, and painstaking but had no sympathy for the natives. It bitterly amused him that this man who looked upon himself as everyman's equal should look upon so many men as his own inferiors. He was hard, he had no patience with the native mind, and he was a bully. Warburton quickly realized that the Malays disliked and feared him. He was not altogether displeased. He would not have liked it very much if his assistant had a popularity which might rival his own.

When he returned in three weeks, the first thing that struck his eyes when he entered his sitting room was a great pile of open newspapers. Warburton sternly asked one of his servants what was the meaning of the open papers. Cooper hastened to explain that he wanted to read all about the *Wolverhampton* murder and so he borrowed his *Times*. He said he "brought them back and knew he wouldn't mind".

Warburton turned on him white with anger. "But I do mind. I mind very much. I wonder you didn't open my letters as well".

Cooper, unmoved, smiled at his chef's exasperation.

"Oh, that's not quite the same thing. I couldn't imagine you'd mind my looking at your newspapers. There's nothing much private in them".

"I very much object to anyone reading my papers before me". He went up to the pile. There were nearly 30 numbers there. "It was extremely impertinent of you. They're all mixed up".

"We can easily put them in order", said Cooper.

"Don't touch them!" cried Warburton.

"I say it's childish to make a scene about a little thing like that".

"How dare you speak to me like that!"

"Oh, go to hell", said Cooper, and he flung out of the room.

Next, Cooper had trouble with his servant boys, and they all left him except Abas. Abas had been with Warburton for 15 years. The others refused to go back. Warburton ordered them to go back.

He explained to Cooper, the next day that they had returned only by his express order. Cooper replied that he would be obliged if the Resident would stay out of his "private" concerns. Cooper told him he had sacked them all again. Warburton explained to him that they weren't private concern and that the Resident was responsible for staffing his home to prevent it from appearing unseemly. He told him that he could not find any other boy servants.

He reminded Cooper that "good masters make good servants" and again told him he behaved "very foolishly" in mistreating them and sacking them.

Then Cooper's boys returned to serve him. But this move by Warburton humiliated him in front of the natives and angered Cooper. Cooper's contempt for Warburton had now turned into sullen hatred.

The two men then began a period of frozen communication except by formal letters sent to and from by his orderly. They brooded over their antagonism. The Resident decided to let him continue work, which he did well, and let native matters take their course. At last, the opportunity came. Cooper was assigned to manage prisoners which meant building roads, repairing sheds, keeping the town clean, and rowing boats up and downstream. The well-behaved prisoners could even be selected as house boys. Cooper kept them all busy, and they performed their tasks well. But then he began to give them useless things to do, and the prisoners behaved badly. In response, he punished them by lengthening their hours which was contrary to regulations.

When this came to Warburton's attention, he gave instructions that the old hours should be kept. White with rage, Cooper went to the Fort and demanded an explanation.

Warburton kept his cool and explained that he had done so because what Cooper did "was harsh and tyrannical, and that he had no power to give such an order".

Cooper claimed he did so out of personal spite—because I wouldn't lick your boots and because you disliked me from the first day and because you are a "damned snob".

Warburton explained to him that he did think of him as a cad but that he was perfectly satisfied with the way he did his work. Then he ordered him out of the house and threatened him verbally with physical violence unless he left.

Cooper, 3 inches taller than Warburton, stronger, muscular, and younger than Warburton who was 54, came up to within inches and put his face in his. "Touch me by God. I'd like to see you hit me".

Warburton's fist flashed out and was caught by Cooper who pushed him back. Cooper gave a short hoot and with a wide grin jumped down the veranda steps and out.

After this incident he wrote to the district officer and requested Cooper's transfer. The DO responded that he understood that Cooper was a "rough diamond" but that hard-working men were hard to find and advised him to be tolerant and try to get on with him.

His boy saw the reply and advised Warburton that if he stayed there "will be a misfortune". Asked the meaning of that, his boy explained that Cooper had been withholding Abas' wages for three months so that he would not run away.

He sent a note to Cooper to ask him to the Fort where he confronted and informed him that Abas complained of him withholding his head boy's wages for three months. He explained that this was arbitrary and illegal. Warburton again warned him that the Malays were sensitive to ridicule and injury and that they could be passionate and revengeful. He warned him officially that he ran a great risk by this action and suggested he might be killed by the boy.

Cooper gave a "contemptuous chuckle" at this and said, "Do you think I'm afraid of a damned nigger?".

Warburton replied, "It is a matter of entire indifference to me".

Then the two men fought a grim and silent battle of wits, nursing a "monotony of hatred" by bouts of lost sleep (Warburton) and by drinking (Cooper). By day, they sat occasionally in their adjoining offices and stewed in their anger.

Next, Cooper accused Abas of stealing some of his clothes. When the boy denied this and demanded his wages, Cooper grabbed him and threw him down the stairs. When the boy confronted Cooper the next morning about his back wages, he struck him with a clenched fist drawing blood from his nose. Rather than face Cooper's patronizing smile and insults, by confronting him with what he did, Warburton decided to let native matters take their course.

At dinner he had asked for Abas and was told by his boy that he had gone to visit his mother's brother in the village. It was quiet that night and the river flowed silently. He walked along the road and saw Cooper's bungalow in which a light burned. He was playing ragtime on his gramophone for which he had an instinctive dislike. At his house, Warburton read and fell asleep. He did not sleep long and had terrible dreams in which he seemed to be awakened by a cry. He lay awake until dawn and then heard hurried footsteps and the sounds of voices. His lead boy burst into the room.

"I'll come at once", he said.

He was led in his pajamas to the bungalow where he saw Cooper lying in bed with a dagger (*kris*) sticking in his heart. He had been killed in his sleep. Warburton started not because it was an unexpected sight but because he felt in himself a sudden glow of exultation. A great burden had been lifted from his shoulders.

He pulled out the *kris* with great effort. It was the one he recognized which Cooper had bought several weeks before. Asking where Abas was, he was told that he was at his mother's brothers'. He ordered the native police sergeant to go there and arrest him.

His boy told him that Abas had been at his house all night. Warburton turned upon him with a frown. "You know as well as I do. Justice must be done".

"You would not hang him?"

Warburton hesitated and though his voice remained set and stern, a change came into his eyes. It was a flicker which the Malay was quick to notice and across his own eyes flashed an answering look of understanding.

The provocation was very great. Abas will be sentenced to a term of imprisonment. There was a pause while Mr. Warburton helped himself to marmalade. "When he has served a part of his sentence in prison, I will take him into this house as house boy. You can train him in his duties. I have no doubt that in the house of Mr. Cooper he got into bad habits".

"Shall Abas give himself up then?"

"It would be wise of him".

It would be an understatement to say that Cooper had zero social skills or TC. Yet he was an experienced veteran of many development projects. Here he was the Resident's assistant or deputy, or the #2 person in charge. But he had no interest or capacity to gain allies,[26] interact with the work teams he managed, or even be civil to the houseboys who did his errands. He was task-oriented but knew or cared nothing about human relations. As noted (2020:15), this lack of interpersonal rapport eventually undermined his ability to manage his assigned tasks and operations done according to the project work plan. In contrast with Warburton who was otherwise arrogant and pompous, he failed to respect or trust the locals and his staff. Cooper failed to leverage diversity and became ineffective and an obstacle to any progress with the teams in Borneo.

What lessons can be gleaned on effective management of personal confrontations from the case of Warburton v Cooper? It seems that Warburton correctly documented Cooper's antagonisms toward him. It is important to keep a record for future litigation or personnel actions. It appears also that Warburton was careful to avoid a full-scale blow-out between them, allowing pressure to build up gradually by limiting the scope and opportunities for confrontation. He also made sure there were witnesses to most of the conflicts. The record he hoped would show that tensions were driven mostly by Cooper's antagonistic behavior. On the debit side, Warburton did provoke him once over the newspaper incident, which Warburton could have avoided by making his quirky newspaper habits explicit beforehand. Effective managers need to make their expectations as well as their limits explicit and clear to all staff.

Questions

As the Resident or general manager of the outstation, was Warburton effective at conflict resolution? How well did he de-escalate minor and major conflicts? How might he have proceeded differently? Was Cooper any better at conflict management than he? What could/should Warburton have done to avoid the newspaper incident? What more should Warburton have done to prevent Cooper's final fatal mistake? Knowing how Warburton felt at the time, is it likely he would have made the effort?

Role-Playing Session #1.3: Dealing with the Recalcitrant Assistant

In Borneo outstation, Warburton is trying to manage his assistant Cooper. He has to reprimand Cooper for the harsh manner in which he treats his team and his house boys. While Cooper gets the job done, he has created a tense working environment. Ultimately, he has to warn him that his life may be threatened. Warburton is summoned to find Cooper stabbed to death, and the suspect is his house boy and confident Abas. He has to meet out justice to Abas. How did he handle both situations? How should he have managed differently to avoid these conflicts?

Finding and Promoting Purposeful Employees

It would be easier if aid field staff could be winnowed with the same thorough personnel hiring systems as formal organizations. Often there is little time, and missions must be put together quickly. Short- and long-term personnel listed in proposals may be unavailable or sick, and fill-in replacements must be found quickly. Project teams by definition stay together for the duration and then disband, going their separate ways. Some are rehired by the same firm for other projects. Others move on to other firms and other projects doing roughly the same types of jobs. In the case of permanent staff, hiring should be done on the theory that they will stay and be promoted. How then should personnel or human resource departments recruit purposeful employees? Traditional hiring systems often amount to box checking, and interview teams are often ill-suited, insulting, and off-putting for really qualified candidates. One option used to sort out problem solvers and alert candidates is leadership scenario analysis.

Action-scenario systems have been used for generations by school districts for planning, training, and recruitment purposes for sudden but frequent events such as snow days and security lockdowns. Use of this method can provide insights into when and what actions should be taken, by whom and with what likely effects? Results can reveal who is missing from the action team, and who should be hired who can deal with these crisis events? How should such people be promoted? Are they in a separate career track, entitled to a space on the organizational chart? Some local education departments use individual types as criteria, e.g., (1) pioneers (mission-oriented), (2) artisan (skill-oriented), (3) operators (meaning from life outside work), (4) strivers (drive for pay and status), (5) givers (improving the lives of others), and (6) explorers (seekers of new experiences). Others focus on candidates' suitability for responsibilities, e.g., "line" technicians (operational systems and skills) vs. "staff" managers less directly responsible for customers, riders, passengers, or patients and more for strategy and planning. Still other recruitment tools try to mix the personality types and institutional roles up with a blend of visionaries that inspire team members and specialists who deliver on the task (IT, AI, logistics, welders, wood-workers, and other craftsmen). What would you suggest for criteria and how would you ferret out candidate qualities in interviews other than through direct questions and body language?[27]

Monitoring Staff Outputs to Strengthen Organizational Cultures and Stimulate Productivity

Organizational leaders may decide that something must be done to increase productivity (output/person hour). This requires two steps: (1) monitoring and evaluating staff to gather data and information and (2) developing and executing a new staffing plan that leads to new assignments that can include no new assignment at all (e.g., being culled).

The first step must be taken clearly, decisively, and gently for best results. Many writers have noted the personnel and management costs of the increasing demand for performance indicators, metrics, benchmarks, and targets. Needed are useful and smart results measures. There are two types: financial and physical. Financial reporting to indicate spending and progress is routine and normal for cash flow management and eventual post-auditing reviews. Physical results measures are helpful but can be an unnecessary burden. For instance, there are dangers to placing emphasis on achieving scores and ratings to assess personal and team performance. Metrics such as numbers of arrests can be gamed and produce goal displacement and must be monitored to convert to useful performance evaluation information. Programs today often target certain roles and types of employees with surveillance techniques. This turns the atmosphere and job into a chain-gang or prison-like setting. Tight monitoring and evaluation based on numbers of tasks completed can be suitable for line jobs where numbers of tasks (on-time bus transit, patients treated, cars assembled, vehicles maintained) can serve as a rough proxy for efficiency but should be supplemented by supporting effectiveness measures.

In aid work, donors often prefer *output* measures (a proxy for efficiency) because these are the easiest to collect, such as classroom hours/student, teacher attendance/day, graduation rates, retention rates, literacy scores. These are important metrics and can aid in redesigning approaches to education, health care, and increasing urban transit ridership. They are not *outcome measures*, of course, such as learning instead of simple graduation or health improvements derived from better transit planning or air pollution controls in a city's limits, but they can lead to marginal project design and management improvements. Some measures might be better targeted to processes, documents, and met deadlines, such as improvements in on-time planning, preparing, and submitting budgets in the economic classification. Instead, evaluators often target reform of systems from input to output or program measurement. Focus on total systems reforms for a two to three year project is typically misguided and results in gamed data and information.

It is well-known that metric target-driven management is susceptible to gaming and distorted incentives consistent with *Goodhart's Law*. That law states when a performance measure becomes a target, it then ceases to be a good measure, e.g., number of patients treated can become a daily target or upper limit of 100 patients. If workers put in 8–10 hour shifts, a tyranny of the metric may combine with that of the clock. Other dangers of metric-driven work include over-emphasis on reporting that actually displaces the work itself, called *goal displacement*. For instance, aid projects require varying degrees of on-job reporting of progress and task attainments. In their novel *The Goal*, Eliyahu Goldratt and Jeff Cox (1984) note that managers frequently cause supply chain bottlenecks by demanding excessive reporting and respond with micromanaging operations. They cause congestion by their need to approve actions, slowing down decision-making, gumming up supply chains, and constraining development project goal attainment and actual results.[28]

The Asian Development Bank (ADB) imposes perhaps the heaviest reporting and micromanagement burdens on their project staff. During my project work in Kyrgyzstan, our team spent far more time writing reports and reporting to Manila HQ than actually doing the work to improve planning, budgeting, and financing systems for health care facilities in two oblasts. The reporting burden for ostensible accountability induced the perverse incentive of displacing the actual work. To avoid goal displacement, managers should combine known industry measures with specific ones recommended by staff. Metrics should be kept to a minimum to avoid wasting everyone's time. It is also well-known that improperly designed targets lead to perverse incentives, e.g. the British NHS target of treating patients within 48-hours ran up against obvious restrictions on a patient's ability to schedule appointments ahead. The metric failed to fit the actual work context. That added to worker alienation, stress, and pressure to meet such impossible metrics. Constant management monitoring and staff reporting requirements made the job and its setting even worse.

The degree of staff alienation is affected by how people are treated by those in charge. Humans have needs that must be recognized and respected according to Theory Z management emphasizing motivation consistent with Maslow's hierarchy of needs consistent with task achievement. This contrasts with Theory X managers who often treat workers as replaceable cogs. Turnover rates are a valuable metric for organizational management. So, how might *bad managers* be described? Important elements typically include, first, impersonal, disrespectful, unsupportive, distant, and tin-eared behavior at the staff or line level, and second, managers incurious to data reported on fiscal discipline, accounting, and control, i.e., cash flow, spending rates and purposes. Bad management usually combines both people and systems—intrusive systems overseen by intrusive people. The familiar adage is that people don't leave bad jobs they leave bad managers—often notable as loudmouth jerks and bullies! Why aren't bad managers weeded out? Often the jerks or bad ones do not behave like jerks around their management superiors up the hierarchy. Rationally, they only bully those below them. The reason jerk managers persist is that they are invisible for long periods of time to the more senior figures to which they report. They are visible to only their staff below them! Why such managerial tragedies last so long is that those above them are the only ones that have the power to weed them out.

Good managers mix: firmness, tact, and humor in their efforts to motivate staff toward goal attainment. A good manager recognizes the role of luck in managing people and groups well. As an Argentine tennis champion once said: "yes I'm lucky and the more I practice the luckier I get." The more one learns from mistakes and successes on the job, the luckier and better they become at managing effectively. Good managers are "bold and humble" with their staff consistent with Klitgaard's (2022) criteria. To narrow these maxims down, the good and effective manager needs to motivate staff toward objectives by being authoritative and commanding but not authoritarian or tyrannical. Common sense suggests that bullying destroys the glue of interpersonal trust needed for effective individual and group performance. To narrow this down, the good and effective manager needs to motivate staff toward objectives by being authoritative and commanding but not authoritarian or tyrannical. An effective manager in any context needs to give his or her team explicit directions and expectations, in written form if possible. The expectations and directions would be criteria for their later evaluation. Such a manager also needs to be sensitive enough to people whom they do not assume they all have to be like themselves. He/she should be flexible enough to differentiate them. In our terms, that would mean a Theory Y type manager. Such managers as Oppenheimer and Warburton (to be discussed) could be considered effective. Oppenheimer managed teams to build the bomb on time; Warburton managed his Borneo outstation well but came up against the difficult team member Cooper in the case below, a truculent and violent person. Cooper disliked Warburton and challenged him at every turn. Explicit reminders to him, even in written form, did not work! Warburton demonstrated effective tolerance of the ambiguity of managing people and schedules in a difficult unstable context. But it wasn't enough. He needed a good management textbook, but more importantly, a good revolver!

It is also the case that an effective manager must oversee their staff by monitoring their behavior. The wider the span of management control, the less personal the oversight. Surveillance and reporting by computer cameras and emails become the preferred means of oversight. Before monitoring and evaluation systems are put in place, the organizational spans of control need to be established. The span of control is the number of subordinates that can be managed effectively and efficiently by supervisors or managers. Norms have been established as rough guideposts for particularly complex and technical public services such as urban transportation to prevent over and understaffing. For example, in New York City, an early childhood education program classroom must have at least one teacher for every eight 3-year-olds or ten 4-year-olds. That is roughly the same norm for other rich-country pre-school programs. Refinement of such ratios and norms is often a process of trial and error to see what works best. As a general rule, for repetitive mechanical tasks, oversight is more mechanical and metric driven, such as items assembled/hour or cases processed/day. Face-to-face and occasional nudges from management other than from impersonal emails are more difficult due to the constraints of time and scale. These often end up being formalistic and mechanical *deus ex machina* exercises. And that often means loss of interpersonal trust and organizational solidarity.

Second, the senior public or private management must devise a new staffing plan from this information. Firms and government organizations perform periodic culls known as "surplussing" or "right-sizing" for cost-cutting purposes. Streamlining headquarters operations and reorganizing at the same time has been done but is often an opaque and complex culling ploy. In the public sector, this is called "State Modernization" or "Functional Review" and has been used mostly for the same purposes.[29] In past decades, many World Bank and UKAID projects have been implemented as part of their governance aid programs. Streamlining and reorganizations are much more slick and sophisticated but with the same basic purpose as the boss inviting you across the street for a chat about the future and a coffee with him! The guiding notion that "getting the right people doing similar functions in the right places where they can work collaboratively to strengthen the company culture for the next 10 years" has been tried many times unsuccessfully by university presidents, government organizations, and private firms and is now being tried by AT&T (billed as a dynamic "return to office" plan with new assignments).[30]

Supervisors then put the data together and devise a new rural technical officer (RTO) plan. This is like most a theoretical plan, full of abstract but crunchy consultant-friendly terms like roles, structures, functions, and expected synergies. It is not management science but rather a form of subjective art with style and flair. It could be science, how to find out? One method is to ground truth the assumptions and premises if that is possible. The result of the RTO, in any case, will be new assignments, which include being guided to the back door. By contrast IDM work is largely conducted in the field with fixed teams, timelines, and budgets. IDM work mostly is line operations rather than major strategic staffing decisions. Field teams normally find out about new staffing assignments on return to their offices. To a large extent the stability and longevity of staff in public, private, or NGOs depend on winning and executing these fixed aid projects, supplier contracts, and/or sales.

Building and Establishing Trust

The trouble is that intrusive monitoring and reporting burdens that support "rule by algorithm" often indicate to staff that they are not trusted. For narrower spans of control where managers oversee fewer but more complex tasks performed, the traditional rule is that oversight should be less intrusive. Intrusive management of a five-star hotel or restaurant, for example, would be an improperly designed management strategy. Management of a good hotel should be unobtrusive but vigilant—allowing for self-motivated task achievement. In such organizations, staff should know their assigned task and perform them to maintain high service standards and to keep customers returning. If managers treat such staff as assembly-line workers, it suggests a weak and insecure organizational culture that would probably show up in high turnover rates. Service standards would drop, and customers would know it. "Digital Taylorism",[31] as it is called, or time management controls via digital surveillance and other supporting systems requires building trust with employees before such systems can be effective. Without prior trust the effort to build solidarity through micro-management, surveillance, and more intrusive progress reporting is simply Theory X management applied to cultural engineering.

IDMs should also reflect on the fact that locals are not there for us to work with to achieve our project metrics and behave consistently with our work plans and timelines. We are there for them and must adapt and adjust our schedules. As I once told my HQ superior on an Albania local government project, we (the project team) often didn't know what we would do or whom we would meet each day. Some days we got nowhere; others we achieved spectacular results, some not on the work plans! The superior, expecting discrete actions and results according to planned timelines, was unable to process this kind of ambiguity, which derived mostly from the unstable country context compounded by bad roads, often non-existent telecommunications and intermittent electricity—all of which was known to anyone with the most basic country knowledge of Albania in the late 1990s. Aid workers and managers need to show locals that we are there for them, rather than any "clients" in Washington, London or embassies in the capital cities.

Empathetic and Humble Management

Effective managers and staff know that interpersonal trust increases morale which encourages good work. A high trust environment makes people feel better and want to work harder for themselves and approval of their colleagues. It is likely that trust is created by the example of working with trustworthy people and emulating their actions more than management training sessions that, for example, encourage willingness to help a colleague in a controlled setting. But most of that is common sense. The CEO at the development firm for which I worked stocked cartons of milk in our dining and break area. He was concerned that because of how badly most of us ate and drank on missions that we were not getting enough calcium. He showed real concern for all of us and we knew it. The firm also was extensively lenient with staff failures to bill enough work[32]. By the cost center system by which expenses are charged to groups or cost centers, one center would subsidize another to make up for the shortfalls—up to a point. I saw one staff last for a year this way, after which he was let go. Other firms would drop a poorly billed staff-member in months or less! These little moves by our firm developed a bond of trust between the firm and us, between senior management and us. They were not gimmicks or canned techniques, they were from the heart. This is consistent with the approaches of Robert Klitgaard's being "bold and humble", and Brenee Brown's to try and open up oneself to being vulnerable in front of staff to attain greater trust and to create a more trustworthy work environment[33]. The development manager above was "humble" as in displays of authentic deference: "I may not be the best person for this job. But I'm doing the best I can do please bear with me and help me to get our work done" And we respected his frequent and "bold" proposals of new objectives and better ways of doing things, and clear suggestions to us of how we could accomplish them.

How's your day been? Bad day with the bank loans...? Trouble starting the car? Kid having discipline problems at school...? Now how do we settle down and teach this class? Prepared? No. Class knows it? Yes. Up for contract renewal this year and need those good evaluations? Level with the class and show you are a mess? No, better keep the facade! So, how's the day been on the North Macedonia local government reform project? You've visited mayors and put in a full 10-hour day. But the time zone in Washington means they are just coming to work. Suddenly USAID chief technical officer (CTO) calls and tells you to come in. You arrive and are accused of bidding on a new project when you had been told not to. You leave, call HQ, and find out the mistake was the CTOs, DAI is not Development Associates Inc which is often mistaken for DAI! But you are handed another request for proposal (RFP) by HQ to get to work on. Then you must be diplomatic with the CTO and avoid blaming her. Level with her? How? Bold and humble? Tell her about your fine day? Would that work to improve trust, or would she have you replaced anyway?

Worse than scenarios like this, failure to establish trust can lead to perverse outcomes such as "ranking and yanking" and an obsession with repetitive technical competence all of which weakens the culture further. For purposes of management control and supervision, the entire organization is treated as an assembly-line operation performing relatively simple tasks. That works well if the tasks are in fact simple and repetitive such as assembly lines. But more complex tasks requiring management expertise and experience require less intrusiveness and allow for greater devolution of authority and responsibility to middle management and line managers. Complex public services such as foreign aid, health care, urban transport, and education fall into this category. But note that more devolution to lower level managers can create clashing incentives. Agency problems occur where "agents" engage in tactical maneuvers to maintain autonomy and independence from HQ "snoops". In foreign aid, project or field workers often view "strategic level" or staff people as time-wasters with their meaningless surveys and box-checking exercises ostensibly to achieve greater output and productivity. Line people often want to be left alone to clash and bicker or just to get on with their jobs! At IMF, for instance, our team of "headquarters-based consultants" (on K Street NW) specializing in taxation and public budgeting bonded together, coming to work often without ties and coats and instead using the communal tie and coat hanging permanently in our office to visit HQ on nearby 19th Street NW for necessary meetings and presentations. The incentives of principals (them) and agents (us) predictably clashed. But it was all in good fun! Everyone knew the rules and that we violated them often out of necessity after coming from the airport straight back from a month mission in Guinea-Bissau!

Remember that *"Taylorism"* is named after the writer Frederick Winslow Taylor (1911) who suggested application of rational methods to encourage greater output. Time management can help. But studies also encounter the real biases of the *"Hawthorne Effect"*—or productivity enhancements caused simply by giving greater attention to the targeted study groups than to control groups that lacked such sudden importance! Nevertheless, as applied *Taylorism*, or the use of time management methods to mathematically streamline industrial workplaces, as noted, was picked up by Marxist-Leninist planners in 1920s and used for the Soviet physical norm system. The Soviet management systems focused on physical outputs and did not measure real financial and human costs. They combined tyranny of the metric with that of the clock! Treating all organizations as producers of simple products and services resulted in defective outputs and products.

Smarter reporting requirements can remedy these defects and lead to a more useful and nuanced form of micromanagement that help employees do better work (e.g., write better contract proposals) and produce more (paid work for individuals and firm profitability). Smarter metrics and reporting systems can also assist in comparing plans with physical and financial results in order to evaluate real costs of production and assessing unit and team performance. Digital Taylorism could also work in the short term for routine assembly-line type jobs that require minimal analytic insight, judgment, or thought. So why then is Digital Taylorism or rule by algorithm spreading and what are its limits? Conversely, how does "rule by algorithm" often produce perverse performance results, such as "ranking and yanking" and obsession with technical competence?

What remedies would you propose for intrusive micromanagement in the form of rule by algorithm in areas such as international aid, education, and law enforcement? For example, switching quotas for reported crimes and neighborhood arrests to cases cleared. The management trick is to build metrics from the ground up or work level and incentivize adoption of them by staff and line officials as a cooperative effort. Reporting burdens are a serious problem for development assistance precisely because metrics are poorly selected and often viewed by aid workers as irrelevant to obtaining real development results. They predictably lead to perverse incentives such as goal displacement.[34] In many aid projects, performative work (or make work) and attention to process become more important than delivering the promised skills and systems to the intended aid beneficiaries.

Facilitating Inter-Organizational Communications between Technical Teams

Organizational trust between individuals and teams is hard to build and easy to destroy. An effective strategy for this problem is to build trust by establishing working relationships between experts and technocrats at same level between adversaries. This works within sectoral areas such as urban transport and security/defense, as well as within organizations. The officials are at the same technical level regardless, and this makes relationships easier to manage as they all speak roughly the same language: solve the problem! These relationships are building blocks of trust within and between similar types of organizations.

This is not a new concept—the notion of organizations as composites of teams that need to be led and managed dates back at least to the Victorian era.[35] The Victorian era model might be set in a school room, with a model leader and manager like the English Headmaster and schoolboys divided into houses. The normative theory was that competitiveness would build character, discipline, team spirit, trust, and ultimately greater resilience to the predictable future setbacks of life and career. Modified for conflict resolution in aid organizations and teams, the idea here is that informal teams of similar backgrounds and expertise can work best at resolving conflicts between other groups and organizations with the same technical missions and objectives.[36]

From onsite research, I found communication channels between similar experts, such as train control and signaling systems, to be an effective trust-builder and problem-solving method for rail authorities in multiple cities such as Toronto, Atlanta, NYC, and Washington. Similarly, such informal cross-organizational communication channels have worked to lower temperatures and avoid major conflicts between current adversaries China and the US. It has been noted that both in China, Russia, and to a variable extent in the US, there are fewer sensible actors, fewer people with problem-solving experience and more zealots in the Anthony Downsian (1967) sense than ever before which raises the temperature for conflicts big and small. Existing cross-organizational channels for trust-building and problem solving to share knowledge should be formalized with a ready supply of new problem solvers, conflict managers, and rational actors to prevent appointment of hotheads and amateurs by senior political types with personal agendas. Such international relations and conflict management luminaries as Henry Kissinger liked small advisers within easy reach of each other working tacitly together to avoid the "policy making bureaucracies".[37] He has been right all along on this point as it also builds trust!

Are there useful insights from economic theories to guide managers in building trust and motivating better team performance? How rigorous or relevant are microeconomic models when applied to softer questions of management and organizational behavior? Models tend to be guided by markets and price signals as determinants of organizational and management allocation of resources and performance. Such drivers are necessary but not sufficient, as administrative fiats often perform the allocations and they work through teams. And regime fiats or directives, decisions, and slogans are hard to link to the right motivators. Indeed, teams are motivated but always by more than economic incentives (rewards—punishments) or the right organizational "governance" structures. Leaders and managers in practice find that it is always more than a tight theory of resource allocation and supporting equations. It comes down to allowing staff to "satisfice" (or combining satisfactory efforts with trying to maximize them), giving employees the space to practice trial and error, perform "piecemeal incremental remedialism",[38] and develop necessary interpersonal, institutional, and cultural linkages that are hard to predict in advance.

Managers like Moses and Warburton in *Cases #1 and #2* wanted loyalty and respect. They wanted staff loyalty with minimum "maintenance" or interventions to keep members on track. Did they earn it? Were they entitled to it as an adjunct of their positions? Theories can't point managers to the right levers in multiple contexts—cultural or personal. Managers must feel their way forward by trial and error with team members, tailoring rewards and punishments. Managers thus manipulate vulnerabilities and needs—vanity, despair, greed, love, hate, intelligent pride, or stupid conceit—to get loyalty and motivation. Whatever works…! Moses used shock treatment to get Silsbee's attention. Warburton tried warnings and then let cultural forces go to work on Cooper. Councilor Mikulin in Conrad's *Under Western Eyes* worked on Razumov's unsettled mind, shaken conscience, and suppressed need for parental affection to gain his loyalty to the state and act as a police informant.[39]

Theory-driven remedies to improve slack staff performance, such as better time management and various intensities of monitoring or "digital Taylorism", typically run up against the limits of "bounded rationality". This means that individual employees have to make decisions with limited information, time, and cognitive capacities—they end up satisficing rather than optimizing. At the shop floor level, teams are motivated perhaps more by their values and attitudes—their political and organizational cultures—than money. Management is about leading, motivating, measuring, and evaluating work in different employment cultures. Nonfinancial rewards and sanctions may motivate staff more than financial ones. And international development managers lean about the most important ones from daily trial and error interactions—from permanent learning experiences. The team manager tries to move local values and behaviors in the right directions to get the tasks done. Use of economic frameworks and theories to identify principal and agent issues and instances of perverse incentives can help if the obstacles can be removed. Whatever tools and theories can help improve management of internal systems and processes, human resource motivation and oversight, and fiscal controls should be used![40]

Managing Tensions and Conflicts: Head-Knocking and Bullying Toward Collaboration?

Lawsuits and legal threats for abuses of power, bullying, and harassment of staff are a familiar problem in aid firms and on aid projects in the field. People "treat each other differently" in different political cultures and what may appear as personnel mistreatment in demonstrative contexts, e.g., Southern Europe and Latin America, and what may appear as crude and antiquarian (e.g., shouting, shoving, and fist-pounding) to Western eyes may just be local commonplaces. The manager may be dealing with high spirits in action, misreading an "intimacy of antagonism"[41] for disorderly behavior or even rebellion. In fact, such antics may be how "others" behave to get the work done. Witness how teams of Latin Americans behave performing construction, roofing, and lawn mowing jobs in residential areas and cities in England and the US. Of course, the other possibilities are toxic team dynamics, loss of managerial control, a nasty ill-placed chief of party, or petty hatreds carried over to the field from headquarters. Any of those personnel problems would have little to do with political culture.

Still, inexperienced (often Western) managers often misread local cultural antics and gestures for threatening behavior demanding a tough response. He/she may fear shouting, growling, whistling, and singing, when in fact this behavior is a necessary accompaniment to work! What would cross the line and need to be sanctioned? Fisticuffs? Knife fights? Some of this may take place with managers and staff participating together in "joking behavior" that cultural anthropologists identify in such groups as longshoremen (violent rough-housing as part of their daily routines).[42] These behaviors have been identified as functional efforts to release tensions from tough jobs—especially those specialists dealing with poor people and facing hopeless situations and clients all day and trying to sleep soundly at night—social workers, mental health clinicians, anti-poverty lawyers, cancer wards doctors, prison guards.[43] How should these differences be treated? One standard remedy that seems to work is making the workplace rules on staff treatment explicit to staff in group and one-on-one explanations.

In addition to tension-releasing, nuanced behaviors and peculiar in-house jargon are useful devices for culture-building. Among themselves, doctors and nurses, for instance, refer to some patients as "*status dramaticus*" types (malingerers), or "ash cash" when they sign cremation forms in the UK. Military, security assistance workers, and fire services teams often refer to victims of firebombing as "crispy critters". Urban transit line officials such as mechanics, drivers, and shop workers refer to HQ and high-level staff people and supervisors from central offices as "suits" or "snoops" and auditors or evaluators as "bean counters". Aid workers in the field use similar terms for such people such as "time-wasters" for those from HQ or USAID who sniff around unknowingly while counting beans and interfering with their work. These in-house terms and behaviors are useful team and culture-building devices for people in difficult contexts doing risky jobs under pressure.

Maintenance of inter-ethnic identities and conflicts are a major problem within countries such as the former Yugoslavia. It is even more of a problem when managing multi-ethnic groups in schools and workplaces. Conflict resolution through defined work and team sports is one successful method. For example, in Gostivar, Macedonia the Inter-Ethnic Project (IPG) utilized unemployed workers from all ethnic groups to work on municipal services such as sanitation collection, park maintenance, and cleaning of streets. According to van Hall (2004:196),[44] the project was a "visible example of multi-ethnic cooperation (i.e. Albanian Muslims-Macedonian Slavs) that effectively challenged some established prejudices that different groups could not work together and that donors were not spending money on anything useful in Gostivar".[45] This was consistent with work the author had done in Albania as part of a USAID technical assistance to five local governments there in 1995–1996. In Pogradec, the author and his team experienced severe problems of after-school delinquency, vandalism, and discovered a complete lack of interest or funds in the city to establish remedial after-school city athletic programs. Wealthier kids in Pogradec were members of "private" sports clubs that provided programs and services for their members. The author worked with the city and a "sports club" that had no funds or equipment to provide after-school football programs. In exchange, the city provided job training for students to learn about such services as water and sewer, sanitation, and parks. The aid project allocated funds to pay an athletic director and coaches for the city program. The athletic equipment was provided to the Pogradec city program by a US NGO free of charge. Vandalism declined and fewer delinquency problems of theft and fighting between groups diminished substantially. One could extrapolate from these group management experiences to the establishment of social cooperation, increasing trust and formation of "social capital", and improved local government institutional performance, by such measures as increased taxpaying and voter support for municipal mayors.[46]

In other cases, aid field managers seeking to reduce tensions and inter-group hatreds simply ignore them on the theory that their causes are complex and may blow over and may even get engaged with groups exhibiting such behavior. Joking behavior such as violent rough-housing to release tensions (e.g., surprise leaps by members on others from the tops of boxes to begin wrestling matches in port warehouses by Portland Longshore-man[47]) can go too far and mask abuses in asymmetrical relations where power differentials are substantial within organizations. Skilled managers must use any and all techniques (often trial and error with specific groups) to prevent such abuses in order to manage the frequently intense feelings of inter-group hatred and distrust. But given tight work plans and intrusion by different organizational personnel, such as donors, firm HQs, and host country officials, it may be that an initial period of head-knocking is required to get everyone on the same page which degenerates into "bullying" by team leaders or members on each other. If work is to be completed effectively, these behaviors need to be avoided. It is well-known that some leaders given tasks of planning and organizing complex events with little guidance on the appropriate means to achieve them resort to knocking heads together, often out of frustration. The atmosphere of some aid projects appears to involve constant mutual bullying!

Questions

What steps should management take to lower tensions? Such managers know they have limited time to produce results. They have to follow work plans and contract specifications or face criticism from their superiors. This problem can be seen in such large undertakings as the Manhattan Project to create the atomic bomb[48] and end WWII, to efforts to sequence the human genome and sequence DNA, to sending a manned rocket to the moon, or to building a road through the western Nigerian bush, as project chief Rudbeck had to do, with Mr. Johnson's creative assistance doing the books and managing the teams. Despite their technical and scientific expertise, such manager-leaders often lacked a clue how to achieve these tasks at the time. The objectives were to develop new technologies. Creativity, boldness, determination, and control were essential ingredients. The team leaders were given resources to hire staff and organize teams to collaborate on producing these objectives. Very soon they became frustrated at encountering known and unknown obstacles—cultural, institutional, personal.

Like many in such positions, Robert Oppenheimer at the Los Alamos lab was also frustrated in having to deal with many qualified scientists and engineers with their own ideas and who wanted to go off in many different directions.[49] He was not considered a bully but was considered a good, effective manager. By contrast his boss General Leslie Groves was known described by Oppenheimer as a "bastard, but a straightforward one!" He was known by his aides as "abrasive, sarcastic and one ho disregards all normal organizational channels. He was also known as 'always a driver, never a praiser'. But he was intelligent and had guts to make timely, difficult decisions". In short, just what was needed to pick Oppenheimer as Manhattan Project director and get an A-bomb built on time! But was Groves a situational bully? Probably....[50]

Must leader frustration necessarily lead to imposing a centralizing economy of scale approach? Denton (2019) notes that inexperienced and often insecure leaders may suddenly demand that all information flow through them and demand constant reporting on and approval of every potential decision. The micromanagement approach is considered old-fashioned time-clock pettiness driven by ego satisfaction. The alternative is to utilize the decentralized approach allowed by technology today. Denton called this the "efficiency trap" where managers reduce strategic uncertainty by mindless pursuit of uniformity in situations requiring inputs of subordinate judgments and a diversity of approaches. How can a leader avoid this "trap"? One effective method is to ask for "sense of the meeting" cloture instead of divisive votes on every move. The change of decision rule can speed meetings along. A more severe remedy is to call for a face-to-face critical review of progress between the team leader and the development agency. The review could result in a series of changes in the COP or team leader's behavior or their immediate replacement. This is often the stage, as in the Pakistan case below (#8), where the "angel of death" arrives for a chat from London or Washington HQ and the leader is "invited to leave". Then begins the process of finding a new leader who has fewer character and leadership flaws than the last one!

Again, it may be that leaders begin with a period of knocking heads together to force collaboration and the approach may work for a short time. For instance, President Biden's scientific advisor (Dr. Lander) was highly praised for integrating biotech laboratories in multiple countries to sequence the genome but was later accused by his staff of bullying and replaced.[51] He achieved much of his initial collaboration by knocking heads and bullying. But his actions were termed "out of sympathy with the times". Leaders of large bespoke or novel projects may fear being cornered and set up for failure. Out of frustration they often lash out at imagined enemies and conspirators in their own staff. They unreasonably bully, humiliate, and blame them publicly and privately. Must there be a stage of bullying precede collaboration for novel, complex, big projects? Should that require immediate team leader replacement as in Pakistan project (*Discussion Case #8* below)? How would you avoid bullying your staff if they consistently disagreed with your plans and team assignments?

In fact, hierarchies give managers the power to weed out poor performers. They have to have this power but need to exercise it reasonably. A common set of legal criteria include "feeling intimidated or threatened" by the behavior of another, often a superior. Are these sufficient grounds? How could they be proven or disproven? Applying them, was Cooper or Warburton guilty of bullying? Did either perform improperly? Why or why not? Should either have felt intimidated by the other? Offended? What role does atmosphere play in deciding if bullying took place? If so, was Moses a bully? What criteria should be used by management in determining if someone is guilty of bullying?[52]

Hypothetical and Further Questions

Suppose you were put in charge of organizing a large, complex conference event for the development industry for competitor firms such as your own and NGOs that would include panels of participants from the major international development donors that finance aid projects on which the invitees depend for their continued existence. It is a two-day event with break-out meetings, speakers, papers, and materials to be produced from presenters distributed, and arranging hotel space and means. You are given a limited budget and permission to utilize home office staff. Suppose also that the staff has experience in this task and many different ideas on how to deliver a successful conference.

What would you do and not do? In the Borneo case below, Cooper was given an additional task by Warburton to clean the town and row cargo and passenger boats up and down the nearby river. His teams worked hard to perform both tasks well and often finished them early. In response, he punished them by withholding their wages! This violates the commonsense rule that if an individual or team is doing its job well, either leave them alone, reward them, or both. Along the winding path to developing the A-bomb, Robert Oppenheimer had frequent run-ins with his scientists, his project sponsor—the US Army, and the lead contractor Westinghouse. He quit his job several times in frustration. He felt like many COPs, that he had multiple uncooperative masters and little real authority to deal with them or to get anything done without navigating a complex time-wasting bureaucratic process of meetings and approvals. Resident Warburton ran the Borneo station and with trust and loyalty from the locals. He paid attention to cultural sensitivities and demonstrated astute "TC". Mr. Johnson gave his work teams financial and nonfinancial rewards that were off the books and technically illegal but got the jobs done for project chief Rudbeck. But note that the objective of building a road was simple, tangible, and had been done before— there was a tangible objective—unlike a moon landing, atom bomb, or sequenced genome which no one had ever seen before. No one had to be bullied, only incentivized properly to build a simple road in their familiar circumstances of the Nigerian bush.

Must there be a stage of knocking heads for large complex and bespoke projects? How can it be avoided? Can sweet reasonableness replace this stage and achieve the necessary team and inter-group collaboration? Is there any evidence that head-knocking can lead to team collaboration? Can the same team leader lead such as transition from Theory X tough management to Theory Y soft management? Are there applicable lessons from Moses, Cooper, Warburton, and Mr. Johnson?

Notes

1 Jonathan Haskel and Stian Westlake (2022) *Restarting the Future: How to Fix the Intangible Economy* (Princeton University Press).
2 Douglass North, C. John Wallis, Barry Weingast and Stephen Webb (eds) (2013) *In the Shadow of Violence: The Problems of Development in Limited Access Order Societies* (New York: Cambridge University Press).
3 Brian Levy (2014) *Working with the Grain, Integrating Governance and Growth in Development Strategies* (New York: Oxford University Press), p.10.
4 Amartya Sen (1999) *Development as Freedom* (New York: Anchor).
5 Francis Fukuyama (2014) *Political Order and Political Decay* (New York: Farrar, Straus and Giroux); Dani Rodrik (2009) "Diagnostics before Prescription" *Journal of Economic Perspectives*).
6 Can "spiritual development" be an end beyond mere economic GDP growth as in the goal of "spiritual development" claimed by followers of Juan Peron in the 1950s–1960s? But Naipaul noted the deep concern of *Peronistas* then over high Argentine rural unemployment. Can sufficient employment then be achieved simply by state fiscal transfers creating state jobs without economic growth? (Naipaul, 1981:117). During the state Soviet period, foreign exchange for growth was earned from trade on the international oil, gas, and wheat markets.
7 *Economist* (2023) "China and Latin America, Comrades across Continents", 6-17, pp.22–23.
8 Joseph Conrad (1960) *Nostromo* (New York: Dell Publishing), pp.347–348.
9 As Naipaul (1981:210, 214) noted for the Zaire nationalizations of Joseph Mobutu, "the nationalizations are petty and bogus; they have often turned out to have been a form of pillage and are part of no creative plan; they are as short-sighted, self-wounding and nihilistic as they appear, a dismantling of what remains of the Belgian-created state". The nationalizations there were done by Mobutists who followed the African nihilist in Zaire toward a "pure, logical world". The reference here is to the Belgian colonial state, but the pattern is the same for most other poor country nationalizations, which are

executed by a new dictator and his mob of followers which may have its catchy slogans but management of needed programs will not be one of them.

10 Albert Guerard, "Introduction" (Joseph Conrad's *Nostromo, 1904*). Conrad was pessimistic about the moral peril of involvement in native affairs by benevolent despots who were often romantic and vulnerable romantic meddlers and idealists from imperialist countries such as England (*Nostromo*, p.13). Such people as Kurtz in *"Heart of Darkness"* believed that they were bringing enlightenment, progress, and order to the locals. These were often "sentimental humanitarians" bemused by generous dreams (e.g., Henry Ford's *Fordlandia* "scheme" (not public purpose "project"!) in the Brazilian jungle for his rubber plantation-based community that featured a healthy dose of moral and spiritual renewal—such as a prohibition against drinking spirits). To their peril, they often became involved in native intrigues and perished. Those who tried to break the spell of such people, such as Kurtz in *Heart of Darkness*, failed because the "high devils" didn't want their spells broken. They morally deteriorated along with the collapsed physical surroundings.

11 V.S. Naipaul (1969) *The Mimic Men* (London: Penguin), p.103 and 176.

12 *Economist* (2023) "Dodging the Resource Curse, Diamond Geyser", 6-10, p.12.

13 Oliver E. Williamson (1981) "The Economics of Organization: The Transaction Cost Approach", *American Journal of Sociology* Volume 87, Number 3, pp.548–577.

14 See George M. Guess (2019) *Building Democracy and International Governance* (New York: Routledge).

15 What is or is not a project? A "project" is a commonly used term in international development. It is the expenditure of funds through a recognized organization for public purpose. That could be a foundation, international donor, or legitimately vetted charitable donor. A project is the smallest unit responsible for attainment of a particular objective, e.g., build and maintain 10 miles of road, or train 100 school officials on teaching through a particular learning script for K–3 students in district 4. The familiar trilogy of public purposes from largest to smallest is policy, program and project (national roads and rail systems), program (secondary and rural roads), and project (Mr. Johnson's road project in Kano sponsored and paid for by the British). A "project" is not a personal "scheme", e.g., a commune or neighborhood garden. The project is distinguishable by the legitimacy of its vetted sponsor and track records in similar work: World Bank and Open Society Institute. Public projects should be distinguished by legitimate sponsorship vs. schemes driven by sudden the inspiration of its leaders and follower. Naipaul distinguishes such projects from Malik's (aka Michael X) black racial uplift schemes which in Trinidad which he calls "hustling projects" organized by "itinerant hustling teams" funded by well-wishing outsiders. V.S. Naipaul (1981) *The Return of Eva Peron and the Killings in Trinidad* (New York: Vintage), pp. 4–5 and 59. Such itinerant schemers have different names in Spanish, e.g., *camelero* i.e., line-shooter or bullshitter who really has nothing to sell you, and *chanta* or an unprincipled operator who will sell you anything, in Argentina (1981:124).

16 Naomi Caiden and Aaron Wildavsky (1974) *Planning and Budgeting in Poor Countries* (New York: Wiley).

17 Wallace Sayre (1958) "Public and Private Management: Are They Alike in All Unimportant Aspects?" *Public Administration Review* Volume 18, Number 2, pp.102–105.

18 *Economist* (2023) "The World Ahead 2023, It's Time to 'Rephrase" How Companies Work", p.120.

19 Chandler Velu *et al.* (2023) *Economist* "The Business of Economics" (letter), p.14.

20 Peter Drucker (1954) *The Practice of Management* (on MBO).

21 Peter Koehn and James N. Rosenau (2010) *Transnational Competence: Empowering Professional Curricula for Horizon-Rising Challenges* (Boulder, CO: Paradigm Publishers).

22 *Economist* (2020) "Bartleby: Why We Need to Laugh at Work", 10-3, p.57.

23 Ceux Qui Travaillent (2018) ("Those Who Work") directed by Antoine Russbach with Protagonist Olivier Gourmet (Locarno: 71st International Film Festival, 8-1-11, p.130).

24 From: W. Somerset Maugham (1963) "The Outstation", *Collected Short Stories, Volume 4* (London: Penguin), pp.338–366.

25 To paraphrase Stendhal in *The Red and the Black*, Warburton viewed his role as a wise leader expected to keep great anger from coming out of petty issues or out of events which rumor transforms in carrying them around (New York: Modern Library, 2004), p.254. In his mind, this prevented petty issues from causing major resentments at the outstation and prevented them from happening.

26 Koehn and Rosenau (2010) *op.cit.*, p.92.

27 *Economist* (2022) "Bartleby: Purpose and the Employee", 1-29, p.52.

28 *Economist* (2023) "Bartleby: The Bottleneck Bane", 5-20, p.60.

29 Guess (2019) *op.cit.*, Chapter 9.

30 Scott Morwitz (2023) "AT&T New Job Plan My Bring Job Cuts", *Bloomberg BusinessWeek*, 6-19, p.14.

31 *Economist* (2020) "Bartleby, Digital Taylorism", 8-8, p.54.

32 International aid firms survive and can thrive on billing "clients" for work. Staff need to bill up to a preset threshold rate depending on the calculated break-even point (see *Chapter 5*). A larger more successful firm with lots of large development projects might require staff to bill up to 30%–40% of their time. A less successful firm might require 75%–80%. Administrative personnel such as project assistants and senior admin staff typically do not bill clients. They subsist on firm "surpluses", or profits, the allowable multiplier for the firm, and the indirect cost charged internally to the organization. See *Figure 5.2*. The audited multiplier rate might be close to 2.0 meaning that direct costs can be billed at double the total proposal amount, providing hefty sums for development firms to cover the period between losses on bids. The length of this period is determined by the "hit rate" of the firm or won-loss score.

33 See Brenee Brown (2015) *How the Courage to be Vulnerable Transforms the Way We Live, Love, Parent and Lead* (Avery).

34 George M. Guess (2019) *Building Democracy and International Governance* (New York: Routledge), Chapters 7 and 10.

35 The notion of organizations as composites of teams that need to be led and managed dates back at least to the Victorian era. There, the model was public schools (i.e. elite private), and it was shown to work if led and managed properly and the teams were selected carefully. It worked spectacularly well (*Goodbye Mr. Chips* by James Hilton and *To Serve Them All My Days* by R.F. Delderfield) and spectacularly bad (*Tom Brown's Schooldays* by Thomas Hughes)! The model leader and manager would be like the English Headmaster, dividing up his boy's school into houses where groups lived, studied, and

played sports against other houses wearing their little emblems. The houses were sources of identity and loyalty, something like regiments.

36 This team structure does the work without the need for the formalities of living, working, and playing together. But they develop anyway among and between groups. At informal gatherings, drinking and eating sessions have recognized as vital and long-lasting incubators of group loyalty. Witness the reunions of German army officers and enlisted members who also invited their US army counterparts that led to strange results, e.g., US army enlisted men supporting their German counterpart families or paying for their medical treatments later in life. In one personal case I knew of this happening between the families of the German soldier who captured the American counterpart and they made friends after the latter was in POW camp—learning each other's language. The informal experiences bond people, families, and teams together in most circumstances.

37 Anthony Downs (1967) *Inside Bureaucracy* (Boston, MA: Little, Brown); *Economist* (2023) "How to Prevent World War III, a Conversation with Henry Kissinger", 5-20, p.17.

38 David Braybrook and Charles Lindblom (1970) *A Strategy of Decision* (New York: Free Press).

39 Conrad, *op.cit.*, pp.255–256.

40 For insights of economists and political economist attempting to explain management behavior with economic theories over many decades, see the writings of Ronald Coase, Herbert Simon, Roger Porter, Elinor Ostrom, Charles Lindblom, Aaron Wildavsky, William Niskanen, Paul Farnham (2010) *Economics for Managers (2nd ed)* (Upper Saddle River, NJ: Prentice-Hall), and Oliver Williamson. Their writings provide for useful insights into the utility and limits of economic tools and frameworks to guide and motivate managers in public, nonprofit, and commercial firms. "Why Economics Does Not Understand Business" *Economist*, 4-8-23, p.65.

41 Joseph Conrad (1965) *Nostromo* (New York: Dell Paperbacks), p.228.

42 Karl E. Weick (1979) *The Social Psychology of Organizing* (Reading, MA: Addison-Wesley).

43 William W. Pilcher (1972) *The Portland Longshoremen: A Dispersed Urban Community* (New York: Holt, Rhinehart and Winston).

44 Albert van Hall (2004) "Case Study: The Inter-Ethnic Project in Gostivar", in Nenad Dimitrijevic and Petra Kovacs (eds) *Managing Hatred and Distrust: Prognosis for Post-Conflict Settlement in Multiethnic Communities in Former Yugoslavia* (Budapest: Local Government and Public Service Reform Initiative of the Open Society Institute), pp.187–205.

45 Another example of an attempt at increasing trust and encouraging ethnic reconciliation was in Vukovar, Croatia which was almost destroyed in 1991 by war between Serbs and Croats. The NGO Info-Klub Vukovar was established to create "mixed public spheres" that encouraged social mixing from all ethnic groups by hosting events such as dances, films, and discussions. The mixing model was offered as an alternative to segregation or ethnic politics which seems to make ethnic relations more strained and tense in many cities and countries, such as Northern Ireland and South Africa. Tania Gosselin (2004) "Info-Klub: Creating a Common Public Sphere for Citizens of Vukovar", in Dimitrijevic and Kovacs (eds) *op.cit.*, pp.68–69.

46 Robert D. Putnam (1993) *Making Democracy Work, Civic Traditions in Modern Italy* (Princeton, NJ: Princeton University Press, p.156-157.

47 William W. Pilcher (1972) *loc.cit.*
48 See *"Oppenheimer"* (1980) 7-part BBC mini-series.
49 "He was a leader. But he was not domineering, he never dictated what should be done. He brought out the best of us like a good host with guests". Hans Bethe gave this eulogy of Oppenheimer at his funeral in 1967. Kai Bird and Martin Sherwin (2006) **American Prometheus, The Triumph and Tragedy of J. Robert Oppenheimer** (New York City: Vintage), p.4.
50 Bird and Sherwin (2006) *op.cit.*, p.185.
51 *Economist* (2023) "Genomics, 20 Years Later", 4-15, pp.68–69.
52 *Economist* (2023) "Bartleby, Dominic Raab, Bully or Victim?" 4-29, p.58.

2 International Management Context and Culture

Context and Problems

International managers may have the toughest positions in which to perform organizational tasks. Commercial firms and private aid contractors like Max Moses' international mining, drilling, and construction companies and non-governmental organizations (NGOs) all have to face constant pressures to (1) cut corners and engage in corrupt practices (tax extortion, kidnappings, phony invoicing, sudden nationalizations, expropriations, and various bribery requirements to obtain contracts), (2) deal with cultural and religious obstacles, contextual insecurity (changes of top in-country supporters, political upheavals), and (3) endure unpredictable bureaucratic obstacles (change in local rules and regulations, micro-managerial intrusions from HQ (headquarter), and donor whims). Carrying on and achieving project goals while having to earn contract profits are exceptional achievements under such fraught conditions. The larger political and institutional context is that their assigned work has to be performed in weak states, beset by populist and ethnic-nationalists forces from all sides, which regularly capture all or parts of their respective states and misappropriate, misallocate, or just steal scarce budget resources that could have been used to solve pressing local problems. Governments of poor countries are typically closed authoritarian systems, riddled with nepotism, isolated, and simply sources of diverted funds, employment, and power to extract bribes in many countries. In this context, delivering services to the populace is often only a residual byproduct.

To learn about real management dilemmas from the ground-up, classical gurus such as Peter Drucker saturated their minds with ideas from great books and novelists such as Jane Austen. By contrast, "outward bound" seminars and motivational workshops from more popular gurus such as C.P. McCormick, George Gallup, Franklin Covey, Frederick Taylor, and Syed often conveyed sound principles, wise proverbs, and clever maxims from their work experience. Are such consultant's workshops and how-to

DOI: 10.4324/9781032670959-2

guides better ways to develop leadership and management skills than "inward bound" approaches that use films and novels to mine ideas and generate hypotheses that encourage relating what you read or see to your own values and actions? Critical parts of the context about which they write are (1) the political culture, (2) the opacity of legal and regulatory rules, (3) corruption as inherent parts of the system of business and government, (4) the weaknesses of public sector and civil society institutions to perform their intended functions, and (5) the instability of top-level official support for management of development programs and projects.

Learning Outcomes

1 To learn the pitfalls of managing in cross-cultural contexts.
2 To distinguish different types of political cultures.
3 To learn the problems of corruption in aid contracting (***Discussion Case #3***).
4 To discuss the problems with the concept of political culture such as how to distinguish symptoms and habits from real behavioral motivators.
5 To explore the case of "weaponizing" political culture through idiosyncratic local versions of history in the Russian war against Ukraine.
6 To compare the cultural problems in managing Northern Irish schools with those of the US (***Discussion Case #4***).
7 To explore the problem of political culture as a static concept unable to explain dynamic change.
8 To examine how misuse of political culture can lead to moral relativism in managing international relations.
9 To explore remedies for macro- and micro-cultural distortions to political culture.
10 To examine remedies for mismanaging organizations in different political cultures.
11 To identify lessons learned from using political cultures as a management tool, such as gaining trust, diversifying staff, and sinking local roots.
12 To examine the issues and lessons for corporate social responsibility (CSR) from the case of Shell Oil in Nigeria (***Discussion Case #5***).
13 To explore the strategy of developing local alliances and sharing risks as a management tool in the case of "Guyana 'Petrostate'" (***Discussion Case #6***).
14 To explore strategies of adapting donor country laws and practices to local political cultures to reduce management problems in the case of "Mr. Johnson" (***Discussion Case #7***) by Joyce Cary.
15 To examine the modern problem of "presentism" when using past literature to understand the workings of local political cultures.

Issues and Cases

Managing in Cross-Cultural Contexts

Concepts of culture and political culture, like mist, are hard to pin down and measure. But they matter! We will speak here of political culture in two senses: (1) as an analytical concept from which researchers can rigorously describe, predict, and explain decisions and events and (2) a loose collection of historic, ethnic, linguistic, and behavioral traits useful for professionals such as aid workers to try and make sense of different overseas contexts. Often in contexts, such as the Central America, it is also a region containing many subcultures, useful to know for predicting variations in country consumer behavior. Similarly, a tropical climate contains many micro-climates, useful for explaining and predicting crop yields and forest species growth rates. In such cases, both types of political culture are useful for business marketing decisions, and for aid project design and management.

Culture has been generally defined as the values and attitudes that affect political behavior.[1] It should be considered all or part of the context in which managers try to accomplish their objectives. In the international development context, political cultures account for the fact that people in different regions and countries view the world differently. The concept has been used and critically discussed for nearly 60 years by political scientists, economists, and management scholars.[2] For management, cultures are the persistent values and habits that affect organizational and institutional behavior.[3] This can be seen operationally and by examples of professional cultures that directly affect behavior. In the wake of scandals where auditors have failed to spot mischief in firms, the British regulator suggests a weakened "culture of skepticism and challenge" that "auditing relies on".[4] Cultural values impede the skepticism and challenge that is needed to motivate determined action and thorough scrutiny of the accounts. The applied research question is to identify the precise "values and attitudes" as well as systems that result in lax investigative practices in particular types of organizations, countries, and regional contexts. This is the soft part on which much work remains before culture can become a measurable independent or at least intervening variable from which analysts can predict practical behavior reliably and validly.

At the present state of knowledge about cultural utility, "culture" is a series or cluster of insights, hints, and habits, such as "the way people treat each other when no one is looking"; or "how we do things around here!" When working as a professor in Jackson, MS, in the Deep US South in the late 1970s for a year, I was often told: "You don't know how things are done around here, do you boy?" Sometimes this was meant politely, sometimes not. Culture can also be like-minded communities of values that influence what rules should be made and how strictly they should be enforced. For aid work, culture is what rules are made and how strictly they are enforced. Managers make rules and enforce them to prod teams toward project or organizational objectives. But they do that in different ways depending on the nuances of political culture that affect behavior. The nuances are the operative values and attitudes at two levels. First, they must operate with the larger macro-political context of institutions and rules. Second, managers make decisions affected by the micro-level local institutions and the character and makeup of individuals and teams.

In contemporary Russia, for instance, managers must read both contexts to keep their jobs. There, the Putin regime strictly enforces loyalty under explicit threats of injury, imprisonment, or death. In Latin American countries, where thuggish past regimes in such countries as Chile and Argentina have used similar tactics, a popular value is "mirroring" where empathy for others facing poverty and uncertainty drives rule-breaking. Mirroring is a workaround to deal with the official enforcement of overly rigid and punitive rules. In Brazil it is called *jeitinho* or "way around" which means shortcuts around the irrationality and hardships of rigid laws and regulations. People "obey but do not comply".

Political cultures are thus variable applications of the formal and informal rules that facilitate local survival. They can be loosely or strictly applied depending on the micro-context. This kind of cultural meaning can be seen in such simple examples as the sport of hunting. Hunters everywhere gather together for social events, shoot hare, boar, and deer, toast their accomplishments, and fill their fridges with wild game. But driven by green values, some French hunters want to ban the sport of hunting on holidays and weekends. This stance clearly upsets hunters who work all week and look forward to their week-end outings. Working hunters complain that wealthy cosmopolitan hunters want to impose their values on working rural people. Are they wrong? This is a simple example of cultural values directly changing behavior through proposed laws. Cultures and institutions combine as the formal and informal rules of the game that structure activities and motivate decisions and actions. The results can be perverse, often incentivizing bizarre chains of command and informal practices, such as the informal protocols in the Nepali and Kazak MOFs. Riggs (1964) described "prismatic societies" where cultures and institutions distort systematic patterns and refract formal organizational routines into horizontal and even non-linear patterns. Chains of command disrupt vertical command structures that overwhelm informal decisions and approvals. That produces the puzzling behaviors that locals know about but leave outsiders baffled. The trick is to describe and predict the real decision-making patterns to explain behaviors using politics, economics, anthropology, and sociology. Along the tortuous path to prediction, one must avoid simplistic and crude stereotypes that over-predict results. A rough summary guide then is that "political culture" is the behavioral expression of language, religious, social values, and trust. All these influence what rules are made and how strictly they are enforced.[5]

Our purposes here are much narrower than an all-purpose cultural explanation. We need to know managerial applications, guides, and rules that might predict local behaviors and indicate behaviors that should be avoided. For example, the link between East Asian values, attitudes, and economic policies is full of rich possibilities. The use of the political culture concept always requires adjustments for moving from individuals to groups to commercial and official institutions. But the composite personal values of deferential obedience to authority, group harmony (something like Moses' management values in the *Oriente*), competitive Confucius-driven discipline, deep personal shame at failure, obsession with order and predictability, neatly add up to cautious risk-aversion, and persistently conservative economic policies leading to lengthy recessions and deflation as has been the case in Japan. Suppose the Chinese realize obedience to centralized authority is impractical for that enormous country of many gigantic and medium-sized cities. Over time, the Chinese have devolved fiscal authority to manage, budget, tax, and borrow to municipal governments within the tight political controls of the Politburo or Communist Party. Predictable inter-institutional rivalries between the center in Beijing, regions, and localities have been managed through a series of competitive incentive programs that have led to enormous national and local growth and development. Political control has been maintained overall by subservience to the Communist Party. The policies and programs have been designed and enforced consistently with the values of its political culture.[6]

Similarly, in the EU, a political culture values-economic policy link (savings vs. spending; fiscal policy, economic growth) can be more explicitly made by comparing debt/GDP ratios in northern vs. southern EU countries. A common assumption is that the German and northern European cultural aversion to debt (*schulde*) has kept their public deficits and debt levels low in contrast with the high-debt southern EU countries such as Italy, Greece, Spain, and Portugal. Along with this over-spending assumption is another that Italians haven't collected sufficient taxes to pay for their debts. The rapid rise in Italian debt to 150% GDP occurred in the 1970s–1980s before the euro began made it easy for southern EU members to borrow cheaply and let northerners pay back their debts. However, since then rules have tightened and the spread between interest yields has narrowed. Italy has run primary surpluses for the past 30 years and public debt/GDP ratios have stabilized. Its tax collection rate of 43% of GDP is now higher than both Germany and Britain. To reduce its debt in the face of inflation and structural problems such as rigid labor markets, countries like Italy need to increase growth rather than impose fiscal austerity. Belgium tried this option, removing structural constraints and increasing growth in order to reduce their debt burden.[7] The suggestion then is that the notion of a political culture policy constraint needs to be updated and may be simply a stereotype leading to over-prediction. It can also suggest that properly designed incentives can change parts of the political culture that do lead to profligacy, over-spending, low collection rates, and tax burdens such as enforceable deficit rules and lower borrowing costs.

Political cultures are included in many management texts as abstract frameworks and typologies and give lip service to managers departing for overseas posts. It is included as a useful tool in the international development management (IDM) toolbox, a set of values and attitudes to identify and predict local decisions when working in different cultures and contexts overseas. It is not meant to be a rigorously predictive quantitative framework for all social and professional occasions but rather a useful descriptive tool to provide guideposts of dos and don'ts to avoid violating local social norms and conflict. Ignored, it can become a serious obstacle to management for such tasks as recruiting staff and resolving conflict.

A novel explicit use of political culture recently has been neither as a rigorous analytic concept or useful perspective on a particular country nor people rather than as a propaganda weapon of conquest and as a military-political justification for war and conquest by a tyrannical regime. Putin's Russian regime has used political culture (without referring to that term) as a tool of domination to justify the Ukrainian invasion. Through a distortion of history his regime claims historical and religious justification to "reunite" by force the current split in both the Orthodox church and states comprising the Ukrainian and Russian Slavic culture.[8] His socio-military plan is neo-Stalinist, to restore and continue the Russian Czarist Empire of the 18th century while stopping contamination of the Slavic race by Western Europeans and their values such as political autonomy, free expression, and dissent.[9] Vladimir Putin has claimed frequently that Western democratic values are "unworkable in Orthodox, Slavic Russia and the Ukraine".[10] Opponents of this narrow view claim that the political cultures of Ukraine and Russia may be intertwined but are distinct, like their cuisine. "They are not a single whole" says President Volodymyr Zelensky, "Ukraine is Ukraine and always will be". Clearly, the distinctive parts of the culture have produced neighborly spats and disagreements but hardly sufficient reasons for major conflicts or war. The manipulation of cultural differences for political gain by demagogues, such as Putin, makes any conflict harder to resolve. The wars appear to occur at historic periods when Russia views itself not as a "laggard" (i.e., post-1990 after the Soviet Union collapsed) in need of aid to catch up with the West, but as a "victim", surrounded by the West which consists of conspirators and enemies (now) intent on taking over Russia.

Historical distortion and the manipulation of the facts are being used to try and turn "political culture" into a causal or independent variable. In the Russian case, this means, eliminating Western values and practices, and regaining territory to reconstitute its fabled and unsuccessful empire. The management quandary is how to deal with a context in which local Russians claim their value distinctiveness distinguish lower order operational and technical values for reform of health or education sectors. What are they and how can those be made to work? As in any country, Russian and Slavic system problems must be worked with and adapted as necessary in order to make sectoral projects work for intended beneficiaries as much as possible. This was the context and challenge for many aid workers encountering Soviet management, budgeting, and policy-making systems for the first time in Former Soviet Union (FSU)/ Central and Eastern Europe (CEE) in the early 1990s through the first decade of the 21st century.

It was found by aid workers then that many Soviet operational systems (which included the near abroad satellites such as Ukraine) were in fact quite efficient and needed only minor tweaks to modernize. The basic values to calculate output metrics were similar even though used for slightly different management purposes. The physical norm system of physical outputs (e.g., #s of students, users, passengers, or patients) was used for each sector and needed only the addition of cost concepts to become useful cost-effectiveness metrics. Their technical skill in calculating outputs and needs in physical units required immense skills which the Soviets had. In some cases, Ukrainian ministries of health and education used units of money for their calculations providing measures which in the West are called "cost finding" metrics that use currency units instead of strict "costs".[11] As indicated, Ukraine used Soviet planning and budgeting systems before the "transition" (Soviet collapse) in the late 1990s. The cost or expense vs. budget expenditure distinction will be explained in *Chapter 4*.

Aid workers in public sector organizations, NPOs, and private contractors need to be sensitive and adapt to the cultural forces affecting their work. They also have to be objective and skeptical of what they are often told about sensitive topics. For instance, the sources of local ethnic passions may be driven in part by "ethnic entrepreneurs" and "grievance mongers". Despite constant calls for overseas workers to update their skills for new contexts, the significance of political culture is often ignored, in texts and in practice. "There is nothing stupider than transferring the personal characteristics of one individual, or even a group of people to an entire nation". said Fandorin in Boris Akunin's *Black City*. While he is right that there might not be a national characteristic, we still need guides to the decision-making styles and contents of other nations and regions.

Without them, the transfer of policy and management lessons from one culture and institutional setting to another becomes even more difficult. Aid workers need to find the smaller bits of the larger culture that can be changed by appropriate incentives and disincentives, such as the modification of norms to unit costs and cost-effectiveness metrics just noted.

Political cultures can raise or lower the transaction costs of getting things done. A more precise definition of the concept concentrates on the rules promulgated by such values and attitudes and how strictly they enforce them. Here, we present a basic framework for classifying cultures, a discussion of how to manage conflict, the concepts of "face" and respect in different cultures, getting to compromises, and context variables that affect expat performance evaluations (Sweeney and McFarlin, 2011), and identifying cultural constraints to reforming institutions. Other important cultural nuances include humor, gestures, and lying: how to know lies, who is lying, and when people are joking. In Graham Greene's novel *Orient Express* (1933:12), Myatt, a self-conscious Jew, employed a rule when dealing with Gentiles, especially English kinds. Following his belief that "the untrained hand gives lie to the mouth" when introducing new themes or posing leading questions, he offered his client-opponent a cigar. If lying, the person's hand would hesitate a quarter of a second before taking it! Not science, but for Myatt it usually worked!

If the cultures are compatible, with shared languages and values (e.g., East and West Germany), reforms can be made and institutionalized more easily. With incompatible cultures (e.g., the US and Saudi Arabia), it is much more difficult. For work in charged places like Lebanon and Northern Ireland, aid workers should try and distinguish *fixed* core social categories and parameters from *variable* personal affiliations and transactions. The object is to connect at the personal level first to facilitate later work. Buy dinners and socialize with your team and its local counterparts, both individually and as a team. Think of political culture as *team chemistry* and ask why it does and does not exist in some countries, peoples, and teams. We noted the effect of missing roles above in the discussion of Moses' construction team. Again, consider cultures as potentially like-minded communities of values (e.g., sects, religions, tribes, ethnicities, races, and elites) that influence what rules are made and how strictly they are enforced. Examples cited were Japanese values of deferential consensus and predictability that underpin long-standing deflationary policies and the persistence of rigid workplace hierarchies such as lifetime tenured jobs. Elsewhere, the effect of political culture on budgeting in different Balkan states can be identified.[12] That paper attempted to identify the variable effects of a common Balkan political culture on the results of fiscal decentralization policy reforms in four regional countries. The perennial question for political culture is whether it is an independent (causal), intervening variable, or a dependent variable. For instance, it is often the case that leadership *defines* the culture which would make political culture an intervening variable. Raudla (2013) found political culture to be only an intervening variable for explaining the fiscal crisis in Estonia.[13]

Typologies

There are many typologies of political culture. They are often broad and combine personal qualities with institutional roles to produce frameworks and scales often progressing from authoritarian and tribal backwardness to growth and development following patterns of Western modernization. An example of a commonly used typology is Kai Hammerich and Richard P. Lewis's *"Cultural Dynamic Model"*[14] that distinguishes three cultural contexts in which one has to manage. They are roughly (1) rich country *linear active* settings, (2) poor country *multi-active* settings, and (3) *personalistic* or *reactive* which managers find in varying mixtures in the first two contexts.

Linear-Active Context

Using their *Linear-Active* cultural context, people tend to focus on time deadlines and schedules, speak what they mean, and are confrontational. The legal and regulatory frameworks are Common Law, Civil Law, and hybrid mixes of both. Rules of law such as criminal and civil codes are transparent and respected. Property, contracts, business, and inheritance laws are clear and respected. Bureaucratic processes are roughly transparent and largely efficient. Such personal and institutional frameworks guide public and commercial management. Civil Law incentivizes cautious, conservative decision-making as active moves are sanctioned unless explicitly permitted. The incentive is to keep one's head down and avoid deviating from the rules. By contrast, the UK and US and their affiliated country networks such as the UK Commonwealth are governed by Common Law which permits proactive management and personal action unless expressly forbidden. The incentive is to act. Some countries such as Germany are hybrid due to US historical influence. The blue-chip and higher income regions are examples of linear-active cultures: North America, the UK and Western Europe, East Asia, and CEE/FSU. Within these regions, wide variation can exist within and between countries, e.g., northern-southern Italy, urban-rural UK, and Russia. In rural parts of these regions, people and institutions move at non-linear time schedules, and systems are "personalistic" or "ascriptive" and require routine corruption payments and personal connections to move processes along. Wide structural gaps between top leaders and lower personnel exist in organizations which affects management efficiency and getting anything done. That is, professional middle managers are missing from the chain of command as they are often distrusted with authority by top-level staff. Such descriptions also fit regions of advanced countries such as organizational cultures in the US Deep South.

East Asian countries such as China, South Korea, Japan, and Taiwan also fit the linear-active cultural category. These are countries with old civil services and strong and successful central states whose policies have led to growth and development. Their deferential and cautious cultures are paradoxical in that they combine tight order and routine with sudden entrepreneurial actions led from both the top or center and bottom-up or localities. The key seems to be smart incentives that induce efficiencies and developmental results. China's vast centralized bureaucracy has had to deconcentrate power and authority to regions and localities or risk institutional chaos. In the last 40 years, China for example has devolved authority to local governments for elections, taxation, and borrowing. This has led to not only a boom in local infrastructure such as housing but also to a debt crisis that has been hard to rein in (Guess and Ma, 2015). This has been in part due to a lack of independent non-state institutions to rate borrower (local bond issuer) creditworthiness rigorously such as Fitch and Moody's. Responding to widened authority, localities have borrowed by bond issuance and off-budget through rural financial authorities (RFAs). This has created tension with the center, normal in federal systems but not as much in unitary systems; in effect Chinese policies of structural decentralization have created a quasi-federal system nested in its 34 provinces including 4 large metropolitan governments and regions (e.g., Beijing, Shanghai) and provinces and thousands of local governments, which frequently challenges central financial and political authority. The developmental success of the Chinese state-guided development model together with its paradoxical culture has made it the leading contender for an alternative development model to Western capitalist democracy.

Multi-Active Context

In their second **Multi-Active** context, institutional and professional relations tend to be much more sociable, consultative, and emotive. Countries in the Latin America, southern Europe, the South Sea islands in southern Asia, and parts of North America such as South Florida and southern California fit this context. Effective management requires trust between overseers and staff in order to get things done. The management role is not simply to drive staff toward the objective on time. If the manager faces time and staff constraints from above and staff dissension within ranks, he or she has to have the capacity in this context to combine incentives and task work plan deadlines. In overseas country contexts, managers also face the challenge of unstable top-level support and legal frameworks and frequent demands of corruption payments by officials, political leaders, and suppliers that cut into project budgets. The latter intrusions can often be managed away by careful attention to the context—befriending local suppliers and paying staff well. Having staff in peacemaker and fixer roles is essential for maintaining these contacts and keeping the wheels greased. But greasing many palms requires side payments which wastes funds that were needed for the project or investment. Moses in the **Oriente** tale handled these secondary tasks well but had to confront trouble in his own ranks. He was insecure, fearful of losing control, and obsessive about maintaining enough harmony and control to finish the tasks on budget and on time. Thus, he backed himself into a corner, requiring instinctively a desperately crude theory X-type show of force-killing Silsbee's dog to try and stop the shirking behavior and re-motivate his team. Warburton in **Borneo** had to deal with a personal conflict between his assistant and him. The Resident was quirky but more sensitive to local values and practices and decided the best resolution was to do nothing and let the local culture work its magic—which it did!

This context may be the most common and most complicated for outsider managers, often recruited from **Linear Active** cultures, for instance, to work effectively. But the unstable and often glacial context contradicts the imported manager's frame of reference and dissonance occurs. For that reason, firms and governments need to focus on the recruitment of culturally experienced managers from a **Multi-Active** country context. Below, in the tragi-comical case of **Mr. Johnson**, we will see how the more unstable and novel the culture is the more difficult it is for those expecting a linear-active context to survive in this surreal and puzzling management context where every day brings unknown surprises.

Given that **Multi-Active** contexts are highly personal and weaker states are part of the cultural context, the constraints of corruption are overwhelming. The state is often viewed as an extension of the family for purposes of favors, employment, and contracts. This is well-known and derives from state weakness as well as the cultural context itself which reinforces this weakness.

Being an effective development manager in corrupt contexts requires an unusual tolerance for ambiguity. IDMs often complain with reason at being responsible for too many subordinates and suffering too many masters. The IDM in fluid, changing poor country contexts must have a high tolerance for ambiguity. This is the plight of many IDMs, and they must deal with these gaps in authority and real power to survive and succeed. It is well-known that many overseas managers do not last long! The tenure of the five to six chief of parties (COPs) for which I worked in multiple countries was often shortened by sudden losses of political support to both subordinates and superiors. A contributor to the loss of positions was the inability to adjust to corrupt systems and cultures without overt protest (a diplomatic mistake!). One of the constants in poor countries is the informal necessity of greasing the wheels to get anything done, big or small. A working definition and guidepost for spotting corruption is the abuse of power for a private purpose (keeping the bribes for personal enrichment) or public purposes (to get around obstructionist and seemingly useless and harmful state laws and rules) to move a project along. Muddying the picture is the fact that as noted corrupt practices that bend rules for favors may be locally excused for empathetic reasons or dismissed as simply personal matters related to family, tribe, ethnicity, or religious sect. Bribery practices and rule short-cuts have been rationalized as "mirroring" (because everyone does it) and *jeitinho* in Brazil (or empathy for those forced to obey but not comply), and by well-known local practices of working around rigid rules generated by Civil Law cultures with colonial histories (everybody does it). In Civil law jurisdictions such as Spain, actions are forbidden unless expressly permitted, while in Common Law Anglo-American systems, managers can act unless expressly forbidden.[15] Viewed as an abuse of official power for private or public purposes, the context and scope of decisions is a critical issue in international public sector management and reducing white collar crime, especially during procurement.

Discussion Case #3: Bribery during Aid Contract Bidding

Suppose a private firm is accused of bribery under the Foreign Corrupt Practices Act of 1977 in order to obtain an aid contract, for example, in the Dominican Republic from the Inter-American Development Bank (IADB). As an audit investigator,[16] what questions would you have? How could you determine whether higher ups or principals knew of the practices? As attorneys for the aid firm, what defenses would you offer for making payments to the host government?[17] Suppose a USAID small business assistance project needed to buy a car locally in Albania, and that market is already saturated with stolen cars at cut down prices (which it has been for years). US rules require formal procurement to buy project cars at market prices. But, like most projects, it has limited funds and a local purchase would allow re-programming of budget savings for other program needs to achieve better project results. What should the chief of the party do?

Reactive Context

The third cultural context in the Hammerich and Smith (2013) typology is called **Reactive**. These are societies where strong senses of dignity, face-saving, and shame avoidance govern interpersonal relations. The tendencies apply to personal relations at family, acquaintance, and organizational levels. It is well-documented that a predominant tendencies and values among Asians are saving face, avoiding shame, group harmony, and consensus. For expat managers in such cultural contexts, establishing trust is difficult since locals tend to tell you what you want to hear. A long historical tradition of treating outsiders as unwanted aliens exists in this region. The British traders and colonialists in the 17th and 18th centuries were treated with polite distance but deep suspicion as permanent outsiders.

Countries such as Korea, Taiwan, China, Vietnam, and Thailand are classified as examples of *Reactive* cultures in East Asia. A common problem in all contexts is for expat managers to treat those who talk, look, and behave like themselves the same. Especially in countries like Canada (lying probably between the first and third type of context), the tendency is serious. Canadians do not like it if they are mistaken for Americans any more than Irish or Australians like being mistaken for British or cockney British mistaken or treated as Australians, and especially now Ukrainians being treated as Russians! Personally, working in those countries I've committed all these mistakes! In parallel with shame avoidance and deference to authority is a tendency toward tight rigidly enforced, similar to Civil Law codes that exclude equity as a softener.

As an older advanced cultural context, East Asians prefer simple, clear rules that can be easily enforced to ensure order and maintain state authority. In contrast with Western rule "of" law by separate and independent judiciaries, the tendency in East Asia is "rule by law" meaning rules that are made and tightly enforced by the state. That is, there is minimal emphasis on due process or justice and more on rules made by unaccountable state bureaucracies.[18] In the current context, Chinese foreign investors and managers have discovered violations of rules, laws, and regulations, which means that alienation from the state means rigid often-arbitrary treatment and subjection to frequent surveillance as suspicious outsiders (i.e., no longer classed as "honored guests"). Paradoxically, as values clash, fear of losing face often works against corruption or at least being caught for it. The penalty in such a case can be self-inflicted harm or suicide as it would be treated as shameful behavior. That would be inconsistent with *Multi-Active* (e.g., Latin or Spanish) contexts since, as noted, the tendency is to "mirror" local behavior and justify rule-breaking and abuses of authority as reasonable displays of empathy for others evading or avoiding arbitrary or unjust rules.

Thus, East Asian cultures like most are inherently paradoxical. Historically and presently, tight group cultural consciousness pervades. This results in conservative institutional recruitment, a strong focus on "credentialism" for hiring, promotion, and enhanced status. People tend to work in large organizations as they provide the greatest status and most group anonymity. They are called "strivers". Individual endeavors were mostly low-status until the past several decades when individual entrepreneurship and enterprise grew to be associated with success and status. This has produced tensions with the state and Communist Party overseers which view individual endeavors suspiciously. For managers, the challenge is to motivate and control a high-energy, hard-working, and entrepreneurial cohort of workers, teams, and local government staff, most of whom are profit-maximizing dynamic people. Also paradoxical despite the cautious conservatism of East Asian cultures are the bouts of aggressive group solidarity via displays of macho late-night drinking sessions. Staff is forced to drink through these and turn up for work the next day as tests of spiritual, physical stamina and mettle. Less surprising is the frequency of such testing sessions throughout Latin America in *Multi-Active* cultures that place a premium on passionate sociability.

Non-Academic Guides

Such broad typologies as just described are useful as rough guideposts for investing, doing business, and managing people. Other useful guides include the Ardo *Culture Shock* series.[19] Published by Ardo, the country and regional guides include chapters on self-images, and living, working, and doing business in each particular country. The guidebooks cover about 60 countries on the dos and don'ts of getting along in different cultures and can help explain why expected tasks and obligations don't work as planned or get done promptly and properly. Additionally, managers posted for long- or short-term overseas assignments will gain insights into the historic and geographical dimensions of political cultures from regional and local marketing books. These books are practical, non-academic, and pointed. Regional guidebooks are also useful to get a flair for differences in histories, behavior, and values by region and within them. For example, Denton (2019) covers the seven-country Central American region individually by country and regionally, historically and presently. Preferences for products and tastes for beer, clothing, and food all provide clues as to political preferences for candidates and voting behavior. They are useful for investing in and marketing products and services.

Problems with the Concept of Political Culture

There are at least three methodological problems with the concept of political culture if it is to be used rigorously or even as a rough guide to behavior. What follows are three related and common misuses of political culture: (1) spreading self-serving versions of history, values, and practices or **weaponization** by cherry picking (self-serving selection) the values and practices of a political culture as noted above, (2) rigid use of political culture as a static concept when some or most values can be incrementally modified by incentives and learning, and (3) spreading these strategic-level distortions as values-free when they are parts of regime-driven aid programs. It is well-recognized that the operational parts of aid technical assistance are largely neutral—i.e., there are no Western vs. non-Western ways to efficiently operate and maintain bus-rail systems. Populist nationalist leaders relish practicing all three mistakes to enhance their power and popularity. Populists often do everything to maintain their power except concentrate on real policies that solve pressing national and local problems. This self-serving behavior represents the triumph of politics without policy. Scholars and analysts need to avoid them studiously. In short, managers should guard against falling into these traps unconsciously or consciously.

First: Definitional Vagueness: Or How to Define the Core Elements of the Culture?

The aim is to avoid "*cherry-picking*", or subjectively selecting out, parts of the culture that may amount to tendencies but are not actual determinants of political behavior. Hirschman and Bird warned against using symptoms or simple habits rather than real behavioral motivators and noted the academic use of a well-known Colombian habit of tearing and folding paper napkins with their noses to indicate backwardness rather than rational reaction to paper scarcity.[20] Defining the core values of the political culture is not easy and very likely debatable. It is perhaps its lack of conceptual rigor (its slippery quality) that has plagued attempts to utilize it as an explanatory research variable that has permitted its misuse. Putin has been able to import historical distortions as essential components of the Russian political culture and weaponize them as transparent propaganda. The propaganda so far has supported his "special military operation" now morphed into a full-scale war. In another case of selective cultural definition, Bangladesh has a deep tradition of pluralism and debate. It has been a secular democracy for the past 50 years. But it has had a corrupt and authoritarian Prime Minister for the past 13 years and a legacy of 29 attempted military coups. It is fair to ask whether it is a South Asian model of solid frugal social development or a "failed state in the making" as

Henry Kissinger called it in 1971. In short, what are the Bangladeshi core cultural values that are not just tendencies or superficial habits?

Other "culturists", such as Harrison,[21] distinguish "damaged" from "productive" cultural behavior in Latin American countries. That has been criticized as the use of a classification that can easily lead to "overdetermination" or of using selected negative habits as indicators for the behavior of the whole political system.[22] In some cases, the results seem consistent across countries of the region. Political culture is likely an important explanatory variable, but decades of "cherry-picking" and hypothesizing and empirical research have gotten managers no closer to identifying what the core variables are. For example, USAID and World Bank programs and projects for the past 50 years stimulated advances from such sectors as forestry: from sawmilling to more sophisticated furniture manufacturing and exporting; and from vast softwood and hardwood forest resources to pulp and paper manufacturing for import substitution industrialization (ISI). Why didn't they take hold of individual project successes and lead to growth and productivity? Now, the same constraints apply to the mining and petroleum industries that should invest their newly discovered profits in the "green transition" in local industry suppliers and manufacturing. In *Discussion Case #6*, this is the constraint Guyana faces now. The same constraints faced by countries in this region for half a century are still operative: absence of skilled labor, weak educational norms and systems, ease of working in the informal sector, and the high bureaucratic costs to employers of hiring-firing formal workers. These are well-known constraints, but why have they persisted and recurred for so long? If political culture is an important explanatory variable, which values, attitudes, and practices are most determinative, and why haven't they changed to mobilize growth and development on national scales? Evidence suggests that the Latin American region is the second least productive behind the Middle East Why is the Latin American region still a laggard in new technology, infrastructure, and educational investment?[23]

Another way of putting the problem of defining the political culture is who is doing the defining? In poor countries often ruled by autocratic regimes, there is at least minimal cultural space between the regime and the citizens. Civil society institutions exist in the intermediate space between citizens and the state. The greater the civil society holds on that space, the more autocratic the fear of loss of power and its control over the societies that they claim to rule. It is the emergence of this space between citizens and state institutions that causes trouble for autocratic control. Civil society institutions, especially the media where citizens can demand reforms, societal changes, and responses to their needs and problems are serious threats to authoritarian regimes. For many regimes, they represent the spreading cancer of "western, liberal values" and "open societies" that must be stopped from corroding their power. Accordingly, regimes treat these institutions as treasonous and state criminals and non-persons. As citizen frustrations increasingly find outlets in such independent groups, they often become targets of regime oppression.[24]

Weaponization and Cherry-Picking

A clear example of weaponization and transparent deniability, as noted above, is the current misuse of political culture by Vladimir Putin and his Russian regime. So, what is the "Russian political culture" and what does it stand for? What are its salient values? Conrad's Razumov noted in *Under Western Eyes* that it was the "land of spectral ideas and disembodied aspirations" where "brave minds turn away from its vain and endless conflicts to autocracy" (p. 35) for peace of their patriotic conscience. Is the key Russian political value then autocracy? If so, Putin may be cherry-picking and weaponizing its real autocratic tendencies to deny countries such as Ukraine the choice of deviating from that determination and creating constitutional republics driven by liberal democratic values. He weaponizes and exports its core anti-Western values. That is, he roughly exports its bad habits and permanent phobias. When I worked in Armenia just after the collapse of the Soviet Union for International Monetary Fund (IMF), my Russian counterpart at the MOF told me a few weeks into my work there: "We have been duped. You are just like us! We thought you were monsters!"

In modern post-Soviet Russia, the "encroachment" by the West upon Russian cultural values to which Putin refers is civil society or the civic and institutional space between state and society. Civil society is represented by the expanding what had been a growing independent media, and more donations to charities and other Ukrainian NGOs including opposition parties that supported independent reportage and free press, environmentalist causes, and that worked against societal corruption. A social democratic Western system would include strong civil society institutions such as media, unions, parties, election administration monitors, and political organizations, all within a state consisting of checks and balances, judicial due process, and independent legal counsel at trials. Such tendencies undermine the Russian regime's chief means of exerting influence and are viewed by Putin as a growing threat. Civil society organizations have been popular in Russia with the younger generation of under-35s that were born in the 1990s period of political liberalization. Among this younger Russian generation, Putin had been unable to employ propaganda to counter their skepticism of his repeated claim that Russia had been a "besieged fortress" encircled by enemies led by the US and the EU that sought to conquer Russia.

But younger Russians have been outside, traveled, know people, and chat with them online.

Perceiving his world surrounded and vulnerable, Putin took the counter-offensive, redefining the Russian political culture as a composite of militant values that must expand and defend the "great" Russian empire of old against imagined encirclement. MRGA (Make Russia Great Again) instead of MAGA (Make America Great Again)! In his view, Ukraine and its "non-people" represent the contamination of these purist Russian values by Western political liberalism[25] and local "Nazis" to which the antiseptic of war must be applied as a disinfectant to rid its society of alien values. In short, the war is a struggle between two definitions of Russian culture, representing its past and future. Or to put it differently, like Conrad's Razumov, one is caught between lawless autocracies of the left and right with minimal political space for an independent center to develop.[26] A centrist Russia would be a movement of young progressives with experience in political and economic social democratic liberalism led by cultured people such as a Gorbachev. At minimum, they would want a republican form of government where power rests with the people or its representatives.

By contrast, the regime's distortion of culture to defend autocratic rule is cherry-picking in action. The Russian war in Ukraine is justified by the Kremlin as a defensive battle against the "meddling international values of a corrupt, sexually deviant Western alliance".[27] The military justification to erase Ukrainian culture as a deviant form of Russian Slavic culture is "cherry-picking" by the Putin regime claiming that tendencies are the actual culture or symptoms rather than causes. After the tsar gained victory in 1812 over Napoleon, the tsar was able to mobilize domestic support after its Napoleon in 1812. Putin is trying a similar tactic to generate patriotic frenzy in support of his military campaign against Ukraine. To do this, the Putin regime employs the revanchist idea of a reunited Slavic culture in service of the re-creation of the Tsarist Russian Empire by "retaking" Ukraine.[28] By this rationale, Ukrainian culture (its Orthodox Church and its citizens in Western Ukraine and along its borders in the east with Russia) would return to the tutelage of the Kremlin. This dangerous and idiosyncratic distortion of history is being used to weaponize the concept of political culture. The merger of distorted history with political culture is evident in Putin's long-term project to prepare public opinion for its war in Ukraine. For this, he has put special emphasis on the Soviet victory on the eastern front over Nazi Germany in WWII, which he regards as the USSR's most glorious achievement.[29] The error of "normative cherry-picking" occurs with this historic focus on the Soviet eastern front victory. The Russian regime stresses privately and in public the constant themes of "tsarist fantasies, power, prestige, and cultural appropriation".[30] These are to be achieved through violence, bullying, and cruelty, turning Russia into a permanent pariah state.[31]

An unfortunate reaction to this hysterical Russian upheaval by Ukraine has been to use Russian literature, plays, and operas such as "The Nutcracker" as justifications for linguistic censorship. These themes are being used by the Ukrainians[32] who have tried to censor Russian arts for these reasons. In short, if not precisely defined, the concept of political culture can be weaponized like this by all sides of a conflict and used as a tool to claim the causation of anything. It is clearly important to avoid the use of political culture as a grand theory that overdetermines and overpredicts rather than serve as a rigorous, theory-based middle-range policy analytic tool, for the description and explanation of specific political behavior and policy problems.

By "weaponizing", as noted, we mean the aggressive distortion of history, values, and actions of a country or people for self-serving ends, usually justificatory and expansionist. But weaponizing the historical element of political cultures in service of distorted or idiosyncratic historical interpretations of them is an uphill battle for any political regime. People adopt and absorb values and attitudes that make them happy, satisfied, respected, and better people, personally and politically. They absorb many of the values unconsciously from civil society institutions and their families. If they have been absorbing values and adopting attitudes like this for most of their lives, the values and attitudes become harder to change. Bangladesh, as noted, has a long tradition of political pluralism and debate that cannot easily be overwhelmed or replaced by an autocratic or dictatorial state. Even authoritarian managers operating in authoritarian conformist contexts eventually must recognize that in demanding political engagement from their staff people do not always choose between the dictates of culture and conscience—they are guided by some of both.

Stalin's "socialist realism" efforts in the 1930s that tried to control theatre, literature, music, and art were in the end a comic farce, e.g., tanks rolling around theatre stages accompanied by drums, trumpets, and bellowing macho choruses to stress the regime value of militant loyalty.[33] The carrots then and now cannot really be taken seriously. In present-day Ukraine, the comic middling talents of the pro-war culture are everywhere obvious. The gray and talentless are trying to take the place of the quality that the state is forbidding, but nobody wants to see or listen to it. For instance, no one listens to the current crop of grotesque rockers such as Shaman shouting out his "I'm Russian" song. Common sense suggests that nonconformity is better and more profitable, i.e., pirated Western films like *Avatar*. The carrots offered by these regimes fail to penetrate everyday routines and repertoires, requiring the use of sticks. So, the regime tried to force the remaining artists and free thinkers who had not fled abroad.

The risks of stepping outside what counts as permissible in current Russian culture are real and growing. But Putin's inept bullying is still a long way short of Stalin's Soviet totalitarianism.[34]

In practice, weaponizing and cherry-picking political cultures by any regime merely perpetuate and intensify violent political conflict, as all sides battle it out over which view of culture or which values are core and which are peripheral, and which should prevail? In addition to Ukraine, the messy policy problem can be seen in the continuing efforts to manage student curricula and staff in public schools, such as Northern Macedonia with its Slav Orthodox and ethnic Albanians (nominally Muslim) over the issue of language, and how to manage the students in Northern Irish public schools in the context of a long legacy of Anglo-Irish conflict?

Discussion Case #4: Northern Irish Schooling

Schooling in Northern Ireland takes place in a culture with an imposed language, controlled politically from London and spiritually by a church from Rome. The Irish cultural-historical context is "lacking independence from English control and powerfully influenced by a religion centered in Rome, where English rule and the British Empire are repeatedly deplored". Like the Jews (whom the Irish have in turn oppressed), the Irish have suffered persecution and enforced exile[35]; the culture is entangled with bloodshed and rebellion as forms of cleansing and sanctifying macho aggressiveness. The inability of cultural realists to deal with "Irish sentimentality and belligerent republicanism" derives from this brutal history of starvation, rebellions, and civil wars that is always just under the surface among the Irish. "Get over it!" is not an option.

Suppose you were the principal of a secondary school in Belfast, Ulster County, Northern Island. In the context of new "troubles" caused by the reaction to Brexit and the newer issue of the "hard border", you are charged with managing student conflicts over curriculum. You need to find ways to integrate students amidst tensions between parents, teachers, and community religious and political groups. How would the long history of religious conflict, racial gerrymandering, and socio-political partition embedded in the political culture prevent conflict resolution? How could you do a workaround and make positive changes at the operational level?[36]

The Second Problem with the Concept of Political Culture Is that It Is Static and Cannot Explain or Predict How or when Parts of that Culture Will Change

Neither culture nor political culture is a fixed category. Both are composed of values and attitudes that change albeit slowly. Cultural anthropologists tend to use culture as a fixed category, a composite of values and practices that cannot be changed. The question of which are the distinctive values that make up the culture is often mixed with the identity issue. Which, for example, are the core values that define the Arab or Moroccan culture? Any notion of Arab nationalism depends on answering this. But that is contentious given religious sects and ethnicities, some of which are not Arab. The identity issue is perennial and intractable. But for governance, the question is which values are pertinent to that object. What are daily routines and ways of doing business? Does the internal culture include compromise, trust, and allowable dissent, or is unanimity to keep the peace? Is pluralism and open debate part of the culture as it is in Bangladesh? In specific regions such as the Middle East and Africa, vast territories are hardly touched by state services. Weak or failed states nominally "govern" territories of atomized tribes, sects, and other groups. Management consists of trying to facilitate cooperation among these groups that mostly focus on their own identity, language, familial structures, and needs. Defining the distinctive values of such cultures requires the use of the assessment tools of cultural anthropology. Even those might not tell managers what to do to get things done! In countries such as South Africa, the governing ANC Party is effectively the state and has a long history of dispensing favors without unaccountability.[37] There is no history of compromise or political culture relying on the tools of democracy to benefit the broader public interest beyond sects, tribes, families, and factions.

As noted, anthropologists largely view cultures as composed of fixed behaviors and practices that are rarely changeable. Political scientists and economists approach cultures as behaviors and attitudes that can be changed by incentives. For the latter two disciplines, whatever the distinctive core values of a political culture are, the fundamental values and attitudes change or can be changed only slowly. For example, in the centralized, authoritarian Chinese culture complemented by Communist Party rule, fiscal decentralization has proceeded gradually over decades driven by the need to plan and finance local works such as housing, transit, roads, and water and sewer projects. Budgeting, taxation, and borrowing to finance local capital assets have proceeded incrementally. Accumulation of massive unsustainable debts by builders and local governments has occurred, many off budgets, so that the central government has had to back many of them, posing a threat to the national fiscal position. The Chinese political economy has adjusted to local needs from bottom-up pressures flexibly without a major crisis. The driving force has been local need and adjustment that has occurred flexibly via national and local regulatory tightening.[38]

In contrast with the flexibilities of the political economy within a unitary governmental structure, the Party and the regime have staked all on controlling the Covid virus through peremptory authoritarian solutions—lockdowns, repeated testing, criminal sanctions for scientific debate or public dissent, and quarantining those suspected of being ill away from home in prison-like conditions. This is consistent with that old-fashioned dictatorship motivated by fear and vapid wartime slogans about victory over the enemy virus and defeating "lying-flat" or defeatist mobs.[39] This didn't work in 2020–2022 so the Party had to spin its way out of a rout. But the arrival of Covid-staked Party prestige on testing, lockdowns, and national vaccines that didn't work and provoked angry outrage. The Party had no political flexibility within the quasi-decentralized system. Party policy had complimented the values and attitudes of an authoritarian culture but finally had to back down from real public pressures. In the last several decades, quid pro quo between the central and local governments (with fiscal and managerial authority devolved in exchange for tighter reporting requirements), incrementally modified part of the authoritarian culture to improve governance consistent with modern financial management standards and practice. The path to fiscal devolution was part of a trend that could not be predicted by reference to the authoritarian culture governing China through the Party.

Similarly, applications of IMF rules and norms have incrementally changed institutional cultures in multiple countries. The Latin American spendthrift culture is well-known and associated with hyperinflation, collapsed currencies, excessive fiscal deficits and debts, high unemployment, and low growth for many decades. Over the past 50–60 years, the spendthrift behavior has changed, and the region has been known for low inflation, and tight fiscal discipline of most state budgets. Countries such as Argentina with nine defaults and even more bailouts have been the exception. The majority of others have performed according to IMF fiscal discipline and budgetary transparency criteria (UN Government Financial System GFS (Government Financial Statistics of the IMF) standards). During this more recent period, donor and bank debts have been repaid, more has been borrowed from donors and private markets, and creditworthiness has improved across the region (Guess and Savage, 2021). The culture has gradually changed induced by fiscal incentives from the IMF that have allowed countries freedom to spend on current and capital needs. During this period, unstable political regimes have intruded on sound financial management and interfered with fiscal and monetary policy in such countries as Brazil and Argentina.

Structural or larger changes in the form or content of regimes and countries cannot be fully explained by concepts such as political culture or individual institutions. Levy (2014:20) recognizes that whether and how institutions change often depends on the interactions between formal and informal institutions, citing North, Wallis and Weingast (2009).

The main distinction is between informal institutions and patron-client relations and personalized transactions and identities. Institutionalized into impersonal codified rules, monitoring, and adjudication and enforcement assigned to third-party organizations such as judiciaries, dedicated to the tasks result in more standardized and formal interactions. By contrast, informal institutions and rules remain at the personal level of patron-client. States become conferrers of patronage rather than by operation of rules of law. The distinction between static and dynamic relations and why cultures can constrain evolution is relatively clear. But, of course, cultures do change and formally developed institutions can result. Levy (2014:10) seeks feasible entry points via reform projects where modest changes in one or more parts of the system can evoke or trigger adaptations in other parts in "an ongoing cumulative process". This is what development experts all want, but the perennial question is "what works and what doesn't?" to "do development" Many have noticed the influence of cultural inheritances such as rules and practices from the Spanish and Portuguese on Latin American colonies, whereupon they evolved in different directions on non-linear paths of development (North, 1990:104). But the cultures and the institutions only partially explain those evolutions.

Generally, rule-driven fiscal institutions in Latin America have evolved and performed well. Similarly, installation and training for Government Financial Management Information System (GFMIS) systems mainly by the World Bank throughout Latin America as well as the rest of the world provided incentives for general ledger and accounting training in exchange for the reduced need to approve individual expenditure and revenue transactions. Electronic signatures provided real-time clearances which has improved the efficiency of governmental operations and eliminated many opportunities for bribery and corruption. Such rule-driven systems serve as incentives to change archaic public sector systems, particularly in treasury and procurement to improve public services. These public financial management systems and programs overall have modernized corrupt and inefficient cultures that had provided poor services, such as health care, education, and transport which has frustrated and demoralized the public.

The Third Problem with Political Culture Is Its Misuse to Claim Moral Relativism by Authoritarian Regimes

Political culture is often used as a self-serving weapon by mostly authoritarian regimes to protect their existing values and practices (e.g., human rights violations) in the name of national "sovereignty". This is often used as a moral justification as part of a claim used to defend "independent non-aligned" states. Regimes use several forms of moral relativism or "see no evil" in local political culture and justify their behavior as "value neutral" or "non-judgmental". This contrasts with Western aid which is often explicitly targeted toward building democracies and regimes with acceptable values and rule of law (as opposed to rule by law). The Chinese, for instance, do business with and support such odious regimes as Venezuela. They also import tropical cedar hardwoods based on dubious cutting permits from sovereign but corrupt regimes such as Papua New Guinea.

Another example of using the hands-off sovereignty defense of cultural values and practices is evident in the US-Mexico mutual war against drugs. The problem as the Mexicans see it is that demand for drugs comes from the north (US) and guns flow to the south (from the US). The current president of Mexico Manuel Lopez Portillo (AMLO) often uses the violation of "sovereignty" defense against US institutions such as the Drug Enforcement Agency (DEA) from seeking advance information on arrests and drug busts in Mexico. In the US view, this means AMLO stands by as the Mexican gangs go about business. The way forward to sharing information and reducing distrust between officials and institutions in this case is to understand that the officials in each country have different calculations. The US is frustrated at Mexican official corruption in the National Guard and local police and the Mexicans are frustrated at the US's refusal to share information. The need is for smart management on both sides to understand the need for systems of arm's length communication.[40]

US aid programs attempt to build civil society, rule of law, electoral, and judicial institutions as part of democratic and governance projects. Authoritarian regimes viewed these as threats to their power, longevity, and of course "neutral values". Projects were in country contexts where rarely people met and compromised, and officials rarely listened to dissenting opinions and responded by changing rules and policies. There was no tradition of pluralism and debate in any of them. The rationale for US assistance was its claim to democracy and freedom—Western universal values—freedom, property, religion, and speech. The claim was that such values should be adopted. Russia after its collapse and during a brief period of political liberalization in the 1990s was in a receptive mode and welcomed Western political and economic advice and assistance. But urging changes to superficial values for recipients was like attending tent revivals to offer salvation. There were no changes to the basic structures of power. Anarchy and tribal warlord governance prevailed often beyond capital cities. Such diffuse structures of organization were left intact in such aid targets as Iraq and Afghanistan. Like aid to Vietnam in the 1960s, they were temporary Potemkin villages built for display by the US military and development assistance (DA).

The West offers a path to democratic values and practices such as elections and the creation of a civil society of unions, independent political and educational institutions, and other intermediary organizations. The premise of this aid (called Democracy and Governance in US aid parlance) is that society needs to be consolidated around these values and institutions. This had largely happened in at least the western part of Ukraine before it was attacked by the efforts of 20 years of Western aid. But it did not happen in Afghanistan and Iraq. Basic economic needs had to be met simultaneously through structural changes to facilitate competition, growth, and incomes. Tyrants pushed back as demonstrated Western freedoms and public institutional accountability values threatened their power bases. They claimed with non-Western prodding, that local democratic values were not inherent or authentic and superficially implanted by Western aid programs to stimulate action against regimes.

Against such claims was and is the reality that a prosperous Ukrainian middle class was demanding these freedoms and failed to see what use a tyrannical regime was to their lives—either as appointed local oligarchs or directly from Russia. Widespread demands for more changes consistent with Western values threatened their power and control in all three targets of the Western democratic values of open societies and open economies.[41] Just as democratic Ukraine was proof that such values were alien to Russian Slavic culture (but could be easily adopted) the existence of a liberal democratic Taiwan was proof that such values were not alien to Chinese culture. The spread of open values and preferences for freedoms is perceived as a threat to authoritarian tyrannical regimes in both Russia and China.[42] More threatening is the reality that the spread of values and practices is mainly through transmission methods: actual demands for alien practices, arts, music, and literature; and rather than by forced assimilation of them.[43] The authoritarian weakness in use of force or weaponization of authoritarian cultural values and practices is that the tactic is transparently artificial and fiercely resisted by captive audiences. The effect can only be temporary. The World Values Survey (WVS) conducted every five years indicates only scant evidence of sociopolitical values converging with wealth and prosperity. In Russia, values may reflect rigid traditionalist preferences. But there is no evidence of a unified Slavic set of values that requires authoritarian rule and export to other countries. Putin has hived off or "cherry-picked" certain opinions claimed to be deeper values as excuses, as political weapons to support his "special military operations". Values are underlying beliefs and motivators not just evanescent opinions that change rapidly. The WVS asks questions that reveal value preferences such as the degree of trust in others and the role of religion in life's decisions.[44]

Remedies for Macro-Political Cultural Distortions

In sum, political culture is the behavioral expression of language, religious, social values, and trust. The concept has been used in an attempt to account for different values and how they affect macro-political decisions. As noted, distinctive cultural values and practices influence what rules are made and how strictly they are enforced. The research task is to more rigorously define the distinctive values and attitudes that motivate political and management behavior. Then identify at the national and regional levels the uses and impacts of specific values on institutional, managerial, and economic change. But instead of trying to understand the transmission of these values into decisions, policy-makers have often distorted political culture for crude political ends. They have cherry-picked cultures for rationales, weaponizing behaviors, and practices as excuses for policies and decisions that are morally suspect. As noted, Bolshevik regimes smothered the Protestant values of Christianity for narrow Communist Party ends to enforce the distorted *Ruskly Mir* concept of cultural imperialism. It is important now that the definition and use of political culture be the focus of identifying and reducing the frequency of misuses. The success of this effort will depend on developing more rigorous definitions of political cultures that identify the core motivating values and exclude those distortions that are not.

At the macro-political level, it is also critical to view political culture as a variable and not a fixed or constant practice or value. And, despite historic efforts to establish political culture as an explanatory variable that suggests causation between societal mores, attitudes, and practices and behavioral changes by individuals and institutions (Almond and Verba, 1963; Putnam, 1993:10), it is at best an intervening variable, though often a very important one. Most values and practices are expressed in institutionalized roles that intervene (Raudla, 2013; Raudla et al. 2018; Mokyr, 2018:23) between cause and effect rather than independent variables by themselves. They are operational values that guide institutional roles. These can be changed with properly designed incentives. Culture, whether political, organizational, or team level, is an intervening variable meaning that it is in part a cause and effect of organizational success. A good working environment reflects a good professional, empathetic management that energizes its teams and staff and facilitates innovative and productive behavior. Turnover is less, and the staff is satisfied, feeling that their work contributes and that their work is meaningful. One can sense this almost instantaneously, as is true with a bad management setting!

For example, "culturists" as Harrison (1985) suggest that societies with deeply held destructive cultural values such as Korean feudalism and historic stagnation, can and have been changed through incremental application of incentives can correct destructive cultural trends. An additional example is observing the deeply held German aversion to debt (*shulde*) and for fiscal discipline which anchored EU institutions away from lending to southern spendthrift countries was modified to allow borrowing for specific purposes such as Covid-19 pandemic relief, support for Ukraine, and against growing energy and consumer goods inflation as well as for carefully targeted conditional grants for specific capital projects. Spending is now more likely to be seen as a solution than a sin even by Germany and EU fiscal rules have been relaxed by Germany and France.[45] In addition to the Next Generation EU (NGEU) recovery fund, the EU will also create a financial instrument to match US Treasuries as a safe asset to underpin a true economic union.[46] But for larger misuses that distort cultural values and weaponized them with aggressive military and territorial ends, the only defense beyond talking with tyrants is military force and aggressive cyber-defense. This has been evident since February 2022 with Russia in Ukraine.

Remedies for Micro-Political Cultural Distortions

To be useful, political culture needs to be able to account for how different values and attitudes affect micro-political behavior for the management of people. To date, typologies such as Kammerich-Smith are employed at both macro and micro levels. The simplest and most fruitful approach to managing people in different contexts at the operational or sectoral-technical level is to assume that they are motivated by the same forces. People like to be trusted to do a good job, praised for doing good work, told clearly of mistakes, and managed by people with integrity.[47]

Managing Organizations in Different Contexts

In order to treat people the same in public sector and commercial organizations and guide them toward the objectives, managers must find the right incentives. They must be motivated to work. In **Oriente**, Moses used fear and drastic action against Silsbee's Labrador dog to motivate his team to build the oil facility on time and within financial limits. Mr. Johnson (below) motivated his crew to finish the road with a combo of material and non-material incentives and made up an innovative accounting system to record his debits and credits to reflect his imaginary world (Cary, 1939).

In Latin America, a major constraint on the effective use of public spending is excessive centralization of finances and obsessive over-control of budget releases as a defense against corruption (Bird, 1992). The IMF arranged a quid pro quo incentive in the Ecuadorian MOF that granted it wider discretion to approve budget releases without ex-ante clearances in exchange for tighter ex-post reporting.[48] This was before the installation of electronic GFMIS systems that eliminated clearance and approval steps, making the new systems vital to Latin public expenditure management.

The Ecuadorian devolution of approval authority within the MOF in exchange for tighter experience-post reporting sped up releases and improved budget effectiveness. The success of this simple mechanism reduced the unexamined cultural values of centralization that impeded effectiveness and actually encouraged corrupt workarounds to make the release system work as intended. The staff was happy in its new and more professional role. MOF budget monitoring staff knew that modern management meant operational flexibility and decentralized command, and they now had at least some of these capacities. But they wanted more. MOF subsequently demanded the installation of a computerized general ledger system (Integrated Financial Management System (IFMS)). IFMSs have been successfully installed with World Bank support and used in every Latin American country MOF and many large city finance departments to monitor and control public expenditures. Such exchange and control systems modified local cultural practices and produced a quasi-decentralized system within the overall context of top-down control systems.

Management Relevance of Political Culture

Management should recognize that the political culture intervenes, sometimes powerfully other times marginally, between their actions, decisions, and directives, and expected results. Unintended and unpredictable results are often the norm. Political culture is thus a contextual intervening variable. At the MOF in Port-au-Prince Haiti, I discovered in 2010 that the highly educated and trained officials that planned and managed the national budgets, and the central bank (Bank of the Republic of Haiti (BRH)) that set monetary policy, were guided partly by Voodoo beliefs (*Voudouist* beliefs). This is a belief that spirits and supernatural forces control what happens in the physical world. Voodoo is derived from African polytheism and ancestor worship. Schedules depend often on what gods and ancestors opine. Officials we worked with believed that their textbook actions actually made little difference to fiscal and monetary policy results. In their minds, calendars, such as annual Santeria festivals and sacrifices, project timelines, and planned benchmarks would be conditional on signs, such as cosmic signals from weather, such as wind and lightning, and animal behavior, like the directions birds flew that day. While Haitian officials politely and eagerly absorbed advice from IMF and World Bank technical teams and knew well how to run the latest treasury and fiscal management systems, the advice could do little to penetrate this barrier between Haitian officials and results. The effect of decades of political chaos in the streets, violence, and instability acted to confirm supernatural Voodoo beliefs (and especially of their priests or *houngan* leaders) that such forces really controlled policy actions and results. For them, religious values in their political culture intervened, if not actually caused, every one of their actions.

Peculiar cultural contexts such as this are a reality in Haiti. They are a real intervening if not causal variable. On the surface all is rational and normal, the offices and computers hum along, officials speak several languages well, and they dress formally as if in Washington or London. But their minds are guided to some or all extent by Voodoo forces. Under such conditions, expat and local managers need to direct and motivate teams patiently and carefully. Despite Voodoo beliefs, they are regular people motivated by trust, trying to do a good job, and happy to receive praise as well as empathetic criticism to do their jobs better. Managers find this out quickly in trying to manage firms or public sector organizations in Haiti or other areas with large Haitian populations, especially in Miami.

Seven Efforts That Can Reduce Distortions

There are at least seven types of efforts that managers can make to reduce problems of cultural conflict and failures to adjust to each other's behavioral norms.

Employ Culturally Consistent Notions of Efficiency

Efficiency is a loaded cultural concept that managers need to be aware of. Achieving "least cost" and highly "productive results" are clearly stable rich country expectations. People in different settings vary in degree of job focus, team loyalty, and motivation by task performance. The constraints and nuances of cultural and behavioral norms often translate "value for money" efficiency notions into "effectiveness" or physical results rather than any notion of cost efficiency. In public sector terms, the managerial question is how much will it cost us to achieve refuse collection for the most dwellings per area? This is different from converting all costs and benefits into monetary value or basic cost/benefit analysis prior to making a decision, i.e., total net benefits. But in different contexts, the emphasis might be on the result itself which is given: effective refuse collection.[49] Or the result may be the pride of completing Mr. Johnson's road through the Nigerian bush, simply getting the job done there and having the road service traders, and pedestrians. The value is the job, service, and result rather than purely the money. In different contexts, employees are often motivated by the task and by its eventual attainment—the money spent is for a given value or objective achieved, metrics such as classroom hour/day, on-time transit performance, fire department or emergency service response time, functioning fire alarm per individual dwelling, homicide clearance rate, rail, and bus operating cost/passenger mile. The managerial emphasis is on the service or project result over the expenditure or expense of cash. All bidders for a given objective, such as the Venice floodgate system or a rail transit system, may be overestimated cost, or even available budget revenues.

Western managers from "linear active" rich region settings, such as Germany, Austria, and Switzerland tend to think of the job as the key objective for workers. They often assume that gaining skilled employment is a sufficient reward and motivation for task performance. Germans often add beer breaks as an essential cultural lubricant that everyone expects and understands. Pure forms of linear active contexts are harder to find as globalization and the mixing of rich and poor countries occur, blending cultural habits and practices. Pure work to attain least-cost efficient results and tasks that mean purely goal and objective attainment are rarer.

Managers must therefore learn the routines and repertoires of the culture and blend them with the efficiency needs of time and cost limits to attain the best available results. Norms and standards such as cost-effectiveness and cost efficiency must be skillfully meshed and fit with the dictates of contexts such as multi-active. In South Asia, managers need to deal with the requirements of empathy, slippery rules, mirroring behavior, and creativity to get the job done. Mr. Johnson in the multi-active context of Nigeria used creativity to the point of blatant illegality to get the road project finished for his British chief. Moses in *Oriente* used cruelty to punish his team of workers to compensate for his own inability to establish trust, gain loyalty, and maintain management control. Cooper in the FMS punished his workers for completing extra, then useless tasks on time without paying them as a motivational device in the Borneo Outstation.

In the unsuccessful attempts to get the jobs done, all except Mr. Johnson ignored the *Reactive* settings where interpersonal relations were key to gaining trust and motivating behavior and results. People are people but their tolerance levels vary, and managers must recognize this. In Borneo, Nigeria, and Ecuador (*Multi-Active settings*), managers must adapt to the softer norms of saving face, shame, political culture, family, and dignity. Somehow, Western managers or those with that narrower frame of reference must blend reactive and multi-active concerns with linear active task-driven efficiency concerns to deal with these kinds of ambiguities.

Managing aid projects within timelines and cost limits is roughly the same for both commercial and public sector project needs. Both must adapt people to tasks within given limits to attain successful results.

Managers apply rewards and sanctions everywhere, but most would like their teams to be "family", driven by the internal rewards of just doing a good job. But both development aid and commercial enterprise managers must make adjustments of available incentives and sanctions according to the expected effects of cultural contexts on results. A problem arises when a manager has a fixed view of their workers, such as Cooper and Moses. In their jaded views, workers were not to be trusted and needed heavy-handed prodding or physical flogging toward mission objectives. That rigid perspective does not work long in linear active rich country contexts.

Denton (2019) recognized this from his applied management experiences in Central America. In his seven-country field research, he found that investing in regional markets requires detailed knowledge of cultural similarities and idiosyncrasies of each country's market. In particular, prospective investors must avoid the efficiency trap of task over-standardization and employing staff that fails to represent the ethnic and racial diversity of the clients to be served. This finding is consistent with that of Mummolo (2023) cited in *Discussion Case #11*. His research into managing large-city police departments in such places as Rio de Janeiro, Sao Paolo, and Chicago found that failure to diversify forces to be representative of poor Black people in the area resulted in greater rates of police murders and corresponding increases in violent crime.

Gain and Maintain Trust

Offices of multinational firms or projects from international aid organizations need to first establish the trust of locals. The organizations must hire locals and work with suppliers for office equipment and for travel and logistics. The aid organizations are viewed both as sources of income, skills, and career advancement and are staffed by local people who view them as tools or means to profitability and success. Development aid firms establishing in-country project offices are not unlike the Dutch and British Trading Firms of the 19th century establishing and staffing their river trading posts in their colonies.[50] But modern projects must have deeper institutional relations than simply for trading (e.g., ivory, cotton). Aid projects must hire local staff on whom they depend for local contacts and relationships with a wide range of suppliers of such services as IT/computer services, office supplies, rental cars, and logistics to find their way around. Two-way trust is essential.[51] Local donor representatives or embassies (e.g., USAID) oversee projects and assist personnel in finding lodgings and other services for which they have established local connections. Project personnel must often be taken around the country to meet ministry personnel and assist in establishing project monitoring units or PMUs for sectoral projects based in particular ministries. For bilateral projects, such as USAID or DFID, the project team meets with their chief technical officer or CTO who oversees the project directly. In the case of DFID, the CTO is actually the ambassador, meaning a much flatter and more personal reporting structure.

As Henry Ford finally discovered with the disastrous experience of his 19th-century *Fordlandia* project in the Brazilian Amazon jungle near Manaus, establishing initial trust was essential, he learned that there were limits to his ability to import modern American management efficiency techniques, such as "time management" from gurus such as Frederick Taylor. Rural Brazilians living in the Amazon bush where rubber was grown would in his mind simply trust his methods, learn, and adopt them without question. Based on his experience with managing factories in industrialized US locales, Ford believed that the application of modern skills, systems, and know-how could tame the forests and turn a profit for him. He laid down Midwestern protestant rural American values of moral purity and probity, such as no alcohol for workers and healthy worker diets of oatmeal, canned peaches, and wheat bread, and fun such as square dancing. The entire operation was imported know-how and equipment. But they had to rely on locals which were the weak link in the chain. The rubber tappers and other workers predictably revolted! Ultimately, despite his brilliance with car manufacturing, Ford failed to innovate and lost the world rubber market for Brazil. This turned his once orderly jungle village into a ghost town for the tropical forest to reclaim…an unintended benefit until rampant deforestation driven by world beef cattle and tropical hardwood markets once again threatened its existence.[52]

Happily, such failures are few and far between as it is well-known by now that local distrust can derail aid projects and diminish commercial operating margins quickly. The investments become expensive failures and negative management lessons travel fast! To its surprise, McDonald's discovered that in Russia changes in regime politics can increase risk calculations without warning! Multinational companies such as McDonald's are the epitome of global trust. If one cannot trust their management to produce the same BigMac quality everywhere, who can you trust? More importantly, their strategy in foreign markets has long been to go native, hewing to the tastes and cultural predilections of local customers.[53] In Russia, the food chain gained trust by building up and training local product suppliers for the bulk of their products: bread, potatoes, and beef. They sent all their employees to their own management training academies, such as "McComplex" near Moscow. Given their enormous customer base and following, by 2020, the Kremlin classified it as a "backbone enterprise" along with such prominent companies as Gazprom and Aeroflot. In 2018, it purchased 4% of Russia's potatoes and 2% "of its cheese, while paying more than $1b in taxes". Unlike Russian firms, it offered fast, friendly service and hot high-quality food (2023:37).

In each country or region, they adapted their menus to local tastes, e.g., Big Mac Croissants in France. They relentlessly trained local staff in the protocols and routines of the parent company. Certified McDonald's managers are some of the most coveted management and sales personnel in the world. Graduates of their management training courses are coveted by employers everywhere seeking staff that move quickly, with alacrity and flexibly to solve the myriad problems that crop up in their busy stores. They learned to treat people humanely and firmly to get their jobs done. They were successful like their Central American counterparts, they differentiated markets and embraced diversity.[54] Similarly, Oreo cookies are also famous for local adaptability and success in not only gaining trust and maximizing sales profits by redesigning some products for local tastes (adapting products to local markets) but also equipping their managers with skills that were transferable anywhere (Reynolds, 2017).

Because DA projects are shorter term and recruitment is often less tailored to country settings, earning the trust of locals is often harder to achieve than with longer term commercial investments. In the overseas aid business, the US provides DA for soft problems, and security assistance (SA) to deal with civil wars and sudden upheavals. DA projects seek to recruit managerial staff with experience in particular countries and regions of the world. As noted in the Oriente story and Mr. Johnson below, even such efforts are often overwhelmed by contextual surprises and the fact that they are based on shorter term scopes of work. The public and public sector providers of aid funds want to know how their overseas aid programs perform. DA programs and projects are evaluated through regular financial reporting and project impact and management analyses. For instance, USAID has been producing evaluations for many decades and the World Bank's Independent Evaluation Office (IEO) performs highly critical analyses of its Official Development Assistance (ODA) projects for lessons learned (Guess, 2019:204–206). Projects are independently evaluated by academics and practitioners for design, management decisions, teaming problems, and contextual obstacles to implementation. Many of the evaluations, especially from IEO conclude that the projects have failed for one or more reasons!

By contrast, evaluations of SA efforts in overseas military conflicts involving US military actions are few and far between. The public has only the sketchiest idea of how SA is being used or its efficacy. Many performance problems are derived from recruitment by poor country armies receiving US SA. Standard US DOD (US Department of Defense) recruitment criteria for armies, navies, and marines focus primarily on their skills and capacities to fight. In SA to weak states and armies, the US approach often ignores the most critical variable in training militaries abroad, which is whether they have the "will to fight". This is critical but often difficult to predict on battlefields. Recruits are typically signing on to risk their lives for what they know are corrupt failed states. In Iraq and Afghanistan, the US found out too late that they won't take the risks! They failed to trust their unskilled and often disrespected officers along with US trainers that had ignored the staffing and trust issues. The problems were predictable all along despite the claims of the US military that the will to fight is "unpredictable" and "unknown!" (Guess, 2019:143).

Recruitment lessons from military SA contexts can be useful for projects that combine development and military or security objectives. They involve taking higher risks with people who may not have the standard qualifications on a routine job description. For example, how should one gauge the right person for a chief of part job (COP) in a difficult overseas context that has not done that precise job before? In the race to develop an A-bomb to try and end WWII, General Groves looked for someone with demonstrated commitment and willpower to achieve something complicated and difficult with often contradictory ends. Most viewed Robert Oppenheimer as the wrong person. One of his Cal colleagues said of him: "He couldn't run a hamburger stand!"[55] But he had put a team together to develop a new field of quantum physics. He had built and managed a new applied research unit at UC Berkeley in a politically charged, hysterical period of suspicion and subversion by Soviet agents in the 1930s. The right COP would be faced with the complex task of running a weapons lab, managing scientists with diverse agendas (e.g., Edward Teller's obsession with a fusion bomb when an atomic bomb was only a goal), integrating these activities into the new Manhattan Project, and building the weapon as soon as possible. General Groves figured that based on his related background Oppenheimer could adjust to tight security rules, conjure up the needed skills, develop new work habits, deal with novel problems, and charm groups of difficult people, enough to please a tough authoritarian Theory X bastard like himself that exercised authority through intimidation, and at the same time get the job done.

But rarely does one confront only one Theory X team leader or supervisor in overseas aid work. We may not build bombs, but we have to suffer arrogant Theory X leaders who tend to humiliate you and challenge everything you've learned about good management. How should you respond to bureaucratic tricks by such supervisors that are calculated to damage you and your career? Oppenheimer survived his recruitment challenge with General Groves perhaps because each needed something from the other party, and they thought they could adjust to each other's peculiarities and control them long enough to get the bomb built! General Groves believed he could leverage Oppenheimer's background of leftist political baggage as a means of controlling him once on the job. But Oppenheimer's unique competence meant he was indispensable, so Groves did not try to intimidate him. On the job, Oppenheimer's charismatic style bred consensus. And at Los Alamos, he became a changed man to fit his new role as director of an industrial enterprise. To manage his teams of theoretical and experimental scientists, he set the tone with the force of his personality and brilliance. He brought out the best of his team's capacities to invent, improvise, and solve problems.[56] He got the job done! Most recognized in retrospect, hiring Oppenheimer was considered an "act of genius" by General Groves![57] A real hire wire act!

The question for management recruiters for DA projects in high-risk and unstable environments is how to distinguish a candidate who can radically adapt and succeed like Oppenheimer from one who can't. His physics colleagues and competitor candidates could not. But Groves could make the right choice! The question is important since adaptability, flexibility, and persuasiveness are needed for effective DA management and need to be spotted by recruiters (usually group decisions, unfortunately!) to avoid the frequent personnel failures that occur on overseas projects. But after the war, Oppenheimer came up against a less empathetic person in Washington who also had a job offer for him at Princeton's Institute for Advanced Studies. The fact is when Potomac fever ends and one almost inevitably enters the arena of practical hardball politics inside the Beltway, men like Oppenheimer quickly shed their naïveté and survive by their charm, wit, and grace. But even he could not deal with the likes of humorless, arrogant intellectually thin-skinned Theory Y types like Lewis Strauss. He was known in the tight-knit Washington foreign policy and overseas diplomatic, security/defense, and aid circles as a dangerous opponent in bureaucratic warfare. It was said if you disagreed with him, he assumed you were a fool. But if you kept on disagreeing with him, you were a traitor! He was widely known as intellectually thin-skinned and arrogant.[58] How can you survive in such an authoritarian environment? Do you "get along" by assuming the lackey role and agreeing with him? But for how long can you stand doing this…?

Despite wartime failures by the US from ignoring lessons learned in the 1970s on counter-insurgency and gaining trust for local intelligence and support, the US is relearning lessons quickly from a smart client for SA: the Ukrainian army. Since the war began in 2022 caused by Russian invasions, the US has supplied the majority of weaponry, equipment, and training to Ukraine. The Ukrainians have fought smartly, with clever nuanced tactics designed to surprise the Russians. They have demonstrated that heavy weaponry can be beaten by inspired grit and invention—unconventional tactics, similar to guerrilla war and counterinsurgency. The Russians, with strength in numbers, have been organized by central command and control, with many recruits lacking the will to fight. They have also had to use the Wagner Group of mostly convicts and street toughs to bolster their efforts. The efforts to integrate this group with the professional culture of Russian regular forces have not gone well. By contrast, the Ukrainians devolved authority to units from the outset which provided the field-level flexibility to fight nimbly. For US SA, such organizational and management lessons on what worked and what didn't were learned in the 1970s but forgotten by the conflicts of the 1990s and into the early 2000s (Guess, 2019:142). Again, Russian military command structures remain centralized, artillery-dominated, and bureaucratic as in WWII, requiring constant clearances to move ahead or take independent actions. Distrust within ranks and of top commanders by regular troops is high. As of March 2023, morale still remains low, and the will to fight is mostly missing from the Russian military. But they are reinforcing with hypersonic missiles, smarter and longer range artillery, and larger numbers of better trained troops. They are also adopting some of decentralized Ukrainian guerilla tactics for greater battlefield success.

There is little or no trust left between Ukraine, Russia, or the US. Some tactical channels remain open at the field level. The question is under such conditions of mutual distrust, how can it be reestablished? Crisis management techniques are widely known and utilized. Many crisis management graduate programs exist to disseminate such techniques for governments and businesses. From such crises as the Cuban Missile Crisis of 1962 to the present, it is clear that the two or three sides need to listen as well as lecture if distrust is to be reduced. In the Ukraine crisis as well as the current state of Chinese-US relations, the sides offer little beyond verbal sophistry and clashing accounts of reality. There is little sense of urgency as if the disputants were merely playing war games. The reckless logic from fearless trading of threats and insults is in part derived from the often-inexperienced ideologue officials that have not lived through real crises such as Cuba or the real Cold War between the US and USSR.

To attempt crisis management under aid projects that are contaminated by staff distrust, managers (perhaps even new ones!) need to get local staff in the loop with weekly meetings to air problems with team leaders. The chief or director needs to maintain contact with working groups and teams. More meetings and emails, of course, would be counterproductive. One example that I was part of was for the project team leader to get on their side. Local staff often views project staff as agents of HQ similar to temporary colonial appointees there to do their bidding and report back to London or Washington. Most staff know that evaluation metrics and teams are useless time-wasters. The team leader should work with project staff to develop quick workarounds to satisfy evaluator needs for data and the larger objective which is to break down distrust within the project. The results in my case were largely effective, perhaps because they were done directly with operational staff and supervised and guided by the team leader.

Diversify Staffing and Operations

There are two common meanings of diversification. The first is racial and ethnic staff diversification which is the most obvious. The aid project needs to avoid the appearance of an occupying force and fit in with the locals. As an example, one of our university staff on the Haitian public financial management and policy master's degree project in 2010 went to Haiti on an official visit for both MOF counterparts and university teams to get acquainted. He attended meetings in short pants and a tee shirt during our visits to the high-level MOF officials. MOF staffers meet and deal with foreign officials such as the IMF and World Bank frequently. Despite being Black, the social gap between an educated US Black person and the Haitians with whom he would work was staggering—and obvious to anyone who knows anything about Haiti. His appearance was clearly an insult to them and created distance for no reason other than a puerile display of ego. That the mission was not given a minimum dress code beforehand was bad management on the university side and showed blatant disregard for their political culture. As in MOFs around the globe, the Haitian values and public sector work practices were formal and well-respected by the public and visiting guests (which we were) to their government and country.

Again, Denton's (2019) research found that diversifying staff can increase trust in local markets and increase the value of commercial investments. To work effectively, as noted above, investors must also avoid imposing the wrong kinds of efficiency objectives. In Central America, the wrong way to manage a large, complex firm (or similar type of DA project) is to try for scale economies, maximizing them to attain predetermined least cost financial and staffing and standardizing product portfolios. The strategy of regional efficiencies ignores or overlooks local idiosyncrasies in the political culture. This sacrifices market growth or effectiveness for short-term, paper efficiencies. The efficiency trap follows standard scale-up thinking: (1) standardize the product portfolio, (2) reduce costs, and (3) improve financial ratios

Denton (*Chapter 3*) describes a fictional case vignette of marketing a FIFA European World Cup championship match to Central Americans where country operational managers were straight-jacketed by rigid sales and financial targets that also limited their discretion to transfer or program funds between country markets to smooth out sales differentials.

Headquarters expected all Central American consumers to behave the same way in response to the marketing promotion for beer. In this, they ignored the fact that beer consumers in the seven country markets were highly differentiated: loyalties were to beers by country not region (as anyone could demonstrate to the HQ executives who actually would listen to advice)! HQ penalized all country managers with across-the-board cuts, meaning rewards for underperformers and financial penalties for exceeding targets! It didn't work for firms trying to succeed in new poor country markets in terms of long-term growth and profitability. HQ tried to scale up and standardize marketing the wrong product (beer) in the wrong place (the whole Central American region). As noted, the top-down imposition of arbitrary targets, penalties, and rigid budget rules worked against the sustainability and development contributions of both the commercial marketing initiative as well as the development aid project of building a road in Nigeria (**Discussion Case #7: Mr. Johnson**). In that case, project developers and field auditors in London expected the Nigerians living and working in different political cultures of values, rules, and behaviors to behave the same way that they would behave in the British accounting and financial management system.

The firm made two mistakes that are also common to development aid projects and provide insights into why they often fail. First, the team leader failed to assess the salient preferences in the political culture for baseball and not primarily football. They did not pick up the market diversity of this region. The successful campaigns were in El Salvador and Costa Rica, the only two countries of seven that the US had not occupied in the last two centuries. By contrast, the others had all been occupied and the football marketing campaign failed: Nicaragua and Panama (as well as Cuba, Dominican Republic, and Puerto Rico). There baseball is king—not football. Second, they used an improper baseline comparison with Mexico which did prefer not only football but also baseball and other sports. This produced a "Mexico Consensus" akin to the "cookie-cutter" approach used in the much-derided "Washington Consensus" of fiscal and financial policies stamped on diverse countries in the 1990s. That is, the policy consensus among donors fell far short on how to satisfy growth and equity standards in poor countries. The firm pushing the marketing campaign in Central America generalized from Mexico to the rest of the seven-country region as a homogeneous entity which it was clearly not.

In short, the right management approach for commercial firms is to recognize market diversity and shun standardization initially to focus on market effectiveness and revenue growth. To understand where efficiencies should be traded off or sacrificed for greater long-term effectiveness, managers need a deeper understanding of local idiosyncratic tastes that differentiate markets. Then the product initiatives can be targeted more precisely. Like McDonald's in Russia and Nabisco's Oreos everywhere, managers should invest in local tastes, train local workforces, pay them well, and treat them well. Such culturally consistent approaches leverage local tastes and widen customer bases. Big beer operations such as AB In-Bev stress local brands consistent with local tastes and values, like *Tecate* in Mexico rather than trying to introduce their internationally known but culturally nowhere brands such as Budweiser. Recognizing distinct local preferences, *Belikin* is not marketed to Costa Ricans where Imperial dominates local tastes.[59] Nor does Imperial try to do the reverse in Honduras, which is Salva Vida territory. Following the same strategy of diversity, Walmart markets local brands at discount prices, differentiating carefully between Central American countries. The same market differentiation errors must be avoided in managing DA and especially SA projects. Time-wasting and box-checking tasks are viewed by locals and most project staff as useless reporting tasks and damage team spirit.

The second kind of diversification in addition to staffing diversity is product diversification, as in McDonald's localized burgers and related items, Nabisco's Oreo cookies, and DA projects which are tailored to country needs and sometimes modified in mid-project to make course corrections for unanticipated problems. A project in Albania decided to substitute small capital grants to cities for technical assistance and training. Our rationale to the CTO: "They already know all this! They simply need equipment and funds!" In that case they needed screens to place over drainage pipes to stop sewage from being discharged into Lake Ohrid. Donors vary in their flexibility to do such things in mid-project with the Asian Development Bank and IADB being the least flexible and the World Bank, UKAID, and USAID probably the most flexible. McDonald's diversified its Russian products by successful import substitution—building up local suppliers and relying on them. The share of local ingredients in their products grew from 25% in 1998 to 90% in 2015. By 2018, the share of local ingredients was 98% (2023:40). A total of 50k Russians were employed by McDonald's restaurants, 100k more by its localized supply chains, and more than 1m Russians ate there daily. When McDonald's sold out to local entrepreneurs in the wake of the global opposition to the Ukrainian invasion, it continued to pay all its former workers for up to two years. This action demonstrated the importance of maintaining as well as establishing trust since the firm may return someday and needs to maintain its positive record with local customers (if not the next regime).

Aid projects also provide products which can be capital assets such as bridges, or softer service-type items such as training skills and knowledge that turn into economic development. But as noted by Moses' actions in *Oriente*, informal benefits such as personal relationships, career guidance, gifts from project members, and even loans of office products can create goodwill that often comes in handy if issues arise later within the community which is served by the project.

Sink Local Roots

McDonald's sank local roots and built-up trust by establishing systems and institutions, such as McComplex near Moscow. That is a worker training institute that teaches both managers and workers in areas such as grinding hamburger beef, churning ice cream, and dispensing apple filling into pies. Graduates of McComplex have been poached by hotels, restaurants, and embassies, and their products purchased by them (2023:38). They differentiated local markets and tailored staff and products to each country or locality. But for other MNCs in the commodity extraction business, and even restaurant chains, results have not been very successful.

Their story seems to end the same way each time. The multinational oil, gas, or mineral resource extractor suddenly discovers it isn't 18th-century era of swashbuckling mercantilism anymore. The firm management can't simply bribe their way in through elite contacts and quietly profit from extracting a country's resources anymore. International capital is no longer king but rather the villain and sometimes even the victim in lengthy lawsuits. Managers failed to assess and understand market diversity and build on local values, tastes, and needs. They treated locals as an occupied population. Now, there is intense scrutiny from such international organizations as the Extractive Industry Transparency Initiative (EITI) funded in part by the Open Society Initiative. After several years of local protests, rebellions, and killings, growing international pressure in most cases leads to settlements and fines for damages. This happened with Shell in Nigeria, Chevron in Ecuador, and many mining companies elsewhere. The firm has to change its ways and act more like a development project. This was always a cheap solution for management compared to the vast profits of commodity extraction with cheap labor and tax breaks thrown in. Usually, the final settlement has little effect on its operating margin.

All the troubles could have been avoided in the first place by sinking local roots and demonstrating goodwill to local communities and the host state. They should have listened to the voices of reason that urged humane treatment of the locals by at least protecting workers and locals from the negative effects of mining, drilling, and deforestation. In many such sites around the world, management is tin-eared, arrogant, and incompetent. Firm officials could easily have avoided the costly pitfalls of time wasted and hefty legal fees by learning from the similar experiences of other firms in exactly the same extractive industries in similar poor country conditions. Current oil extraction efforts in Guyana (*Discussion Case #6*) seem to be the product of management finally learning from the accumulated successes and failures and being forced to work for the mutual benefit of both the country and the firm.

Discussion Case #5: Shell and Corporate Social Responsibility in Nigeria

Shell Oil gained a concession to drill and extract oil in the Niger Delta from the government (GON) as early as the 1980s. Much of their activities were controversial involving protests by locals which were repressed by the GON and the Shell police force. Drilling took place in an area populated by the Ogoni ethnic group (in Ogoniland) who were represented eventually by MOSOP. The military government cracked down hard on this group. A group of protest leaders called the Ogoni Nine had been tried, convicted, and executed for seditious treason by the military. In this period of the 1980s–1990s, intense worldwide public criticism focused on the MNC giants that extracted resources in poor countries and maximized profits but enriched small corrupt elites in each country, such as Shell, BP, Exon, Nike, Rio Tinto Zinc (RTZ), and Mobil. The oil "resources" were labeled "curses" rather than development assets that benefited anyone but a small corrupt elite in each country. The "resource curse" (rather than a blessing) became a popular thesis for why efforts to develop poor countries with renewable or non-renewable natural resources must fail. Under these conditions, the question in Nigeria was whether Shell should continue or pay damages for leaks and spills (which the company claimed often correctly were sabotages) and for failure to generate socioeconomic development in the Ogoniland area. Shell had built clinics, schools, and hospitals and built roads and other infrastructure. But MOSOP claimed it was insufficient and often enriched administrators and their GON contacts.

The fact was the development projects were often shoddily executed and left incomplete. In contrast with other MNC resource firms, Shell developed a new policy of "Corporate Social Responsibility". In this new outreach phase, Shell held public environmental-developmental workshops with community leaders and other stakeholders invited. Shell integrated human rights concerns into its internal management protocols. Shell clearly tries community outreach and more development expenditures as well as employment opportunities for locals to "sink roots" deeper and avoid more public relations disasters and repressive tactics against protesters.

Questions

How could Shell mend past relations and further reduce distrust by the communities? How could large mining and oil investments such as Shell in Ecuador and development aid projects avoid getting caught in the "efficiency traps" (such as those noted in Central America) of scaling up and over-standardizing its activities without alienating local communities near project activities? What can project management do to avoid these traps and problems if HQ executives continue to ignore their exercise of "voice"? How could the GON ensure that development projects are implemented fully, on budget, and on time? Suggest ways that project monitoring and evaluation could be done more effectively. Should reliance be on the public sector or NGOs to perform these functions? How could the MNC sink its roots deeper by relying on local organizations for these functions reporting abuses and project progress or obstacles?[60] Why does resource extraction often coincide with bad governance and corruption? How have relations worked out with MNC extractors in other countries such as Namibia?[61] How could the resource curse become a blessing as intended? To which elements of the Nigerian political culture should Shell (and the Government of Nigeria) have been sensitive prior to investment?[62]

Develop Local Alliances to Share Risks

Locals would also like to see a risk-sharing partnership between any MNC and their government. They want agreements with the MNC to be transparent and to be persuaded that all the benefits of the drilling and mining operation will not flow to the MNC and local elites and officials, confirming another instance of a "resource curse". In the next case, the jury is still out on whether the Guyana oil bonanza will be a blessing or another curse for that poor and underdeveloped state. Locals there want to see tangible evidence from Exxon that it is more than a revenue generator for the Government of Guyana (GOG), by at least sinking real roots into the populace and not simply sinking rigs into the ground or sea to supply the MNC with most of the profits.

Discussion Case #6: The Guyana Petrostate[63]

One of the new Faustian bargains with the devil in 2023 has been a large, short-term investment in fossil fuels in return for promised development benefits for the recipient country. Billions of dollars of oil were discovered were discovered in Guyana's waters by ExxonMobil in 2016. It is up to President Irfaan Ali to manage the new revenue windfall for growth and development in the future. The previous President Jagedo, whose term ended in 2011, was hailed as an ecological superstar and received the "Champion of the Earth" trophy from the UN for the world's first "bilateral carbon-trading" scheme with Norway to set aside its forests in exchange for carbon credits. A total of 85% of Guyana is tropical forest and the swap with Norway also received UN support. So, to environmental critics, the switch back to fossil fuels to fund development appears contradictory.

Nevertheless, the discovery of oil is a lifeline for this small undeveloped country. Guyana has 400k residents, half of which live in Georgetown on the Caribbean coast. It is one of the poorest countries in the Western Hemisphere. Almost 60% of its GDP was wiped out in 2005 by a tidal surge. If the globe continues to warm from consuming fossil fuels, the sea will rise six inches six "submerging its sea wall that partly protects it from flooding".

In 2015, Exxon Mobil discovered billions of barrels of crude oil worth hundreds of billions of dollars, one of its largest global discoveries since then. The regions of Guyana, Suriname, and the northeastern Brazilian Amazon are known as the "Equatorial Margin" which could hold as much as 30b barrels of oil (of which 25% should be recoverable). Guyana wants to use the revenue windfall to build more durable infrastructure ironically powered by renewable energy. Currently, a 40-mile auto trip from Georgetown to Anna Regina takes 3 hours. This year, with a 100% increase in its capital budget, the GOG is building connecting roads to the other two countries noted in the Equatorial Margin: Brazil and Suriname. Many new homes as well as existing homes will be connected to reliable water and energy services. The 2022 Guyanan GDP should increase by almost 60%, and oil has already reached nearly 60% of GDP (2022:37). The GOG created an oil account in the MOF, and it plans to fund its projects such as a new grid that will run on renewable energy. Fossil fuel opponents argue that Guyana should leave its new oil in the ground to avoid contributing to global warming. The GOG rejects this and considers oil as part of its sustainable strategy to manage growth. As noted, 85% of Guyana is covered in forest which sponges up tons of carbon. It protects this resource for which Norway already paid $250m. In exchange, Guyana receives carbon credits to offset its overall emission totals, in the world's first bilateral carbon-trading scheme (2022:38).

The oil contract signed in 1999 with Exxon shares profits 50–50 and pays a 2% royalty to the GOG. Inside the contract are concessions, such as on any taxes paid by the GOG. Mobil Exxon will claim such payments as tax credits in the US. Exxon will also pay itself from current oil revenues to repay itself for future decommissioning and abandonment expenses, costs unlikely to be incurred for decades. Exxon may also repay itself now for additional exploration costs for work anywhere in the area, not just the area under lease. In 2018, recognizing its lack of expertise in dealing with large MNCs, the GOG hired an expert Vincent Adams to run its EPA who was born in Guyana but worked for the US DOE for 30 years as an energy sector monitor.

Exxon promised the GOG that its oil drilling would not flare natural gas at its rigs but instead be reinjected into the ground. Adams found a complete lack of petroleum engineering depth to support him in the Guyana EPA, meaning Exxon is able largely to regulate itself. Adams was then sacked, and GOG announced that instead of requiring Exxon to cut production to manage flaring, it would fine it for $45/ton of carbon emitted. Touted as one of the few taxes on flaring in the world, however, it actually acted as an incentive to increase production. The new 2016 Exxon contract provided for a GOG signing bonus which was deposited in a new extrabudgetary account that was not subject to audit (2022:40). Fear began to surface that Guyana would be subject to another "resource curse" from signing an unfair royalty concession. The demographics almost make exploitative relationships that plunder the country of its resources unavoidable.[64] Only 2.3% of locals have at least a bachelor's degree of which 89% leave the country for better work. A total of 40% of the population lives in poverty and subsists on less than $5.50/day. The average adult has only six years of education. In 2016, Guyana became a member of the EITI which requires accounting transparency and regular reporting of financial flows including how and whether earned royalties are spent for developmental benefits. But so far progress in generating local incomes and employment from the production of oil and gas has been slow. There is little evidence of corruption or misappropriation of funds so far. But pressure is building to show developmental results besides funds paid to the GOG by Exxon.

Questions

It is unclear from the case how much expertise Guyana gained from EITI when negotiating its oil concession contract with ExxonMobil. It apparently left itself vulnerable to explicit and hidden conditions that could cost it development benefits and substantial treasury losses. International tax lawyers, often working for such large firms, are experts in avoiding taxation by their clients. US states, for example, have a long history of providing billions of dollars in tax credits and other business subsidies and handouts such as site preparation and infrastructure to lure potential investors to its tax jurisdictions. Many did not work out! Historically, incentives average about $5k/job created and for such investments as electric vehicles it is $10k. But having been burned on loose contract and concession language, more recently states such as Georgia include conditions that require, for instance, 80% of its commitment to invest $5b and create 7,500 jobs by the end of 2028 or pay back the tax credit. The firms must also invest in infrastructure and job training as part of the tax breaks. Thus, even if the investor fails, the state gains in increased job force capacity, infrastructure, and site preparation. Another user can quickly come along and absorb the capacity almost free of charge. An additional part of Georgia's incentive package was that the state would issue revenue bonds to help finance the investments by Rivian EV-maker. But the state court invalidated the bonds as a high-risk speculation by the state pointing to Rivian's record as a loss-making start-up.[65] In short, there are many applied lessons out there for similar countries with valuable resources that need to protect their financial worth from aggressive and experienced investors and to guard against unnecessary risks to the fiscal condition of the country.

Can Guyana meet its environmental commitments for sustainable development through fossil fuel revenues? How is Guyana preventing oil from becoming a "resource curse" for the country? Does Guyana really have the institutional strength and regulatory capacity to absorb oil and gas revenues and spend them effectively for needed development projects?

Adapt Donor Laws, Systems, and Practices to Complex Local Political Cultures

Often, expats from major donor countries and institutions need to manage projects in complex, puzzling legal contexts and under unstable political conditions. Staff of religious ethnic and varied habits need to be directed and motivated to get the project work done. Often rich country codes are rigid and designed for countries with developed rules of law. These must somehow be mixed with poor country practices and habits to complete projects. Laws are often bent and subject to standard corruption accusations that may not be strictly legal but actually quite effective in the context of having to get at least something done. This will be evident in the following case of British colonials trying to manage a road project in West Africa (Nigeria) in the 1930s (*Mr. Johnson*, London: Thistle Press, 1939).

Discussion Case #7: Mr. Johnson

In the 1939 Joyce Cary novel (and film in which Pierce Brosnan plays Rudbeck https://www.youtube.com/watch?v=vADRHPoGjH4), the action takes place at another colonial station near Kano in the Muslim part of Nigeria. Johnson is a wily local (whose native name is Bauli) who works for Rudbeck the political officer or ADO who likes road-building. The district officer (DO) Blore deals with tax collection and is also a judge—he suspects Johnson of no good; Bulteel is an old hand who likes roads and wants to see the 100-mile Dorua road project go north to Fada to link with Kano. He learns of Johnson's embezzlements but sympathizes with him, recognizing that in the bush the UK rule of law environment is not the same. The context consists of a British project to build a road and pay and account for it in multiple cultures governed by different treasury, accounting, and judicial institutions with different values and practices: British colonial accounting and auditing from London and local Muslim and tribal practices many of which are informal. These parallel but contradictory rules and institutional practices were not sorted out before the project began. Nor were supervisory roles clarified for both British and native staff. For example, Rudbeck is the COP but has a variety of roles from judge to budgetary spending approvals. Johnson has ingratiated himself as native staff with an undefined supervisory role he calls "road treasurer" and a right-hand local man to Rudbeck. Johnson was a delightful dreamer and believed in his own words as soon as he invented them. That was the origin of his financial dexterity, respect by the natives, and his longevity as he kept the construction project moving. In this context, the British fail to appreciate that the local Muslims actually oppose the road and the *zungos* or temporary work camps that could become permanent and threaten their native authority. But the parallel Muslim locals like to have the British source of loosely accounted-for funds for their occasional enrichment. As a kind of double agent, Johnson is able to facilitate side payments to locals from road project funds by creating his own system of project accounting.

Soon enough, Tring the regional UK regional auditor becomes suspicious of Johnson, since the project is having repeated cash flow problems. He suspects that many of Johnson's approved road payments are being drawn from both the British and native treasuries. He finds that Johnson is moving funds freely around between accounts, capital and current, personnel and non-personnel, and even fiscal years to pay workers from journal entries based on fictitious or non-existent ledger accounts. For example, Johnson enters the purchase of a cow as an expense for personnel milk supplies. But instead of a payable or incurred liability from a legitimate vote in the chart of accounts, he enters the commitment in a made-up exports account because he expects it to become a hide. Why not one might ask? Johnson has a rich imagination and only limited book-keeping knowledge. But he knows math and is able to move money around to cover cash flow problems, e.g., buying uniforms and paying next fiscal year (modern forward funding!) or replenishing the temporary deficit with revenues from a temporary road fee. From such fees he would keep small commissions for himself which he used to pay debts to native officials. He also pays native officials, such as the Emir of Dorua, from the British Treasury. This is a conflict of interest facilitated by the lack of internal controls that require approvals for payments from the vote (appropriation) accounts to be valid. But Johnson draws pay orders or phony invoices and approves them without out real invoices which are more conflicts of interest facilitated by his vague road treasurer role.

Tring and Bulteel make an audit report and find Johnson guilty of over-spending accounts and making unauthorized payments for which he is sacked. Rudbeck was also reprimanded in Bulteel's report not for fraud/embezzlement which is what Tring wanted but rather for "unorthodox accounting" and "overspending votes". Actions such as stealing from Rudbeck's cash drawer are all petty embezzlements that he makes in good faith to get the road completed. In his imagination they are all justified. He is sacked by Rudbeck and goes to work at Gollop's store, where he excels because of his financial dexterity, salesmanship, and mathematical skills. However, he is robbing Gollop's safe or doing ("good robberies") in order to finance booze parties in the store after-hours with his native friends from town and the project. In one instance, he is caught in the act and stabs Gollop to death. Tried by Rudbeck who is also the local judge, he is convicted and shot. As a postscript to Johnson's short career as project financial accountant and manager, Bulteel notes that British financial control regulations were too rigid, and if followed there would have been no Dorua road or even a British Empire!

Questions

Describe the parallel cultures, diffuse local roles, and conflicts of interest that allowed the road to be completed despite Johnson's embezzlements, as well as his "good" robberies and "bad" robberies.

What should Johnson have been found guilty of? Was he a good man set up by a bad system?

What rules and systems should have been in place to control spending, complete the road, and be consistent with the UK and native institutional cultures?

Was Mr. Johnson a more effective road project manager than Rudbeck? Why? Was Rudbeck a financial manager? Did Rudbeck's lofty slogan— "order, rules, progress" pertain to the road project's finances at the operational level?

Which of Mr. Johnson's actions were legal according to local customs and practices but illegal according to Western budgeting and auditing rules (e.g., GAAP)? His financial shenanigans kept the project going. But did not his payments to the native treasury likely amount to embezzlement and were they not illegal or corrupt according to GAAP and British rules? What were the institutional issues of *internal control/audit* (National Audit Office or NAO vs. project unit); *cash management* (budget management flexibility); and *accounting*? For example, as noted, Johnson made up ledger accounts as "road treasurer" and posted transactions such as cow purchase as a reimbursable expense to be placed in export accounts as a future hide.

Describe the political culture(s) here. How were the locals locked into systems of patronage and tribe? What were their values and what behavior(s) and practices resulted? How can a project manager deal with the larger policy conflict between roads or railways for national connectivity and nation-building vs. the concept of roads serve only atavistic local cultures? How can he/she avoid it? Gandhi saw railways as perpetuators of the British Raj, importing diseases and exporting locally produced grains that would produce famines. By contrast, Nehru saw railways as essential to building an independent India. Note also how sectarian and religious strife destroyed the contextual stability necessary to construct and manage the Taurus and Orient Express RRs through the Middle East (begun originally by the Ottomans), affecting larger regional structures and relations, especially trade and commerce.[66]

Use Literature to Understand Political Culture

Overseas development managers try to decipher the values and practices of present political cultures with references to the accumulated values and practices from the past. As the novelist L.P. Hartley once said, "the past is a foreign country: they do things differently there". That points to the value of reading the classical novelists who wrote about their experiences in some cases more than a century ago. Aid workers and managers today will enter overseas worlds that exist now and not as they should be. "The world is what it is", said V.S. Naipaul in his 1979 novel *A Bend in the River.* To deal with this dissonance, tolerance of ambiguity, and re-thinking of learned values and behaviors are essential. Pretending that the past should be like the present (or "presentism") is ahistorical and a flawed approach. As to deleting or changing 19th–20th-century expressions, words, and language, it is this author's view that any deemed "offensive" should be "explained why they read the way they do" but not modified or eliminated by modern publishers or "editors".[67]

Classical writings such as Cary's *Mr. Johnson* reveal societies with often racist, imperialist, ethno-centric, sexist, and anti-Semitic leanings which we reject as inconsistent with our modern cultural values and practices. This is a mistake. Think of works by Greene, Wharton, Maugham, Conrad,[68] Kipling, Hemingway, Gogol, Dostoyevsky, and Whitman as "time machines". Orwell was actually opposed to British colonialism and imperialism despite the recognition that in some cases, there could be forces for good. Such writers are conveying cognitive models of their world to us. Cary's work does that in *Mr. Johnson*. We are traveling there to find out what made those societies and characters what they were. They had much to offer despite their often-pinched views. In their novels, post-colonialist writers such as V.S. Naipaul seem to touch every key discordant to the oversensitive eyes and ears of "presentists". Nevertheless, reflecting that neither the authors nor the characters are traveling here to the present allows us to avoid being complacent ("it can't happen here"!).

Seeing these people as creatures of their age allows us to see ourselves as creatures of our own. As with reading classical languages and the classics themselves, you enter their world rather than trying to haul them into the present age.[69] By reading these authors we are invited into their worlds, not to judge or change them to suit our current opinions but to understand the values, beliefs, attitudes, and habits of our future companions, adversaries, and employees on aid projects. If you reject their systems and beliefs or disbelieve the author's observations, perhaps IDM is not the profession for you. The insights of these writers should be critiqued and updated. But they cannot be rejected or denied, as racial and cultural behaviors are extant or just under the surface of those whom you will manage and work with. Remember also that "literature is often meant to be provocative". These people wrote in the 19th-century era when the dominant thinking was often Victorian: the need to impose order by diffusion of values and how states tried through imperialistic and nationally driven enterprise efforts with typically military back-up to impose that order. Religions often exported their doctrines and strictures by adding "God's Will" to colonial justifications for imposing order on the "lesser peoples" of the world.

Notes

1 For rigorous identification and measurement of the values component of the political culture concept, they must be distinguished from opinions. The World Values Survey (WVS) surveys attempt to do this. Permanent "values" are distinguished from evanescent "opinions" that can be selectively cherry-picked by populists and weaponized to mobilize supporters in support of false historical and territorial claims. Putin has been doing this to support his special military operation in Ukraine for more than a year.

2 Lucian W. Pye and Sidney Verba (1965) *Political Culture and Political Development* (Princeton: Princeton University Press, republished 2105 by Princeton Legacy Library).

3 For management purposes, there is no need to tackle a multiplicity of motives and circumstances that determine a decision or cause an event. Managers need simple rules of thumb to guide them to action. There are no frameworks that can explain the many motives that, for example, caused Miss Julie's suicide. This has long been the topic of intense debate among theatre critics. Strindberg explains that the "soul is rich and complicated" and personalities manifold (August Strindberg, *Miss Julie and Other Plays* [Oxford University Press, 1985]), *Preface*, p.58. A manager just needs a few do's and don'ts for recurring actions—meetings, supervision, recruitments, and firings.

4 *Economist* (2023) "Professional Services: The Too-Big Four", 4-22, p.54.

5 Ronald Inglehart (1988) "The Renaissance of Political Culture" *American Political Science Review* Volume 82, pp.1203–1230.

6 George M. Guess and James D. Savage (2022) *Comparative Public Budgeting: Global Perspectives on Taxing and Spending (2ⁿᵈ ed)* (Cambridge: Cambridge University Press).

7 *Economist* (2022) "Special Report, Italy Spreadeagled".

8 Juan Peron played the cultural unity card in 1950s Argentina, but it was exclusionary: mixed races enriched by the blood of native Indian ancestors. Naipaul (1981), *op.cit.,* pp.112–113. This was an early example of "blood and soil" populist nationalism by an elected dictatorship. In a modern twist, Vladimir Putin has defined the limits of Orthodox Slavic political and religious culture inclusively as a political weapon to be dealt with by Russian force. In his definition, Orthodox Slavs are "unified" despite boundaries and borders on maps; political and religious breakaways violate and insult cultural norms. Breakaway political systems, e.g., such as Georgia, Ukraine, and Chechnya (Grozny), must accordingly be dealt with by force to re-create Imperial Russia with its vast Eurasian territories and the Russian Tsarist Empire of 1721–1917 with Putin as a neo-tsar.

9 *Economist* (2022) "Briefing "The War in Ukraine: The Cult of War"", 3-26, pp.17–18.

10 In fact, much of Western aid presupposes a vibrant civil society where it is in charge of democracy not the army, regime, or the presidential administration. Aid technical assistance and training, especially in budgeting and financial management, recognizes that through candid revelations and examples of how Western government programs and institutions are often subject to error, betrayal, and incompetence. The Western value, hope, and question is whether the target country's systems of aid projects can allow for timely scrutiny and accountability of their own officials and institutions. Nemtsova argues Ukraine's culture of democratic resilience is precisely what makes it radically different from Russia—and that to be more effective and "workable" it should increasingly scrutinize the failures of (its own) officialdom. Anna Nemtsova "Ukraine Reveals its Secret Weapon: Self Scrutiny" *The Washington Post,* 8-19-23, p.A19.

11 George M. Guess and Stoigniew J. Sitko (2004) "Planning, Budgeting and Health Care Performance in Ukraine" *International Journal of Public Administration* Volume 27, Number 10, pp.767–798.

12 George M. Guess (2001) "Decentralization and Municipal Budgeting in Four Balkan States" *Journal of Public Budgeting, Accounting and Financial Management* Volume 13, Number 3 (Fall), pp.397–436.

13 R. Raudla (2013) "Estonian Budgetary Policy during the Crisis: How Explain the Outlier?" *Public Administration* Volume 91, Number 1, pp.32–50.

14 Kai Hammerich and Richard P. Lewis (2013) *Fish Can't See Water: How National Culture and Can make or Break Your Corporate Strategy* (New York: Wiley).

15 Colonial histories are very much part of the institutional context of transitional and developing countries. The colonial systems and practices persist, in bureaucratic processes such as purchasing, treasury operations, public budgeting, taxation, trade, and commerce, and need to be taken into consideration by current aid managers. For example, we divided up the historical and institutional environment into five "cultural clusters" affected by the main colonial influences over fiscal, bureaucratic, and political institutions: (1) French, (2)

Iberian, (3) US, (4) Great Britain, and (5) Former Soviet. Of course, in particular country cases, the influences are multiple, e.g., Dutch, English, and French. But usually one predominates in all or part of the country. (George M. Guess, William Loehr, and Jorge Martinez-Vazquez (1997) "Fiscal Decentralization: A Methodology for Case Studies", *CAER Discussion Paper #3* [Cambridge, MA: Harvard Institute for International Development].)

16 Private audit firms such as Ernst and Young (EY) are hired by firms to certify the truthfulness of their balance sheets, income statements, and cash flow accounts for investors and regulators. A well-known "expectations-reality" gap exists here between guaranteed truthfulness and the reality that frauds are often sophisticated and hard to detect. The same gap exists for public sector accounts where phony invoices, unregistered expenditures, and unreasonable levels of accrued tax receipts take place. Samples of source documents have to be examined before they are entered into ledgers to be fully truthful. Auditors rarely have the time for such "forensic audits". Accounting, Why EY? *Economist* 4-8-23, p.57.

17 From: *Economist* (2018) "Corporate Graft in Europe: Cleaner Living".

18 Francis Fukuyama (2014) *Political Order and Political Decay* (New York: Farrar, Straus, and Giroux).

19 Szuzanna Ardo *Culture Shock Hungary: A Guide to Customs and Etiquette* (New York, Ardo, 2000).

20 Albert O. Hirschman and Richard Bird (1971) "Foreign Aid: A Critique and a Proposal" in Albert O. Hirschman (ed) *A Bias for Hope: Essays on Development and Latin America* (New Haven, CT: Yale University Press).

21 Lawrence E. Harrison (1985) *Underdevelopment as a State of Mind: The Latin American Case* (Lanham, MD: Center for International Affairs).

22 Following Harrison (1985) and others that use political culture as an independent variable, Naipaul (1981:213–214) witnesses the breakdown of municipal services and administration, the jobs not done, the garbage uncollected, in places like Kinshasa (Zaire) and suggests that "a kind of underdevelopment issues from the habits of people and attitudes toward life and society". He concluded perhaps harshly that these failures are not caused by the colonial past but by present egotism.

23 *Economist* (2023) "A Land of Frustrated Workers", 6-10, pp.27–28.

24 *Economist* (2023) "Militarizing Russia, the Home Front", 2-25, pp.23–26.

25 In Conrad's *Under Western Eyes* (pp.178–179), the noble feminist high priest of revolution Peter Ivanovitch explains to Razumov that the chasm between Russia's past and future can never be bridged by "foreign liberalism" or any "foreign-bred doctrines". It can only be bridged by the genuine Russian peasantry led by leadership from its nobility.

26 This was the student Razumov's dilemma in Joseph Conrad's *Under Western Eyes* (Penguin, 1964, p.71). He saw his stable, politically centrist future determined and menaced by either a lawless autocracy of the right (roughly Vladimir Putin now) or the lawlessness of leftist revolution (Stalin and totalitarian Communism). It would be menaced by perennial competition for Russia's future between Utopian visionaries (p.85) "who work their everlasting evil on earth" inspiring "in the mass of mediocre minds a disgust of reality and a contempt for the secular logic of human development" (p.85). In this context, how can the Western occidental values of open societies and markets be reconciled with Russian values and attitudes? Natalia (the revolutionary Victor Haldin's sister) believed Russians would find a better form of national freedom than through the Western "artificial conflict of parties" (p.94), a type of "disembodied

concord". But to her English tutor, Russians lifted every understandable problem "to the plane of mystical expression" (p.93). He believed Russians to be hopelessly cynical and scornful about what they saw as an "irremediable life" (in a strict religious sense). Her pessimistic conclusion was that antagonisms between Russian and Western values and practices (i.e. "political cultures" or values linked to political behavior that historically oscillated between autocratic extremes) would have to be "cemented by blood and violence" (p.94). That is, they cannot be resolved at the same level of analysis and must lead to bloody stalemates or worse (e.g. Ukraine).

27 Philip Kennicott (2022) "Putin's Brutality against Ukraine Complicates Our Appreciation of Russian Culture" *The Washington Post* December 18, pp.E2–E3.

28 The claim of historical destiny attempts to rationalize his cultural weaponization. In a 1999 speech, Vladimir Putin compared the post-Soviet "time of troubles" ("transition") to the uprisings, famine, and invasions of the 16th–17th centuries. He promised stability, prosperity, and state restoration. His hyperbole grew further by casting then-President Boris Yeltsin as Pushkin's *Boris Godunov* (the Russian regent who restored the legitimate state and later became a tsar) and himself as the beginning of a line of new tsars (Alexander Pushkin (2007) *Boris Godunov and Other Dramatic Works* [London: Oxford World's Classics]). But the values in this new reform package would be pure Russian values not the decadent Western decadent values of freedom, independent judiciaries and media, and rule of law as opposed to rule by law. But his role as head of state has been threatened by his mistaken decision to invade Ukraine, and the intensity of rival clans and militias vying for control of state power, i.e., the FSB security service, the recent Wagner Group mutiny, the regular Russian army and technocrats who make things work. "Putin's Time of Troubles" *Economist* 7-1-23, pp.39–40. As the state fragments into rival armies and clans, he has failed at state restoration. Western post-transition DA to the Russian state constructed a strong economic and fiscal state that was respected by global creditors for its management quality. It was politically legitimate, creditworthy, and eligible for more loans and grants from bilateral and multilateral aid agencies.

29 Lee Hockstader (2023) "Europe Has a Monuments Problem of its Own", *The Washington Post*, 2-9.

30 For Pushkin, Russia's "most cosmopolitan" playwright, cultural and political nationalism or "Russianness" meant a hybrid: "the ability to refract, integrate, condense and translate everyone else". To Caryl Emerson in her "Introduction" to *Boris Godunov and Other Dramatic Works* (London: Oxford World Classics, 2009), the operative word is "cosmopolitan". Stalin and other wannabe clones such as Putin are decidedly provincial, mid-level security bureaucrats rising to power and glory that they are unable to manage beyond the realm of their own egos See also: G. Guess (2010) "Close Shave in Ukraine: Stalin's Barber" review in *The American Interest.*

31 Timothy Snyder (2022) "By Denying a Ukrainian Culture, Putin Flattens His Own" *The Washington Post*, 4-10, p.B1.

32 Hockstader, *op.cit.* (2023); George Guess (2022) "A Hallmark of Tyranny", letter to the editor: *The Washington Post*, 9-3, p.A20.

33 This was spelled out in hilarious detail by the classic book on Soviet socialist realism: Abram Tertz's (Andrey Sinyavskiy) *The Trial Begins* and *On Socialist Realism* (Vintage, 1965).

34 *Economist*, "Russian Art in Wartime: Culture in the Time of Z", 2-18-23, pp.75–76. See: George M. Guess (2014) review of *Stalin's Barber* by Paul M. Levitt (New York: Taylor Trade Publishing, 2012), xiv + 378 pp, "Close Shaves in Ukraine: The Well-Groomed Autocrat" *The American Interest*, March 30.
35 Cedric Watts (1987) "Introduction" to James Joyce (1987), *Ulysses* (London: Wordsworth), p.xxxii.
36 From *Economist* (2021) "Northern Ireland: Unhappy Anniversary", 4-21.
37 *Economist* (2022) "A Bitter Life for All", pp.39–40.
38 George M. Guess and Jun Ma (2015) "The Risks of Chinese Subnational Debt for Public Financial Management" *Public Administration and Development* Volume 35, pp.129–139.
39 *Economist* (2022) "Xi Jinping's Covid Retreat", 12-17, p.38).
40 *Economist*, "El Chapo: The Sequel", 1-28-23 p.28.
41 Correspondingly in Ukraine, Russia conquered the southeastern provinces acting to install instant Russian villages that held sham referenda after which the Russians claimed them as its own legitimate territory. Schools and media were now taught, and broadcast in Russian and Ukrainian was prohibited. By force Vladimir Putin imposes his view of Russian values: obedient, state-dependent, Orthodox, and militantly nationalist under Russia as one re-united culture that includes Ukraine, purged of Western moral and political impurities. Patriarch Kirkus, head of the Russian Orthodox Church, has provided the faith-based justifications for Russia's expansionist aims—*Ruskly Mir*—a Russian word for the Russian world which encompasses Ukraine. But many Ukrainians reject this wing of the Church and now celebrate Christmas on December 25 according to the Gregorian calendar instead of January 7 according to the Julian calendar.
42 Authoritarian regimes, e.g., the Chinese Politburo, argue Western values are not universal after all—not everyone wants the freedom and responsibility to fail or to go through the tedious process of debating and forging consensus repeatedly. Party/regime forged consensus more orderly, efficiently, and usually effectively. These are enticing arguments or rationalizations in favor of absolutist and tyrannical rule.
43 Aid managers and workers normally do not think of guiding principles behind their TORs for technical assistance and training to strengthen systems—tax, budget, procurement, and elections. They would accept that there is no "one best way" and often encourage lively debate and critique of the very systems and tools being transferred. But the base purpose of Western aid and its aid programs is the protection of individual rights through what it considers "universal" values"—accountable and transparent governance, independent courts, free speech, multi-party systems, and free-fair elections. Even aid workers that claim "they don't do democracy" admit this. The values are on offer as public goods like clean water and not as an imposed system, such as "socialist realism" imposed on art and literature by Stalin. Western aid follows this path of theory and ideology "light" and best practice "heavy" Where that varies, such as in the crude attempts by Western aid workers to lecture or sermonize about the wonders of "democracy and governance", the host reactions are mostly skepticism at best and laughter at worst.
44 *Economist* (2023) "Thinking for Themselves", 8-12, p.47.
45 *Economist* (2021) "Whatever it Took?", p.48.
46 *Economist* (2021) "Down to the Wire", 4-3, pp.17–19.

47 According to Grosse (2023) despite cultural differences, people then are really the same for purposes of management (Robert Grosse [2023] *People are People—A New View of Cross-Cultural People Management* [New York: Routledge]). His views and findings are similar to those of Klitgaard in *Bold and Humble* (2022).

48 George M. Guess (1992) "Centralization of Expenditure Controls in Latin America" *Public Administration Quarterly* Volume XVI, Number 3, pp.376–394.

49 R. Gregory Michel (2001) *Decision Tools for Budgetary Analysis* (Chicago, IL: Government Finance Officers Association), pp.59–77.

50 The function of 18th- and 19th-century commercial trading companies and their outstations was to somehow bring as the slogan went: "faith, light and commerce" to the poor and backward but resource-rich countries as part of colonial expansion. Colonial-era writers like Conrad repeatedly divided the world into "civilized" and "uncivilized" countries rather than rich and poor. His provocative distinction today would certainly demand definition, clarification, and measurement! In those days, "trade" really meant mercantilism (the policy of extracting local natural resources and exporting them unprocessed to home countries [logs, ore]). Colonial powers did this rather than invest in local industry that processed and exported into world markets. It was a simple plunder facilitated by trading stations. Mercantilist policies did not stimulate local growth or development, nor did they intend to! Rather, they contributed to underdevelopment! Belize was a test case for British mercantilist policy effects on local growth and development. My research there in the 1980s under a Fulbright grant noted the extraction of mahogany and export from Belize City to London of unfinished logs (George M. Guess [1982] "Institution-Building for Development Forestry in Latin America" *Public Administration and Development* Volume 2, Number 4, pp.309–324). No local forest sector or industry for secondary manufacture of wood products developed. Few jobs were created in the primary sawmilling sub-sector. One novel industry developed to insert cocaine and heroin into the logs and transship them to the US without detection. Otherwise, the country remained a backward monoculture that failed to take advantage of its forest resources. USAID concentrated its aid on developing businesses and commercial training institutes; UKAID made few inroads into developing a robust forest sector for development.

51 Development projects, as noted, seek wider and deeper socioeconomic benefits such as income, employment, and quality of life. To accomplish project ends, staff and workers must be trained, instructed, and managed to perform many complex tasks on schedule. Kayerts (the chief) and Carlier (the assistant) appointed to run the Congo River trading station in Joseph Conrad's "*Outpost of Progress*" (1897) did not train or manage any of the staff but simply concluded that "the men won't work" and that they were "no good at all" (Dover Thrift, Mineola, NY, 2019, p.13). Knowing how the chief of station felt about him, Makola (the staff assistant), and the rest of the station workers, nevertheless, to prevent the company director from "growling" at them for the evident deterioration of the station when he returned in a few months, Makola quite sensibly traded the ten of the workers away for more ivory. After all, ivory was the most valuable local "product". And his risky decision to buy more ivory from an untrustworthy warlike and savage tribe from the coast did mean more "trade" and more commissions for the chief and his assistant. Nevertheless, Kayerts and Carlier fumed at him for this idiocy. But in Makola's mind, he was

only doing them a favor! Makola had not been trained, instructed, supervised, or managed properly—a predictable failure due to their own inexperience and incompetence. Unlike Moses and his crew in Ecuadorian Oriente, Kayerts and Carlier failed to establish contacts with the locals or to recognize the personalistic basis for the few allies they had. Makola was their only link to the locals and he detested them. Despite their long-term status as residents, they remained incurious to the people or their local happenings. They tried to isolate themselves from the local culture and endure the experience until they could leave and head home. In my view, it was not the culture that resulted in their moral and physical degradation—rather they were unsuited to overseas life and work. They failed to prepare themselves or anticipate what could go wrong. They completely lacked "transnational competence" (Koehn and Rosenau, 2010).

The destructive effects of overseas cultures on modern Western managers and experts are familiar themes in literature, e.g., Conrad's *"Heart of Darkness"*, the film was famous as *"Apocalypse Now"* with Marlon Brando as Kurtz! and often makes for an exciting if depressing read. "Outpost of Progress" and other tales like this reveal the stamina, constraint, and discipline needed for overseas aid work should be part of any recruitment screening for IDM candidates. Often the recruiters miss this and later blame the difficult culture or conditions for project failures. The resultant "curse" is the lack of individual qualities rather than any "resource" or local cultural constraint. Some people thrive under such difficult conditions; others clearly do not! The trick is to pick the right ones!

52 *Economist* (2022) "The 2 Brazilian Booms that Bookmark the History of the Car", 12-24, p.11.
53 Melissa Rainey (2023) "I'm Leavin' It" *Bloomberg Businessweek*, January 9, pp.35–41.
54 Mark Denton (2019) *The Efficiency Trap: Maximizing Business Growth in Central America by Embracing Diversity and Avoiding the Pitfalls of Over-Standardization* (San Jose, Costa Rica: Bloomberg BusinessWeek), p.50.
55 Kai Bird and Martin J. Sherwin (2006) *American Prometheus, The Triumph and Tragedy of J. Robert Oppenheimer, op.cit.*, p.186.
56 Kai Bird and Martin J. Sherwin (2006) *op.cit.*, p.218.
57 Kai Bird and Martin J. Sherwin (2006) *op.cit.*, pp.187–203.
58 Kai Bird and Martin J. Sherwin (2006) *op.cit.*, p.362.
59 Denton, *op.cit.*, Chapter 3.
60 From: *Shell in Nigeria: CSR and the Organi Crisis*, Pew Foundation, Georgetown University Institute for Development Studies, Case #267, 1995.
61 *Economist* (2017) "Namibia's Economy", 4-22. http://www.economist.com/news/middle-east-and-africa/21720932-such-policies-did-not-work-out-well-zimbabwe-namibias-president-flirting
62 See: Albert O. Hirschman (1965) "Obstacles to Development: A Classification and a Quasi-Vanishing Act".
63 "Guyana Petrostate", From: *Bloomberg Businessweek*, November 21, 2022, pp.35–41.
64 Isabella followed the example and advice of Jamaica on its Bauxite royalty concession renegotiations (Naipaul [1967] *op.cit.*, pp.217–218). Until the 1960s the Isabella concession was opaque and its terms and values were hidden from both the Isabella government and its public. Jamaica demanded and got transparency from the mining firm. EITI as noted in the text now provides technical assistance on resource concessions to equalize the playing field

when powerful multinational mining companies deal with tiny resource-rich countries that lack skills, expertise, and negotiating experience. The use of Jamaica as a policy model with regional experience, expertise, and aggressive leadership was a successful example of sharing vital knowledge to convert a curse into a valuable natural resource by increasing its royalty revenues. This is precisely the purpose of EITI. 218

65 *Economist* (2023) "The Incentives War", 2-25, pp.29–30.

66 *Economist* (2021) From: "Railway Lines Once Connected the Middle East", 12-18.

67 Washington Post Editorial Board Opinion (2023) "21st-Century Editors Should Keep Their Hands Off of 20th-Century Books", 6-14, p.A22.

68 According to Albert J. Guerard (1960), his stories "play on our sensibilities" and "tamper with our convictions". They "demand more complex sympathies than we ordinarily need". By re-reading his intimate novels such as *Nostromo*, he improves through our acquaintance with him. "Introduction" (Dell, 1960) p.5.

69 From: Brian Norton (2019) "Past Tension: Why We Should Read Works That Offend Us" *New York Times*, 1/13.

3   Managing as Problem-Solving

Context and Problems

Managing as problem-solving means motivating and directing operational teams at the line level of an organization where issues arise 24/7. This is especially true in sectors, such as health care and public transit where perennial supply shortages or thefts, personnel absenteeism, and equipment breakdowns plague service delivery. As noted, supply chain constraints can arise from bad policies that cause internal congestion and overwork or even from "pissing contests" between managers over who has the right to make decisions that delay actions.[1] Managers are supposed to lead their employees to tackle practical problems, such as the case of evaluating a USAID project portfolio in Pakistan (*Discussion Case #9*). Managers for aid projects like Pakistan, financed by firms and government donors, oversee expatriates, local hires, and subcontractors with expats often as in that case, beyond their direct control. To focus resources, managers need to target their resources to defined, actionable problems. A policy problem is an important issue affecting the public on which it is deemed funds should be spent and for which laws and regulations may be enacted. At the management level the actionable problem is an important issue that affects the delivery of public services or construction and rehabilitation of a capital asset, such as sewer pipes, irrigation canals, bridges, or railways. Management of development programs or projects takes place at the implementation level of motivating teams and ensuring that organized efforts lead to the achievement of contract scopes of work (SOW) or terms of reference (TOR) tasks on time and within budgets.

For example, a development assistance (DA) contract might be to strengthen municipal fiscal institutions as part of a fiscal decentralization aid program to support existing public policies in country X. The project manager would break down the problems of tax, budget, and borrowing systems and provide modules of training and on-the-job technical

DOI: 10.4324/9781032670959-3

assistance to the finance department in ten target cities. A training course for this project might last for five days, covering five to six topics on public spending: budget formats, fiscal and project analysis, accounting and reporting, implementation, and spending evaluation. Such a course would need two to three instructors and 35–40 trainees assigned from finance departments in several targeted project cities. Specifically, long- and short-term specialists from the project would be assigned to deliver specific modules according to the work plan over the five-day period. The instructors might select four to five of the best performing trainees for advanced pedagogical training to become future trainers, thereby ensuring that institutional training capacity stays in the country after project completion. Operational problems often arise, requiring management attention. For instance, instructors are often sick, buildings and classrooms are suddenly unavailable, equipment breaks down, training materials are not ready, and students may be called to perform other duties. At the institutional systems level, budgets may often be approved late which interferes with planned spending and creates cash flow problems during the fiscal year. Other systems, such as allotments, need to be reviewed for approval inefficiencies that delay spending by the technical departments. Procurement systems for supplies and equipment are often problematic with inefficiencies due to weak internal controls, opaque bidding processes, and fund leakages that allow misappropriation of funds.

Thus, along the implementation path of this one- to two-year project such as this broken into multiple tasks according to estimated schedules for delivery and completion of each, there will be management problems that must be carefully identified and defined. The "problem" definition is often incomplete in that for some people, problems are sometimes management opportunities. A problem could be a symptom of other underlying problems, e.g., drug trafficking in Mexico is one symptom of deeper problems, such as weak courts and corrupt police. At the operations level, especially in municipal services, managers have to deal with fact-driven, everyday service delivery issues and respond effectively. Disagreement is intense at the initial phase of the program or management review because it is often hard to get an analytic consensus on a workable problem definition. Institutional frameworks emphasize "analysis" and "conflict-resolution" between stakeholders which often generate options but produce little consensus on either actionable problem definitions or especially a preferred option. This difficult and often flawed process often leads to implementation failures. In the first of four phases of this cycle, problems should be identified and distinguished as short- vs. long-term, directly-indirectly actionable, strategic vs. operational, and structured vs. messy. Development managers in the field are often surprised to find that some of the same problems identified in the host country as topics for technical assistance and training, often constrain project performance as well, such as the failures by donor and/or headquarter development firm prime contractors to release funds on time, intrusions by time-wasting micromanagement and monitoring efforts performed by unqualified generalists and so on.

Learning Outcomes

1   To explain the policy-making and management cycle: problem-identification, development of scenarios and options, implementation, and evaluation.
2   To distinguish why management consists of four sub-systems of the strategic policy-making cycle: organizational processes, human resources and personnel, budgeting and financial management, and sectors such as transport, education, and the environment.
3   To discuss why public management and policy problems should be real, public, quantifiable, and actionable.
4   To exemplify and distinguish: well-structured, moderately structured, and ill-structured or messy problems.
5   To examine obstacles to problem identification: false analogies and incomparable cases.
6   To learn the strengths and weaknesses of the Xavier (1998) "matched-case" method for preventing the use of incomparable cases.
7   To learn methods for selecting preferred solutions to complex problems: simplify the problem.
8   Discuss the elements of a public management problem through the four phases: forestry and international development.
9   To draw lessons from *Discussion Case #8*: are non-governmental organizations (NGOs) a preferred solution to the messy perennial problems confronting Haiti?
10   To discuss and draw lessons on the obstacles to DA effectiveness.
11   To discuss the attempts to increase DA effectiveness: the 2005 Paris Accords on Aid Effectiveness.
12   To discuss and draw lessons from the facts and issues in the *Pakistan Case #9* concerning: personnel and staffing, security, local and international politics, and management.
13   To examine the facts and draw practical lessons from the paradox of the seeming inability of African countries to develop their substantial natural resources *(Discussion Case #10)*.
14   To explore the strengths and weaknesses of delivering DA through commercial enterprises, such as in Cabo Delgado, Mozambique *(Exercise #3.1)*. To explore under what conditions private DA might work and not work.

Issues, Topics, Cases, and Exercises

The Importance of Identifying, Structuring and Prioritizing Problems:
The Management and Policy Cycle

IDENTIFYING AND STRUCTURING POLICY PROBLEMS

The four-phase policy cycle (*Figure 3.1*) also applies at the management level. Policy-making and senior management take place at the strategic and broad national level for areas such as transportation, education, environment, health, and fiscal policy. The management level focuses on improving one or more of the four sub-systems noted above: (1) organizational processes, both internal such as procurement and external, maintaining and operating schools, hospitals, and roads; (2) human resources, such as recruiting, interviewing, hiring, and firing; (3) budgeting and financing, such as planning budgets, cash management, and financing services and projects; and (4) sectors such as urban transport, education, and the environment. Management focuses on the narrower sectors and program operations at a technical level within policies and programs, such as rail programs, overseas aid technical assistance programs in infectious diseases programs, and public financial management (PFM) systems. Projects, such as rail systems for specific cities, are developed with separate TORs within both policies and programs. The objective at the management level is to install systems, use techniques, and devise methods to make sector programs work more efficiently and effectively.

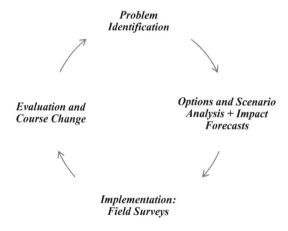

Figure 3.1 The Policy Cycle.
Source: Created by author.

To do so, problems must be rigorously defined to avoid misdirected analytics, data, and information. Badly defined problems result in wasted human and fiscal resources. Funds are spent developing options and forecasts for the wrong technical systems and projects. The unneeded technical system might be implemented efficiently but the total effort would be ultimately ineffective. Our view here is that problem identification and definition is the most important phase in the cycle. It is easy to come up with options and solutions if one has never faced and worked through complex operational problems, such as financing and operating an urban transit system, managing a hospital budget, or staffing and running an urban public school.

Policy-making takes place at the strategic level and long-term; management is short-term, high-pressure, and quick feedback, at the operations level, such as raising bus fares or cutting particular routes. Both policy and management problems need to be defined mainly by experienced people who have dealt with similar issues in comparable contexts. Only they can know what can or will go wrong. It is critical that problems meet four criteria before appearing on the public agenda for funding and execution. First, problems should be real (urban congestion measured by traffic density and speed vs. normal everyday traffic jams). Second and third, they need to be public and quantifiable (health risks of Covid-19 virus spreading vs. genetically modified (GM) food bans from fear of future genetic risks; tilting high-rise in Russia as described in the film by Bykov).[2] Fourth, they should be actionable (a light rail transit line or LRT selected among quantifiable cost-benefit and cost-effectiveness analyzed options).[3] If a problem meets the first three criteria but is not deemed actionable—it might be divided up into phases or sequences. Break it down into discrete smaller problems, smaller steps, or smaller phases. Then it can be acted upon sensibly and more successfully. This is often the tactical method for dealing with international diplomatic and conflict problems (e.g., Cuban Missile Crisis of 1962) and battlefield actions in wartime. Divide the problem up so one can decide what to do in logical priority.

In short, as noted in *Figure 3.1*, before developing options and forecasting their probable consequences—operations managers and/or policy-makers must first define the problem(s). It is the manager's responsibility to direct the analyses and discussion and deliver the unit or team report on each of the four sub-criteria that will identify and define the management and policy problem. Problems should be *real, public, quantifiable, and actionable.*

Problems Are Real and Public

A real problem is one that is public and quantifiable, for instance, urban congestion measured by high traffic density and low-speed vs. annoying private complaints—-or normal traffic in most cities! Options to fix this problem by responding to public needs include traffic-sensing traffic lights and more expensive options such as an LRT line to move people fast and reduce congestion and air pollution from idling cars, trucks, and buses. For institutions like the British health service (NHS), the need would be to distinguish: normal annoyances, such as decrepit buildings and facilities, from real public problems, such as a waiting list of 6.8m for medical treatments, from even bigger public problems, such as the lack of staffing to fill open NHS positions: a shortfall of 11k medical doctors and 46k nurses!

Suppose you are a plumber living in a 30-story bloc of flats whose pipes have burst, and in the process of dealing with them, you discover that your building is badly tilting and could fall over at any minute. On closer inspection from the roof, you discover that the building is decrepit and could fall, killing or injuring its 500 residents and perhaps others on the ground and in neighboring flats from the falling building. But your landlord and the city officials who own the flats do not want to pay for evacuation and face lost rents. They say the building is fine and only needs minor maintenance. How would you prove it is a public problem and a hazardous risk to public welfare? Suppose it were a Russian city! The 2014 Russian film noted by Bykov dramatizes exactly this problem and the personal dangers of being an honest citizen speaking out against injustice on behalf of the other tenants and the public. After the pipes burst in his high-rise building of flats, small Russian town plumber Dima finds they are not only endangered by the pipes but also by the building itself which is tilting and is bound to collapse and fall over. He tries to convince municipal authorities to relocate the tenants to abandoned state buildings. But this threatens the corrupt real-estate moguls who profit from both their abandoned buildings and city contracts. Several of Dima's supporters are murdered, and he narrowly escapes death several times fighting corrupt bureaucrats. Even the smallest attempt to rectify routine problems with building inspections becomes impossible because these efforts threaten established ways of state business and would challenge existing authority.

Related to the issue of real problem identification is who has defined them and are they symptoms rather than actual problems. Or are they just planning to offer solutions to yet more problems that they come up with? Enormous potential for conflicts of interest exists in problem definition. Often multiple layers of government and institutions delay and confuse the process. The planning processes typically allow "public comment", meaning often that potentially corrupt intrusions into the process are likely to happen, confusing the final definitional product even further. Some conflicts of interest in defining the problem are easy to spot and could lead to identifying the symptom rather than the real problem.

For instance, often the very supplier of their own equipment is in a position to recommend their products or services. That would be easy to avoid. Consultants and equipment suppliers try this all the time for public sector contracts. But suppose your dilemma as administrator for the City of Venice is that only one feasible option is available and even that one may be your only chance for even a temporary remedy to build resilience and to survive as a city.

When the problem of flooding in Venice was bid out for definition and remedy, all bidders were makers and purveyors of floodgates. The city then predictably bought a new set of advanced floodgates from the Consorzio Venezia Nuova (CVN), the winning consortium which built the new system. The problem of flooding was defined by the CVN consultants as an absence of floodgates, precluding other available and perhaps cheaper options and solutions. But other feasible options did not exist and still do not as of 2023. And the old adage that all solutions lead to new problems holds! The 78-hinged steel floodgates (running roughly 1 mile along the seafloor) that now protect most of the city from floods at high tide are costly to use and must be retracted when the tides retreat to avoid blocking maritime traffic. As sea levels rise, the gates will have to be raised more often. Maintenance is also costly—removal of sand from the machinery as each floodgate must be "defouled" every five years. Finally, a related problem is that raw sewage flows into Venice's canals. When the new floodgates are raised to hold back rising tides, the lagoon turns from a bathtub into a sewer. To deal with this problem, Venice is now planning to raise the city by pumping seawater underground to raise up the land. This is an even more expensive option that despite precedent from the oil and gas industry that stores gas underground to raise oil lands might not work here. The other option being "floated" is to move the city![4] What now?

Similarly, but with less severe consequences perhaps, if heavy rail and other rails systems engineers are working in the bidding entity for an urban transit capital project financed by the national government, one could easily predict heavy rail to be favored and recommended by the urban transport agency procuring the system. That was precisely what happened with Miami Metrorail in the 1980s. The Metro-Dade Transit Administration (MDTA) engineers talked to other engineers about the best technical design for the reclaimed urban swamp area and then selected their "preferred option" of elevated rail for the 20-mile system. To distort the procurement further, the request for proposal (RFP) from USDOT (then UMTA) excluded other feasible and cheaper options preferred by transit systems in rich and poor countries worldwide such as bus rapid transit (BRT) and LRT. These would have been cheaper for both grantors and for taxpayers in the grantee city. It would also have blended in more easily with the tropical architectural surroundings and led to significant economic development along that corridor (Guess, 1985).

Another real and public problem in many countries is that of stray dogs. They are considered a major health and safety problem in many Central and Eastern European countries, such as Romania (Guess, 2005, 2020), and Ukraine (Webne, 2019). The causes of the problem are multiple and complex but result in large populations of roaming dogs some of which attack humans and spread rabies. Stray dogs are classified as a "well-structured" problem (Guess and Farnham, 2011; *Figure 3.1*) because the outcomes should be calculable. Dogs are stray/owned, captured or stray, dead or alive. But the stray dog problem can get "messy" and become "ill-structured" fast if the wrong policy solutions are applied and it becomes a public media fiasco. This has happened in cities when they panic and adopt quick solutions such as "catch and kill" that are inhumane and empirically documented to be ineffective (Webne, 2019). In Sochi before the Olympic Games there, dogs were shot and beaten unsuccessfully to reduce their population as public spectators watched in disbelief and fear, and the media caught it all on camera. Purveyors of culling equipment, used for other animals as roaming urban deer, peddle the same hardware as the best solution. The use of deer as an analogy by the suppliers to peddle their equipment is an example of misuse of a common tool for problem-structuring: the use of analogies (Dunn, 2008, 4th edition). Misusing this and similar analogies (that defy common sense), the sales pitch is that stray dogs are said to be caused by the absence of dart guns, clubs, and metal tongs. More effective related options for strays include sheltering or placing them in pounds, vaccinating, registering, and either putting them up for adoption or tagging and releasing them if space is short. But unfortunately, these are costly and longer term solutions, mostly adopted over time by wealthier countries such as the US and even Hungary.

A final example of equipment suppliers confusing and distorting problem structuring is in the area of tax administration. Tax collection is a complex and hard technical profession requiring managers (especially line tax inspectors) to balance incentives for citizen payment, systems to detect avoidance, and application of transparent and rule-based sanctions for evasion. Note that such transparent sanction systems would need to be mandated in tax "policies" which would guide tax "administrators and managers" in enforcement. In Armenia during an IMF technical assistance mission from the Fiscal Affairs Department in the 1990s, we were asked by the tax department within the MOF for help in giving them more tools to enforce tax collection. They asked for the usual training and better FMIS systems with which to record revenue collections. Then they moved to hardware: wooden batons and electroshock machines. It was well-known that the tax department there had been staffed with recently downsized staff from the KGB, and they needed new work. The ones we chatted with fit the part: pock-marked scarred faces, wearing black leather jackets and dark shades as they talked with us. Their implicit pitch was that the absence of tax administration efficiency and effectiveness was due to the absence of batons, electroshock, and other persuasive enforcement hardware. IMF was the potential supplier in their minds!

Problems Are Quantifiable and Actionable

To be actionable, that is a candidate for spending state funds for effective action problems must also be real and quantifiable. Several years ago, the EU banned GM seeds and foods based on presumed risk. But the risk of long-term damage from GM seeds was and is not a real quantified, measured, or documented problem. Rather it was a fear not a measured risk and hence not an actionable problem. The EU had banned GM foods based on a known public fear that had not been measured or quantified according to existing food safety standards. By contrast, public fears of risks caused by nuclear accidents and the known effects of radiation poisoning are real and quantifiable (if small). The banning of nuclear power generation after the measurable effects of the Fukushima accident a decade ago was therefore rational and debatable logically with empirical support for and against it. Similarly, the British NHS has real, quantifiable types of problems in delivering efficient and effective health care services. As noted above, patients suffer from decrepit facilities that are under-maintained and decrepit. They suffer real health risks or problems from the measurable medical treatment backlogs of 6.8m people! Patients suffer from an even larger problem of an institution that cannot keep itself sufficiently staffed. As of 2023, it has been unable to fill 11m medical doctor positions and has 46k nurse positions unfilled. Some of this is due to its lethargic personnel processes and systems. The rest is due to a substantial shortage of medical staff and nurses worldwide as the result of the Covid-19 pandemic.

In addition, the problem of stray dogs is real and quantifiable as well. But as noted by Webne (2019), hard data is difficult to find with which to measure the scope and intensity of the problem. Baseline data on the number of dogs have to be estimated by indirect proxies, such as the number of hospital admissions for rabies and attacks due to dog bites. Proxies such as these are used to allocate dog patrols to deal with them with the variety of methods noted above by Webne (2019) and others. But the absence of a real-time, objective baseline makes it difficult to identify the type of problem and to rationally tailor appropriate management responses. Responding to the stray dog problem with dog pounds and improved regulations are the best available actions and short-term solutions (Guess and

Element	Well-Structured	Moderately Structured	Ill-Structured or Messy
Decision-makers	One or few	One or few	Many
Alternatives	Limited	Multiple	Unlimited
Outcomes	Certainty/risk	Uncertainty	Unknown
Probabilities	Calculable	Incalculable	Incalculable
Examples	Controlling city rats (what is baseline population?); replacing rail rolling stock; replacing v repairing bridges	Pension cost forecasting & financing; prisoner dilemma: both confess get lesser sentence, one confesses gets probation, other gets max. Rational choices lead to collective irrationality due to informational uncertainty.	Bosnia, Northern Ireland, Ukraine; Cuban missile crisis; dogs (sub-problems could be well structured!).

Figure 3.2 Structuring Management and Policy Problems.
Source: Created by author.

Farnham, 2011, :46). Note in **Figure 3.2** that stray dogs are considered both a well-structured short-term and messy or long-term problem. As suggested, it can be either or both depending on what the data indicates (and recognizing that poor baseline data is part of the problem!) its severity, and urgency to be. It is a usually messy problem but in theory could be fixed quickly in the right context, usually a resource-rich country with a determined problem-solving regime.

In the process of identifying an actionable problem, the known constraints to remedial action should be rationally anticipated during the planning phase of the policy-management cycle. The implementation constraints should be recognized to ensure that the target problem remains actionable and is subject to manipulation by managers in the short or medium term (Guess and Farnham, 2011:46). The analysis may prove that a real public problem is not in fact actionable due to the high long-term costs of implementing its solutions (see **Figure 3.1**). The obstacles to implementation and effective completion are usually known (despite pleas of surprise that they were unknown and could not be anticipated) and in a strict sense added to the upfront project costs (diminishing the benefits of using particular options for a management solution) if benefit-cost or cost-effectiveness analyses are required.

For example, the 1967 inter-governmentally financed and managed economic development program in Oakland faced a series of bottlenecks that impeded scaling up to the state and national levels. By 1969, only $3m of the $23m allocated for the federal program had been spent. It was found that the program was impeded by complex multi-step loan application transactions, the inability to commit budgeted funds, and the many decision approval points that were well-known at the initial program planning stage. The Oakland training program required approval by nine separate organizations. The program was riddled with required clearance points which added to the probability of stoppages and delays (Pressman and Wildavsky, 1984:143). These authors noted long ago that US national government fragmentation is similar to the problems faced by US officials providing overseas DA, such as corruption, kleptocratic and unstable regimes, and budgetary instability that later impeded program results (1984:141, 145–146). Prior transaction analyses could easily have revealed such known bottlenecks, for instance, in licensing, procurement of office furniture, and other capital equipment as well as recruitment, hiring, firing, and promotion of personnel (Guess, 2019:168). Each of these transactions and supporting systems had been set up to produce a decision product vital to the success of the planned economic development program. Despite this, the costly federal local economic development program was planned either by ignoring the obstacles, assuming they would be fixed during implementation, or denying that they would be much of a constraint to implementation. Such known features of institutional underdevelopment would impede efforts to eliminate them and generate development in the few years of this program. Again, this was hardly surprising in retrospect. That this mistake is repeated with similar domestic and overseas aid efforts many years later is a wasteful tragedy.

As in Oakland, aid programs and projects around the globe are rendered ineffective by constraints to action and known bottlenecks that could be identified, anticipated, and cost out for thorough forward planning. Management and their superiors at the policy-making level should make certain that this vital review step is part of their problem-structuring process. Of course, program and project managers argue (correctly) that if the constraints were spelled out, donors would not commit funds for predictably futile efforts to eliminate them! Officials routinely know the constraints and ignore or deny that they are serious problems in the hopes that this time it will be different! In this nightmarish scene where an infinite regression of problems continually jumps out at you, even after the right policies and more professional management arrive, other constraints remain. That means, in short, many known problems cannot simply be managed away. The constraints are often well-known and could have been removed if the political will had existed! But in many countries (as well as the US), the will is lacking, and management (despite well-documented efforts) has been unable to reduce or eliminate the bottle-necks and obstacles.

Sub-Saharan Africa (SSA) is a modern example of the same kinds of ig-nored constraints that beset the Oakland project in the late 1960s (and many domestic and overseas development aid projects since then): unnecessary bureaucratic complexity for simple transactions and general corruption. As is known, the SSA region has abundant natural resources that consistently are not exploited for growth and development to benefit the poor major-ity of countries in the SSA region. Many economic policies and supporting rules are simply the wrong ones and should not have been approved, or if they were, canceled long ago. For example, SSA has 13% of the world's natural gas reserves. But exports of liquid natural gas (LNG) to meet surg-ing European demand are constrained by inadequate port terminals. For-eign domestic investment (FDI) to build these terminals and ports is scarce because it is repeatedly scared off by the endemic violence and instability in most SSA countries that are attracted by big foreign investment projects. In-vestors tend to write these countries off as hosts of high-risk, ill-structured, and intractable problems, cost out or not. Investors often claim, validly, that there are not enough "bankable" projects in the SSA.[5] Political insecurity and lack of contract enforcement add to investment appraisal risks of pro-jects that mostly fail ROR or ROI tests for fiscal viability. These required test criteria are lowered for need, allowing development financiers such as the World Bank's IFC, DFC, and Dutch DFI to ease loan approval condi-tions. But investors know that DFI projects will mostly be money-losers.[6]

Nigeria is the biggest regional SSA oil exporter. But it is well-known that kleptocratic oil elites waste funds on oil subsidies for mostly middle-class citizens and hive off the rest for vanity projects and personal use. Currently high world market oil prices fail to contribute to Nigerian devel-opment because the costs of providing subsidies are actually higher than the amount of revenue generated. Potential FDI to build processing and exporting terminals in order to avoid robberies along roads is dissuaded by political instability and extortion in building most capital facilities. The numerous elite vanity projects have increased Nigeria's debt burden with left it with little capacity to pay back the loans. The bulk of public SSA budgets consists of debt service costs, and few funds are left over for basic needs such as infrastructure and education. In Nigeria, because of vast debts, servicing them generally eats up 80% of annual budget revenues, and 96% of them in 2022!

The problem for development managers is that they know how hard it is to manage bad policies to try and make them efficient or effective. Managers implement policies that are inappropriate or flat wrong. The constraints on management are overwhelming. This is a major dilemma of aid projects and qualified, well-meaning local professionals caught in bad systems. Managers refer to this problem as "being dealt a bad hand". The heavily criticized consumer gas subsidy eats up 2.2% of annual GDP to keep consumer retail prices low (subsidy price or Ps in *Figure 3.3*). But the low subsidy price induces consumers or users to overconsume resources, whether gasoline, electricity, heat, or tropical hardwoods (Qs in *Figure 3.3*). The opportunity costs of this are immense in potential development investments in education, health care, infrastructure, and wasted services such as heat and electricity. Predictably, the low retail price of $0.40/liter or about $1.60/gallon is so cheap (world market price or Pw in *Figure 3.3*) that neighboring countries smuggle it across their borders causing shortages at home in Nigeria. At the same time, underinvestment in technical staff and the infrastructure of the state oil firm results in inefficient and costly production. Increased oil export levels to take advantage of higher recent prices do not save the state firm from both cash flow and investment shortages. Again, Nigeria, an OPEC member, fails to capitalize on its oil revenues after paying its subsidies.

Retail consumer electricity prices are also subsidized with a similar negative dynamic. Half of Nigerians, mostly in the north, have no access to electricity, and even in the south where there are power lines, factories suffer from frequent blackouts, requiring the purchase and use of expensive diesel generators. The whole of Nigeria consumes about as much energy as San Antonio, Texas, a medium-sized US city. Again, bad policies play a big role, keeping electricity fees artificially low, meaning utilities lose money and investors in private power are put off.[7]

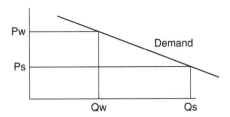

Figure 3.3 Producer and Consumer Subsidies. State Oil, Gas, and Electricity Producer and Consumer Subsidies (above Line Graph). State Marketing Boards Pay Producers (Farmers, State Oil Firm, State Utility) Pw to Ensure Supply; and Subsidize Consumers to Ps. Differences between Pw and Ps = Budget Subsidy (Caption below Graph).

Source: Created by the author.

Another wasted developmental advantage in the SSA is that it is 94% self-sufficient in food. It need not import any major foods. To grow the food, however, requires fertilizer, decent market roads, favorable climate and sufficient rainfall. For some crops, such as timber for furniture and building products, and tomatoes for export and home consumption, secondary manufacturing and processing facilities are also required. But SSA must import fertilizer and fuel because its bad roads make it difficult to profitably build domestic processing and manufacturing facilities. Food prices have risen because existing farm-to-market highways are unsafe to ship produce even to other SSA countries, few of which trade with each other because of tariff and non-tariff barriers tariffs. These constraints have been there for years but few leaders, governments, or project planners have successfully tackled them by generating cost-effective investments that would contribute to local or national development.[8]

Problems Defined on False Analogies and Incomparable Cases

A final challenge to rigorous and thorough problem identification and structuring is the use of false comparative cases and analogies, often as evidence to make one's case for a preferred option. Policy planners and managers begin almost automatically to try and find comparisons with successful examples locally or elsewhere to save time and money in the analysis of options and their costs and risks. This is sensible behavior given the lack of available time and tight deadlines. But the objective should be to define the right problem and make sure they have solid empirical bases in reality. In an example of irrational futility, Gulliver's mad scientist spent eight years unsuccessfully trying to extract sunbeams from cucumbers and promised to spend eight more! Repeating the same mistake for that long is by definition "insanity" (Guess and Farnham, 2011:48; Dunn, 2008, 4th edition). At best, Gulliver's scientist was defining an unreal problem.

Thus, the challenge to problem structuring is to apply the right analogy or comparative case to assist in defining the "real" problem. The challenge is also to have strong management reviews that challenge a preferred but perhaps unreal, incomplete, or inappropriate definition of the problem at hand. The EU ban on GM foods, as noted, was based on fear, or unknown risk, and therefore an unreal public problem. By contrast, the known and real risks of nuclear power have been dropping for decades to the extent that its benefits probably outweigh its real and potential costs in most contexts. Nuclear technology has vastly improved in safety and cost-effectiveness in the past two decades. Data and analysis of safety risks have vastly improved as well as the technology to meet higher construction and use standards. In addition, the growing current need for secure and reliable energy has increased. Nuclear power has graduated into a well-structured problem from a messy ill-structured one over time. It is now considered a real solution to a redefined and updated problem by many countries and US states.

Suppose you were in charge of an analytical review team that needed to develop a set of criteria by which to reject analogies and comparative cases. You need to find a preferred option to recommend for a nuclear plant and need to know how to accept and reject the many cases and analogies that your team will propose during the discussions. A simple methodology known as "matched-case" was proposed by Xavier (1998) and is to be used here. The two steps and their rationales are as follows:

The comparative cases and analogies presented must refer to the same systems and have been from the same kinds of contexts. That is, first, the similarities must be isolated. Comparing the performance of two LRT systems in China and Ecuador would be tempting. But the cultures, work ethics, and ethnicities are far different. The contexts could render the comparison invalid. Better to find cases in the same region with roughly the same values, attitudes, and practices, e.g., the Andean region that might include Peru and Ecuador, or by contrast China and Japan in East Asia. Comparable examples mean examining the same type of system in similar contexts. With enough similarities to counter skeptics, one can safely focus on the differences in the target technical system, analytic method, or managerial practice. Xavier (1998) was targeting the performance of two PFM systems reforms in two British Commonwealth countries: Australia and Malaysia.

He found the contexts and systems to be similar, both professional states in the Commonwealth trying to succeed at PFM reforms that mainly consisted of reforms to the budgetary systems within the larger PFM systems first. That is, the focus of the reforms was the two budgetary systems which were both through the efforts to implement the reforms to become performance-program type budgets. The reform objective to install performance-program budgets was similar in both countries. After the reforms, he found the performance of the Australian systems to be superior in design, support, and implementation to the similar system in Malaysia.

The two-step matched case method just described controlled for rival explanations that the performance differences were actually due to contextual features such as culture, language, population density, or political system type. With rival explanations largely controlled, he could then focus on the features of the PFM systems. What this meant is that any performance differences would be due to characteristics of the PFM systems, such as their design and implementation, and not something external such as political system or culture. Specifically, the design of the Malaysian PFM system ignored the need for institutional and management support by providing staff incentives to implement and later use the new system.

The project design lesson for managers is to include management training in supervising using financial and non-financial incentives to motivate the staff to install and use the new system. To summarize the lesson of the matched-case method, if the important similarities of the representative cases are greater than the marginal differences, one can draw preliminary but rigorous lessons from the target system or project.

A simple Xavier-type matched case methodology could be applied to much weightier matters than budget reforms in only two country cases, such as the criteria for establishing or entering a currency union. Argentina is trying to avoid a tenth sovereign default and has proposed a currency union with Brazil as its solution. Like Xavier (1998),[9] Robert Mundell (1961)[10] proposed two conditions beginning with economic similarities. The union countries should have similar central bank policy rates with business cycles roughly synchronized. His second condition is that people and money should flow across borders without interference by capital controls or poor infrastructure. Admission to a union without meeting such conditions means here that Brazil would be forced to bail out Argentina and Argentina would have every reason to continue irresponsible spending. Entry into a union without meeting such basic criteria would make it difficult to manage debt and economic relations between union members since analogies and lessons from other countries' experiences would likely be false and incomparable.

Thus, analogies and cases presented as similar or pertinent to the discussion not exposed to a representative case match or quasi-experimental test are suspect and should not be used. They could be turning up oranges when apples are needed, e.g., elevated heavy rail where LRT would be cheaper and better; cross-roads where roundabouts would be safer and move traffic faster; hardline theory X management where empathetic Y-type managers who managed cash flows and watched balance sheets to avoid destabilizing and abrupt cutback decisions during the fiscal year would be more effective.

Developing Preferred Solutions for Complex Problems

To conclude, managers should take the following steps to deal with problem identification and structuring:

> First, simplify complex problems. Divide up the issues to make it easier to decide what to do first and later. As indicated in *Figure 3.1*, the more alternatives and institutional jurisdictions involved the more obstacles, messiness and less structure. The process becomes more opaque. Dividing problems up makes them more actionable, such as solving climate change v dealing with flooding rehabilitation and

resilience projects here and now. Second, state the problem simply and tangibly. For example, illegal logging for pasture and profit destroys forestry potential to contribute to growth and development (*Figure 3.4 below*). Third, brainstorm and develop action scenarios for anticipated problems. School systems and hospitals do this for emergencies as it teaches how conditions dictate actions and reactions. Using action scenarios for anticipated problems allows administrators to focus on the trigger points for each option. Doing this

I. *Forestry and Development Problem Identification:* Deforestation destroys resource, soil cover, eliminates carbon sinks, habitats. It is a well-structured or moderately well-structured set of problem(s).

II. *Develop Actionable Policy Options:* not plans but action scenarios, forecasted costs and risk or each, as well as the do-nothing option. What responses to similar conditions, here and elsewhere, what results?

-       ***Fiscal incentives:*** small farmer pulp and paper; Reduced Emissions from Forest Degradation (REDD) payments to poor countries not to deforest; debt/nature swaps (Bolivia and Costa Rica)

-       ***Regulatory:*** strengthening forest services; fines and TA for integrated land use planning (traditional forestry including palm oil); laws to increase tenure security

-       ***Mixed economy: exploitation & conservation*** (e.g., agro-forestry).

-       ***R&D*** on tropical forestry management results and impacts

III. *Develop Preferred Option and Measure Policy Impact*

-       Changes in measures of policy problem, short-long term, e.g., deforestation rates

IV.   *Implementation, M&E* — imagery verification via ground surveys, redefinition of problems and basic concepts (e.g., actual forest in India!) make policy

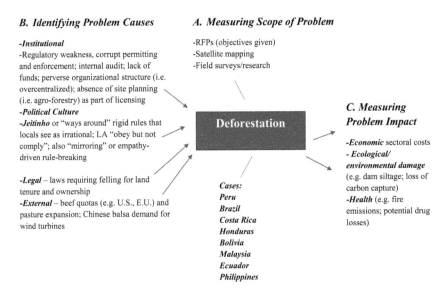

B. *Identifying Problem Causes*

-Institutional
-Regulatory weakness, corrupt permitting and enforcement; internal audit; lack of funds; perverse organizational structure (i.e. overcentralized); absence of site planning (i.e. agro-forestry) as part of licensing
-Political Culture
-Jeitinho or "ways around" rigid rules that locals see as irrational; LA "obey but not comply"; also "mirroring" or empathy-driven rule-breaking

-Legal – laws requiring felling for land tenure and ownership
-External – beef quotas (e.g. U.S., E.U.) and pasture expansion; Chinese balsa demand for wind turbines

A. *Measuring Scope of Problem*

-RFPs (objectives given)
-Satellite mapping
-Field surveys/research

Deforestation

Cases:
Peru
Brazil
Costa Rica
Honduras
Bolivia
Malaysia
Ecuador
Philippines

C. *Measuring Problem Impact*

-Economic sectoral costs
- Ecological/ environmental damage (e.g. dam siltage; loss of carbon capture)
-Health (e.g. fire emissions; potential drug losses)

Figure 3.4 Forestry and Development Problem.

Source: Created by the author.

exercise allows institutions to see in advance what could go wrong with their planning and management plans. Finally, to simplify problems and polish up responses, managers need to use appropriate cases and analogies for what has worked and not worked in similar contexts. *Figure 3.4* illustrates how one might structure the deforestation problem in nine potential countries that have extensive experience with this problem and remedies that have worked and not worked. Aid programs and many projects could be and have been developed by donors such as World Bank and USAID for the causes of deforestation: institutional, cultural, legal and external markets.

There are at least three problems with identifying problems inside and outside of organizations. Inside, management may reflect a societal eagerness to assign blame and liability for the many accidents and incidents that result in physical and mental injury. Plane, transit, bus, rail passenger, and freight accidents occur daily. Along with these, systems and personnel failures occur regularly: especially computer and cyber-security systems, structural failures (wind turbine blades, faulty building, and facilities construction), transit and city policing, unfit or overstressed pilots, mechanics, and drivers, and bad decision-making.

The first constraint to problem identification is the lack of an institutional barrier to making snap judgments and establishing the pertinent facts (e.g., proximate and remote causes). The need is to establish the facts and not assign blame at the outset. In some cultures, blame is almost immediately assigned by sect, race, ethnicity, or partisan affiliation. Independent institutions rarely exist to investigate fairly and withhold snap judgments. Managers and staff both assign blame, oversimplifying what went wrong, or over-generalize in the rush to point the finger.

Institutions such as the US National Transportation Safety Board (NTSB) are explicitly designed to avoid assigning blame or assessing liability and can be used as institutional models in developing programs and projects. Their institutional role is to promote collective learning and to prevent such accidents from repeating themselves. Forensic units such as insurance companies exist for assigning blame as well as courts, juries, and judicial systems. NTSB uses a system of mutual finger-pointing by industry stakeholders to establish the facts. In aviation crashes, for example, engine builders, aircraft designers and builders, aviation mechanics, air traffic controllers, pilots, and passengers meet behind closed doors away from the often-inflammatory media, review the facts to date, assess them, and assign blame. As group representatives defend themselves, a definition of the problem and a clearer view of the contributory facts are established for purposes of the final report. Institutions like this should exist for high-risk industries such as aviation and health care safety. But they are rare.

The second constraint to rational, textbook problem identification is management. People in positions of authority may be more likely to assume that workers have choices and therefore are to blame. Blameless postmortems have long been part of the culture at Google, for example, which has templates, reviews, and discussion groups for examining individual vs. process causes and assigning blame and the areas where processes must change. Managers need to ensure that a "blame culture" does not exist or if it does, at least by example, make sure that it is dismantled.[11]

The third constraint to problem definition is weak capacity for data analysis. Where is the data that leads to this problem and its definition that available methods can produce a practical solution? Is the data valid and reliable? Does it produce conflicting solutions and why does the preferred solution lead to this problem? Bad data or failure to probe its patterns and nuances often leads to a mis-definition of the problem(s). This leads to bad policies that often build in perverse incentives that are beyond the capabilities of management to alter.

An important target for ODA spending is to ensure that social assistance is targeted to the truly needy, and that they receive and spend it properly. One of the most common benefits is the disability or incapacity benefit. This "welfare" benefit is politicized in many countries between the defense of the hardworking poor by liberals vs. their description as deadbeats and layabouts by conservatives wanting welfare "crackdowns"—all inflamed by popular tabloids and populist leaders. Bad management informed by bad data along with the often-perverse incentives that eligibility requirements create also diminish the effectiveness of social assistance in OECD countries, playing further into the hands of right-wing populists.

British data has shown long waiting lists for health care treatment and high rates of successfully claimed incapacity benefits. Blamed initially on NHS incompetence, the waiting lists were found to contain mostly non-working-age people. But in the mid-1990s, policy-makers toughened up requirements for incapacity benefits to guard against welfare fraud. The result was a number of high-profile suicides by mentally ill patients denied incapacity benefits. Policy-makers reversed gears again making it easier for claimants to receive benefits. But by accident rather than design, policy-makers eliminated the distinction between limited and permanent long-term-incapacity benefits. People were encouraged by the faulty measure, which allowed twice the cash benefit if they claimed permanent incapacity (neither working nor looking for a job) rather than partial (partially able to work). Even the possibility of limited remote employment was eliminated by this blanket eligibility measure. The faulty policy and management metric became a powerful incentive to claim long-term incapacity benefits and has served as a perverse incentive to create real labor shortages across the UK.[12] Soluble problems must be defined to prevent goal displacement by such means as excessive reporting burdens or by perverse economic incentives that waste time and public money.

Discussion Case #8: Managing Development Assistance for Haiti: NGOs as Solutions or Part of Messy Problems?

For over a century, Haiti has suffered from natural disasters and internal political threats to its governance and development efforts. Hurricanes hit the island with almost annual regularity varying recently in 2010 by the first earthquake in almost 150 years. The country must deal with perennial political regime instability and a weak state that is incapable of delivering such basic services as health, education, water and sewerage, sanitation, electricity, and public transport. It is an enigmatic, tough, and exceptional case of a persistently weak and corrupt state that has left its people in poverty and ill-educated misery despite years of US DA projects and NGO field work (Downs, 1988). The brutally corrupt and tribal weirdness of the Duvalier (Papa Doc and Baby Doc) years has left an almost permanent legacy of centralization, customary misuse of funds and bribery, and a central government with a lack of capacity to absorb and properly use aid funds (DA).[13]

US DA amounts to about 40% of the GOH budget. Despite the US amount, it only adds up to about 0.7% of all ODA to Haiti. Note that bilateral ODA is also dispensed globally by other aid agencies, such as Australia (AusAID), Swiss Development Corporation (SDC), Canada (CIDA), Sweden (SIDA), and the UK (UKAID). Roughly 50% of US DA or ODA passes through to 800 private voluntary organizations (PVOs)/NGOs for a wide variety of development projects. Since 2010, Haiti has received $3.8b in relief from all sources. While NGOs and aid agencies work around the GOH by receiving and spending their funds directly from their donors, they often are loans rather than grants. Non-traditional donors, such as the Venezuela-Petro Caribe Fund, not only work directly with GOH but also contract loans rather than grants. Such loans now amount to about 84% of GOH debt!

Whatever micro- or sectoral reforms and successes take place at the project level few of them have been scaled up to strengthen the state and to ensure effective governance. For example, a PVO implementing an agro-forestry[14] project distributed 11m trees to 20k peasants in two years. PVO staff showed them how to prune the fast-growing species and ensure that they were used as shade for their coffee plants. Other tropical agroforestry schemes utilize *lerchern* trees (a pine species that sheds its leaves in winter) to cover more stunted cocoa trees and coffee bushes. But in Haiti little of this knowledge was scaled up to the Ministry of Natural Resources or to other communities across the country. This was part of the ongoing tragedy in a country famous for deforesting most of its tropical hardwood trees for charcoal and pasture. Similarly, multilateral donors utilized Project Implementation Units (PIUs) in the sectoral ministries (as is normal) to monitor and implement its sectoral projects such as in health and to ensure that those ministries gained technical knowledge after project termination. But very little technical knowledge was diffused to the ministries. Part of the problem is that ministry staff lacked the minimum technical expertise in the first place.

Largely because of the lack of technical expertise in sectoral ministries, multilateral and regional donors distrust the GOH to spend their funds directly and rely instead on NGOs as a workaround. Haiti has been noted for its reliance on NGOs to deliver basic education and health services which have had few spread effects that built up state capacity.[15] A stable functioning central government has not existed for years.[16] As noted, an otherwise very successful central bank, American University (BRH-AU) project to build precisely such state capacity in PFM and policy analysis, was ended by a devastating earthquake in 2010.

For good reason, countries such as Haiti are called "NGO republics" while frequent attempts to take power and rule the hollowed-out state result in ongoing competition for power by gangsters, warlords, and even murderers. Eventually despair or resentment seeps into the development aid systems when it is unable to establish legitimate states. Experts from different aid agencies have been crawling for many years on projects all over countries such as Nepal driving their new Land Rovers and sporting their alphabet soup of aid abbreviations such as "UNDP". All the while, corruption and underdevelopment persist. The resentment from locals occurs when the country is flooded by Western experts with high salaries and extravagant perks such as new trucks to drive on their bad roads. The effect of this aid theatre can be destructive.[17]

For DA to be effective, more efforts need to be made to find state institutional partners that can drive the reform process. DA depends on functioning states in target sectors; aid programs are often designed with their initial assistance and support. There have to be local partners and government officials, in MOFs or sectoral ministries, that are supportive throughout project implementation. In countries such as Haiti without functioning states, NGOs can be partners but often have few links to actual government officials who can make and execute future policies. As noted, Haiti has been called the "Republic of NGO" for this reason—it receives substantial ODA but little of it has improved state capacity.[18] Because of criminal insecurity, many senior GOH officials live in Miami. This makes it hard for would-be donor projects to get GOH approvals when officials are not in the country. NGOs work in-country on smaller projects with their own sources of funds that can be approved for disbursal quickly by lower level GOH officials. In short order then DA is expected to create function-ing and effective states when politics intrudes and counterpart officials in weak states, such as Haiti, are regularly removed or left. Top-level support to move aid projects forward is severely lacking. This destabilizes both the state and the aid programs.

In a tragic paradox, DA to improve state effectiveness depends on a minimum level of stability and effectiveness that are a precondition to im-prove them. Operational DA projects are expected to create big long-term things like democracy and economic growth that depend on effective states when, as noted, there are too many links in these causal chains that DA cannot control. Despite the reality of unstable or failed states with which to work, the public aid debate is captured by the abstract conceptual jar-gon of the international aid community—civil society, sustainability, insti-tutional and state modernization, and "development" itself—which often leads to exaggerated expectations. Should a representative and legitimate state partner not be found, it could be argued that the aid funds should not be disbursed in the first place. Regime buy-in is essential to prevent disbursement of funds that otherwise lead to waste, fraud, and abuses of power.

Naturally, this many attempts via overseas aid to improve matters in Haiti, with so much money disbursed over so long a period of time, have produced a robust explanatory industry. Theories of failure range from (1) racism (the other side of the island is the Dominican Republic which is mostly white and prosperous if corrupt); (2) political culture (the per-sistent belief and practices of Voodoo even by MOF and BRH profession-als with PhDs from such places as Oxford and Harvard) works against rational progress. The Voodoo beliefs place a supernatural, fatalistic, and deterministic variable between policy cause and attributable and measur-able effect. That has produced unpredictable, bizarre, and damaging re-sults; Harrison (1985) calls these beliefs and practices part of a "damaged culture" that has impeded development and quality of life for almost a century there. The effect of collective Voodoo is similar to the random and destabilizing effects on governance by narcissist-driven populism. (3) Divine judgment (another bizarre theory attributes Haitian misfortunes to divine judgment). US religious fanatics such as Pat Robertson blamed Hai-tians for the 2010 earthquake as divine retribution for a profligate living! A more sensible explanation might just be its incredibly bad luck—in 2010 just weeks before the earthquake, Haiti was noted by many international observers for its development progress which according to them had never before reached that stage of advancement. All these explanations have sur-face plausibility but divine judgment. But even the last one adds to the fatalistic part of the political culture and prevents positive action. And the effects of a damaging local culture quickly wear off with emigration. As is known, Haitians in Miami have thrived for many decades to the envy of many poorer and often Black Americans living in the same parts of town.[19]

How can international disaster relief avoid treating host governments as bystanders? (Guess, 2019, *op.cit.*, Chapter 1). What are the macro-political and economic constraints to effective governance? What are the micro-constraints to program and project effectiveness? Why haven't aid project successes been scaled across the country to local governments or upwards to the central government?

Discussion Case #9: Managing Development Projects in High-Risk Environments: The Case of Pakistan

George M. Guess and Dennis DeSantis[20]

Abstract

This case describes the relationships between the field workers of a development project in Pakistan and their overseers in the local USAID mission and their firm's home offices in Washington. The case has three purposes. First, it intends to demonstrate the political and technical issues of managing a project the objective of which was to monitor and evaluate other projects. Monitoring and evaluation of projects by USAID, World Bank, and other donors is a large and important area of practice. Second, the case provides important issues for discussion in the area of development business: bidding, winning, and executing projects in increasingly high-risk countries and regions of the world. Third, the case intends to generate a discussion of the rewards and risks of different management options to mitigate personnel, security, and political problems that arose during the execution of the project.

Background

USAID History, Purposes, and Development Assistance

When the United States Agency for International Development (USAID) was created, it brought together several existing foreign assistance organizations and programs. Until then, there had never been a single agency charged with foreign economic development, so with the passage of the *Foreign Assistance Act of 1961* by Congress, US foreign assistance activities underwent a major transformation. Leading this transformation was President John F. Kennedy. President Kennedy recognized the need to unite development into a single agency responsible for administering aid to foreign countries to promote social and economic development.

On November 3, 1961, USAID was born and with it a spirit of progress and innovation. November 3, 2011, marked USAID's 50th Anniversary of providing US foreign DA. The USAID workforce and culture continue to serve as a reflection of core American values, ones that are rooted in a belief in "doing the right thing".

The modern-day concept of international DA took shape after WWII ended in 1945. George C. Marshall, the Secretary of State from 1947 to 1949, provided significant financial and technical assistance to Europe after the war. Famously known as the Marshall Plan, this was a successful effort that allowed Europe to rebuild its infrastructure, strengthen its economy, and stabilize the region. It has been argued that international aid became and continues to reflect and drive US foreign policy that the lines between US foreign aid, trade, and broader policy are blurred.[21] Building on the success of the Marshall Plan, President Harry S. Truman proposed an international DA program in 1949. The 1950 Point Four Program focused on two goals: (1) creating markets for the US by reducing poverty and increasing production in developing countries and (2) diminishing the threat of communism by helping countries prosper under capitalism. From 1952 to 1961, programs supporting technical assistance and capital projects continued as the primary form of US aid and were a key component of US foreign policy. During this time, government leaders established various precursor organizations to USAID, including the Mutual Security Agency; Foreign Operations Administration; and the International Cooperation Administration.

In 1961, President Kennedy signed the Foreign Assistance Act into law and created USAID by executive order. Once USAID got to work, international DA opportunities grew tremendously. The time during the Kennedy and Johnson administrations became known as the "decade of development". In the 1970s, the USAID began to shift its focus away from technical and capital assistance programs to more specific needs. In this period, US DA stressed a "basic human needs" approach, which focused on functional or sectoral programs in (1) food and nutrition, (2) population planning, (3) health, (4) education, and (5) human resources development.

By the 1980s, US foreign assistance sought continued to broader and deeper concerns of currency stabilization and strengthening financial systems. It also promoted market-based principles to restructure developing countries' policies and institutions. During this decade, USAID reaffirmed its commitment to broad-based economic growth, emphasizing increasing poor country employment and income opportunities through revitalization of agriculture and expansion of domestic markets. In this decade, development activities were increasingly channeled through PVOs, and aid shifted from individual projects to portfolios of projects within larger sectoral programs such as health care.

In the 1990s, USAID's top priority became sustainable development or helping countries improve their own quality of life. During this decade, USAID tailored DA programs to a country's economic condition, which meant that (1) developing countries received an integrated package of assistance, (2) transitional countries received help in times of crisis, and (3) countries with limited USAID presence would receive support through NGOs. USAID played a lead role in planning and implementing programs following the fall of the Berlin Wall in 1989. This was the beginning of USAID programs that overtly attempted to establish functioning democracies with open, market-oriented economic systems and responsive social safety nets.

The 2000s brought more evolution for USAID and foreign assistance with government officials once again calling for reform of how the agency conducts its business. With the Afghanistan and Iraq wars in full swing, USAID was called on to help those two countries rebuild government, infrastructure, civil society, and basic services such as health care and education. The Agency began rebuilding with an eye to getting the most bang out of its funding allocations. It also began an aggressive campaign to reach out to new partner organizations—including the private sector and foundations—to extend the reach of foreign assistance.

As of 2016, USAID staff work in more than 100 countries around the world with the same overarching goals that President Kennedy outlined more than 50 years ago—furthering America's foreign policy interests in expanding democracy and free markets while also extending a helping hand to people struggling to make a better life, recover from a disaster or striving to live in a free and democratic country. It is this caring that stands as a hallmark of the US around the world.

USAID plans and administers the country's *bilateral* DA program. Other bilateral aid agencies represent countries such as Britain (DFID), Australia (*AusAID*), Canada (CIDA), and Sweden (SIDA). The US program is delivered through USAID via the Department of State parent organization. The components of the $55b 2011 program are (1) direct economic and development aid (DA) ($23b); (2) DOS—embassies and Foreign Service ($11b), (3) military aid ($11b), (4) international organizations ($7b), and (5) USAID operations including food aid ($3b). DA projects fall within the current functional program categories of health care, agriculture, education, economic stabilization and public finance, infrastructure, natural resources, and democracy and governance.

Broadly, there are three types of aid (1) military, (2) humanitarian (such as UNHCR), and (3) development (DA). The US provides the largest amount of DA (with grant projects for the longest periods) of any DA Club (DAC) member. While the $23b economic and DA proportion of the US aid budget is the largest amount of any country, it represents perhaps the smallest percentage of GDP (only 0.2%) or roughly that of Japan (JICA) which provides only $11.0b mostly in tied aid projects. As indicated, most DA consists of unconditional grants. Policy conditions may be attached by Congress and operational requirements must be met before DA is approved, such as functioning internal controls and reporting practices consistent with USAID requirements for sound financial control. It should also be noted that US DA projects are relatively large budget and long in duration, compared to other bilateral or even multilateral donors. US DA projects run from $1–2m to $100m and last about three to five years. The sustained effort for multi-year projects is needed to successfully tackle development problems, e.g., Ethiopian fiscal decentralization. But the amount available in the RFP, often a product of normal multipliers and fees, drives up total project costs and acts as an incentive for corrupt transactions.

By contrast, most aid grants for development projects were smaller and shorter. Many of the applied policy analysis and management improvement projects that my unit at the Local Government Initiative of the Open Society Institute in Budapest (LGI/OSI) developed lasted for up to a year and were small, the largest being $100k (most were less than half that). Fees and "multipliers" were disallowed which kept projects (and bidders) small. Nevertheless, these ground-level policy and administration projects were enthusiastically implemented and produced books, papers, workshops, and articles that had substantial spread effects in the host countries in which the NGOs, universities, and charities worked. Funded projects covered such topics as training effectiveness, health care efficiency, educational reforms, budget and tax systems installation and use, and participatory budgeting for capital projects (Armenia). The honor and pride in implementing an OSI project was an important factor for success. See, for example, *Grupo Propuesta Ciudadana* (2006); Staronova (2007) and ICHD (2006[22]).

By contrast, *multilateral* aid organizations such as IMF provide a balance of payments assistance, bail-out contributions, and conditional aid (loans in exchange for meeting conditions) such as a recent $2b loan to Jordan in exchange for cuts in fuel subsidies and numbers of civil service positions. IMF does not plan or administer DA but many of World Bank's programs and projects fall into the category of DA. That other multilateral and regional aid agencies allocate funds for country projects can limit the ability of the USAID program to exert leverage where needed to achieve its development objectives, especially where other programs work at cross purposes. For instance, Chinese infrastructure loans and lease-purchases of farmland in countries such as Congo or investments by Kuwait in Cambodia for the same neo-mercantilist purposes often result in pasture expansion and increased deforestation that work against the objectives of USAID programs for better forestry and natural resources management.

It may be helpful to think of aid flows through the energy policy metaphor: (1) *generation* of programs and projects takes place through national-international budgets of bilateral-multi-lateral aid agencies, (2) project grants and loans are *transmitted* and allocated via contractual arrangements, and (3) they are *distributed* via local systems, e.g., NGOs, government ministries, local governments through such mechanisms as conditional transfers to individuals or grants to institutions for specific USAID programmatic purposes.

USAID programs/projects are disbursed by grant instruments that allow varying degrees of discretion to country officials, i.e., MOF and sectoral ministries. About 90% is still disbursed through *direct budget support/task orders (DBS)* that are almost totally managed by USAID. This is termed *centralized aid.* About 10% of US DA is disbursed through *implementation letters* (ILs) and *fixed-amount reimbursements* (FARs and expanded FARs). These provide for cost-sharing in exchange for achieving performance targets. They rely more on country PFM systems for disbursement and control. This is more *decentralized aid.*

While the terms "assistance project" and "development project" might sometimes be used indiscriminately, it helps in understanding USAID's work to distinguish between (1) the development projects of local government agencies and NGOs, such as their projects to improve public health services or schools for a particular beneficiary group, and (2) USAID's assistance projects, which support local development projects. The key to successful assistance is how well it fits the needs of local development projects, while the key to a successful development project is the institutional capacity of the local government agencies and NGOs, including the professional ability of their staff members.

When a local development project's assistance needs have been identified, USAID arranges the agreed assistance through funding agreements with implementing organizations, often referred to by USAID staff as "implementing partners". Private firms and nonprofits bid for these projects. *Practical Concepts in Development* (PCD), the implementing organization in this case, is discussed below. A variety of different kinds of funding agreements can be used by USAID to support implementing partners. Also, USAID sometimes finances several different implementers to provide a number of different inputs to a single development project.

To illustrate, a multi-faceted assistance effort supporting a single development project could include the following types of funding agreements: (1) budget-support grants to a government agency, (2) contracts with a firm for support to USAID, (3) grants to a local NGO serving the beneficiary group, and (4) grants to an international NGO to strengthen the operations of the local NGO.

First, *budget support agreements* to government host country agencies take the form of a letter from USAID's Mission Director, countersigned by the recipient agency, explaining the agency's objectives, the amount of USAID's financial commitment, the specific expenditures to be financed by USAID's grant, and other operational aspects of the agreement. USAID's technical office would assign a staff member (US or local) to oversee progress in the agency's implementation. USAID's financial management office would transfer funds to the agency, in tranches as needed. Audit under this kind of government-to-government (G2G) financial assistance is usually performed by the host government's own audit agency. USAID may sign technical assistance contracts with government agencies. As a government agency is usually specialized in services to its beneficiary population (medical services, for example), its staff may not be equipped to undertake investments called for in the agency's program, such as construction, acquisition of equipment, or management of training and study tours. The government agency might therefore request USAID's assistance in these areas, and USAID could respond by contracting with a firm to supply the services or technical assistance requested.

USAID's technical office collaborates with the government agency and stakeholders in drafting the specifications for what is needed (generally referred to as a "Statement of Work" for the contract) and in conducting market research for available sources and potential bidders. USAID's Contracting Officer would then advertise for bids, manage the selection of a contractor from among the competing bidders, sign the contract, and assign a technical office staff member as the Contracting Officer's Representative to oversee the performance under the contract. (If the workload permits, this staff member might be the same person who oversees USAID's financial assistance to the government agency.) The contractor supplies technical assistance directly to the government agency so that in monitoring contractor performance USAID relies substantially on the agency's evaluation of the contractor's work.

Second, USAID may provide *grants to NGOs*. NGOs are, like their government counterparts, usually already engaged in service provision in areas where USAID wants to assist, and they often have unique abilities that complement public programs. Therefore, USAID technical-office staff might set aside a budget and, with the help of the mission's contracting office, publish a solicitation for applications from NGOs for financial assistance to their programs. One or several grants could be made to select NGOs by the contracting office's "Agreement Officer". Similar to the case of a contract, a USAID technical-office staff member would be assigned as the Agreement Officer's Representative to monitor progress in the NGOs' implementation and to arrange for external evaluations. USAID grants require recipient NGOs to contract for external audits.

As some local NGOs may be small and young organizations with no prior experience in receiving awards from USAID, the USAID mission's financial management office conducts a careful review of grant applicants' administrative systems to ensure that they are capable of managing USG funds. Where necessary, USAID can devote part of the grant to the NGO's internal organizational strengthening to help the NGO qualify for USAID's financing and build the capacity of the organization in the process. Disbursement of the portion of USAID's grant financing of the NGO's project would follow completion of the NGO's internal organizational development.

Third, USAID may provide *grants to strengthen a local NGO* so that it can deliver services needed by USAID. International NGOs have their own development projects and capabilities. If USAID and its counterparts determine that development objectives can best be met by supporting an NGO project, the relevant USAID technical office will draft a program description and the contracting office will issue a request for applications to solicit responses from the international NGO community. The process is used if grants to local NGOs would not be able to achieve the USAID Mission's objectives or if local NGO capacity is not yet sufficient.

Fourth, International *NGOs also frequently make unsolicited proposals* to USAID, requesting funding for their own planned assistance activities. Where NGOs or business enterprises are dedicating a substantial amount of non-USG resources to their projects, they can receive USAID funding through "Global Development Alliance" grants, provided that the non-USG resources are at least equal in value to USAID's grant. In general, USAID provides financial assistance (grants) to support other organizations' programs when those programs correspond to the areas that USAID wants to support, while USAID uses contracts to procure products or services requested by the leaders of local development projects.

USAID in Pakistan

For more than 60 years, the US and Pakistan have worked together to forge a relationship that benefits the people of both countries. This cooperation has produced transformative ideas and institutions that are still considered landmark accomplishments for Pakistan.

In 1947, the US was one of the first countries to recognize an independent Pakistan and to extend considerable assistance for the establishment of key institutions. With US support, Pakistan was able to undertake many notable development projects, such as the Institute for Business

Administration, Jinnah Postgraduate Medical Center, the Indus Basin Project, Faisalabad Agricultural Institute, and a variety of other efforts that laid the path for Pakistan's Green Revolution.

In the 1960s and 1970s, the US was a major donor for the construction of the Mangla and Tarbela dams, which at the time of their completion accounted for 70% of the country's power output. In the 1980s and early 1990s, the US helped build the Guddu Power Station in Sindh and the Lahore University for Management Sciences, which is now considered to be one of the nation's top business schools.

More recently, US civilian assistance to Pakistan has delivered real results on issues of greatest importance to all Pakistanis: energy, economic growth, stability, education, and health. In addition, when natural or manmade disasters threaten Pakistan, the US has been quick to respond. Over the past decade (2006–2016), the US, through USAID, has given Pakistan nearly $7.7b of funding. Pakistan remains one of America's largest recipients of foreign assistance, a sign of long-term partnership and commitment.

USAID's 2016 programs in Pakistan focus on five key areas: energy, economic growth, resilience, education, and health. All of USAID's efforts in these five sectors incorporate the cross-cutting themes of gender equality and good governance.

It was noted that DA is a tool of foreign policy. According to Markey,[23] this became clear in the 1990s when the US dropped aid altogether and imposed sanctions on Pakistan. During the Cold War, Washington intended Pakistan to serve as part of its defensive bulwark against the Soviets' southward expansion into the Persian Gulf, first by drawing it into a treaty alliance and later by using it as a conduit for sending money and weapons to the Afghan *mujahedeen*. All the while, Pakistan's leaders—usually dominated by the military—pocketed resources for the fight against their principal adversary: India. In the 1990s, Washington's policy concerns shifted to nuclear non-proliferation, but neither threats nor costly sanctions dissuaded Pakistan from testing, weaponizing, and even sharing its illicit technologies with other states like North Korea and Iran. In the late 1990s, the first author of this case worked on designing a fiscal decentralization project in Pakistan for the Asian Development Bank (ADB). Under the required heading of project failure risks, he listed nuclear war with India which became a real threat a short time later, requiring his evacuation from the country!

Issues with Development Assistance Effectiveness

Questions about the effectiveness of US DA to achieve policy or even operational objectives have been perennial (see Guess, 1987).[24] At least eight major problems in planning and DA implementation are outlined as follows:

1 *Civil Society is Lacking or Banned*: Civil society consists of those institutions between the state and the rest of society, such as religious organizations, labor unions, craft guilds, and charities. DA works best through enablers that either already exist (local NGOs) or that have to be created (local associations). But often civil society is a threat to local political regimes, e.g., Ukraine, Russia.

2 *DA is often Short-Term*: Most projects are small and last a few years at most; often they are not followed up by host governments, e.g., provision of school running costs after training and construction of schools. Nevertheless, DA is often unfairly evaluated for long-term contributions at the strategic level where it can have the least effect. This is especially true in the US where the amount spent and expected impact is widely exaggerated through ignorance and a deadlocked political system cynically engaged in partisan point-scoring. The result is that operational DA projects are penalized with minimalist budgets.

3 *Lack of Effective States*: DA depends on functioning states in target sectors; aid is often designed with their initial assistance and support. There have to be local partners and government officials in MOFs or sectoral ministries who must be supportive throughout project implementation. NGOs can be partners but often have few links to actual government officials. But in short order, DA is expected to create functioning and effective states when politics intrudes and counterpart officials are removed or leave. The paradoxical constraint on DA is that minimum stability and effectiveness are a precondition to improve them. Operational DA projects are expected to create big things like democracy and economic growth that depend on effective states when there are too many links in these causal chains that DA cannot control. Despite the reality of unstable or failed states with which to work, the public aid debate is captured by the abstract groupthink concepts of the international aid community—civil society, sustainability, institutional and state modernization, and "development" itself—which often lead to exaggerated expectations.

4 *Conditional Aid is Ineffective*: In addition to the ODA from the US, an additional $900m annually is allocated for policy-level conditionality activities through the Millennium Challenge Corporation (MCC). This is called the GOP alternative to USAID and allocates funds on the basis of the country's achievement of gains in big-ticket policies such as good governance, reduced corruption, and better macroeconomic performance. MCC spends money on such activities as school construction

and improved business registration systems. MCC provides merit rather than needs-based aid. In some cases, MCC policy-level objectives are achieved through the support of operational systems such as health, education, and anti-corruption, e.g., internal audit and procurement systems. Other areas such as macroeconomic improvements, which are advised by multiple donors such as IMF with their own conditionality, are harder to attribute to MCC spending. Moreover, according to Hirschman (1971:205),[25] there are doubts about such conditional aid as a catalyst for "virtuous policies". Often, he argued, aid-hungry governments accept conditional aid at variance with their own policy or program preferences and then backslide later or sabotage any measurable results attained later (1971:206). Nevertheless, there can be achievements at the operational level if the aid is both conditional and run through country systems (decentralized) without unnecessary reporting burdens. For example, USAID spends on PFM improvements and fiduciary risk (FR) assessment systems at the operations level. PFM improvements improve efficiency but do not necessarily lead to better macro-policies. At a minimum, fiscal databases and information sources are improved and made more transparent. As in other policy areas, the PFM goal is a long-term aggregation of skills leading to more analytics, better data, and more circumspect decisions based on comparative research of what happens elsewhere. But the reality is that security and policy-level rationales are always a better political sell than the often-invisible drudgery of improving operational systems. In sum, longer term strategic-level aid usually has less direct effect than shorter term operational aid that builds needed systems for the future.

5 *Problems in Training and Capacity-Building*: The fact is that locals trained through DA projects often leave the country or move to the private sector. Some are recycled from other previous aid projects. DA capacity-building is subject to the same limitations faced in military training. Officials will only risk life, limb, and/or career for those whom they respect. If respected senior managers or officers are replaced by hacks, the "will" to fight, reform, or deliver results disappears. So, states remain weak and may degenerate further into failed status despite good DA projects—additions of unqualified personnel damage capacity for which DA is often blamed. But the development of policy-level personnel (senior-level management) is rarely the field intent or in the realm of technical possibility given the smaller amounts spent per project, their relatively short time spans, and the frequent lack of counterpart support or follow-up.

6 *Failure to Understand Constraints to Economic Growth*: Growth is often constrained by structural supply-side factors (these are persistent rather than cyclical). DA cannot change deeply ingrained laws

or policies; operational DA can only create a knowledge base and some support for those changes over time—it cannot change "structures". DA is also expected to generate economic growth when this depends on for starters on (1) strong states that (2) can control macroeconomic policy and (3) which have the political will to make the necessary structural supply-side changes, e.g., elimination of laws restricting hiring and firing of personnel. Strategic level results depend on the willingness of governments to solicit and adopt lessons over time from DA advisors. Ukraine illustrates that this often does not happen. Two decades of DA lessons were largely ignored by the central government, mostly in the western part, and adopted only by selected cities. In some cases, minor changes to forms are considered "structural" and require new laws; a government financial management information system or GFMIS is a management system yet requires parliamentary and/or presidential approval for design, bidding, and installation in most countries, e.g., Jordan and Honduras. In other countries such as Bulgaria, reform of program or PPB budgeting systems varies by city. DA work with receptive mayors produced dramatic and almost instant results; other cities never reformed their systems despite TA and capacity-building by the same teams from the same DA project. In Nicaragua, frequent changes of counterpart personnel at MOF finally led to the derailment of the PPBS project there.

7 *Invalid Political Evaluations*: Most DA by the US is planned, executed, and reported as if it were a policy-level, strategic operation with direct support of Congress to which it is accountable for big results. USAID evaluations based on what Congress asks focus mainly on program and functional-level expenditures (planned vs. actual), not project-level resource allocations. Projects are the building blocks of the DA program but are aggregated into functions/programs without further explanation to demonstrate DA policy-level results. Project budgets are broken down by traditional categories: direct costs (i.e., wages, fringe, expenses such as classroom and equipment rentals, travel, telecommunications, materials, copying, and food services) and indirect costs (30%–50% of direct costs) rather than operational vs. reporting and administrative tasks. Projects may still achieve important results, but despite what personnel actually must do. This emphasis on programs and functions explains why most annual reports are compendia of glowing field successes or excusable failures (e.g., floods, wars).

Evaluations often reflect the major mismatch between strategic policy evaluations which are broader, long-term and overtly political, and short-term DA objectives, e.g., systems that are invisible in the short-term but can deliver results in the medium-long term if supported such as girls school enrollment, promotion, and graduation in exchange for fiscal transfers to local governments (i.e., districts) in Pakistan. Instead, direct costs reflecting what should be operational activities are displaced by performance reporting which produces the very reports that impress Congress and strategic-level policy officials but waste project time. Moreover, the institutional delivery structure for DA integrates policy operations, with USAID reporting to DOS and Congress. The MCC must also report to Congress directly (without the DOS intermediary) and allocate funds conditional on reported indicator progress from the country level. Most MCC results depend on operational systems changes but the emphasis is strategic results—politically friendly, stable democracies. But the activities of small, shorter term MCC projects cannot really be linked to these deeper, long-term results. As noted, in USAID ODA financing is by country with the most strategically important to USFP receiving the most DA: Israel, Pakistan, etc. DA performance results are reported to Congress and DOS with at least some interest in effectiveness, e.g., hundreds of parliamentarians trained leading dramatically to more democracy. This confusion between short-term operational needs and longer term strategic results impairs valid evaluation with the results that funding is wasted on longer term programs (or the fluffy proportions of operational-level project activities) that produce few needed results for growth and development. But they look good on paper.

Centralized Aid Allocations and Management Control

The *2005 OECD Paris Accords on Aid Effectiveness* formalized the aid decentralization objective. The rationale was (1) to increase a country's stake in aid outcomes and (2) to encourage locally designed programs that would be more flexible and responsive to needs. World Bank had used PIUs as PFM enclaves to ring-fence projects with special accounts and units within ministries. But these did not achieve the first or second objective. The core issue is trust between donors and host countries: will the host country misuse or steal the funds as has happened in the past? This boils down to how effective the government's financial controls are. How can these systems and practices be changed through modification of aid incentives? For comparative purposes here is a breakdown of the degree of centralization of aid (ODA) delivery. The percentages of aid disbursed for countries using national PFM systems are US 15%; UK 53%; World Bank 36%; and Norway 56%. The percentages of aid disbursed for the government sector are US 30%; UK 45%; WB 62%; and Norway 57%. The percentages of aid for procurement using country procurement systems are US 11%; UK 51%; WB 30%; and Norway 66%.

Consistent with the *Paris Declaration*, USAID now believes that by shifting allocations from direct budget support or DBS to fixed-amount reimbursement or FARs and implementation letters or ILs mechanisms, aid can be decentralized and become more results oriented by encouraging (1) local PFM ownership of aid programs and (2) local efficiencies which would save USAID funds and allow reprogramming funds to other sectoral programs and projects. The shift has to occur within a framework of ongoing tight internal control/audit supported by USAID mission controllers.[26]

The question is how do make this aid policy shift without permitting further losses of funds due to leakage/corruption? There are two ways: (1) measure PFM *fiduciary risk* and permit decentralized aid only to lower risk countries and (2) encourage higher risk countries to reduce their PFM risk levels. FR is the danger that funds allocated from the budget may *not*: (1) be controlled properly (i.e., leading to corruption), (2) be used for purposes other than those intended, and/or (3) produce efficient or economic programmatic results. It should be noted that the World Bank program for results (P4R) lending now includes PFM/FR. Its PEFA reviews have been reformed multiple times in over 100 countries and include measures for FR that guide the conditions used on later project lending based on that risk. Higher risk countries receive lower scores and thus pay a price with fewer loans/grants through country systems.

The Need for Smarter Soft Power

Despite these problems, the case for "smart soft power" has never been stronger. With increasing state fragility and failure around the world, foreign aid is needed for stabilization, and it can provide it at a lower cost and greater effectiveness than, for instance, security assistance (SA). SA began in 1949 to provide new allies with equipment as a bulwark against the Soviet Union.[27] The mission of SA has expanded from a tool of security influence in fragile and failed state contexts to the naïve and unrealistic expectation of it being able to win wars by equipping and training foreign military personnel. Like SA, DA is faced with the unrealistic expectation that it can re-create Western representative democracies in poor countries without national loyalties and no traditions of responsive governments.[28]

How does DA then provide stability? Even this advantage sounds wrong to Congress, the media, and officials with little experience or understanding of the endemic problems of underdevelopment, sectarianism, and state capture in poor countries. Aid stabilizes, "by allowing rulers in fragile states to maintain stable patronage systems to buy off opponents in order to keep the peace. A dramatic decline in revenue from a drop in aid would decimate the tenuous links that keep countries whole, as happened the last time foreign aid declined precipitously—in the immediate cold-war period".[29] Of course, that leaves DA open to the charge of encouraging corruption! That reflects the naivety of not only DA planning but SA as well. Military aid or SA often ignores the "soft factors" of establishing cultural rapport and understanding local routines as well. An example is the failure to appreciate that partners or counterparts have sectarian or tribal loyalties that outweigh national patriotism.[30] There is no nationally legitimate government which magnifies the problem of disbursing either DA or SA from Washington without allowing for the cultural flexibility by either aid personnel or country counterparts that can facilitate achievement of the aid's narrower project objectives.

Case Introduction and Overview

PCD is a fictional for-profit, Washington, DC-based international development consulting company specializing in private sector development, evaluation, and health.[31] PCD was 15 years old in 2010, employed nearly 100 people, and had worked in 65 countries implementing both long- and short-term development projects for multiple international donors. PCD would be considered a mid-sized development firm. Large US firms execute about $150–$200m in projects yearly and employ 400–700 people. They have been collectively known as "beltway bandits" because of their proximity to the funding source (USAID) from their DC and the Virginia and Maryland suburb offices. Over the past five years, the firm has enjoyed steady and sustainable growth, reaching $40m in annual revenue, with profitability above the industry average. PCD's reputation and status in the development community have been growing, and the firm feels that it is on the cusp of breaking into the top tier of development firms. The culture of the firm is entrepreneurial, growth-oriented, and technical. The management style has been evolving from a centralized owner/manager approach to a collaborative, decentralized approach to broaden management skills and opportunities.

PCD's main client is USAID, which provides 85% of its contracting revenue. The remainder is from a variety of sources including the World Bank, the State Department, and the US Trade Development Agency among others. In 2010, the firm won a USAID competitive bid for $25m over five years to implement the evaluation of the $500m USAID Private Sector Development portfolio in Pakistan. It was noted that US DA to Pakistan focuses on issues of greatest importance to all Pakistanis: energy, economic growth, stability, education, and health. Consistent with the emphasis on growth, the private sector development portfolio is implemented by 14 different contractors, and PCD will design and conduct a monitoring and evaluation project to efficiently identify and track a set of standard project and development indicators. The project, based in Islamabad, has five long-term expatriate staff members, 25 local Pakistani staff, and a large number of short-term expatriate and Pakistani consultants.

PCD won the contract in part because of its superior past performance on similar projects. For instance, in Afghanistan, it had successfully evaluated several projects for USAID. In Pakistan, the TOR required the contractor to develop performance indicators and a system for monitoring USAID's portfolio across all projects which included micro-credit, banking and financial sector development, and commercial enterprise financing and development. Monitoring and evaluation of project impact would proceed according to its approved management plan in Pakistan by collaborating with the 14 contractors implementing USAID's projects in these multiple sub-sectors of the private sector development program. Evaluation would be based on the results of measures derived from indicators agreed between PCD and implementing contractors. They measured progress and results through such indicators as on-time performance of project objectives; personnel turnover; actual spending vs. projected spending; reduction of unemployment; and sub-sector growth, operating margins, and profitability.

PCD was noted as a for-profit international aid firm. Since USAID began delegation of DA implementation to contractors decades ago, the largest bidders in the development business have been for-profit, e.g., Chemonics International and Development Alternatives, Inc. (DAI). Nonprofits, such as World Learning or International City and County Management Association (ICMA), find it easier to bid as sub-contractors for teams led by for-profits. To perform the prime contractor or team leader role requires a much larger scale and the ability to manage large, complex USAID projects according to USAID's detailed accounting and reporting rules. "Profit" meant the firm bid on contracts for clients such as USAID and would charge an agreed-upon, fully audited "multiplier" that was roughly twice its operating costs. It would then add another small percentage to that figure for profit. Such profits would be distributed to shareholders in firm stock, often firm employees and others that could purchase it as a private firm. PCD was not a "public" firm or listed on stock markets. By contrast, a "non-profit" firm, such as ICMA, was mission driven and less bureaucratic than a private firm. NPOs also made profits ("retained earnings" consisting of revenues over expenses), but they were treated as "reserves". In practice, other than for treatment of "income" by the US tax code, this may be a distinction without a practical difference since both must report project progress to clients in the same way. The reporting burdens are the same.

Like most bidders, PCD bid on mainly USAID contracts with particular TOR or TORs to implement them through field projects around the world. It is also possible to submit unsolicited proposals to USAID with novel approaches to particular development problems in specific countries. These are often funded but the projects are much smaller, and it would be difficult for a firm to remain in business and meet payroll based on a portfolio of such projects. PCD had a staff of around 100 consisting of proposal writers, contracts specialists, procurement specialists, subject and regional area experts, and project support staff. At any time, it would be bidding on several USAID projects in order to smooth out its revenues and ensure that cash management problems did not occur from sudden gaps in revenue flows in the face of fixed expense obligations. That meant that PCD personnel had to perform reconnaissance on upcoming bids, travel to target countries, locate local firms and personnel, meet with donor clients, and return to prepare the proposals by the due date. This was high-pressure work and required the use of teams of diverse personnel focused on winning the project for the firm. PCD would grow depending on how many wins it could obtain, thus maximizing its revenues and ensuring positive cash flows during the fiscal year. In this way, PCD could hire more personnel and increase its capacity to bid on more projects with the hope of obtaining even more wins.

Upon award, the project became the "jewel in the crown" for PCD, becoming the largest overseas implementation project with a high profile in an important country, with potentially a large amount of follow-on work both in Pakistan and throughout USAID. It was also a practice that PCD had been trying to "grow" into by winning more project bids. Monitoring and evaluation were a popular technical practice area for international development work and especially that financed by USAID. Other donors such as DFID and World Bank also financed evaluation work but that was much harder work to "win" for a medium-sized US firm with most of its experience and funding from USAID. Nevertheless, PCD now had an opportunity to showcase its management and technical expertise and ability to work in high-risk environments. In addition, once PCD successfully performed on a large contract in Pakistan, given geopolitical policy realities, the likelihood of winning more work in evaluation and other practice areas would be increased.

As luck would have it, a few months into project implementation, problems began to emerge from three sources:

Personnel and Staffing Issues

Andrew, a first-time Chief of Party (COP), was specifically requested by the USAID Project Officer, Kathy during the proposal development stage. The operative oral phrase often used by USAID is they would "look favorably" on PCD's bid in such a case. While technically not allowed under USAID contracting, this is not an infrequent back-channel request. Kathy was in her first assignment with USAID and in charge of the historically high-budgeted Privates Sector Development portfolio. Kathy's position was the Chief Technical Officer (CTO) or person in the mission to whom USAID project implementers would normally report on technical/physical progress. The perverse incentives operating at this stage were fairly clear. PCD wanted to win the contract. Senior PCD staff likely knew of the conflict of interest if told by those preparing the proposal, putting the team together, and negotiating the contract with USAID which meant both personnel and budget issues. But they also hoped it would all work out during successful implementation. To have protested at this stage on moral, conflict of interest grounds would have been naïve and self-defeating. It might have scored points with moralists negotiating the final contract at USAID but might have raised broad questions about PCD's competence for future work.

It soon became apparent that:

1 Kathy, while familiar with the Pakistan environment, had a weak grasp of USAID contracting regulations and protocols and was inexperienced in development practice. In other words, she was an area specialist but not into the time-consuming complexities of USAID reporting requirements, some of which are onerous and can even lead to the goal-displacement of important project work in the field by bureaucratic process requirements. USAID places a premium on performance by such experienced field hands on its projects.

2 On the basis of their personal friendship, Andrew became more responsive to Kathy's management rather than PCD's home office, which often led to arguments bordering on insubordination with the Washington senior manager. Effectively, he was reporting to her and viewed her as his superior rather than the home office PCD. This is the dual reporting problem faced by public sector managers who have to serve multiple masters.

3 Andrew entered into a personal relationship with Sarah, who was one of the long-term expatriates, and they moved in together. Sarah then became his live-in partner and subordinate on the project. Such relationships are not uncommon in the tight camaraderie of development teams working in the tight quarters of development projects. At the end of most of them, a realistic tally would consist of #s of marriages between staff, # of children born to these and other project personnel during implementation, and #s of staff living with each other. Some chiefs of party of COPs even claim their more successful projects have higher numbers reflecting greater camaraderie which led to better project results.

4 Pakistani staff complaints were increasing that Andrew was abusive to Pakistani staff and that he lacked sufficient management and technical experience. Project feedback channels are formal and informal. COPs may have a set time for weekly complaints; often serious ones come from back-channel sources that want to remain anonymous. A good COP will listen to both, investigate them, and make personnel changes accordingly.

5 Andrew's progress in getting the 14 contractors to agree to a standard set of measurable indicators was slow. These contractors lacked confidence in Kathy's approach to reaching an agreement through Andrew on a final set of performance measures that would apply to them. Since knowledge of how to evaluate presumably won PCD the contract and USAID evaluated his qualifications positively, one has to assume he must have known that uniform indicators for the contractors would be an essential first step for the project to go forward. The contrary incentives here should be obvious: contractors seeking indicators that would make them look good; COP needing performance indicators that also would produce valid and reliable data fast.

Environmental and Security Issues

1 Street bombings and kidnappings were increasing, as were roadblocks and the presence of the Pakistani military to guard against possible terrorist strikes. Curfews were imposed by the government. Security problems were more nascent in the mid-2000s. They are much more serious now in 2016.

Security costs increased more than 100% over budget to comply with office, vehicle, and staff housing security standards implemented by USAID. This was clearly a large increase from the planned and approved budget. But to have budgeted 100% more for security on the chance that security would deteriorate further could have lost PCD the contract on cost. Guards, hard structures, hard vehicles, and security equipment were needed. In this case, USAID did not want to cover these additional security needs and costs by increasing the budget or redirecting funds from the technical component. The original budget did not include actual "hardware" equipment costs and trained personnel. It focused on the "software" of security procedures for project personnel with curfews and flashlights which were much cheaper. With the changed context.

2 PCD engaged USAID in a discussion of several security cost issues without reaching final decisions. PCD wanted to know who would hire the security personnel and who would train them. Who would own the guns and the ammunition and then what would be done with them

after the project ended? Who would pay for kidnapping and personal liability insurance? The insurance oversight is odd since as of the early 1990s, firms had such insurance for such events. The firm for which the first author worked (DAI) carried kidnap insurance for him to work in Pakistan. When asked for how much, the president told him that it was secret as they could torture out the figure—a sensible response. These discussions and negotiations are more common now as most USAID target countries increasingly have security risks for aid personnel. Estimated additional costs of security were now around $500k/year. PCD would make about 7% profit on the $25m contract or about $1.75m which breaks down to $350k/year on the five-year project. Thus, PCD's coverage of all extra security costs would wipe out all of its project profits and produce a five-year loss of $750k. There would be little incentive for it to continue under these constrained circumstances. The cost coverage issue depended on USAID's treatment of "foreseeability" or whether the costs were "unanticipated" and "unforeseen". Decisions on this issue by the USAID IG (the Inspector General) or the Professional Development Association lobby group would take about six months. In the meantime, USAID wanted its TOR implemented at the original budget and the clock was running to achieve milestones in the PCD management plan for its project. The question for PCD at this point would be whether to walk away from the contract to preserve its company profitability and risk future USAID work or continue as good professionals and fight it out later with USAID.

3 Electricity blackouts surged in the summer, and required more generators and renovations, in response to increasing security risks.

4 Expatriate staff, led by Andrew, resisted restraints on staff movement during off-hours and tighter security standards. Sarah was reported by ISI (the Pakistani Inter-Service Intelligence military agency) to be going out at night, taking taxis, and generally "going native"; she was becoming a "loose cannon" to PCD and to the project. While civilian and military governments alternate, nearly all civilian political leaders play along with a dominant army to form a permanent establishment that protects its narrow interests at the expense of the vast majority of the population.[32] The ISI is part of this army establishment and still concerns itself with the Kashmiri issue as well as monitoring foreign personnel working in Pakistan. During the first author's ADB project work in Pakistan in the early 2000s, it became evident that their driver couldn't drive. He ran over at least one bicyclist and roared through red lights regularly. Recognizing that we would all be killed at some point, he approached the project assistant (or RHM right-hand man as we called him). The RHM met with the security chief in Bhutto's Palace (our project's central office) and came back with the explanation that

the driver was a "spook". I told him that was fine but to have the chief find a spook who could drive. We had a new spook that could drive the next day. Negotiation can work wonders even at this low level of operations.

5 It became impossible to travel to parts of the country to visit sites, and increasingly difficult to travel to contractor meetings.

6 USAID was under lockdown, requiring two days' notification to enter the facility under very strict security procedures. USAID staff could not leave the facility. This is not unusual. Even under "normal" conditions in Pakistan, one could not enter the USAID compound without authorization beforehand. In the first author's case, it wasn't a problem since the project was funded by ADB and we only went to the USAID facility to eat cheap hamburgers. For the PCD project, it was a problem since the CTO was there. The way around this fortress problem was to meet the CTO informally in a restaurant and report over lunch. That USAID officials couldn't leave the building was less of a problem given their intense paperwork routines. One USAID official in Honduras told me once they rarely traveled outside and got most of their country's information from the Peace Corps.

Political Issues

1 A Special Ambassador was appointed for Afghanistan and Pakistan, ranking above the US Ambassador to Pakistan, adding another layer to the official bureaucracy.

2 The Special Ambassador, a known micro-manager, took de facto control of the USAID Program, severely limiting the control and input of the Country Director. All checks written over $1k had to be approved by him! The Country USAID Director remained accessible to US contractors. But he had no discretionary budget control which limited the flexibility of all USAID projects to achieve their objectives. This micro-control of financial transactions centralized the flow of US DA in Pakistan even further than noted above.

3 The Special Ambassador wanted to contract directly with Pakistani consulting firms, eliminating the implementation and oversight of many US contractors, and putting the PCD project at risk. That is, he wanted USAID to directly plan and deliver DA, which was the original intent of foreign aid in 1961. The requirements of scale to perform these tasks, as noted, resulted in the gradual delegation of the implementation of DA contracts to private contractors and NGOs. To eliminate PCD in this case as well as for other USAID projects in Pakistan meant in practical terms finding "certified" local firms, re-bidding all

contracts, and training cadres of new people—a process that would take years. The notion that local personnel could do the project better than US contractors and that LOE (level of effort) should be allocated to them is a perennial issue. Some fear that US foreign aid would lose its political clout in Congress as a supporter of US firms (e.g., "buy America" procurement provisions and other examples of "tied aid") and employment if the policy were changed. Others argue that if locals knew how to perform these tasks, they would already have done so and that international assistance from any donor is therefore not needed. For comparative purposes, regional donors such as ADB working in Pakistan have smaller, shorter projects and do use a greater percentage of local LOE to implement its projects.

4   The Special Ambassador shielded himself from direct contact with US contractors.

Management Issues

1   Given the loss of control over personnel and angry feedback from staff, it became apparent that PCD would have to replace the COP. This is not an uncommon situation: COPs are replaced all the time on USAID projects usually with the rationale of moving ahead in a different direction with a different leader. The question is how should PCD proceed. Andrew as COP had authority over the checkbook and the lives of 100 people. Angry COPs can and have sabotaged projects before. Andrew was already "dissing" PCD among Pakistani officials and local staff. He was clearly out of control.

2   To sack him, a proverbial team of "angels of death" was organized which included the CEO of PCI. It then set up a meeting with Andrew at which USAID and Kathy were present. In this meeting, PCD notified Andrew and USAID simultaneously that he was being fired. Later, Kathy was notified separately by USAID that she was fired as well.

The project raised interesting questions about how all this might have been avoided in the first place. What should PCD have learned? What might USAID learn about procedures to implement projects in dangerous or "current-conflict" situations?

Questions

1   *Management:* Simulate or assign the roles of Andrew, Kathy, Sarah, USAID, and the USAID angel of death team to classroom participants around the issue of Andrew's termination and what should follow.

What should USAID require of departing project COPs? How can USAID be assured that the COP actually leaves the country?

- Did Andrew, Sarah, or Kathy manage their teams (projects) effectively? Did they act as if management was a verb or a noun? Were they cognizant of the roles each team member played, and did they try to motivate them?
- How did that lack of rule clarity and the failure to anticipate this limit the ability of Andrew to actually manage the project? Which rules should have been clarified or replaced? How did this rule ambiguity lead to the larger management issues that finally derailed the project?
- What management options existed for Andrew on the issues of security and personnel? What would you have done given his circumstances and why?
- What was the quality of Andrew's decisions? Did he rely on staff for advice? Was there evidence of team collaboration, such as team meetings, social events, solidarity gatherings, and responsiveness to project member suggestions or complaints?

2 *Project Planning*: How would you improve the TOR for this and similar projects? What language should be included to clarify liability and security rights and obligations for all parties to the contract?

- Often planning and implementation issues are settled but not resolved, and they re-surface on other development projects in other contexts, leading to more problems. Is there any evidence that USAID produces "precedent" from its projects and re-works its rules accordingly?

3 *Content:* Despite successful bids, all USAID projects require approval of a work plan by the CTO in country before work begins. Contractors must deploy personnel almost immediately and have around 30 days to produce an approved work plan. Some projects even founder at this stage, and USAID terminates the agreement with the formerly successful contractor. What should the work plan in this case have provided before USAID approval?

- It is often argued by contractors that the project SOW is ill-structured and makes no sense to implement as it stands. Contractors can make these points during formal comment periods before bidding after seeing the TOR. They can also make the points after the successful bid but during final negotiations with the CTO and USAID personnel while preparing the project work plan. Was there any evidence that this was done here? What issues should have been raised?

4 *Diplomacy and Negotiation*: Diplomacy is needed to resolve issues and reduce conflict through realistic, arms-length negotiations. There must be a clear framework with explicit rules to guide issue resolution. For instance, ISP cases #205 and #262 which the first author assigns his graduate classes focus on the design of IMF structural adjustment programs for Zambia and South Korea, respectively. IMF provides clear rules with program design driven by the explicit, transparent, and often debatable assumptions of its macroeconomic models. Local MOF officials often disagree with IMF demand, but most issues are resolved given the relatively tight fiscal framework and the need for valid and reliable fiscal data in support. Local officials are left with the choice of means to attain IMF program objectives if they want more loans and continued access to international credit markets. By contrast, for USAID project implementation, rules, and criteria to guide management are often vague or non-existent. Field guidance is provided by USAID/PCD for financial transactions and financial and physical progress only. Issues must then be settled ad-hoc through formal and informal meetings. Issue resolution is also constrained by the need for aid contracting firms to maintain profitability and the USAID's need to maintain credibility and political capital with the US Congress.

It is clear from the misunderstanding and miscommunication on this project, at the outset with the TOR, at the personnel appointment stage, during implementation with the staff, and for the final replacement of the COP, the diplomatic element was missing from this project. Diplomacy can be high or low: it may be required during a Cuban missile crisis with high stakes involving top officials or more commonly at the other end of the scale resolving lower level field conflicts on projects that involve personnel and higher level country officials + the home office. This is the triangulation problem commonly faced by aid people from companies and NGOs executing development projects overseas.

- How might conflict resolution mechanisms have been improved for the management of this project? How could PCD have had better field intelligence on the project and anticipated what was happening? Aid personnel often complain about supervision and evaluation of their work by inexperienced generalists often interested in power and personal games. Would the provision of personnel by both USAID and PCD of personnel with greater technical expertise and experience have improved communications here?
- Overseas aid or DA should be a diplomatic tool. Lasting personal relationships are forged over the course of long projects. Locals learn about the US development business and often fit perfectly while others become cynical of the entire business. Locals also gain insights

into the functioning and operation of a USG institution working overseas. They witness the relations between home office project personnel, the COP, and themselves. What conclusions can you draw on these themes from this project? How might USAID improve its delivery of aid as a diplomatic tool?

- How could USAID design its programs for evaluations and private sector development to reduce ambiguity and potential conflict? Could the evaluation process be formalized to produce faster and more accurate agreement on program objectives, means, and results? Could the private sector development program include grants to small businesses and local NGOs to design criteria and eligibility requirements and suggest evaluation measures? What other suggestions could you make to reduce conflict and ambiguity between the key project partners (i.e., USAID, PCD home office, PCD field staff, PCD local project staff, local private firms, and local NGOs) in this case implementing these programs? (Guess, 2019).[33]

Discussion Case #10: The Paradoxical Mismanagement of African Development Resources

Poor countries often cite the absence of funds to explain their underdevelopment—lack of funds for health care, educational systems, city planning, and decent roads from farms to export and domestic markets. But is poverty really just the absence of funding and available income? What of the absence of backup or redundant administrative and operational systems? What of excessive bureaucratic processes and rule complexity requiring bribery to obtain permits, licenses, and services? What of insufficiently qualified professional staff by poor country governments? Regions such as SSA contain substantial natural wealth such as minerals and ideal conditions to grow almost all its own crops for food. Yet the resources are not exploited for local development?

The problem of underdevelopment is usually not just the absence of money. Other deficiencies contribute, such as stranded wealth and wasted pools of excellence unable to be deployed toward growth and development. Deeper dimensions of poverty contribute to uncertainty in planning and delivering public services and building infrastructure, attracting commercial investments, and maintaining macroeconomic stability.[34] In most African countries, for example, the energy sector produces excess electricity, but blackouts occur everywhere. Ministries of health and agriculture often fail to spend most of their annual budgets despite weak health care systems and dependence on imports for most food items.

Many countries in this region lack decent infrastructure such as pipelines, ports, roads, and rail systems while bank and donor financing is available for construction. But most countries also lack lists of bankable or feasible projects (i.e., capital improvement programs) that meet economic and financial criteria for successful implementation. A more serious constraint is that the main productive sectors in SSA are state owned and managed. For years, the 40% of state enterprises that run the railroads, ports, and utilities have been unprofitable. For example, the Eskom state utility in South Africa has daily blackouts. It is staffed with mostly unqualified party cronies who mismanage and pillage the SOE budgets via overpriced contracts. Transnet runs the ports, pipelines, and railroads in the SSA region. While world market coal prices reached record highs in 2022, South African exports were at the lowest level since 1993. In many cases, Transnet failed to get the mined ore to ports resulting in at least $4.7b lost in coal exports. As noted in the article, SOEs don't lead development in SSA, they actually arrest it.[35]

Questions

What are the causes of these perennial development paradoxes, and why haven't they been addressed as actionable policy and management problems?[36]

Exercise #3.1: Private Development Assistance for Mozambique

Recall that project managers in Oriente, Borneo, and Kano faced internal tensions and cultural constraints. Suppose the context is a fragile, quasi-failed state in the context of extreme external threats by guerrillas (called "rebels" here). This is even a more extreme case than the Pakistani state failure noted in **Discussion Case #9**. The Cabo Delgado LNG project operated and owned by Total Oil of France was shut down by guerrilla ISIS attacks two years before. Recent joint efforts of neighboring Rwanda and other nearby countries flushed out most ISIS insurgents and the region has returned to a tenuous peace. The Government of Mozambique (GOM) and the provincial government in Palma where the project is based are still dysfunctional. They cannot provide permanent security, education, health care, or social service coverage to the Palma province region, the northern coastal area which is the poorest in Mozambique.

Instead of a full-fledged DA push to rebuild, with some World Bank support, Total Oil is providing several basic governance functions. For example, Total has created a $200m endowment fund to cover food aid and for the reconstruction of many destroyed facilities, roads, and electrical supplies. Total is also providing K–12 education and training of local workers for future jobs in the LNG facilities of Total and for the nearby Exxon LNG project which has just returned to operational status. The renewal is far from complete, but World Bank and Total are working hard, and the population has rebounded to more than the 75k residents it had before the conflict. Its main hotel was the scene of the ISIS attacks on Cabo Delgado where more than 100 people sought refuge two years ago and ten were killed. The hotel has even resumed Sunday pizza nights! It is estimated that the two LNG projects when operational should supply the EU with one-third of its natural gas imports, which will help wean it from dependence on Russian gas. Britain's Centrica and the French electricity utility have signed long-term purchase contracts. Environmentalists have protested that the LNG plants will contribute to major increases in greenhouse gases.[37]

Questions

Suppose (as an experienced aid person) you were interviewed by Total Oil for a position to provide them with a list of needed skills for the tasks ahead to provide private sector DA. Knowing the constraints and problems of delivering effective DA from the Pakistan case, what would you recommend? For, as noted, Mozambique is a high-risk fragile state environment like Pakistan where DA has floundered over the years as described in *Discussion Case #9*. What aid partnership arrangements are possible with donors, charities, and commercial firms to provide needed basic services and technical assistance to modernize central and local governments? How should security services be provided? Why did they fail before?

Notes

1 *Economist* (2023) "Bartleby, The Bottleneck Bane", 5-20, p.60.
2 Yury Bykove (2014) *Durak* (The Fool), Locarno: 67th Annual Festival del Locarno.
3 George M. Guess and Paul G. Farnham (2011) *op.cit.*, Chapters 4 and 6.
4 *Economist* (2023) "Climate Change, Water Works", 5-27, p.69.
5 Chinese firms, state banks, and official policy institutions have finally learned this as massive debts pile up from projects that were not appraised by standard ROR, creditworthiness, or break-even standards before committing funds. This was a lesson absorbed long ago by Paris Club members on SSA projects. China's projects now focus on commodity hotspots for rare earth metals to supply its EV industry. The "aid" vehicle is partnerships between Chinese SOEs and local mining operations in poor countries of SSA and Latin America. *Economist* (2023) "Changing Cash Flows", 2-25, pp.73–74.
6 *Economist* (2023) "Helping the Poor, Cautious Pioneers", 4-22, p.63.
7 "The World's Toughest In-Tray", *Economist* 2-18-23, pp.41–42.

8 *Economist* (2023) "A New Source of Sustenance: *World Ahead 2023*", pp.65.66, and "A Suffering Sluggish Giant", p.67 (in Guess, *op.cit.*, 2019:168).
9 J. Xavier (1998) "Budget Reform in Malaysia and Australia Compared" *Public Budgeting and Finance* Volume 18, Number 1, pp.99–118.
10 Robert Mundell (1961) "A Theory of Optimum Currency Union Areas" *American Economic Review* Volume 51, Number 4, pp.665–675.
11 "Bartleby: Faulty Reasoning, Why Pointing Fingers is Unhelpful, and Why Bosses Do It More Than Anyone" *Economist* 1-21-23, p.56.
12 *Economist* (2023) "Britain Isn't Working, Welfare and Economic Inactivity", 9-16, pp.47–48.
13 For background on ODA and US DA purposes, planning, and implementation, see Guess (2019), *op.cit.*, Chapter 7.
14 It should be noted that pasture is not a complete trade-off for tropical hardwood forests. As far back as the late 1970s, the Tropical Science Center in San Jose, Costa Rica, performed tropical forest management trials financed by USAID. Strips of secondary tropical hardwoods were cut into the forest. Several years later, the strips were naturally reseeded and the original species were replaced. That is, in principle the deforestation strips preserved the original species. The method allows the forest to recover naturally. Additionally, fast-growing pine trees (seven years to maturity and less for thinning to serve as fence posts) for poles and pulpwood have been successfully planted for years as shade trees for coffee crops in countries such as Costa Rica.
15 As noted, the case study by Charles Downs on how DA can be disbursed most optimally in a country without a state partner is: "Negotiating Development Assistance: USAID and the Choice between Public and Private Implementation in Haiti" (#117) (Pew Case Study/Institute for Study of Diplomacy, Georgetown University, 1988).
16 loc.cit.
17 In Ghana, I was once approached by some locals in a cafe who wanted to chat. Soon they discovered I was with the World Bank and on a civil service mission. That was all they needed to know, since bright young locals know of what these programs and projects do, trying to reconcile or match salaries and positions to people only to discover vast pools of ghost workers. The result is invariably that both government positions and people are cut, downsizing the entire state structure. In poor countries, the civil service employs most people in the formal sector, and downsizing the bureaucracy means eventual unemployment for them and loss of support for their families. Future retraining: yes. But for what jobs are there in a poor country with minuscule private sectors to absorb them? Through channels I was rightfully declared *persona non grata* (rightsized!) or put on a list not to be "invited to return". But civil service programs and other missions continued elsewhere as part of multilateral donor development aid. Other variations of "colonial aid" projects and programs from the British, French, Dutch, German, and quasi-colonial US are provided mostly by grants (not loans). These projects do provide sound technical assistance and training projects in sectoral areas such as forestry and local taxation for improved public services. But the imported experts have to tread lightly and avoid marketing their own political systems and state systems by avoiding displaying their perks to avoid appearing as new versions of the great colonial master. Naipaul (1967, *op.cit.*, pp.209–210) noted the emanation of "disingenuous parables from lower ministerial civil servants" about "black and white keys working together to create harmony" in order to explain the

purpose of their work. If I had tried that in Ghana, I would have been laughed out of the country! The tragic paradox of establishing effective governing state institutions in aid-dependent poor countries, he noted, was that sadly given local power games, locals actually preferred to be served by expat aid experts because they were no threat to them and would eventually return to their own countries at the end of their contracts.

18 An exception to this litany of aid failures at the project and program level in Haiti was the 2009–2010 project between the Central Bank (BRH) and American University's School of Public Affairs to provide in-country public financial management and economic policy analysis courses leading to MPAs for the 20 students initially selected. The $400k project was paid for by the Government of Haiti. Students were in-service from other ministries such as MOF and Health and would return to their positions after graduation adding to state capacity. The second group of 40 students had been selected for 2010–2011 by BRH when the earthquake hit destroying the BRH classroom building and killing several program staff as well as students. Success for this short period was due mainly to (1) top-level GOH support, (2) establishment of direct IT and library systems linkages between AU and our BRH program which gave them access to full AU services in Haiti, and (3) in-person delivery of classes by AU faculty in Haiti. After the earthquake, AU ensured that some of the students could continue their MPA-MPP studies in other US universities paid for by the project.

19 Guess (2019): *op.cit.*, p.176; from: "A Time to Sow" *Economist* (2017), 6-10. Consistent with *Discussion Case #8*, the argument is that governance is constrained structurally by weak government or state. Could better public management make a difference in policy results here? What are the problems with aid to Haiti? From: "Aiding and Abetting, Foreign Aid Has Done Little to Help Haiti" *Economist* (2022) 2-5; also from: "A March Around the Institutions" and "Unhappy Anniversary", *Economist*, (2015) 1-17, p.14 and pp.35–36.

20 Guess and Dennis DeSantis (2019), Pakistan case, *Appendix A*. Dennis DeSantis is the founder and CEO of *UkraineAid*, an NGO that procures and delivers non-lethal equipment to Ukrainian troops. DeSantis explains the work of his charity on the Virginia public television show: "Hometown Heroes" (6-23): www.ukraineaid.group.

21 George M. Guess (1987) *The Politics of United States Foreign Aid* (New York: St. Martin's), p.1 (republished by Routledge Development Library Edition, Volume 7, 2011).

22 See, for example, Grupo Propuesta Ciudadana (2006) *Seminario Internacional: Democracia, Descentralizacion and Reforma Fiscal en America Latina y Europa del Este* (Lima: GPC); International Center for Human Development (ICHD) (2006) *Citizen's Participation in Local Government Budget Policy Development: A Case Study on Involving Citizen's Voice Into the Policy-Making Process* (Yerevan: ICHD; Budapest: Local Government and Public Services Reform Initiative); Staronova, Katarina (ed) (2007) *Training in Difficult Choices: Five Public Policy Cases from Slovakia* (Bratislava: Institute of Public Policy); and George M. Guess (2007) *Training of Trainers for Local Government Public Financial Management* (Budapest: Local Government Initiative of the Open Society Institute).

23 Daniel Markey (2016) Subcontinental Drift *The American Interest* Volume XII, Number 1, pp.88–90.

24 Guess, *op.cit.* (1987) Chapter 2. "Critical Perspectives on Foreign Aid".

25 Albert O. Hirschman and Richard Bird (1971) "Foreign Aid: A Critique and a Proposal" in *A Bias for Hope: Essays on Development and Latin America* (New Haven, CT: Yale University Press).
26 George M. Guess and Thomas Husted (2011) "Fiscal Incentives for Decentralized Aid Management", paper presented at American Society for Public Administration (ASPA) conference, Baltimore.
27 Justin Reynolds (2017) "Training Wreck" *The American Interest* Volume XII, Number 4 (March/April), p.95.
28 Guess (2019) *op.cit.*, pp.139–143.
29 Seth Kaplan (2017) "Risk Cascades and How to Manage Them" *The American Interest* Volume XII, Number 4 (March/April), p.109.
30 Reynolds, *ibid.*, p.94.
31 The people, companies, and events detailed here are fictionalized for teaching purposes but are based on the authors' many years working in international development.
32 Daniel Markey (2016) "Subcontinental Drift" *The American Interest* Volume XII, Number 1, pp.88–90.
33 Used with permission of Routledge—Taylor and Francis Group LLC, from George M. Guess (2019), *Building Democracy and International Governance*; permission conveyed through Copyright Clearance Center, Inc.
34 Ironically, since rich countries are often unable to deploy their wealth and resources for these reasons, poverty and uncertainty can impede poor as well as rich countries. See: *Planning and Budgeting in Poor Countries*, Naomi Caiden and Aaron Wildavsky (Wiley, 1974).
35 From: *Economist* (2023) "Africa's State-Owned Firms, Arresting Development", 1-21, p.11–12.
36 From: *Economist* (2022) "*The Paradox of Untapped Riches*", May 7, p.42.
37 Matthew Hill and Borges Nhamirre (2023) "Reviving Dreams of Gas Riches" *Bloomberg Businessweek* 6-12, pp.30–31.

4 Fiscal Management

Context and Problems

We turn now to the third form of management. Managers, whether overseas or domestic, must first be able to manage processes and internal systems such as IT and security; second, they must be able to deal with personnel, managing teams of people and motivating them toward objectives; and third, they must know how to manage organizational finances. This is especially important for revenue-generating utilities, nonprofits which often deliver social services such as specialized health care and meals for the poor, and city or state funds and enterprises which run and maintain transit systems and water and sewerage services. Starting in this chapter, we turn to sectoral management, explaining the use and of the specific tools, methods, and skills necessary to manage sectors such as national and local budgets, urban transport, education, and the environment. The four sectors were selected from many because they provide important tools and skills that are used in managing other sectors, such as security assistance (SA), rural agricultural development, and humanitarian aid.

Growing pressures to spend for climate change, defense and security systems, and for pandemic controls, require databases and metrics for managers to control national and local fiscal balances. Public financial management (PFM) skills and systems need to be strengthened for countries to stabilize and grow. Solid empirical baselines, benchmarks, and anchors are needed on which to base all sectoral programs and policies, such as education or transport. These skills and systems are needed as foundations for maintaining creditworthiness based on accurate data on fiscal position in order to generate investments and loans to finance growth and development.

Russia realized the need for fast PFM assistance in its "laggard" or supplicant period of self-doubt and introspection as the Soviet Union

DOI: 10.4324/9781032670959-4

collapsed in the late 1980s. During that political and fiscal liberalization period lasting about 20 years, Russia worked with International Monetary Fund (IMF) to adopt Western PFM (GFS) standards and to develop institutions that would ensure fiscal discipline that give it access to capital markets and enabled Russia to achieve spectacular growth. Before the Ukraine invasion, Russia was one of the IMFs star pupils. Even during this war, it has maintained fiscal discipline despite international sanctions on its main revenue sources (oil and gas).

IMF upgraded Russia's status in the early 1990s, enabling it to borrow more cheaply. For instance, it adopted a strategy of "fiscal authoritarianism" or defensive macroeconomics with a tight fiscal rule that budgets would be based on $40/barrel of oil (Brent oil value in 1/23 is $80/barrel). Russia has also maintained its star pupil status with IMF with its positive macroeconomic performance: budget deficit only 1.1% GDP (Gross Domestic Product) and current account balance +12.3%. But largely due to sanctions and the Ukraine war, its GDP has dropped by 3.7% (*Economist* "Economic and Financial Indicators", 1-14-23). Nevertheless, Russia has withdrawn and adopted a stance of the "victim" surrounded by enemies, where the autocratic leaders of its current authoritarian regime view former enablers, benefactors, and donors in the EU and West (such as IMF!) as bullies, enemies, and conspirators. That global capital markets, banking, and financial institutions have now shut their taps off to it only feeds its self-image as mistreated victim. But even at war, Russian budgets still need to be based on facts: financial trends, cost analyses, and physical performance information. Though PFM can provide these inputs, CEOs, and senior managers need to take these periodic reports into account before allocating resources to services, programs, and projects. That is why receipt of financial information is so critical to effective management. PFM then is a key system and also a skill, like proposal-writing, needed by both generalist senior managers and departmental financial managers.

An important sub-sectoral target for aid grants and loans has been to strengthen local governments. All countries, whether unitary or federations, have local government units to serve its citizens with services such as education and transport and goods such as infrastructure. The focus of aid starting in the early 1990s was to strengthen management capacities to plan, budget, finance, and monitor service delivery and project implementation. Local governments to be effective must have the fiscal authority, managerial responsibility, and political institutions be held accountable. Aid programs, particularly US DA funded and directed by USAID (US Agency for International Development) projects, have attempted to strengthen the managerial competence of local governments to spend, collect revenues, and to finance services and capital projects. The aim has been to devolve revenue and expenditure authority to provide local government fiscal and political autonomy. These projects have been effective in upgrading managerial capacities to spend for needed services and to finance budgets through revenue mobilization for current and capital expenditures with taxes, fees, fiscal transfers, and debt.

Similarly, support by USAID and the Open Society Institute (OSI) to local governments in the Former Soviet Union (FSU) and Central and Eastern Europe (CEE) to devolve revenue, expenditure and borrowing authority have been very successful. Local Government Initiative (LGI) research in the 1990s documented many changes in PFM systems in local government budgeting, accounting, and financing that took place since the transition in the early 1990s–2006. The effect of multiple pressures from USAID, World Bank, and LGI efforts to encourage budget transparency and creditworthiness to gain access to capital market financing made substantial improvements in the fiscal conditions in Kyrgyzstan, Bulgaria, Romania, Hungary, and Armenia. The reforms and upgrades to fiscal systems have improved the quality of life at the local level. The demonstration effects of successful reforms have encouraged local mayors and finance directors in many other countries to copy the successful practices of their neighbors to their advantage.[1]

In short, such aid efforts seek fiscal decentralization, where intergovernmental roles and responsibilities are defined and devolved to lower level governmental units.[2] The programs have been an important source of projects and programs for USAID and UKAID, particularly in the FSU/CEE region. Technical assistance and training have been provided to strengthen the local administrations, particularly mayoral, finance departments, and city enterprises to deliver services efficiently and effectively. An important budgetary process innovation from Porto Alegre, Brazil, was participatory budgeting which has been transferred to local governments around the world since the 1970s to guide planning and execution of local capital projects. Participatory inputs in planning and budgeting processes by individual citizens and other stakeholder groups have improved local government responsiveness and increased their legitimacy. Citizens support incumbent mayors and administrations that serve them with needed and useful projects and services by increasing levels of taxpaying. As the result of these programs, mayors and finance directors have developed a wide range of creative capital finance methods for these projects, including tax increment financing (TIFs), municipal bond financing and concessions such as BOTs (build-operate-transfer of assets) and private public partnerships (PPPs). Local and national capital markets have been deepened which has contributed to improved fiscal condition and the increased sustainability of national public finances.[3] Other options for buying capital assets include direct borrowing from commercial banks or issuing bonds. Bonds finance acquisition of assets either directly or through capital leases. Lease payments for long-term periods of five to ten years are treated as a long-term commitment like a home or building mortgage. Since lease payments are technically not debt, they are subject to annual re-authorization by legislatures which adds risk to the lease transactions.[4]

Financing environmental resilience infrastructure in poor countries, such as seawalls, flood gate control, and sewerage systems to deal with coastal flooding, and for traditional assets such as roads, railways, and electricity generation, transmission grids, and distribution systems, relies on the same sources. Countries can utilize all or some of these financing options for each project: own-source revenues for pay-as-you-go, and capital financing: bond markets, bank loans, donation from special source foundations, and private investments in PPP arrangements to plan, build, and operate public transit systems. For instance, Belize, Guyana, and Indonesia used funds for their resilience assets to deal with climate change from alternate sources to the multilateral and regional banks, such as US Development Finance Corporation and the Nature Conservancy to arrange bond sales on the capital market. These funding sources supplement local tax and fee revenues which are typically very low in poor countries. More importantly for effective capital financing is to have a formal capital improvements process (CIP). In this 10–12 step annual process, projects are identified and subjected to cost-benefit and cost-effectiveness tests to winnow out the uneconomic ones. The final list of needed projects is then matched with available funds to arrive at an actual capital budget for the fiscal year. That budget should consist of both capital and operations and maintenance (O&M) costs charged to the current budget over a medium-term framework of three to five years.

To be useful, the CIP system of arriving at projects requires project appraisal and procurement skills and systems. This process must also be real reflecting the actual projects that will be financed by varying sources of funds. That ensures that extra-budgetary funds are not used distorting the actual country fiscal position with hidden fiscal commitments. The CIP process should not allow leakage of political projects onto the list that have not been ranked according to transparent weights and scores into a proper rank-order list.[5] In this comprehensive and public capital budget document, it displays sources of funding for each project so that the local own source funds are identified as well as external loans, grants, and donations.

PFM consists of two skill areas:

1 *Government Budgeting* or public expenditure management (PEM) requires a set of tools using multiple formats to provide revenue and expenditure data and information to executive officials, citizen watchdogs, credit agencies, legislators, and auditors. These are topics of this chapter. Whether public sector, commercial, or nonprofit organization, budgeting is based on timely and accurate accounting systems information. Accounting professionals enter transactions and track public outlays using transparent and consistent accounting categories. Without frequent reviews of charts of accounts to make certain that budgetary accounting and reporting formats are consistent and uniform, governments cannot track their own budgetary progress nor measure their fiscal positions. Accounting and reporting systems provide the figures to assess creditworthiness for loans. Internal control systems operate to control commitments, outlays, and payments throughout the fiscal year. The controls are reviewed periodically by independent internal audit institutions. Failure to strengthen these basic control institutions allows the growth of creative and often corrupt systems which no outsider understands except someone like Mr. Road Treasurer Johnson! Successful "*shock therapy*" based on restructure budgetary and accounting systems was done in Poland in the early 1990s and Hungary a few years later through the "*Bokros Plan*" (named after its designer: minister of finance Lajos Bokros). As discussed below, in the early 1990s, the IMF also tried this approach in Russia in the late 1980s and early 1990s and in South Korea in 1997 (*Discussion Case #15*). Successful austerity rescue or "fiscal consolidation" efforts typically require major disruptive programs that cause social disruption and massive unemployment for a few years to get control of the public finance institutions through austerity programs. They require strong political support for the duration which is not always available.

Austerity programs often include spending cuts, higher taxes to generate balanced operating budgets, and increased interest rates to allow defense of the local currency and maintenance of reserves. The programs fuel almost immediate resentment and populist rants against the IMF as "fiscal fascists". In Russia, they are now recalled by Putin and other autocrats as evidence of "Western neo-Nazis" institutions that conspire against Russia. As will be seen, such fiscal fascists actually set the framework for Russia and other countries to grow and prosper if the funds are efficiently allocated to local needs. But they often wasted on military adventures and rewarding corrupt political cronies. Wiser leaders, such as those of Ghana, play the international credit and assistance game well by making some required fiscal reforms, running up more debts, then returning to the debt trap later by borrowing more from donors. The disruption of Ghanaian society by IMF austerity programs is predictably blamed on the IMF to politically cover local political leaders by prior agreement. This regular cycle of borrowing, reforming, and repaying to keep up its international credit standing is played out without any widespread whining about fiscal fascism. This mature approach satisfies donors such as IMF which gives the green light to credit markets to deem it highly creditworthy. Almost on cue, in 2023, Ghanaian GDP/person is expected to grow 38%, while countries such as Nigeria and South Africa are expected to grow by 0%.[6]

2 **Public Sector Costing and Pricing** requires use of analytic tools for management, such as break-even and flexible budget analysis. These are needed for rapid analyses of proposed capital projects and for monitoring annual cash flows. Costing and pricing are tools that one can teach to host country professionals and officials when working overseas on technical assistance missions for donors. They are also tools that a financial manager needs to analyze and manage the finances of NGOs, firms, and public sector organizations, especially state or city enterprises and public utilities. This will be covered in **Chapter 5**. Those with professional interests in the international fiscal management area should consider the US Treasury Office of Technical Assistance (OTA) program of overseas resident advisors, which provides technical assistance in budgeting and taxation systems to strengthen local ministries of finance (MOFs) and treasury institutions.

Learning Objectives

1 Students will be able to define and distinguish each of the five principles of healthy public finances.
2 To present and explain the elements of and linkages between the economic-object of expenditure budget and capital budget classification or format.
3 To explain why the **Medium-Term Expenditure Framework (MTEF)** is an important fiscal management tool (designed by Malcolm Holmes and colleagues in the Australian government in the late 1980s and widely implemented overseas by World Bank and IMF in member countries) and how it is similar to the capital budget format.
4 To discuss the fiscal problems IMF-World Bank missions face before developing country loan and rescue programs.
5 To discuss responsibilities for PFM technical assistance missions (**Table 4.1**) and how they are assigned to achieve their field objectives in two to three weeks.

Table 4.1 Guidance on the Selection, Preparation, and Management of Team Members for a Technical Assistance Mission for an International Fiscal Agency

Mission Size, Membership, and Duration

- Four to five members (including the mission chief) is the optimal size of a mission team.
- A four- to-five person mission team should have no more than two inexperienced members since this situation will invariably impose, inter alia, additional editing burdens on the mission chief when reviewing their draft contributions to a mission report.
- Missions will generally have durations of 10–14 days.

Mission Preparations

- Ensure that all mission members are recruited at least four weeks prior to the mission and that their contracts include two to three days mission preparation time.
- Provide copies of all relevant background documentation to mission members (once recruited) and indicate, where practicable, the main areas where the mission will focus its work.
- Signal, where feasible, the particular topics/areas where individual members will be expected to contribute to the mission work.
- Provide individual "face-to-face" briefings, especially to inexperienced mission members, to explain their mission roles, tasks, and expectations regarding preparation of a mission report. Emphasize mission comportment expectations, awareness, and respect for cultural differences, ensuring no actions will breach agency ethics and standards (e.g., no excessive alcohol consumption, no "hookups" with prostitutes, and similar actions), requirements to work weekends, and touristic outings only on a "time-permits" basis.
- Involve mission members in the preparation of a mission questionnaire, transmit the questionnaire to country authorities, preferably three weeks before the mission commences, with a request to the authorities to complete and return it one week before the mission commences.
- Transmit to country authorities in the same timeframe a detailed draft agenda for meetings (including parallel meetings on different topical issues), covering the first seven to ten days, and seek early confirmation of availability of key officials for proposed meetings. Leave three to six days free on the agenda for follow-up meetings and report preparation.
- Provide to inexperienced mission members, model chapters, and sections, from approved reports that demonstrate the expected writing style (e.g., the topical highlighted "first sentence", and short paragraph style). Invite them to practice writing in this style even before the mission commences.
- Follow-up authorities to ensure that the questionnaire is delivered on time and the proposed meeting schedule is confirmed.

Conduct of Mission

- Conduct introductory meetings with the Minister and an assembly of key counterparts to introduce mission members, outline mission objectives, confirm mission meeting schedule, and identify any outstanding data requests from the questionnaire.

(Continued)

Table 4.1 (Continued)

- Assign responsibility for meetings on assigned topics to experienced mission members and ask them to prepare one- to two-page outlines of the questions they will ask and circulate to all mission members the day prior to the relevant meeting. Invite all mission members to comment on/contribute to those outlines and "tag-team" inexperienced team members to experienced members to provide back-up during interviews.
- Ask inexperienced mission members to prepare similar one- to two-page outlines on their assigned topics in advance of relevant meetings, and follow the same approach on feedback, as above. "Tag-team" inexperienced with experienced team members to conduct their topical interviews, especially if and when the mission team divides to conduct parallel interviews with different counterparts.
- Meet with mission team each evening prior to dinner to review discussion outcomes and highlight key issues that might be covered in the mission report. Ensure that outlines of interview questions for the following day have been completed. Try to ensure that mission members "stick together" for dinner outings since the team that dines together is less likely to engage in problematic behaviors in their free time.
- Encourage inexperienced team members, in particular, to start their write-ups on their assigned topics, at the end of each day when relevant interviews have been conducted.
- At the conclusion of all initial meetings scheduled, prepare an outline of the mission report with input from all team members and finalize in a team meeting, including assignment of any topics not previously allocated. Ideally, the main body of the report (excluding attachments) should not exceed 25–30 pages (since no one will read it if it is longer!).
- The mission leader should set the timelines for completion of individual written draft report sections and edit those drafts. The leader should also take responsibility for the preparation of the report's two- to three-page executive summary which will be the critical minimum mission output delivered to a minister (and agency heads) at least 24 hours in advance of a "close-out" meeting.
- Present full report and conduct close-out meetings with the minister (and agency heads) and with other senior counterparts. Invite feedback and comments within an agreed timeframe (minimum two weeks).
- Provide feedback on mission performance to all mission members.

Source: From author's anonymous International Monetary Fund (IMF) colleague

6 To demonstrate the value of written reform commitments by top country and sectoral ministry officials for aid managers. To discuss the ingredients of a hypothetical technical assistance reform commitment (*Table 4.2*). To examine the predictable obstacles to aligning host country official needs with donor mission purposes before obtaining a commitment?

7 To review the core functions of PFM and discuss why budgeting is the lead function.

Table 4.2 How Not to Manage a Technical Assistance Mission

---

1 *Accentuate the positive.* Fail to share with the responsible minister and senior officials, critical information regarding likely major challenges in, and obstacles to, the implementation of planned reform measures.

2 *Boilerplate is best.* Provide to the authorities a "boilerplate" reform project implementation plan that takes no account of local conditions, including political constraints, legal requirements, and limited capacities.

3 *Travel cannot broaden the mind.* Do not encourage, or provide funding for, visits to regional and/or other countries that have implemented the same or similar reforms to learn about their implementation experiences, including project "pitfalls" and "derailments" that have occurred there.

4 *No ownership, no problem.* Provide all of the funding to cover all implementation costs (e.g., foreign and local consultants, IT hardware and software requirements, and other project expenses), so that authorities effectively have no "ownership" of reform measures and have no "skin in the game" (i.e., no significant counterpart funds and own resources).

5 *Act in haste, repent at leisure.* Assign fulltime advisors to in-country roles supporting reform implementation before project implementation plans have been finalized, related local resourcing requirements have been agreed with the authorities, and those resources have been assigned.

6 *Warm bodies are better than no bodies.* Recruit and assign "experts" to the reform project quickly even if they have limited, if any, specialist knowledge in the particular reform area, or indeed, in the delivery of reform projects.

7 *Part-time is better than no time.* Accept officials' assurances that local personnel assigned by the authorities to a project can undertake major project work on a part-time basis over an extended period, even as they required to carry out the responsibilities of their existing full-time positions.

8 *What's special about reform project work.* Assume that local personnel assigned to a reform project by the authorities have all the necessary skills and experience (especially in project management, business processes design and engineering, and IT), appropriate financial incentives, and the critical motivation to work effectively as members of a project team.

9 *Support local IT developers, of course.* Agree that IT requirements to support reforms can be developed by local firms located in-country, while ignoring the ready availability of "commercial off-the-shelf" (COTS) software and services from reputable international vendors.

10 *No progress, no consequence.* Ensure not only that project benchmarks and deadlines are <u>not</u> closely monitored via regular meetings of a high-level project steering committee, but also that there are no adverse consequences for the project team leader and members if they consistently fail to deliver agreed outputs according to the project plan.

Source: From author's anonymous International Monetary Fund (IMF) colleague
The important thing is to avoid responsibility for both implementation and results!
Ten top tips to ensure that a reform project will <u>not</u> be delivered on time and/or on budget

8   To learn how to use the Object of Expenditure budget to assess fiscal discipline.

9   To learn how to use a performance budget to assess both technical efficiency and efficiency of budget allocations between departments and functions.

10   To learn what functions a computerized financial management information system (FMIS) performs.

11   To learn how an *integrated financial management system (IFMS)* or *Government Financial Management Information System (GFMIS)* enhances the performance of the general ledger as well as budget preparation and execution.

12   To learn how the Ghanaian growth and expenditure model works and why it might be a rational response to the system of international development financing (*Discussion Case #11*).

13   To compare policing methods in Rio v Sao Paolo *favelas* and explain their differences (*Discussion Case #12*).

14   To discuss the question of whether the high Black police killings in Brazil and elsewhere is a product of racist history and inequality.

15   To discuss why development aid efforts to strengthen CEE/FSU local governments have been largely successful, in contrast with fiscal and management efforts with central governments.

16   To examine options for tax reform in Colombia that can minimize or prevent violent backlashes (*Discussion Case #13*).

17   Costa Rica lurches from fiscal crisis to crisis and IMF program to program as it struggles to maintain its well-known democratic social welfare state. The objective is to examine options for reform consistent with its political culture and history as well as IMF suggestions (*Discussion Case #14*).

18   Is Costa Rica following the lessons of Ghana in managing its public finances and dealing with the IMF?

19   Argentina has had 21 stand-by loans and programs with the IMF in 60 years. It has defaulted on its loans roughly 12 times. The objective is to discuss what the IMF might do differently to be more effective in wealthier transition countries such as Argentina and Costa Rica. The discussion should also generate options for how such countries might comply with structural reform suggestions and conditions without setting off violent backlashes.

20   To discuss answers to the question of whether in fiscal reform program design (e.g., South Korea), if economic recovery is threatening to democratic development, which reforms should take precedence? (*Discussion Case #15*). Refer to the Russia program in the early 1990s where donors, especially USAID, gave precedence to democratic reform.

21   To discuss how far IMF rescue packages should intrude on local economic management. Is it appropriate for IMF rescue packages to require far-reaching reforms such as opening its economy to foreign investment or economic liberalization?

22   To identify the proper contexts when structural reforms are necessary to restore access for such countries as South Korea (*Discussion Case #15*) to international capital markets.

Background on Public Financial Management

The macro-fiscal theory proposed by international donors consists of five simple budgeting principles based on the normative theory that fiscal discipline stabilizes fiscal conditions and leads indirectly to growth and development. Budgetary discipline leads to lower borrowing costs, more money to spend and invest on basic needs and capital assets. This leads to fiscal stability and growth of income and employment opportunities. Application of tested, orthodox fiscal policies and a professional state to enact socioeconomic policies and to manage relevant programs and projects are needed to stimulate and maintain growth. A professional public sector is needed to establish databases, supporting fiscal information systems, and the authority to generate real-time data for reporting balances and cash flows to facilitate fiscal management.

From the notion that a strong professional state is needed to guide and direct growth and development efforts, five fiscal management principles follow for healthy finances. They are simple and applicable for states and firms as well as personal finances.

First, Negative Balances or Fiscal Deficits on Current Spending Should Be Reduced to the Extent Possible

If large unplanned drags on revenues occur, the shocks must be responded to with stimulus spending, such as for the Covid-19 pandemic. The larger objective is to close the output gap (GDP before/after the external shock) as much as possible. The fiscal standards stressing discipline reflect the early *UN Government Financial Statistics (GFS)* standards established in the postwar 1940s at Bretton Woods and carried forward into IMF and rating agency borrowing criteria for rating and scoring prospective debtors. They are now part of *EU Stability and Growth Pact* fiscal criteria (deficits no more than 3% of GDP) that has, for example, moved countries such as Ireland and Denmark from agrarian backwaters to service economy powerhouses. The EU budget rule is a conservative but flexible standard to keep members on a rough course to budgetary rectitude and debt sustainability.

Object of Expenditures – Economic Classification

1. Salaries (e.g., 35% in RSA v 11% in OECD)
2. Fringe Benefits (80% payroll and pensions – Brazil)
3. Supplies (small equipment)
4. Operations and Maintenance (O&M) (travel and minor repairs)
5. Subsidies (price: e.g., explicit payments to producer or consumers of food, energy)
6. Fiscal Transfers/Individual Grants
7. Arrears (overdue payments to suppliers = forced financing)
8. Debt Service (annual interest portion of total repayment) (e.g., Ethiopia 40% of PY revenues)

----

9. Capital-Rehabilitation (infrastructure/major repairs)

Figure 4.1 Economic Budget Classification: Objects of Expenditures.
Source: Created by the author.

Second, Governments Should Try to Maintain Primary Surpluses

This means maintaining fiscal surpluses net of interest expenses in order to contain the debt trajectory from becoming unsustainable. Revenues should match expenditures less debt service (see *Figure 4.1*). That notion of primary balance is that often debts are run up by fiscally incontinent regimes for personal reasons such as building large expensive vanity projects and handing out cash to win elections. Many Arab States, such as Egypt, Jordan, and Tunisia, have debts of 90%–100% of GDP and little hope of paying them back or even covering periodic debt service. In places such as Egypt, debt service payments can swallow up to 50% of current revenues leaving little left over to pay the salaries and running costs that are needed to maintain services such as health, education, public transit, and sanitation.[7] In Ethiopia, debt service amounts to 40% of past year revenues (*Figure 4.1*). The goal of primary surplus criteria is to relieve fiscal pressure on poor countries and to stave off debt default as long as possible.

Third, Capital Investments Should Be Increased for Growth

Capital assets such as ports, bridges, roads, ports, water and sewer systems, and rolling stock for rail systems increase economic activity and stimulate growth. The process of planning capital projects, ranking, and financing is called the CIP. The analysis of financing options and rationales for ranking projects must be carefully managed to avoid intrusions by special interests. The construction and later rehabilitation of capital assets are considered below the line (line item #9 in *Figures 4.1 and 4.2*) and should be financed by long-term vehicles such as sovereign and municipal bonds or long-term loans and even long-term (e.g., 99 year) leases. They are not current expenses because they will benefit future generations in the long term (Guess, 2015: Chapter 4). The capital budget planning (1st FY + 4 more) is also used by

Capital Improvement Program (CIP)	Capital Budget (Appropriation)		Capital Program			Total
Year	2022	2023	2024	2025	2026	
Local Hospital	$500,000	$150,000		$3,000,000		$3,650,000
Local School Rehabilitation		$100,000	$50,000	$1,000,000		$1,150,000
Local Clinic			$75,000		$2,000,000	$2,075,000
Total	$500,000	$250,000	$125,000	$4,000,000	$2,000,000	$6,875,000

Figure 4.2 Capital Budget Planning Framework.

Source: Created by the author.

aid donors and called the MTEF. The concept is to plan out current and capital spending needs for the five-year framework and aggregate them into planned deficits. With these figures, the MOF can then roll the fiscal planning framework and decide which items and projects need to be reduced, delayed, or eliminated if forecasts of spending levels exceed revenues unsustainably.

Donors such as World Bank provide low-interest loans for capital and "development" assets that are often a mixture of current and capital assets such as schools and teachers. The debt structure of many poor countries has changed from traditional donors such as World Bank and now consists of mostly Chinese and commercial bank loans which often charge higher interest. Chinese loans are extended to less creditworthy borrowers, e.g., Pakistan, that collateralize its new assets, such as ports, for the loans. Several poor countries have gained new assets but eventually lost them to their new creditors which take over management and control. Due diligence and analysis of the costs and benefits of loan agreements should precede signing adhesion or one-way contracts that unreasonably cost the borrowers their futures.

Fourth, Make Fiscal Policy Counter-Cyclical

Fix the roof when the sun shines! Build up savings for the next storm! Cut expenses when times are hard! These maxims are roughly those of a small farmer reliant on a single crop for survival. Firms cut expenses to the bone to save and out-compete rivals. But when external shocks appear, sudden storms that require, for instance, airlines to cancel flights and rebook passengers, their textbook strategies of cost-cutting run up against reality. Failure to build up positive redundancy can damage operations and cripple firms. Cutbacks that lead to staffing shortages can also paralyze operations. This is true for governments that need to fill coffers when revenues are high, perhaps due to high commodity prices. But they have to recognize the necessity of maintaining core staff in order to continue operations when their revenues dip. They must manage their yearly cash flows to ensure funds are available from banks or their own reserves to quickly to fill gaps and pay their bills. They cannot (or should not) borrow long term to finance annual budget expenses, so sound cash management is crucial to their fiscal position (Guess, 2015: Chapter 5). As noted in the discussion of problem identification, revenue and expenditure shocks must be anticipated and planned for through such exercises as rolling plans and conducting regular and realistic fiscal scenarios. Part of the zero-based budgeting (ZBB) systems that dated from the 1960s was integrated into many state and local budget planning processes. This budget method and system required empirical assessments of: what is needed now (baseline services), what would be required with 15% fewer resources, and what could be done with 15% more.

Fifth, on the Revenue Side, Tax Bases Should Be Widened and Rates Lowered. (See Discussion Case #11: Implementing Tax Reform")

Modern systems incentivize taxpaying. The objective of tax policy is to generate tax collections through incentives to pay. A major incentive to pay and not to avoid taxes is a reasonable rate. Excessive rates actually lower collections and encourage both avoidance and evasion. Oppressive rates and archaic methods discourage taxpaying. Poor countries typically have low tax efforts/GDP precisely because of excessively high rates and cruel, archaic and ineffective tax collection systems. Indirect levies work well for such poorer countries as China and their Communist Party, because they lower citizen demands for democratic representation and provision of public goods. Levies on land sales, SOEs and VAT, or sales tax levies are the main sources of Chinese state revenue. By contrast, richer countries rely on direct taxes on individuals and corporations to finance spending needs[8]. Unlike authoritarian states, officials must answer to critics in an independent media and voters in regularly scheduled elections.

It was noted above that in the early 1990s the Armenian tax service used cattle prods and clubs to encourage tax collections through fear and random inspections. An important means enabling lowering rates is to widen the tax base as much as possible. This encourages widespread taxpaying rather than targeting the rich with high rates. In that way, the system is viewed as fair by all taxpayers. Another obvious way of encouraging widespread tax compliance is for the government to provide high-quality services and infrastructure. Consistent with counter-cyclical fiscal policy, consumption taxes (e.g., sales and VAT) should not be raised during recessions when many are unemployed. People are encouraged to pay for what they can clearly see is an exchange for goods and services. They trust their governments as legitimate and accountable providers of quality services.

Modernizing Public Financial Management Systems

Multilateral donors such as World Banks and IMF regularly perform fiscal reviews of member countries to identify structural and sectoral problems and recommend fixes, both short and long term. The trilogy of standards which the public finances should meet are fiscal discipline, allocational efficiency, and technical efficiency. The Fund concentrates on *budget discipline* which is essential for growth and macroeconomic stabilization, while the World Bank focuses on allocational and technical efficiency in order to stimulate economic development. Fiscal discipline refers strong financial management institutions to ensure minimal budgetary imbalances over the medium term (around 3% of GDP) and sustainable gross public debts (around 60% of GDP). Emphasis is placed on strong fiscal reporting, internal accounting controls, and internal audit institutions to minimize accounting leakages.

Allocational efficiency refers to budget allocations between sectors and the efficiency of those choices for poor countries and those in transition. Funds allocated to sectors without using basic marginal productivity analyses, such as excessive wages over funds for O&M or defense over social safety net urban transport, and education. Arab state budgets allocate scarce funds to unproductive line-items and sectors. Lack of basic cost-benefit or cost-effectiveness analyses as well as political pressures by special interests explains the pattern. In Egypt wages amount to 48% of discretionary spending. This leaves a much smaller share for allocation to schools, hospitals, welfare, and public services than a decade ago. Public sectors should provide public services absorb the unemployed, indirectly help expansion of the middle classes and reduce inequality. Arab states are not doing these tasks effectively despite their availability of ample budget funds. The average wage bill in rich countries is 20% of the budget, 30% in poor countries, and 40% in Arab states. The average share of public sector employment is 18% in OECD countries and 20% in Egypt. In Tunisia it is 60%, Saudi Arabia 58%, and Jordan 48% according to IMF.[9] Excessive funds are allocated to state civil services, including militaries and state enterprises, leaving social services and O&M needs badly underfunded. Excessive and distortionary budgetary allocations to state wages, state enterprises, and to defense sectors are inefficient from the growth and development perspective. The distortions away from basic services and social welfare are inefficient and make them harder to manage.

The third fiscal performance standard is *technical efficiency* which refers to the problem of under-maintained and poorly managed assets. That contributes to poor public services and lost development opportunities since capital assets and infrastructure are essential for growth. For these reasons, the Bank focuses on country provision of regular O&M in order to ensure that assets built with donor loans do not deteriorate. The basic PFM functions are budgeting (both current and capital) which is considered the lead function and central incentive system of government since budget composition and implementation are driven by local regime and electoral politics. The other core functions are treasury (payments and maintenance of state fiscal position), accounting (the foundation of budgeting which should cover consolidated government receipts and expenditures, i.e., enterprises, funds, off-budget entities, local governments), revenue (tax policy and administration), procurement (purchasing of current supplies and capital equipment), internal control and audit (ensuring that accounting systems function properly and maintaining vigilance against waste, fraud, and abuses of power of public expenditures and tax collections). The Fund and Bank seek to ensure that PFM functions work together smoothly. Many well-crafted fiscal policies have been derailed by weak PFM systems. For example, if budgetary accounting is weak, unrecorded cash transactions later turn into treasury commitments. Unauthorized payments then turn into outlays that are part of total uncontrolled expenditures. Audits discover that surprising levels of uncontrolled expenditures exceed originally planned budget expenditures. They contribute to increased fiscal deficits and their aggregate totals which become increased gross public debt burdens. Higher debt service payments of course crowd out other needed services from the current budget. As noted below, because of reckless borrowing for vanity projects and other public investments of little value to growth, Egypt's annual debt service payments are now 50% of the state budget!

Donor Reviews: The Trilogy of Fiscal Challenges and Standards

Ultimately, as a member of a donor technical assistance mission you are trying to beef up the transparency and consistency of budgetary and financial accounting. The main purpose of IMF missions and loan-driven stabilization programs is to stimulate growth. For instance, Nigerian GDP growth (2015–2021) has been only 1.1% with 0% predicted for 2023. Only economic growth can eliminate the cycles of fiscal stress and borrowing by a country such as Nigeria. The first step is to put the budget classification in order so that deficits and debt which hold back growth can be reliably ascertained. In its classification review, the mission wants to ensure that the budget covers all expenditures and revenues, and that they are classified according to GFS format standards. Thus, the IMF missions initially review the budget categories to make certain they measure only what they say they are covering. In FSU systems, budgets were simple accounting entries of cash debits and credits in journals and ledgers for use by the ministries of planning (MOPs)—there were no MOFs. Early missions to the FSU worked on reconciling the broad expenditure categories with the specific GFS economic budget format. This was absolutely essential to fiscal deficit and debt calculations from which annual performance could be gauged.

Wages and salaries, for instance, measured current and capital salaries for all government, including state enterprises as well as general government civil service. Instead of separate O&M in a current budget, spending and maintenance were included in capital expenses, both recurrent and periodic meaning capital rehabilitation expenses. These broad data entry categories made it difficult to distinguish what government expenditures actually were for in a fiscal year. Thus, the first job is to use the economic classification (*Figure 4.1*) as a basic framework for rational and exhaustive categorization of expenditures. In initial IMF missions to FSU countries, the task was essential to determine the meaning of the existing "economic" classification and how much or little the budget covered. For example, often social security and state enterprises for water, sewer, and transportation were included. Other times they were not. Fund missions had to work backward from expenditures and translate them into the UN Government Financial Standards "economic classification" or what we in the West consider a standard budget format.

Armed with data reported from these categories, budget totals provide a picture of budget discipline as evidenced by country income or operating statements, broken into sectoral allocations evidenced by use of a functional or sector budget classification (*Figure 4.3*) and spending toward the maintenance of assets and operations of services. For O&M spending efficiency, the member country can provide evidence by presenting line-item budget data in the economic classification as well as unit cost measures and ratios (i.e., O&M spending/% of total spending) *(see Figures 4.1 and 4.4)*. These basic data categories allow for more detailed expenditure analysis (Guess, 2015:Chapter 3). Some jurisdictions provide the public

| ($000s) | Program Services | | Support Services | |
	In Hospital Care	Clinical Care	General & Administration	Total
Salaries	$60,000	$13,700	$5,200	$78,900
Supplies	11,300	3,100	1,000	15,400
Rent	2,500	500	100	3,100
Other	2,300	200	100	2,600
Total	$76,100	$17,500	$6,400	$100,000

Figure 4.3 Functional Budget Classification: Hospital. Functional Budgets focus on major functions performed by an organization. This format is often used to report to outsiders. Note the line-item detail or object of expenditure detail in column 1.

Source: Finkler (2010:104) and from sources created by the author.

Figure 4.4 Performance Budget Format: Social Assistance Department. This Chart Provides the Operating Details, Financing Requirements and Resources for the Social Services Program Which Is in Part the Responsibility of SSSAD. From the Perspective of Departmental Program Management, SSSAD Could Then Be Viewed as an Organizational Subunit or Cost/ Responsibility Center with Three Major Sub-Programs, i.e., (1) Administration, (2) Social Services, and (3) Capital Investment. (a) Object of expenditure. (b) Performance. (*Continued*)

PERFORMANCE BUDGET ANALYSIS

DEPT: Social Service Assistance Department (SSSAD)	FUNCTION/ACTIVITY: SOCIAL SERVICES	FUNCTIONAL CODE: xxxx

Describes the duties and responsibilities of each program cost/responsibility center.

FUNCTIONS/ACTIVITIES DESCRIPTION:

(Formal and informal program/departmental duties and responsibilities)

SSSAD performs regulatory, oversight, monitoring and evaluation of social services. The Department is responsible for the staff functions pertaining to social services. It develops and makes proposals for regional operation of social assistance facilities, such as homes for disabled, elderly and children. The Department is responsible for advising on the level and composition of the annual recurrent and capital investment budgets for social services.

Nonfinancial program issues are identified that constrain effective performance.

PERFORMANCE ISSUES:

(Identification of key variables affecting program, basic data that indicate magnitude of problems or issues)

The demand for elderly, handicapped and children's homes exceeds supply by x%. The target population is x of which the program is only able to satisfy y # of clients or z %. The future demand is growing at the rate of x% and we can expect a target population in 3 years of y. In addition, the condition of x% of the facilities is poor and requires rehabilitation. This affects the quality of service to clients of social service homes. Part of the problem is that intergovernmental responsibility for social services is shared: 100% of capital funds are provided by the state budget while 100% of maintenance is a local responsibility. Only x% of funds are available from other support funds. The condition of facilities is difficult to monitor or evaluate on a regular basis due to the absence of a facilities condition monitoring system of personnel to utilize it.

Both quantitative and qualitative performance data are presented.

PERFORMANCE OBJECTIVES AND INDICATORS:

(Principal purposes of program and major quantitative indicators. Identify a few (1-3) workload measures) that can be monitored, e.g., # facilities maintained in good condition, link to operating costs or expenditures, and establish results measures, e.g., 90% coverage of potential demand for social services. Multiple performance indicators/measures should be developed, if possible, for: (1) *demand*—e.g., number of inspections, number of home residents; (2) *workload*—e.g., person months, passenger kilometers, bed days; (3) *efficiency*—e.g., operating cost/client, non-wage costs/home resident; and (4) *effectiveness*---e.g. cost/quality patient day, cost/5% increase in service coverage).

Qualitative measures are used to show how well a service is provided, and the level of customer (public) satisfaction.

To provide quality room and board to elderly, handicapped and children who meet legal requirements. To increase quality coverage of services in Fiscal Year 2002 from 70% to 85% of eligible clients. To improve monitoring and evaluation of facilities condition by increasing the number of inspections x % in FY 02. To reduce waiting lists for homes. To reduce unit costs of facilities operation to comparable systems or jurisdictions

SERVICE REVIEW	PAST YEAR ACTUAL 2000-2001	PAST YEAR ADJ. BUDGET 2000-2001	CURRENT YEAR 2001-2002	PROPOSED 2002-2003
QUANTITATIVE MEASURES OF SERVICE:				
Program Cost per home resident	$141.21	$190.25	$174.26	$204.43
% demand responded to within 1 month	New	New	72.5%	70.0%

Source: Created by the author.

# of facility condition inspections	16	20	17	24
# of recommendations for change or citations issued	6178	6487	7241	6616
% client service coverage met	65%	70%	75%	78%

FINANCING	PAST YEAR ACTUAL 2000-2001	PAST YEAR ADJ. BUDGET 2000-2001	CURRENT YEAR 2001-2002	PROPOSED 2002-2003
REQUIREMENTS:				
Personal Services	31,893,635	40,157,534	36,370,021	43,073,374
Non-personal Services	3,718,429	5,969,621	5,878,156	6,338,646
Interdepartmental Charges	148,733	330,542	307,536	513,186
Capital Outlay	6,844	0	0	0
Prior-year Encumbrances	6,694	2,011	98	0
TOTAL REQUIREMENTS	35,774,335	46,459,708	42,555,811	49,925,206
PERSONNEL QUOTA	30	23	23	25
RESOURCES:				
Fines, Forfeits, & Penalties	0	2,800,000	1,272,217	1,459,000
Rev from leases/rents	0	0	101	100
Revenues from Other Agencies	380,928	125,000	122,262	25,000
Charges For Current Services	0	0	295,143	310,000
Special Fund Revenues	17,371	1,000	34,387	200
Interfund Chgs for Svcs	857,261	1,442,182	1,684,847	1,177,220
Intragovt Fund Chgs for Svcs	0	0	9,897	373,323
General Fund	34,518,775	42,091,526	39,136,957	46,580,363
TOTAL RESOURCES	35,774,335	46,459,708	42,555,811	49,925,206

Figure 4.4 (Continued)

with spending in both classifications, to allow a rough "crosswalk" between object of expenditure and performance data by service that allows a reasonable estimate of service efficiency.

Performance budget formats and reporting practices, such as *Figure 4.4,* aim to increase service efficiency. Note that for the social assistance services target planned versus actual output results, as measured indirectly by # of customer complaints and responses to them. This is important information to gauge unit costs and service outputs. But experience suggests that substantial amounts of efficiency information can also be gleaned from detailed analysis of spending by line-items and subline items for non-personnel services, such as O&M and procurement, contracting, oversight, and utilization of equipment. Internal audit reviews of services using comparative data from other similar jurisdictions also provide insights into service efficiency and effectiveness. The advantage of using supplemental formats, such as functional (***Figure 4.3***) and performance categories, is that they incentivize collection and analysis of unit cost and outcomes or effectiveness in one annual process presented in one document transparently available to the public. They can serve as an alternative perspective on gathering and reporting line-item input data. Output and outcomes data can also provide supplemental information on both technical and allocational efficiency between departments and functions.

An implicit danger of spending staff time on generating output and outcomes data is that it overburdens the system filling out performance forms that should be spent on producing the results and efficiency outputs themselves. In other words, the result-oriented budget system contributes to goal displacement and wastes management time. For this reason, pressure in the UK is growing to eliminate such systems, for instance, abolishing its decades-old NHS Quality and Outcomes (Q&O) framework. This pay-for-performance framework incentivizes earning points for chasing 72 targets from chronic disease management to taking aspirin. It incentivizes goal displacement as general practitioners (GPs) have traded valuable time with patients for paperwork and potential pay increases. Patients are less likely to receive quality such as continuity such in seeing the same doctor. The core funding formula for allocating GPs to regional and local hospitals is also based on age not patient needs. The formula misallocates resources. The Q&O framework is viewed by most patients as an expensive waste of time.[10] Most importantly for results and performance budget systems, at the end of data generation, even if the measures are gamed by staff to produce the desired results, there is no incentive to actually use the information to manage an increase in service productivity. Funding is not linked to increases or decreases in results information by cost center, department, ministry, or organization—but it should be.

To continue with the task of assessing fiscal discipline, IMF considers budget discipline to be a valid record of maintaining deficit targets in a medium-term period. Installation of MTEFs in many member countries facilitates planning and reporting of progress in meeting spending targets. Monitoring and reporting progress is a good indicator of budget management capacity. Also critical is that member countries maintain sustainable debts. That means controlling debt service payments to sustainable levels (Nigeria's GDP is currently 111% which absorbs most of its current budget) and demonstrating measurable progress toward reducing gross public debts (typically by running primary surpluses or revenues minus spending less debt service). Ghana has been on an IMF diet of required primary surpluses for years and it confirmed the validity of this remedial approach with a projected 38% growth in GDP/person for 2023.

Functional budget formats are easy to compile since they are a combination of object of expenditure and expenditures classified into functions.

They are useful tools for quick assessments and analyses of the financial management of hospitals or similar revenue-generating organizations. Such organizations have relatively stable expenditure flows and constant need of accountability for results by unit or department. In *Figure 4.3*, the vertical columns are by results or outputs and the horizontal ones are by line-items or objects of expenditures. It is important that all budgets report minimal amounts for an "other" category. All expenditures should be accounted for if possible in comprehensive categories to determine maximum accountability for output results.

To continue with donor reviews of the budget management, the reviews focus particularly on the "plumbing" systems of budget execution. Timely and accurate reporting of revenues and expenditures must occur so that policy-makers can make plans knowing that the baseline figures are accurate and spending does not vary excessively from the plans. See *Figure 4.1* and refer to budget execution progress, outlays, and reports. In its *Public Expenditure Reviews*, for instance, World Bank drills down to gauge the quality of accounting and reporting systems at the sectoral as well as the national government levels. This provides useful information on country creditworthiness or ability to finance its budgets and repay its debts that is used by rating agencies such as Fitch's and commercial banks to assess loans. Newer donors, such as China (which is now a larger creditor than the IMF or World Bank), through its state entities such as its Development Bank, have suddenly become more interested in creditworthiness data as many of their past loans have soured on poorly appraised projects that might have been strategically important but were economically and financially unsound,[11] leading to China pursuing a new debt-relief approach.[12]

Thanks to funds from World Bank and other regional donors such as Asian Development Bank which also conduct expenditure reviews, much of the manual work of accounting and reporting has been converted from manual work by computerized financial management systems. These are called variously: GFMIS, IFMSs, or FMISs and are computerized multi-module general ledger systems. The multiple modules collect and control data in functional areas, such as treasury, purchasing, accounting, and budgeting which can be shared between them, i.e., inter-operability. In the national and/or local governments of over 100 countries, they take the form of packages that contain some or all PFM functions called modules.[13] As indicated in *Figure 4.5*, they integrate budget execution data and allow comparison with planned expenditures in real time. Cash flow balances are instantly available as well as payables and receivables in the balance sheet (BS in *Figure 4.4)*. Computerized links between budgeting, accounting, and treasury functions allow real-time coordination and inter-operability, exchanges of data, and daily balances into a treasury single account (TSA) for whole-of-government reporting (see *Figure 4.5*).

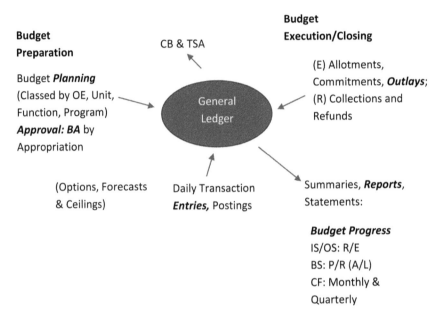

PFM Transactions with IFMS Support

Figure 4.5 Budget Transactions with IFMS Support.

Source: Created by the author.

The main computerized platforms are available from SAP and Oracle that install the systems and train MOF as well as spending ministry personnel. Such systems also reduce corruption in that approvals are real time by computerized signature which eliminates the manual steps that for centuries have delayed work only to be prodded along by side payments and bribes.

As noted, *Figure 4.5* illustrates the application of an IFMS to the key phases of the budget year: preparation, execution, and closing. Budget institutions, such as MOF and ministry of public works (MOPW), have to be linked up as they are often separate silos and impede fiscal accounting and reporting of consolidated figures. The data for periodic financial progress and closing reports is maintained now in real time. This allows for timely assessments of cash flow (monthly and quarterly), income balances (from the income statements), and payable liabilities and receivable assets as accrued commitments from the balance sheet. Such IFMS-generated data is extremely valuable for assessment of fiscal condition and quality of fiscal management by donors, creditors, auditors, and rating agencies.

To properly gauge the status of fiscal discipline, the quality of revenue forecasts must also be included, such as the capacity of the tax administration system to collect forecasted revenues and ensure that they are deposited in treasury accounts. This means the PERs and IMF Aide-memoires must be able to identify any sources of fiscal leakage, whether from failures in expenditure system plumbing or inaccurate revenue forecasts and faulty tax and fee collections, which could be caused by corruption. Poor countries typically have low tax efforts measured as a % GDP compared with richer countries. For example, the tax revenues collected as % GDP in Pakistan (12.5%) and Nigeria (3.6%) compare unfavorably with democratic well-managed countries such as Costa Rica (24.1%), Colombia (18.1%), Botswana (14.0%).[14] Citizens in the former two countries, for example, lack trust in their governments that fail to allocate tax revenues to needed services. Low taxpaying rates from such weak tax administrations and corresponding high individual tax evasion rates mean that overall tax rates are excessively high and tax bases are narrow. This means that the few wealthy people in such countries provide most of the tax collections that finance budgets, which is unfair and inefficient. That is exactly opposite of a fair, efficient, and effective tax regime which should consist of low rates and wide tax bases. Again, this revenue incapacity keeps poor states weak and illegitimate in the eyes of citizens and voters. Services must be financed by fiscal transfers from central government and donor loans and grants.

All this keeps states and their local governments financially weak and dependent on funds from the central government or from overseas loans. Such conditions favor populists with their simplistic and utopian solutions, political instability, frequent unplanned changes of political regime, and instances of mob rule. Development aid focused on strengthening tax administration and fiscal controls provides technical assistance and training to beef up MOFs and local finance departments. Past and current aid from IMF, World Bank, and USAID missions and programs increases local revenue and expenditure managerial efficiencies but often fails to penetrate or generate the political will needed to enforce tax collection and widen tax bases. Few candidates can be elected on a tax efficiency platform and the cycle of fiscal instability continues!

At the most basic mission management function, the technical assistance review missions must be staffed with experienced quality personnel to complete their scopes of work on both the expenditure or revenue assessment missions. It is important that the team leader knows who and how to select people that will maximize synergies and achieve the most for their efforts in the limited time of the mission. In *Table 4.1* there are tips and suggestions by an experienced team leader (and former colleague of mine) for staffing his IMF technical assistance missions.

Other multilateral organizations such as OECD and bilateral donors such as USAID conduct regular in-country fiscal assessments, which also include expenditure management and revenue collection systems. Donor missions in PFM are staffed using criteria and with expectations similar to those contained in *Table 4.1*. USAID, for example, has conducted over 60 fiduciary risk assessments since 2011. As noted in the introduction to the Pakistan case above (#8), international development assistance from the US has historically been centralized. Allocations are made in Washington and devolution of authority to country officials is virtually non-existent. This means that aid contributes to allocational inefficiency by excluding country officials and public opinions on where US aid should be allocated. Other donors devolve substantial amounts of their development assistance to country financial management system: Norway (56%), UK (53%), World Bank (36%), and the US (15%). The amounts and longevity of US DA projects are mostly much higher and longer than the other three donors.[15]

Further, to improve allocational efficiency and the value for money of overseas aid, ways should be found to devolve authority for planning and spending this aid to host countries. The risks of mismanagement, theft, or misuse of funds could with PFM reforms to accounting and reporting to USAID be outweighed by the benefits of giving locals stakes in the planning as well as the use of aid funds to their country. This would be especially important for grants as well as loans that add to their country's debt burdens. Devolution of aid to country financial management authorities encourages locals to increase the *technical efficiencies* of spending for O&M, since they would choose spending from their own country operating budgets. Their stake would be to spend for maintenance of their own hospitals, buses, schools, roads, and clinics.

Managing PFM Systems Reforms

It is often said that baseball is a good model for International Development Management (IDM). That is because team chemistry and cohesion matter most to winning and succeeding. Managers who are good at creating chemistry among their players and between the team and themselves seem to produce the most cohesive and successful teams.[16] Some of this applies to managing successful aid projects. In the early 2000s, as part of a five-year USAID local government budget and tax reform project in Romania, I led a five-person team of local specialists to devise and install reforms in 15 cities. We worked with mayors and finance directors to install multi-year budget formats and corresponding databases. The team members knew their areas of expertise: computerized finance systems, tax, fee and budget forecasting methods, and capital financing methods. We added the MYEP format and combined current and capital budget information, as well as the written descriptions of local fiscal conditions and threats on the horizon to growth of tax and fee revenues. Our plan was to replicate useful parts of Official Statement (OS) used for bond issuance by municipal borrowing and MTEF rolling expenditure plans to support local asset borrowing in capital markets. The team was enthusiastic, and we worked long hours together. I was able to introduce finance directors to regional CEE representatives of Fitch rating service to facilitate demonstrations for what these cities were doing. The results were successful as cities developed their intended budget reforms, databases, borrowed on capital markets, repaid three- to five-year loans, and mayors were re-elected!

The team and I got on well—we socialized in the towns, ate together, drank together, and kept in touch after we went our separate ways after project completion. I once asked a colleague at IMF when I worked there, why this kind of camaraderie developed. Besides the experience of working together on specific tasks, he mentioned that it was like camping out. People from all over come to your campfire at night, you drink, eat, and share stories and then you go your separate ways, vowing to stay in touch, but usually don't.

From my team leader end, I supported their ideas, bantered with them and met their families, and, of course, liked them. The vibes must have been mutual as the work far exceeded our expectations. I should say "our" expectations because we did what was needed for the objective—modern budget systems and database reforms and actual usage by city officials in future year budgets. From the city end, they used the reformed documents and systems to obtain loans to finance assets such as roads, bridges, schools, hospitals, and equipment such as vehicles for police, fire, and sanitation services.

It should be added that much of our camaraderie may be attributed to our feeling of achieving these ends in spite of our "clients": USAID and HQ people in Washington or staff from regional offices, such as Bucharest for CEE. We found them to be intrusive and focused on progress metric surveys with measures made up by generalists in far of places that we felt had never actually worked in PFM. That made us work around them, often break rules gleefully, in order to satisfy the mayors and finance directors and get the jobs done.

Issues and Cases

Discussion Case #11: IMF and Ghana: Deadbeat or Star Performer?

For years, Ghana has repeatedly overspent its state budget and run up unsustainable debts. But in a peculiar pattern, it often plans to overspend and happily welcomes the IMF and its conditional austerity programs.

Since 1957, it has had 17 IMF austerity programs for debt relief. In 2021, 44% of annual budget revenues went to pay debt service on foreign loans. It has an unsustainable gross public debt of 84% of GDP. Inflation is now 18%, the highest in 18 years. Annual fiscal deficits are the well-known product of deliberately high spending and a low tax effort of only 12% GDP. The African average ratio of tax revenues to GDP is a low 15%, but that is still higher than Ghana's. Other poorer countries such as Colombia, Chile, and Costa Rica, all of which are political democracies, have much higher tax effort ratios of 18.8%, 24.1%, and 20.2%, respectively.

In this familiar context of fiscal crises and timid policy responses, officials of such poor countries such as Ghana use the IMF as cover for accepting fiscal austerity conditions that they know they need but are afraid of the political costs and inevitably blame for the social unrest that typically follows the publicity that accompanies signing the IMF program documents. One conclusion is that democracies have stronger institutions enabled by constant pressures of elections, media criticism, and citizen demands for representation and public goods than in weaker African democracies and authoritarian states.

Yet, Ghana is a functioning democracy and maintains social cohesion by spending borrowed IMF funds on schools, roads, and hospitals. Institutional graft is relatively high, derived mostly from rent-seeking by police and religious leaders. But graft is high or higher in most other African regional countries. Ghana's GDP/person is expected to grow 38% in 2023. Rating agencies have in the past penalized Ghana for its fiscal misbehavior. But it does pay its debt service payments on time. Given the predictable regularity of fiscal crises, IMF programs, fiscal policy, and management reforms to cut spending and strengthen controls, followed by overspending, leading to new IMF programs, lenders wait in line to lend the Government of Ghana more funds. Everyone stays in business and all parties are reasonably satisfied. As chief of party of a new IMF fiscal review mission, draft a memo to your team members on the "terms of reference" of an approach that might be taken to define its fiscal and economic problems, develop and analyze options, and to recommend preferred actions to the Ghanaian MOF.

What is Ghana's unorthodox public expenditure and growth model? Is it surprising given how donor development financing works? Should it be copied elsewhere in Africa? Is it copied already? What are causes and consequences of deficit spending in Ghana? What are Ghana's actionable fiscal problems? Which ones should they tackle first and how? Should it be considered racist to criticize deficit spending there as the minister of finance asserts?[17]

Discussion Case #12: Police Budgeting in Brazil: Defund or Reallocate to Adopt More Modern Methods?

Background and Problems

Police killings of Black people in poor areas of Rio known as *favelas* are extremely common. Rio is divided into the rich whiter area of Zona Sul that includes the Ipanema beach community and the poor favelas of Zona Norte. "Black" here means *negros*—brown, mixed race, and indigenous Indians or roughly *morenitos, mestizos,* and *Indios* in Spanish. Overall, 80% of those killed by police here are then "Black". Police killed 8,400 last year of which 1,800 were killed in Rio alone. The murder rate in Rio is twice that of all the US which has a population 19 times larger.

Experts attribute the high rate of Black killings to three causes:

History and Racism

Brazil was the last country in North and South America to outlaw slavery. Today, Black people are 56% of the population but 70% of the poor. Unemployment for Black people is 17% and 12% for whites. White people earn two times the level of Black incomes. In Rio's Black favelas there is no sewerage, jobs are mostly informal, lots of drugs are for sale and consumed, and teens walk around carrying AK-47s despite the location of police stations nearby. Reported crime often results in encounters between locals and heavily armed police units. Enforcement tactics are the "iron fist" (*mano dura* in Spanish) yet violence levels have stayed the same or increased, especially after such encounters. The Black Lives Matter movement in the US, starting several years ago, placed racism and racialist policing and communities on the management and policy agendas in many countries, and especially US, Brazilian, and UK cities.

That the recent beating and killing of an unarmed Black motorist in Memphis (TN), for example, was perpetrated by five Black policemen suggests that police supervision and management is a much more actionable explanation for Black killings in urban places such as Rio and Memphis with high concentrations of poor Black people than racism, poverty, or inequality. As found by Phillip Zimbardo's experiments in the 1970s, institutional roles and the aura of authority determine violent individual behavior far more than had been thought.[18]

Inequality

The legacy of 1930s laws still on the books created what many Brazilians term a "racial democracy" or a segregationist attempt to deal with obviously stark inequalities.[19] By this description, Brazil is not racist but rather a place where races segregate themselves with state policy assistance. Favelas lack running water, connected sewer systems, and access to basic services such as transit, clinical services, and quality schools. Social and cultural projects have been constructed but suffered budget cuts in 2019 after they were built for the Olympics as showcase efforts. Police pacification units were also created as part of the efforts at community policing. But most pacification and community policing units were cut from the budget. Such units in wealthier white areas as Ipanema still exist and are extremely successful at maintaining contact and building trust with locals.

Archaic Police Methods

Most blame the tough enforcement by civil and military police for the spate of Black killings. Black people remain three times more likely than whites to be homicide victims than whites. Most of the killers are Black. But not all experts buy the racist policing as the main explanation for the high levels of Black murders. Sao Paulo has retained its community policing methods and anti-racism training. They have made incremental reforms such as having ambulances on call and preventing local schools from being bases for police units during raids. Sao Paulo still requires police to wear body cams. The Black lieutenant colonel in charge of the reform effort there notes that 1/3 of the police are Black but amount to 2/3 of the police deaths. In the wake of such reforms, Black killings by police in Sao Paolo have dropped dramatically. But overall, police retain their old tough enforcement methods and continue to make heavily armed appearances in Black favelas. They resist accountability for killings enabled by abolition of the internal affairs units and the security secretariat that oversees police management and actions.

Recent empirical studies from similar urban contexts with high poorer Black populations such as Chicago by Mummolo (2023)[20] confirm the need for diversifying the police. Evidence from Chicago comparing the number of arrests and uses of force between Black and Hispanic officers in black high-crime areas found that White officers used 60% more than Black officers and that White officers used force with a gun 50% more than Black officers. In short, officers of different racial, ethnic, and gender identities do their jobs differently. Diversification is one of many reforms, but as found in the Brazilian and US cities, it can help reduce the use of gun-related force and the number of physical confrontations in the process of arrests.

Remedial Options

Remedies tried and often discontinued include community policing which had worked demonstrably better in Sao Paolo but discontinued in Rio and major cities around the world. The rate of Black city killings by police in communities with pacification tactics, such as with body cams, anti-racist policing training, and high proportions of police in favela districts with large Black populations worked well, in contrast with cities such as Rio. It is also evident that police do need to carry arms but not patrol in large military-type occupation forces on a routine basis. That tactic only reinforces the separation of the police from its surrounding community and perpetuates distrust. An additional remedy is to weed out the rotten apples from police forces that have poor leadership and ingrained toxic cultures of bullying and brutal policing methods. For example, in the 1980s a culture of bullying trainees and new recruits known as "initiation rites" had taken hold. This was eradicated through severe an uncompromising disciplinary action. In one unit, the commanding officer was sacked along with a swath of the unit's hierarchy not because they had participated in the abuse but because they had not prevented it. In the 1990s, the Canadians disbanded an entire regiment when it was found to have been infiltrated by neo-Nazi groups. It was found that such actions, boldly cutting off the rotten heads, actually reinforced the essential values and purposes of the police organizations.[21]

It is also clear from the Brazilian case that police in high-crime Black urban areas must be prepared and have the authority and equipment to respond to violent attacks, mediate, call in social or mental health workers to do whatever it takes to pacify the area. Underfunding of favela cultural centers, athletic equipment and facilities, basic services, and community police units suggests the need for funding formulae that give extra weight to poorer, higher crime areas in major cities such as Rio and Sao Paolo.

Mayors in cities such as Rio have the authority to modify their funding formulae to target and upgrade services in their favelas and informal communities. The Brazilian federal system, like others in Mexico and Argentina, devolves substantial tax, budget, and borrowing authority to mayors and local governments as independent layers of government. Under existing fiscal decentralization laws in such countries, Brazilian mayors are expected to work with local inhabitants and community leaders to provide needed services. Unlike most mayors in other regions of the world, Latin American mayors are directly elected and not appointed by the federal government. That means they are responsible and accountable to voters in those districts. Mayors frequently use innovative financing methods to create and upgrade infrastructure to their voters such as Betterment Districts and tax increment financing to pay for new assets from the property appreciation in their districts. Latin America is the most urbanized region of the world with 81% of the population living in cities. This means crime and policing problems will only worsen unless mayors face them and use their authority to act.

Policing poor areas of wealthy cities is a major worldwide problem and many reform models have been applied. Which ones have succeeded and failed? Why? How should funds be spent for *favela* security in Rio de Janeiro? Review how successful remedies, such as community policing units, police pacification units, and police body cameras, have been in reducing violence in similar urban contexts.[22]

Discussion Case #13: Implementing Colombian Tax Reform

President Ivan Duque presented a tax reform bill to the Colombian Congress in 2021 based on standard fiscal austerity principles. Its main components were an increase in income taxes, elimination of many VAT exemptions, and lowered threshold for income taxpaying, and taxation of pensions. To compensate, the bill would increase social spending substantially. Most experts agreed that Colombia's tax regime needed reform. The fiscal deficit had climbed to 8%/GDP and its tax effort/ GDP (both rates and collections) was one of the lowest in the OECD. Its tax-to-GDP ratio was only 19.5% compared to the OECD average of 32.9%.

The context of this crisis was that Colombians had just endured a long Covid-19 lockdown and businesses had to be temporarily shuttered. Overall, 80% were opposed to this bill and called for more radical spending measures such as for guaranteed incomes. Violent protests followed introduction of the bill and 800 police and civilians were injured. Duque sent in the army to restore order. Despite Duque's campaign pledges, crime was also rampant, and lack of public safety was evident in poor health, security, and welfare services. The 2016 FARC peace deal was largely holding but rural peace and development was threatened daily by terrorism and killings by other splinter groups. Duque withdrew the tax bill and called for a national dialogue. The finance minister resigned the next day. Gustavo Petro, a leftist who had campaigned for the central bank to print money and spend it on programs for the poor and to ditch any ideas of tax increases, was elected President one year later in 2022.

Often political leaders, especially in Latin America, freeze when facing severe fiscal crises and are unable to compartmentalize problems, put them in priority, and seek out comparative examples of what worked and what didn't (ignoring or not knowing about such simple techniques as the *Matched-Case* method) (discussed in **Chapter 3**). They often go boldly ahead proposing short-term fixes and get into deeper trouble as President Duque did here. Weak governments are often loth to widen their tax bases and lower their tax rates (consistent with *sound fiscal policy principle or practice #5*) in order to try and collect more revenues from fear of political and social repercussions. The rule that consumption taxes should not be raised during a recession is part of that same fifth principle. More practical principles and options for designing a sound tax reform program and implementing it effectively are needed before it can be sold as parts of standby arrangement and structural adjustment/austerity programs especially in Latin American countries.[23]

Managing tax increases, either by rate increases or new taxes by cutting fuel subsidies, are potentially high-risk politically fraught decisions in all countries. Countries with ballot boxes and regular elections can eliminate sound leaders who are unable to sell tax increases without, for example, adding increased to minimum incomes through cash transfers or increasing the minimum wage by laws or regulations. In countries, such as Nigeria with serious security problems as well as ailing economies, leaders must proceed cautiously and compensate any tax increases with additions to income. In Nigeria, for example, in addition to rescuing the economy newly elected President Bola Tinubu has to deal with separatists in the southeast and clashes between herders and farmers in the center, a jihadist insurgency in the northeast, and rampant kidnapping gangs in the northwest.

Questions

Several basic management principles have been identified to support economic reforms in such diverse cases as defending free trade against the protectionist British Corn Laws in the 1840s, and modern efforts to preserve modern democratic institutions against populist tyrannies worldwide, as well as the recent Nigerian effort to implement elimination of costly fuel subsidies. For many Nigerians, cheap subsidized fuel is the only benefit they get from the country's vast oil wealth.[24] On the other hand, because of the high costs of drilling and production and price ceilings, the state oil firm Nigerian National Oil Corporation (NNPC) pays nothing into the national treasury to support budgets and currency reserves. The oil sector is a drain on growth and development. Four tried and test economic reform principles are well-known (1) clearly explain to the public what the reform is and what steps will be taken, (2) organize a broad coalition and creatively use the social media, (3) go for small victories to gain momentum, and (4) demonstrate tangible public benefits. How have these principles been applied or not in the case of Colombian tax reform?

Discussion Case #14: Costa Rica: No Longer Top of the Class; Argentina: Still at the Bottom

Costa Rica was known for years as the Switzerland of Latin America. Since the late 1940s it established the first rate national educational and health care system that produced a healthy, highly literate population. It has a broad social safety net, including a national pension system. In those early days, the army was also abolished and spending for education, health, and welfare mandated in the constitution. Like other LA countries such as Uruguay and Chile that contrast with regional neighbors, it is a stable social welfare state. It manages its energy and tropical forests well and generates substantial revenues from ecotourism. Hydropower provides almost 100% of its energy needs. It was one of the first to take advantage of debt-nature swaps (DNSs) that preserve its carbon-absorbing tropical forests in exchange for offset payments. Its HDI (UN human development indicator) score is very high at 0.77. Its government is ranked effective (67%) by World Bank Governance Indicators. It is an older functioning democracy with contestable presidential elections and orderly changes of government every six years. Parties represent all interests in an inclusive state and there have been no fringe populist presidents or violent protest movements to disrupt politics and policy.

But it costs a lot to provide this high quality of life. Its gross public debt is 68% of GDP (third highest in Latin America) and debt service payments are 8.1% of GDP. Like Ghana described in *Discussion Case #11*, it lurches from fiscal crisis to crisis and borrows heavily from donors. It is a high-spending high-service state. For instance, 2,200 of its 305k state employees (for a population of 5m) earn twice as much as the President—currently Carlos Alvarado. In January of 2021 it negotiated an IMF stabilization loan of $8b. Costa Rica spends 7% of GDP on education, paying public school teachers seven times the level of private school teachers. Yet its state students rank second lowest in international PISA scores. It spends more than 50% of its budget on state salaries, the highest in the OECD. Costa Rica needs structural reforms to avoid default, such as cutting tax evasion, increasing taxes, and selling off state monopolies such as the telecoms authority (ICE). Without them, it risks becoming a politically unstable deadbeat like its Central American neighbors: Nicaragua, Honduras, and Guatemala.[25]

Meanwhile, one of IMFs regular customers and slower learning pupils, Argentina, continues to perform poorly. But unlike Ghana, it borrows without abiding by reform conditions and it has trouble repaying even the debt service on Fund loans. Despite multiple loans over many years, Argentina has had major problems getting its fiscal house in order. Argentina has had 21 standby arrangements (loans for reform promises) with the

IMF over the past 60 years and it has defaulted seven times. A new IMF loan negotiated 2018 was conditioned on dropping its fiscal deficit from 3% to 0.9% by 2024 through more efficient tax collections.

But it defaulted again in 2020, leaving the 2018 loan agreement in limbo. Current negotiations between the Fund and the Argentinian government are trying to revive the 2018 loan agreement and delay repayments on it, such as the $40b it currently owes! The 2018 loan was the largest in Fund history and premised on reassuring markets that it would get private capital funds flowing again in the form of foreign investment to Argentina. For its part, the Fund did not expect to disburse the full loan as market conditions in Argentina improved. But markets remained wary of investing there and the Fund had to disburse $44b of the $57b loan.

President Mauricio Macri (a "liberal" fiscal reform advocate) lost to Cristina Fernandez (a Peronist or populist spender) in 2019. Fernandez promptly canceled the 2018 Fund loan and tried to restructure $100b directly with foreign currency debt by using private creditors. But international market conditions were tight. As GDP dropped by 8%, commodity prices also weakened for exports of wheat and beef cattle, and the fiscal deficit climbed to 4%. The current macroeconomic and fiscal context is grim: inflation at 50%, overvalued exchange rate (5% of parallel market or black market rate). But it has shown some progress in the fiscal area by cutting the 2021 primary deficit from 9% to 3%.

At this time, IMF did an internal review of the 2018 loan fiasco and found that it was mostly to blame itself. It concluded that the Fund cannot demand more conditions that won't be met because of structural and political obstacles. For example, the Fund can demand as it has many times before cuts to utility rate subsidies, cuts or elimination of price controls on 1,400 imports and items for domestic consumption, and elimination of bans on beef exports. Local politicians blame each other as they have for years. The clock is ticking for real fiscal reform as falling into arrears on Fund loans will cut them off from other multilateral lenders and international capital markets. Argentina currently owes the IMF a debt service payment of $40b! This is roughly 20% of annual expenditures.

A related but less known problem is that the IMF repeatedly imposes conditions on lenders such as Argentina but does not enforce the commitments. The Fund later finds itself faced with borrowers in arrears without realistic recourse—it cannot realistically impose more conditions.

For instance, without firm and enforceable country commitments in Argentina, the IMF has for many years conditioned loans on demilitarizing its economy. The army owns and operates most of the non-strategic sector such as fish-farming, olives, mineral water, gas stations, and car-making. These army-state enterprises pay no taxes or customs fees. Like Argentina, Egypt, which is the IMFs biggest debtor after Argentina, has asked for a fourth bail-out in six years. Egypt pays 50% of its annual budget revenues to service its debts that are an unsustainable 90% of GDP. The Fund has conditioned past loans on demilitarization yet failed to enforce the commitments. For donor management failures such as this, and others mentioned in its own report on Argentina, the Fund deserves blame.[26] As in Argentina, the old joke in Egypt is leave for ten days and everything changes; leave for 20 years and everything seems the same!

And Argentina stays the same, in large part, because of its consistently bad trade policies. Given its long pattern of peculiar policies and bad results, one might say that its plight is the result of the self-inflicted pain of bad domestic policies and judgments rather than IMF strictures. Management is about solving fixable policy and institutional problems that impede development. Remember: trade and investment fortified by aid should lead to more growth and development. But in Argentina trade has been deliberately stunted by agricultural export taxes (one of only a dozen countries in the world to impose such as tax. Trade amounts to only 33% of GDP, one of the lowest shares in the world. With annual inflation at 114% (the 3rd highest in the world), 43% of its citizens cannot pay for basic foodstuffs.[27]

Meanwhile, as noted, Argentina has had 21 standby arrangements with the IMF in 60 years. Yet the country has defaulted on all its loans almost a dozen times (nine going on ten if the latest IMF negotiations fail) and its public finances and investor confidence are still in shambles. The annual inflation policy rate is 113% and the market rate is 113%. Has the IMF been too neocolonial (bossy) or too neoliberal (free market hubris) with Argentina? The obvious background question is: if IMF is known for lax enforcement, what incentives do its borrowers have to comply with its loan conditions? Is the Fund-Argentina problem: local economic and financial mismanagement, policy failures, political culture, or a combination of all of them? Should the pupil make more effort to reform in exchange for all the money it has received over the years? Why has the IMF been more successful in countries such as Costa Rica and even Ghana?[28]

We should stress that development management can occur without the deus-ex-machina of external aid projects. Country policy-makers and officials can and do make useful decisions to improve governance. They need not wait for IMF conditions or externally financed development projects to make sensible and better policies. They can strengthen their own states. But Argentina "stays the same" because these decisions are often not made, and if they are they are reversed or not implemented. A shrink might ask: what causes such repetitive self-defeating behavior?

**Closing the Reform Loop: Detailing Responsibilities
and Expected Results**

Fiscal assistance (one example of ODA) in support of loans such as
those to Ghana and Argentina is designed and targeted through the
efforts of missions to assess needs, define problems, and offer best practice remedial systems, tools, and methods. Fiscal managers from donors and host countries must report progress, monitor progress, and
evaluate host or counterpart efforts. An important tool for this used
by aid managers is the written "reform commitment". Technical assistance missions work with top- and mid-level country officials for several weeks at a time over requiring multiple visits, to obtain approval
and demonstrate commitment to recommended reforms as well as to
report on implementation progress. An example of a country reform
commitment is *Table 4.2* for a tax administration system to improve
revenue collection. Another common fiscal reform is for installation of
performance budgeting systems (see *Figure 4.4*) that measure results
and outputs of expenditures. Such systems improve the efficiency of
public budgeting systems and make progress monitoring more meaningful than simply tracking raw outlay or input spending. Reform commitments have resulted in the installation and use of many successful
Performance and Program Budgeting systems at national and local levels of government.

But there have been spectacular fiascos and one cause is the failure to
assign and enforce responsibilities for discrete tasks to counterparts. Here
are sardonic tips from an aid "old hand" on what to avoid when managing
a technical assistance mission.

More Questions

Suppose you are on an IMF or World Bank mission to review the public
finances and recommend needed improvements for these two countries.
Applying the principles and practices presented of sound fiscal management noted previously in this chapter, how and why should Costa Rica
manage its public finances differently to decrease its fiscal deficit and public debt?

For instance, one means of cutting deficits is to increase the efficiency
of expenditures. As a mission team leader you might have developed a
budget reform in which the budget data would be reported in outputs
or units costs by function in addition to object of expenditure inputs.
These reforms have been very common for local governments in CEE
and other Former Soviet "satellite" Republics. Some have been very
successful such as in Poland.[29] Others in hard line Soviet system institutional hangover cities in such countries as eastern Ukraine and Balkan

states such as Bulgaria have not been.[30] To install them successfully you and your team would want to ensure that your mission counterparts reform the reporting formats from inputs to outputs. An important task is aligning the charts of accounts and budget codes. In addition you would want to have the ministry of finance improve staff incentives to report unit cost output performance data by service (e.g., urban transport). Incentive, such as reduction of redundant data reporting elsewhere in the budget process, can free up time wasted on reporting meaningless fiscal data of no practical utility to fiscal or physical results. Finally, you would expect the host country budget staff to actually use the new budget data for analysis to develop budget totals for the next fiscal year.

Financial Management and Fiscal Control

IDMs are often frustrated and discouraged when they know serious country problems exist and can be addressed by rather simple and effective tools if the will is there within their own development organizations and in the countries themselves. Dysfunctional turf-ego-power problems persist everywhere that divert funding from where it is most needed. The need is to stay focused and fight for one's agenda, e.g., often a remedial project. It is important that, like Warburton, one not give up and to keeping adjusting to the constraints of the political culture that make internal factionalism much more intense.

As noted, fiscal discipline is critically important for effective financial management at both national and local levels. And, it is well known that devolving spending and project planning and implementation authority to local governments in Latin America is fraught given their small size and lack of fiscal capacity. They have never managed anything but transfers for the central governments. Despite this, the share of expenditure controlled by subnational layers of government has doubled to 25% between 1985 and 2015 on the theory that local governments are more responsive to local needs and more democratic. Mostly authoritarian central governments have long provided their meager funds via fiscal transfers that covered few of their needs. Thus, an important Peruvian reform in the early 2000s ruled that 50% of corporate tax revenues should be earmarked to the local communities in which copper (mostly) mining and fossil fuel drilling took place. This was an enormous fiscal windfall to the many small towns (60% of district municipalities have fewer than 5,000 inhabitants) that had little or no services management of financial control experience. A recent study found, for instance, that poor cash management of sewerage projects was causing accidental releases of waterborn pestilences that killed many infants all due to the inability of localities to complete projects or spend the budgeted funds as scheduled. New funds caused greater local fiscal corruption and social conflicts as local factions fought over spending priorities.

The lack of local fiscal and management capacity was recognized early on by the MOF and local government NGOs such as the Red de Municipalities Rurales del Peru (REMURPE). LGI financed a team including the author and two colleagues from the Andrew Young School of Policy Studies at Georgia State University to assess the fiscal capacity and control problem and develop a multi-year capacity-building program. The goal was to make fiscal decentralization work in Peru and in similar context around Latin America. The intent was to attract follow-on support from World Bank, Inter-American Development Banks, and other nonprofits and foundations. The recent study suggests that such efforts were not effective. One notable finding was paradoxical that to be effective fiscal decentralization programs must be managed and controlled by a strong, legitimate, and trusted central government which, at the very least, must be capable of seconding personnel to communities that receive windfall transfers to manage and control their finances and capital projects until capacity becomes sufficient. This has been the basis of success for the fiscal devolution regional programs in Chile, Bolivia, and Colombia as well as in Southeast Asia in the Philippines.[31]

Discussion Case #15: "Structural Adjustment and Local Partners: Managing the Asian Meltdown: The IMF and South Korea"

Background and Core Problems

"In the 1970s, South Korea industrialized and grew under the stimulus of President Park's program of chaebol (industrial conglomerates) expansion driven by heavy borrowing from banks with state loan guarantees. The chaebols borrowed far beyond their worth, averaging debt equity/ratios of about 4:1. By 1980, the rice crop failed, the '79 oil price shock hit world markets, and chaebol debts became unpayable, triggering state loan guarantees that added to fiscal deficits. South Korean GDP growth fell by 5%. An IMF austerity program in that year stabilized the economy. To finance growth and adjustment, South Korea continued to borrow more in private capital markets, increasing its debt burden. But the economy regained growth through its increased exports. While the IMF economic and political liberalization program required South Korea to open its markets to foreign investment and begin holding democratic elections, nevertheless, the unions and chaebols retained their privileges, such as connected lending, and were able to acquire yet more loans.

In 1997, in the context of the Asian currency meltdown, IMF imposed another austerity program on South Korea much more severe than that in 1980 to stabilize the economy. This one was a $57b rescue package (the largest IMF program for any nation at the time). The conditions required severe public spending cuts, raising borrowing rates, and raising taxes. The negative economic and social shock was almost immediate. Unemployment shot up to 8.5% from 1996; 10k workers/day lost their jobs; small business bankruptcies reached record highs; and small business owner suicides averaged one/day; even large chaebols went bankrupt from their inability to repay or reduce any of its debt/equity ratios that reached 22:1 (e.g., the Hambo Steel Works debt for its new mill). The chaebol and small business bankruptcies threatened the banks such as Korea First that had lent to them with state guarantees through "connected landing" or state driven loans. Independent creditworthiness and due diligence standards had not been imposed on bank lending by IMF programs previously even though widespread connected lending practices were evident even in 1970. The South Koran current account (like a national checking account) suffered from loss of exports and the currency (won) continued to dive. Other Asian currencies collapsed from efforts to defend their collapsing currencies due to similar over borrowing and inability to repay their debts, e.g., Thailand (mostly property debts), Malaysia, and Indonesia.

In 1998 IMF programs were judged to be failures due to the collapse of basic industries and their disastrous socioeconomic consequences. Critics argued that the fiscal economy problem had been badly defined and improperly identified in the case of South Korea. Its basic indicators of 8%, GDP growth, only 3% employment, low 3.9% inflation, and sustainable budget deficits suggested a sound economy in 1997. Instead, many argued, it faced a *liquidity crisis* or cash flow problem that required cash support from IMF to defend its currency. That is, at that point it was not a *solvency crisis* or bankruptcy that required major structural reform. Opponents of the solvency problem definition argued that South Korea's growth model of chaebol and gradual political and economic liberalization was working at the time. These critics charged that the IMF austerity rescue package of higher taxes, lower spending and higher interest rates was based on faulty problem assessment and was the wrong remedial program and set of conditions at the wrong time for South Korea. It was claimed to be a continuation of the IMF-World Bank "cookie cutter" approach also called the "Washington Consensus"".

It was charged, for example, by Jeff Sachs and Martin Feldstein that the core problem was the banks and chaebol lending, and that short-term debt was greater than foreign exchange reserves. But total foreign debt was only 30% of GDP. IMF had misdiagnosed the problem which was illiquidity and required a bridge loan not complete structural reform or shock treatment. Short-term debt needed to be restructured in their view to stem the loss of foreign exchange. The paradoxical but predictable effect of the austerity program was to convince investors that Asian markets were headed down—like shouting fire in a crowded theatre. South Korea was not insolvent—it could repay its debts on time as it had been. It did not need a structural adjustment austerity loan package (Corning, 2011:8).[32]

Criticism

Critics of the IMF's role in propping up high-risk country borrowers and competitors with US firms logically included US industries and opponents of US foreign aid. This was the *moral hazard* critique that the IMF subsidized bad investments in poor countries because the investor had every incentive to invest and loan money knowing that the IMF would repay them if they lost it. For example, the US semiconductor industry was an early critic of IMF rescue programs.

IMF's director Stanley Fisher responded that the austerity package was not a short-term fix to restore confidence in the won but to stimulate longer term growth. To do that required: (1) increasing institutional transparency especially of the workings of crony capitalism and nepotism at the top, such as the heavy flow of connected loans between the state and its client banks which risked both institutions as it did here. They had become routine monopolistic anti-competitive chaebol practices and (2) increasing bank supervision especially state-directed lending rather than via internationally recognized creditworthiness criteria. South Korean financial institutions were weak and systemically self-serving. They needed structural reform, similar to those implemented in Indonesia and Brazil at the time or not implemented well in Russia which provided the Fund with practical lessons on what and what not to do. One of the clearer ones was the necessity to maintain the cutbacks and economic pain in such countries as Poland and Hungary for at least one to two years to bear results.

Fisher also argued that the Fund's rescue packages were not moral hazards to incentivize poor investing decisions but rather intended to pay off existing short-term debts and create investor confidence by rebuilding country reserves and recapitalizing its banking system. It was also clear that investors would not return to South Korea unless they believed their funds were not simply enriching crony capitalists and high-risk propositions regardless of what the IMF might or might not do. Structural reforms were therefore needed. South Korea needed cash to pay off the short-term loans that were creating the liquidity crisis. It also needed structural reform to prevent further deterioration into insolvency where it could not pay its bills to both foreign and domestic investors.

Results

Consistent with Fisher's defense of Fund austerity rescue and structural adjustment programs, roughly two years later (by 1999), the won stabilized and investors returned to South Korea. The current account returned to surplus as exports picked up, inflation dropped significantly, reserves returned to the level of about $56b, and short-term foreign debt dropped 50% by value from pre-crisis levels. Conglomerates such as Daewoo failed but that was likely an indirect objective of the IMF program to rid the economy of monopoly chaebol. In short, comprehensive and rapid adjustment rescue programs, like those in Poland and Hungary, required several years of economic disruption and pain, as well as social costs that required social safety net programs to cover the resultant unemployment and other social costs of eliminating anti-competitive conglomerates. South Korean GDP growth shot up 8% the following year and has largely continued since then.

Questions

1 What are the lessons of this case for IMF adjustment and austerity program design to prevent the South Korean meltdown problems in the 1990s, and for other countries such as Ghana (***Discussion Case #11***)?
2 How does chaebol contribute to anti-competitive practices (such as pricing and jobs for life) and financial opacity?
3 What is "connected lending" and how does it create systemic financial risk?
4 What were the initial impacts of the IMF South Korea rescue program?
5 For fiscal reform programs, if economic recovery is threatening to democratic development, which should take precedence? Refer to the Russia program in the early 1990s.
6 Is it appropriate for IMF rescue packages to require far-reaching reforms such as opening its economy to foreign investment or economic liberalization?
7 Was structural reform necessary to restore South Korean access to international capital markets?
8 Under what conditions would an IMF rescue program create moral hazard?

Notes

1 George M. Guess (2007) *Fast Track: Municipal Fiscal Reform in Central and Eastern Europe and the Former Soviet Union* (Budapest: Local Government and Public Service Reform Initiative of the Open Society Institute), pp.4–8.
2 See Guess *op.cit.* (2019) Chapters 5–6.
3 In the context of a common political culture, largely successful aid efforts in four Balkan states to decentralize taxation, spending and borrowing authority varied by country. The variation was due to differences in the technical fiscal management systems and their applications. George M. Guess (2001) "Decentralization and Municipal Budgeting in Four Balkan States" *Journal of Public Budgeting, Accounting and Financial Management* Volume 13, Number 3, pp.397–436.
4 Steven A. Finkler (2010) *Financial Management for Public, Health and Nonprofit Organizations (3rd ed)* (Upper Saddle River: Prentice-Hall),pp.235–239. The sale and leaseback option allows the government (usually local) to sell the property to investors and simultaneously lease it back by the government for its use (e.g., buses or rail cars). This permits taxpayers to receive investor tax incentives such as asset depreciation. The benefits are shared with the private "lessor" in exchange for which the government receives lower lease payments. For specific facilities such as water and sewer or building renovations, the overall capital costs can be lower than incurred by debt financing. John E. Petersen and Wesley C. Hough (1983) *Creative Capital Financing for State and Local Governments* (Chicago, IL: Government Finance Officers Association of Canada and the U.S.), p.83. For development financing, local authority must have borrowing authority and sufficient discretion to manage their budgets and raise taxes and adopt fees. That means sufficiently advanced level of fiscal decentralization, meaning local government autonomy or functional devolution rather than basic deconcentration of local fiscal roles and responsibilities.
5 *See* Guess and Husted (2017) *International Public Policy Analysis*, Chapter 3 (New York: Routledge).
6 Bloomberg Businessweek (2023) "Can Nigeria Get Back on Track?", 1-16, p.16.
7 *Economist* (2023) "World Ahead 2023: Middle East", p.62.
8 Tom Hancock (2023) "Taxing China", *Bloomberg BusinessWeek*, 6-19, p.26.
9 *Economist* (2023) "Arab Bureaucracies: The Incredible Shrinking State", 3-11, pp.33–34.
10 *Economist* (2023) "The NHS, Dr. No Go", 1-14, pp.48–50.
11 China has recently agreed with Paris Club donor to share the losses on its loans to countries nursing unsustainable debts. African countries, for instance, average debt service payments of 17% of their annual revenues. While Chinese loans are for traditionally vital infrastructure such as roads, rail water and sewer, power, schools, and hospitals (like those from Paris Club) in the past China argued these are not loss-making projects and thus should not contribute to paying consolidated gross country debts. But such loan repayments stymy efforts to budget for socioeconomic development. African countries have had to cut back on health and education because stifling debt service payments prevent them from paying for needed current services, such as teacher and health care wages and maintaining existing infrastructure.
12 The compromise now is that China will contribute to losses and in exchange World Bank will extend more concessional loans and grants to poor countries.

The test case for the new debt-relief approach is Ghana. *Economist* (2023) "The Debt-Relief Duet", 5-20, p.10. China is regularly accused of lending for infrastructure then foreclosing and confiscating local assets as collateral for non-payment. But finances aside, the assets stay and contribute to local development. And without Chinese loans, many poor countries would lack first-class road and rail systems as well as reliable power and clean water. They would lack them because many loans are appraised as uneconomic or financial duds and rejected according to creditworthiness criteria. So, as one who was once rejected for a home mortgage loan by a bank, the Chinese are now acting fairly as a participant in the international development financial system. The Bank-Fund Credit Union gave me one despite being my uneconomic status at commercial banks!

13 Cem Dener, Johanna Watkins and William Dorotinsky (2011) *Financial Management Information Systems: 25 Years of World Bank Experience on What Works and What Doesn't* (Washington, DC: IBRD).

14 Heritage Foundation (2022) "Tax Revenue % GDP by Country".

15 George M. Guess and Thomas Husted (2011) "Fiscal Incentives for Decentralized Aid Management", p.10.

16 Thomas Boswell (2023) "These Nationals are Fun and Scrappy and They Seem To Be on Their Way Back" *The Washington Post*, 5-12, p.D1.

17 *Economist* (2022) "Making a Success of Failure", 5-8.

18 It should not be forgotten that race and its priority classifications are different beyond US borders. For instance, there are six races in Singapore: Malay, Chinese, Tamil, Bengali, Japanese, and English. Distinguishing them officially for censuses and targeting social benefits is called "racialism" in that part of the world. Racism is an American term distinguishing Blacks from whites pejoratively as historical and present domination of Blacks by whites. The historical edifice of racism is founded on the alleged superiority of educated white men. In much of Asia such as Malaysia and India, which became multicultural/ multiracial after independence, the official policies are that one must "adapt" to the dominant Malay or Hindu culture. In many Asian countries, open talk of discussion of race and racial norms and values is banned to prevent racial finger-pointing (i.e., "weaponizing") and misuse of the issue by rabble-rousing populists *Economist* (2023) "Banyan, Race to the Bottom", p.30. Managing racial relations among staff in programs and policies in Asia and much of the world is a powder keg! Fringe theories of special racial hierarchies based on pseudo-science have been used for centuries in multiple regions of the world to justify dehumanizing Black people, Jews and other races, and ethnicities.

19 Similar to Brazil's "racial democracy", Ethiopia is called an "ethno-federation" or ethno-federalism that segregates by tribes and sects (not races). The existing asymmetric federation provides a weak institutional compromise in the semblance of vertical separation of powers but paves the way for the next wave of ethno-nationalist Ethiopian conflict, Guess (2019), *op.cit.* p.28.

20 Jonathan Mummolo (2023) "Don't Give Up on Diversifying the Police", *The Washington Post*, 2-5-23, A23.

21 Simon Diggins (2023) "Reforming the Police", *Economist* 2-4, p.14 (letter).

22 *Economist* (2021) "One City Two Worlds", August 14.

23 *Economist* (2021) "Protests in Colombia: Taxing Times", May 8, pp.35–36; and *Bloomberg Businessweek* (2021) "Austerity Backfires in Colombia", 5-17, pp.38–39.

24 *Economist* (2023) "Bye-Bye to Bungs", 6-10, p.41.

25 *Economist* (2021) "No Longer the Top of the Class: Costa Rica Is Struggling to Maintain Its Welfare State", 4-15.
26 *Economist* (2023) "Egypt, Debt on the Nile", 1-28-23, p.14.
27 *Economist* (2023) "It's Still the Economy Stupid", 6-24, pp.23–24.
28 *Economist* (2022) "Argentina, Blood on the Dance Floor: IMF Cannot Solve Argentina's Dysfunction", 1-29.
29 Kurt Thurmeier (1994) "The Evolution of Local Government Budgeting in Poland: From Accounting to Policy in a Leap and a Bound" *Public Budgeting and Finance*, Volume 14, Number 4, pp.84–98.
30 George M. Guess (2001) "Decentralization and Municipal Budgeting in Four Balkan States" *Journal of Public Budgeting, Accounting and Financial Management*, Volume 13, pp.397–436.
31 *Economist* (2023) "Local Governance, Sub-National and Sub-Optimal", 8-19, p.29.
32 Gregory Corning (2011) "Managing the Asian Meltdown: IMF and South Korea", Case #235, Washington, DC: GUISD Pew Case Study Center.

5 Managing International Transportation

Background and Context

This fourth section of the book combines the three management activities (process, human, resources and budgeting and financing) to focus on particular sectors: urban transport, education, and the environment. Managing budgets and financing them should also be considered a central sector in that it is responsible for the planning and financing of service delivery by the service sectors. Thus, the four sectors may be distinguished as *program* (transport, education, and environment) and *support* (budgeting and financial management). Thus, in this book we cover management of four sectors. Managers of urban transport systems must know managerial and financial accounting and reporting in order to perform such tasks as costing out and pricing their yearly budgets, tracking expenditures and revenues, examining their cash and fiscal positions in real time, and moving routine organizational processes such as purchasing forward to achieve timely and efficient results. Effective financial and organizational management, specifically public expenditure management (PEM) managed by the MOF or central treasury, is needed for routine transit operations, such as managing construction of capital projects and monitoring maintenance and rehabilitation tasks. To perform these vital purposes, managers in urban transport typically work in public authorities funded typically by special and proprietary funds. Such funds are like enterprise funds that allow tracking of accrued payables and receivables regularly over the fiscal year and at year's end in the closing balance sheets.

In this chapter, we examine management problems and prospects in two related transportation arenas: (1) international between countries in the same or different regions and (2) national in cities and between rural and urban areas.

Internationally, one could expect countries in the Latin American, European, Asian, and Middle Eastern[1] regions to be connected by roads, rails, air, sea, and telecommunications. But often they are not. The ability

DOI: 10.4324/9781032670959-5

of trade and investment to contribute to development depends on these regional linkages. Without connectivity, markets cannot function and flourish, and investments are higher cost and risk in the first place. Infrastructure facilitates growth and development. For regional development, the infrastructure has to connect with similar facilities across national boundaries. Otherwise, countries are left dependent on DA aid grants which allow survival and provide skills training that presume trade and commerce linkages exist. But the aid by itself can make few real differences to sustained growth and development. Aid loans can make an important difference to growth if targeted to real need and due diligence ensures that the loans do not threaten fiscal sustainability and can be repaid. The bulk of aid loans are for transport and communications infrastructure. Without functioning inter-country transport linkages, international transport management can only focus on national and urban corridors, which is an extremely pinched perspective on a much wider problem.

Famous inter-country overnight trains such as the Orient Express that passed through seven countries for 80 years between Paris and Istanbul (Constantinople) were finally eliminated by wars and country squabbles. A cut-down version between Paris and Vienna operated by Austrian OBB *Railjet* still runs today. The "City Night Line" ran for 140 years between Zurich and Budapest and served among other purposes to provide an escape route for Jews fleeing the horrors of the Nazi regime. The Night Line runs today operated by the state railway of Hungary (MAV) and the Austrian OBB. But gauges between Europe and former Soviet countries still vary, impeding the flows of freight and passengers. Recent projects such as the Rail Baltica project to link the Lithuanian port of Klaipeda on the Baltic Sea by a 500-mile-high-speed rail to Thessaloniki on the Adriatic Sea have floundered after decades of revised and canceled plans. Roads and rail connections between the provinces of former Yugoslavia are either highly treacherous or non-existent. Political suspicions run high and impede commercial flows except by air or internet. Many countries are landlocked and need access to the sea. The perennial regional squabbles prevent coordination of schedules for bus, rail, and air. Regions are littered with the remnants of grand projects linking rails between countries for freight and passenger travel. In short, political geography for centuries has kept inter-country commerce fragmented and almost impossible to manage except by workarounds. The problems seem simple challenges for management to craft win-win solutions. But they are at root messy, ill-structured, and difficult to manage.

Next to international problems are those at the national and regional levels within the same country. National and regional laws and operating regulations within countries can severely obstruct transport of people, commerce, and trade. For instance, US environmental and preservation laws prevent energy transmission lines which obstruct economic development.

Energy infrastructure in the form of power generation plants, transmission, and distribution lines need state and often local permits before construction can begin. For high-voltage transmission lines, this can take ten years or more. Such attempts to transport electricity via transmission lines from wind-rich and sparsely populated states such as Wyoming to densely populated states with high energy demands such as California and Nevada can wait at least ten years as in the case of TransWest Express, the proposed line by Anschutz Corporation between the two states.[2] Without abbreviating and simplifying this process, green infrastructure cannot deliver more than traditional generation plants without more transmission and distribution lines to customers.

Permitting reform requires managing the trade-offs between special interests (e.g., animal rights and preservationists, tribal claims to sacred lands, not in my backyard opponents), and the wider public good. Often government agencies responsible for regulating and managing such conflicts, such as the US Federal Energy Regulatory Commission (FERC) can avoid trying to manage such conflicts by claiming they can regulate pipelines but not transmission lines! Like many agencies they often avoid such explosive conflicts between green energy infrastructure and fossil fuel interests. Managing requires weighing and deciding among trade-offs and opportunity costs. That means real management that takes risks and field public criticism to come up with real solutions rather than second and third—best remedies that leave no one better off. Every interest wants extra-special status. As discussed in **Chapter 3**, problems need to be structured to allow devising remedial options. These options must be weighted according to beneficial effects net of detrimental effects and scored to develop a workable and transparent rank-order. Criteria and scores can then be debated rationally among stakeholders and policy-makers. The result as indicated in the tables of **Figures 5.1 and 5.2** should be a weighted

Alternatives		Rail Car A		Rail Car B		Rail Car C	
Criteria	Weights	Score	Weighted Score	Score	Weighted Score	Score	Weighted Score
Cost	.60	4	2.4	6	3.6	7	4.2
Reliability	.90	6	5.4	2	1.8	2	1.8
Speed	.40	5	2.0	4	1.6	8	3.2
Total Weighted Score			9.8		7.0		9.2

Figure 5.1 Weighted Scores for Three Fire Engines.

Source: Michel (2001:16) and from sources created by the author.

Capital Repair Project	Cost Sharing: or Available Funding 2-hi/1-some/0-none	Benefits: or Forecasted Demand 2-high/1-some/0-low	Need: 0-minimal/1-increased level/2-higher level of service	Location: 2-rural/1-semi-rural/0-urban	Investment: 4-new/replace/3-utility support/2-rehabilitate/1-complete construction	Cost: 3-less than 850,000 som/1-850-1 million/0-greater than 1 million	Occupancy: 2-75-100%/1-50-74%/0-less than 50%	Score
A								
B								
C								

Figure 5.2 Weighting and Scoring Matrix for Three Health Care Investment Projects.

Source: Guess (2015). Created by the author.

score (column 2 weighted criteria for each project × column 3 score from stakeholder grading) for each project and its ranking among all proposed projects in a formal Capital Improvements Plan (CIP). It is not a perfect methodology or solution. But it allows policy-makers and managers to follow the trail back to the rationales for weighting and development of scores more sensibly.[3]

The State of Urban Public Transport

Internationally, more than half the world's population lives cities. In addition to increased pressures on municipal services and the capacity to finance them, this has led to crises of public access, mobility, increasing congestion, and pollution in cities large and small. With increasing urbanization, frequent deterioration of municipal infrastructure, and more expensive transport services, the movement of people within cities becomes increasingly costly and difficult. Not paying for infrastructure is a huge opportunity cost in that $100b in investment typically translates into a 0.10% addition to GDP growth. Moving people between and within cities may be the most visible and perhaps the important sectoral public policy or program.

Functioning and affordable urban transport is demonstrably important for the survival of governments, regimes, and constitutions. For instance, frustrated Santiago (Chile) bus passengers, upset by abysmal bus service, decades ago commandeered two buses going in different directions and took them home. More recently, in 2019, widespread Santiago protests at a small subway fare increase forced the national government to step down, amplifying demands for improved services, a new constitution, and more equal redistribution of resources. Specifically, the four most critical urban transport problems worldwide are (1) fragmented organizational and management responsibility structures; (2) weak capital planning systems; (3) lack of systems financing; and (4) weak public transport authority accountability and low citizen participation.

Urban socioeconomic development depends in great measure on the efficacy of urban transport—to move people to jobs, schools, hospitals; for police and fire to respond to emergencies; and for the operation and maintenance of related services such as electricity, water-sewer, and sanitation. In spite of this importance, land use patterns and urban transport systems are rarely well-linked or managed in most cities of the world. Better budgeting and financial management could help. Managers often know their cash positions and levels of expenditures. But few know their expenses or the market costs of resources consumed. Instead, managers budget expenditures, not costs, which sacrifices efficiency.

For these reasons: land use distortions, lack of maintenance, negligent cash management, even successful urban transport systems seem to deteriorate over time from underfinancing and mismanagement, suggesting that institutionalization of management and policy lessons has not occurred. European and North American cities are acquiring many Third World transport features, including poor planning, underfunding, clogged roads, and air quality problems caused by trucks and cars. Conversely, many Third World cities have come up with innovative solutions to increase social mobility and access for both the poor and middle classes. Political focus only on inputs such as rigged elections cannot prevent the rise of populist demands for instant and simplistic solutions to complex urban problems. These real and actionable problems must be managed by skillful professionals. People demand fair outcomes such as social mobility, especially urban mobility (vertically and horizontally across geographic space). European and North American systems have also developed innovative responses to urban transport policy problems. It is important that these management and policy lessons be identified and transferred to systems around the world to improve systems performance. The lessons must be scaled up to central governments and transferred across urban jurisdictions.

Learning Outcomes

1   Why managers need to guard against disconnects between financial management and operations management. A disconnect between the two often leads to a failure service delivery and of accountability.
2   To distinguish between managerial accounting and financial accounting. Managerial is prospective; financial is accounts reporting.

3 To distinguish general fund governmental expenditures from special fund and enterprise costs or expenses.

4 To explain the contents and structures of grant or contract proposals.

5 To understand the capital budgeting process, the major steps in CIP review and separate institutional responsibilities for planning and oversight of the capital budget.

6 To understand the budget management uses of variance analysis.

7 To explain and exemplify: fixed, variable, semi-fixed, and semi-variable costs.

8 To understand how flexible budgeting (FB) tool helps management understand how changes in costs, prices, and volume affect transport service break-even calculations.

9 To understand why public transit is called a natural monopoly average cost industry.

10 To explain why public transit always needs a subsidy and why well-managed systems employ fiscal rules to limit the public subsidy obligation to transit, e.g., Metropolitan Atlanta Rapid Transit Authority (MARTA).

11 To understand how to calculate the break-even ticket price of Martell Orchestra in *Exercise #5.1* and discuss ways to lower its break-even point.

12 To calculate break-even prices for New City Subway in *Exercise #5.2*. To explain how break-even analysis (BEA) and FB tools can be used for typical management problems of setting prices and service levels.

13 To demonstrate how IFMS tightened preventive controls over corruption in public procurement.

14 To demonstrate in *Discussion Case #16* anti-corruption successes and failures in procurement (successes with EITI, Romania DNA, US General Accountability Office, UK Comptroller & Accountant General of the National Audit Office or NAO) and the Ukrainian anti-corruption high court (HACC), and failures (Guatemala CICIG) and to try and explain the differences.

15 To explain what private-public partnerships (PPPs) are and how they operate in Europe, Latin America, and US states and cities. Their role in adding complexity and opacity to transport projects will be described.

16 The problems of complex rail projects and use of PPP to save time and money will be described in the US case of the inter-county LRT called the "Purple Line" in the Washington, DC area.

17 To distinguish in *Discussion Case #17* the role of domestic vs. international constraints to building cross-border linkages and managing them.

18 To identify management lessons from the case of Tel-Aviv LRT and Israeli SOE operations of its heavy rail freight and passenger rail services.

19 To compare the management strategies and their effectiveness in managing transit problems in Tel-Aviv, Washington, DC, Rio, and Chicago.

20 To identify the roles of SOEs such as Transnet in obstructing commerce and trade in South Africa and what managers can do for workarounds.

21 To draw practical lessons for overseas transit technical assistance from *Discussion Case #18* which explains the differences between the Japanese (Japanese International Cooperation Agency [JICA]) aid work with the Vietnamese Ho Chi Minh (HCM) rail line and the Chinese efforts with the Hanoi line.

22 To discuss the differences in approach and results in designing, procuring, financing, and construction of the lines and managing operations afterward between the Japanese and Chinese in Vietnam.

23 To draw managerial lessons from *Discussion Case #19* of how Bogota managed to turn a successful and cost-effective transport policy into a costly failure.

24 To examine whether Bus Rapid Transit (BRT) is a more cost-effective solution to congestion, mobility, and safety for cities in poor countries than rich.

25 To explore ways poor country governments can resist pressures from international transit engineering firms can control local decisions on transit planning and operations of large rail projects such the Hanoi and HCM lines in Vietnam.

Concepts and Tools for Fiscal Analysis and Management of the Transport Sector

Transit managers should recognize that public sector budgets are divided into general fund and special fund accounts and budgets. Budgeting for general government departments and ministries is *general fund*: simple cash-based tracking of expenditures and revenues. The format is the object of expenditure budget (*Figure 4.1*) which tracks inputs classified into line-items that cover a 12-month fiscal year. Accounts are kept in income or operating statements for the same period (called "IS/OS" in *Figure 4.5*). As noted, some output measurement is possible with cash-based general fund budgeting by, for instance, examining expenditure/O&M spending ratios. That tracks the financial dimension but would not give management the actual O&M results in the physical condition of capital assets. More importantly, it would not tell managers if the work was actually done or how well. For that, one would have to focus in on results by department, ministry, or other unit of general government.

Budgeting and accounting for special funds (i.e., those units given dedicated sources of revenues such as fares, tolls, fees, charges, tariffs, and fines) is used by: NGOs, nonprofit organizations (NPOs), fee-charging city-state enterprises such as utilities, SOEs, and water and sewer authorities, and especially by transit or city-state transport authorities. The term used for special fund budgeting and accounting is managerial cost accounting and applies to special and "proprietary" funds. Expenditures and revenues are called expenses and receipts as will be explained. Expenses and receipts accounting is performed by accrual rather than on a cash basis. Accruals mean payables or amounts owed, and receivables refer to funds to be collected from suppliers and other debtors. Transactions are not just cash out and in the accounts as for general funds. Budget progress, meaning the hundreds if not thousands of expenditures made and revenues received, is recorded in the balance sheets (called "BS" in *Figure 4.5*). All such transactions are tracked in the three financial statements: income or annual operations, accrued balances, and annual cash flows (CF in *Figure 4.5*). These statements give managers a three-dimensional and comprehensive picture of how the organizational financings are performing—called its fiscal position.

Transit and other special fund enterprise-type organizations especially need to know how to deal with cost, price, and volume issues in order to effectively manage operations. They constantly have to monitor budget and account progress to make informed decisions that take into account their main stakeholders: oversight boards, riders or passengers, and labor unions. The intense pressures from these groups demanding changes to service, fares, and capital plans make transit management a highly politicized profession.

Rationale for Financial Management

All public sector organizations need sound financial management to operate effectively and efficiently. By multiple measures, for instance, the Washington, DC, school system was once associated with about the worst pupil performance in the US. This is discussed further in *Chapter 6, Case #21*. The school system performance was achieved in spite of having the far highest $19k/pupil expenditures compared to the US average of only $11k. The school system Chancellor Michelle Rhee received information from the system internal auditor that classes in most DC schools lacked textbooks. Internal audit is a core function of public financial management (PFM) systems as noted in *Chapter 4*. The independent internal auditor found that school warehouses were in fact full of textbooks that accounting records revealed had been ordered, and paid for, but never delivered to classrooms. Rhee uncovered a systemic failure of the interface between financial and operations management. While the accounting entries for procurement, O&M, and inventory each showed textbook transactions that resulted in their deliveries to inventory, they were not transferred by administrators from inventory to classrooms. This she discovered using "management by walking around" (MWA), an informal technique to check whether accounting matched reality, which in this case did not! She instituted a tight accountability program with real financial consequences for administrators and teachers for failures such as this. The DC schools case underscores the need for two related types of financial dimensions of budgetary accounting: *managerial* and *financial*. A senior manager (CFO) should be responsible for both. Accounting is the foundation of budgeting. Without timely and accurate reports of expenditures and revenues clearly defined, budgets and budget totals can easily be misinterpreted. For this reason, the two dimensions are distinguished.[4]

Managerial Accounting

It is prospective, forward planning for the annual budget. Managers cull information from the budgetary accounting system to establish a baseline for forecasting revenues and expenditures and to provide analytics to deal with expected issues for both the current and capital budgets. Important policy and fiscal issues should undergo cost and consequence reviews for each option through a locally adapted version of zero-based budgeting (ZBB). Many state and local governments develop their own review systems to assess prospective outputs for issues such as capital investment options of leasing vs. buying equipment; cutting vs. adding rail and bus service, size of labor force, and their effects on fare box revenues. For example, the Atlanta rail and bus system (MARTA) has for years used a fiscal rule for budget planning: it can use no more than 50% of the dedicated sales tax revenues of 1% levied by its three counties. MARTA must adjust fares, service, or staffing levels to ensure that operating revenues cover at least 35% of projected operating costs (Guess, 2015:72–73). Fiscal rules such as this place a premium on getting the funding formula right that, in turn, requires accurately reported budgetary accounting information to develop annual baselines.

The IFMS-supported budgetary accounting system supplies real-time cash revenues and expenditures data for budget planning. Simultaneously, data are recorded in the financial statements: income statements, balance sheets, and cash flow statement (see *Figure 4.5*) for internal management, the public, and regulators. Daily budget spending and revenue receipts transactions are also recorded as assets or receivables and liabilities or payables derived from source documents invoices for orders and shipments and tax receipts that have been recorded first in journals and then ledgers. All accounting figures enter the general ledger in real time and are classified according to the chart of accounts. They are also registered nationally in the treasury single account (TSA) to allow measurement of the current fiscal position.

As noted for the MARTA fiscal rule cited above, managers rely on the PFM revenue module for accurate revenue data to develop their budget baselines. This indicates revenue available or forecasted to be available to use in building the budget for the next FY. Available revenues for many public sector organizations, national and local, rely on funding formulae. If the formulae have been miscalculated, the revenue estimates will be erroneous as well. Education ministry CFOs, for example, need to make sure that the formulae components such as tax revenues and number of students are accurate before submitting their budgets. For FY 23, the one state department of education submitted a revenue estimate based on an outdated formula that needed to exclude receipts from the state tax on groceries. This error amounted to a $202m loss for Virginia state districts that rely on the funding formula. The oversight penalized poorer rural districts that relied on the formula revenues for 80% of their budgets. The formula included property tax revenues which wealthier districts used to make up for their funding shortfalls. But poorer districts lacked this option.[5]

Financial Accounting

It is retrospective, looking back at budget execution and ensuring that all fiscal events have been recorded in the accounting system. It is the financial plumbing system that ensures that all transactions have been reported and accounted for all. As noted in *Figure 5.3*, financial accounting is vitally

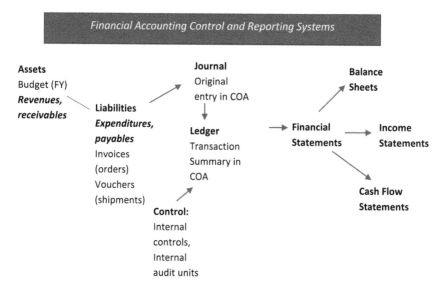

Figure 5.3 Managerial and Financial Control Systems.
Source: Created by the author.

supported by the system of internal controls. These are the core accounting rules that are maintained by personnel who rotate in their roles to avoid conflicts of interest, such as approving both pay orders and treasury outlays. The internal control system, in turn, is supported by the internal audit units which checks the accounting controls to ensure that they are functional. The internal audit unit also reviews fiscal performance, assessing whether waste (such as the DC schools case noted above), fraud, or abuse of power is occurring.

Basic Budget Management Concepts

A basic distinction that is often flouted is between expenditures and expenses. Expenditures are the commonly used term for cash spending or outlays by general government budgets from their general funds. Expenses, by contrast, are used for special fund, enterprise-type organizations such as utilities and transit agencies that charge fees. NGOs also budget as enterprises in that they pay actual costs to deliver goods such as meals for homeless people. Thus, for the latter, enterprise accounting is more precise for pricing, charging fees, and assessing costs of production to measure inputs and resources consumed or purchased during periods to produce services and goods. Special fund organizations have to budget and price for their actual costs of production. General fund organizational expenditures from ministries and departments are then termed expenditures and outlays but are not strictly accounting costs.

Expenditures are useful in presenting budgets and receiving cash for general government. Commitments and outlays are expenditures not accounting costs. Output efficiency can be roughly measured by using "expenditures/unit" as a proxy for efficiency. But as noted expenditures are not strictly costs. Expenditure add-ons are used to comply with legislative rules (e.g., Buy America provisions) to arrive at "fully-loaded costs" used in grants and contracts (*Figure 5.2*). An example of the distinction can be seen in the health sector. The US health care budget "expenditures" per person are the highest in the world. But "costs" of drugs, meals, nurses, and doctors are much lower so that the actual costs of production are really much lower than public expenditures for health care. General fund expenditures are made by quarterly plans with no cost or price considerations.

Capital Budget Institutions

As noted in *Figure 4.2*, capital budget planning is multi-year, while the actual spending for capital is on a fiscal year basis. A formal capital budget calendar and system includes a capital improvement planning (CIP) process. This process is a multi-step review of project rationale, costs and benefits, financial affordability, and expected rates of return. The final step of a CIP should be to rank projects by transparent weighting and scoring criteria (*Figures 5.1 and 5.2*). A problem institutionally is that ministers of finance and CFOs often view capital as non-core and performed by a separate institution such as ministries of public works (MOPW) or ministries of planning. But their decisions commit current budget expenses such as O&M and add to debt service costs. Often capital planning calculations, assessments, and analytics are excluded from regular budget calendars. This causes many surprises later in white elephants, poorly bid projects that have to be abandoned, and expenses that contribute to gross public debts and annual fiscal deficits. GFS describes four budget formats that are in standard use around the world: economic (*Figure 4.1*), functional (*Figure 4.3*), administrative, and program/performance (*Figure 4.4*). Administrative means budgeting by departments or ministries. Program means output or performance-type budget of which many varieties have been used, e.g., ZBB by cost center, performance budgets by department or ministry, program budgets by program structures aggregated from sub-programs and elements all of which aid financial managers in establishing accountability for results. All formats use general fund expenditures rather than accounting expenses. Managers typically will employ multiple formats for analysis of budget plans and results. The numbers for all four budget types add up to the same amounts and can be "cross-walked" between formats, e.g., programs to line-item objects of expenditure (*Figure 5.4*).

Financial managers use many tools for analysis of budgets and for tracking their progress. Here, we discuss three commonly used ones: (1) variance analysis, (2) FB, and (3) BEA. As noted, PFM consists of operational data

Public Contract or Grant Budget
Proposal Format

    A. Projected Gross Revenues
    B. Direct Costs or Projected Expenses
        Salaries
        Fringe
        Program Travel, Expenses and Materials
    C. Indirect Costs (e.g., 50% add-ons for instructional grants; 30% for non-credit)
    D. Total or Net Project Costs (surplus/loss to organization)
        (D = A − B + C)

Figure 5.4 Public Contract or Grant Budget Format.

Source: Created by the author.

modules that facilitate the financial and service performance of government organizations. Budgeting is the lead system.

Variance Analysis

Financial and budget managers need to know the differences between actual expenditures and the originally planned and approved budget. Reviewing their line-item, economic classification budget formats, they need to know the year-on-year and month-by-month spending differences for comparative analytic purposes. Three main reasons can be cited for spending above or below past fiscal years or quarterly periods. First, variance analysis can be used as a monitoring and evaluation tool for implementation analysis. It can signal "red flags" or major deviations by specific line-item when compared to past budget executions. The manager would want to know why. Second, if budget execution is deviating strongly from past years, it can allow short-term cash management corrections to avoid shortfalls later in the year.

Third, it is a tool for gauging departmental and managerial fiscal capacity. A problem for overseas aid is the absorptive capacity of host country institutions. Aid allocations for sectors such as transportation, education, and environmental protection run up against the problem that local institutions are unable to spend the grant or loan money effectively. Poor countries often suffer not from lack of funds but from inability to spend them. Variance analysis can pinpoint where the weak ministries and subunits are that have capacity problems. Problems may be internal, such as local budget processes that delay releases of approved budget funds from MOFs to departments responsible for aid programs and projects over minor technicalities. Conversely, overspending by administrative units can be a problem of weak internal controls, or failure of MOFs to properly control apportionments of approved funds.

Figure 5.5 indicates a simple method for performing variance analysis that can easily be applied.

Budgeted 2023	Actual 2023	$ Change
$780,000(B)	$610,000(A)	-$170,000

What is the percentage variance?

$$\frac{BY\ 1(B) -- BY\ 2(A)}{BY\ 1(B)} = \frac{780-610= 170}{780} = --21.8\%$$

Figure 5.5 Budget Variance Method.
Source: Created by the author.

Flexible Budgeting⁶

Public transport managers need to know how costs, prices, and volumes behave for break-even/subsidy calculations. Such managers are responsible for advising transit boards on what and where to set prices and service levels. They know that mistakes here can lead to serious backlashes as transit managers in Santiago (Chile) found out recently! Thus, they need to provide sound advice on where to set prices, service levels in the face of costs, some of which vary in intriguing ways as volumes increase or decrease. Decisions are vital as riders and unions have low flash points for even the smallest infringements of their wallets. Managers in such cases often use "flexible budgeting" which is a simple form of "what-if?" analysis.

This method recognizes that planned costs and revenues for a fiscal year will change in different proportions for changes in service levels or workload volumes. FB uses the current or operating budget as a baseline to examine the cost, price, and revenue implications of varying workload levels. It provides managers with a dynamic look at how the three main variables behave and enhances confidence in decision-making.

A basic starting distinction is between variable and fixed costs (see *Figure 5.6*).

Variable Costs

FBs recognize that for differing workload volumes, some costs vary proportionately such as meals, O&M, supplies, and fuel. Others vary in

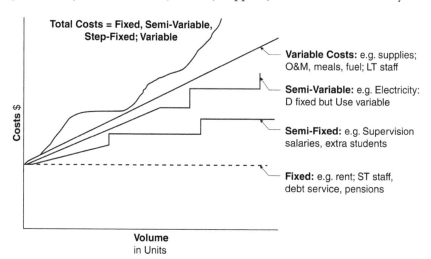

Figure 5.6 Cost Behavior for Volume Changes.

Source: Created by the author.

step-grade with long-term staff costs as safety inspectors, teachers, and supervisory personnel. *Step-fixed costs* are those that must be added to maintain efficiency and effectiveness, such as more teachers for more students and more health workers to serve patients for outbreaks of diseases. This can be seen in *Figure 5.5* whereas volume increases, the fixed costs step upwards with variable and fixed components.

Fixed costs: Other costs are fixed and do not vary with changes in volumes or workloads. Examples are pensions, rent, debt service, and most short-term personnel.

For FB, use the operating budget and vary the workload volume to arrive at a new cost figure. Suppose the number of meals bought and delivered by the NPO Meals for the Homeless (MFH) happened to be greater or less than expected. The workload volume for MFH is its number of meals delivered. See the MFH flexible budget in *Figure 5.7*.

The CFO knows that the city will pay MFH a flat rate of $1.50/meal. He needs to know the actual cost/meal to MFH. How does he figure that out from the FB in *Figure 5.7*? Fiscal managers always make working assumptions. With so much in flux, they become specialists in making assumptions! Making assumptions is fine as long as they are stated in footnotes that allow auditors to retrace the steps in calculating the costs. Here it is reasonable to assume that all supplies are meals or $87,500 for 35,000 meals (=$2.50). If that is acceptable, the MFH cost is $2.50/meal. Given the $1.50 city reimbursement, that adds up to a $1.00 loss/meal! MFH meals delivered only cover 2/3 of their actual cost (1.50/2.50 = 0.60). What should the MFH CFO

Meals for Homeless
Flexible Budget Example

Meals Delivered	35,000	40,000	45,000
Revenues			
Donations	$105,000	$105,000	$105,000
City	52,500	60,000	67,500
Total Revenue	$157,500	$165,000	$172,500
Expenses			
Salaries	$46,000	$46,000	$46,000
Supplies	87,500	100,000	112,500
Rent	12,000	12,000	12,000
Other	6,000	6,000	6,000
Total Expenses	$151,500	$164,000	$176,500
Surplus/(Deficit)	$6,000	$1,000	$(4,000)

Figure 5.7 Flexible Budget Example.

Source: Finkler (2005:84, 2nd edition) and sources created by author.

do? But with real costs facing him from the operating budget, he cannot just assume the meal losses away! He has to review the costs, divided into fixed and variable, and revenue sources in order to make nuanced choices that can keep MFH going without penalizing the hungry too severely by cutting back meals for them.

Looking over the costs and the revenues in the FB example, the manager first needs to figure out a "ballpark break-even point (BBE)" where workload increases will break the budget. If more meals are needed than the BBE allows, MFH must lower the break-even volume so that more meals can be delivered. Where is the BE volume for MFH?

Referring to the FB, the answer is 41,000 meals. It can be seen from *Figure 5.5* that at 40k meals delivered MFH is still running a $1k surplus. That means, if the costs are roughly in proportion to those reported in the FB, that MFH could deliver 1k more meals and break even = 41k.

Break-Even Analysis (BEA)

BEA is used to calculate subsidy requirements for activities with revenue potential. For instance, the French government railroad (SNCF) used BEA to calculate public subsidy requirements for its high-speed TGV rail before building it. The requirements have worked out roughly as planned. By contrast, the Spanish state railroad did not use BEA to calculate subsidy requirements for the AVE country-wide high-speed rail system. Instead of calculating financial returns or losses, the Spanish used the planning method of forecasting net benefits of economic development. The forecasted benefits of economic development are widely speculative and subjective when compared to forecasted riders, volumes, running, and investment costs. The Spanish forecasted benefits but not expected costs according to transit industry financial norms. Their method was roughly that of calculating physical norms used in the former Soviet planning system.

BEA is also useful to appraise rates of return on investment proposals and projects for build operate and transfer concession proposals (BOTs); PPPs for capital projects such as rail lines and toll roads, contracting out for services such as sanitation, facilities maintenance; public swimming pools financed partly by user charges, orchestras that survive on patronage fees and donations, museums, urban transit systems, schools, hospitals, and early child care services.

In short, BEA analysis can reveal such management essentials as costs/rider, costs/student, costs/job created, costs and returns for sanitation projects and waste management services, government contracting out proposals, costs/conference attendee, costs/meal, costs and benefits of retaining vs. selling public hospitals, and making or delivering vs. contracting out recreation programs.

Nevertheless, public transit financing and pricing is inherently paradoxical: it cannot provide needed services profitably. The paradox is that the more service volume the transit system provides, the more variable costs it incurs. This paradox is a problem faced by all public transit systems worldwide. They inherently lose money no matter what managers and policy-makers come up with as solutions. Convincing the general public to pay for transit as part of a direct income tax is practically impossible anywhere. The benefits of transit are diffuse—reduced congestion and better air quality from time saved by rail-bus commuting are hard to attribute empirically or in the public mind to more reliable or cheaper transit service. On the other hand, the costs of paying for better transit are concentrated; riders are directly affected by service cuts and increased fares to try and cover transit system deficits.

All urban systems face the problem of trying to cover transit deficits. All of them try raising fares with predictable results; some of them use indirect sales fees or portions of general sales taxes (e.g., Minnesota and Georgia); all systems rely on state or federal subsidies; a few use earmarked revenues from their state emission cap and trade systems (California); a very few lucky transit systems can rely on supplemental revenues from commercial real estate profits, such as Hong Kong. Even reliance on multiple sources of funding rarely is sufficient to finance annual budget shortfalls. And the more service urban transport systems provide to generate more revenues, the more step-grade-fixed costs they incur. Caught in a tragic managerial conundrum, average costs and unit costs always grow faster than revenues. The system's unit costs always grow faster than revenues/unit. The transit manager is faced with the dilemma that he "cannot make it up in volume". Various tactics are tried to lower the break-even volume. But a subsidy is always required to run the urban public transit service. Some require less than others; some contract out particular lines to lower service costs. But full-service urban public transit still requires a substantial subsidy.

This is called the "natural monopoly" problem. It is inherent in high "average cost" industries such as urban transit and provision of water and sewerage. Greater service volumes still cannot cover growing average costs. Managers lower fares to increase rider demand to cover marginal costs. But as noted in P2–Q2 in *Figure 5.8*, this sensible tactic still cannot cover the average costs that inevitably keep on growing. Transit demand is elastic. That means, raising fares loses riders which require service cuts that alienate even more riders, lowering revenues and raising unit costs further in the familiar vicious cycle. By contrast, lowering fares should increase ridership which it usually does but not enough to break even. Transit is not inelastic like cigarette pricing where the good is so valuable to the user that they keep on demanding more smokes. As hinted above,

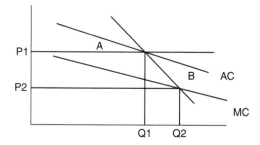

Figure 5.8 The Urban Transit Natural Monopoly Problem.

Notes: **Natural monopoly** used to prevent duplication of I's in UPT, W&S type industries. But increasing **returns to scale**, @P2/Q2 NM cannot generate enough $to cover AC (TC/#units = AC). At P1/Q1 efficient but cost/unit > revenue/unit. Q1 too low to generate BE revenue. At P2, can generate normal ROR but Q required is inefficient. Context requires regulated monopoly + subsidy prices + other revenues.

Source: Created by the author.

the transit paradox managers face is that lowering prices to attract more riders is also inefficient as noted in P1–Q1, and AC > MC. As indicated in *Figure 5.9*, to keep services reasonably effective, a public subsidy is required to price affordable and service volumes high enough.

The natural monopoly financial problem means that the preferred or most efficient solution is institutional: a regulated monopoly, such as the state authority in Atlanta known as MARTA with a dedicated source

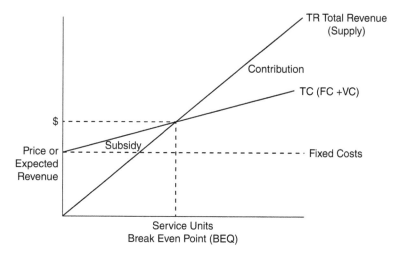

Figure 5.9 Public Transit Requires Subsidies.

Source: Created by the author.

of revenue and an annually enforceable rule to maintain its fiscal discipline. Increasing scale alone is not a solution to the natural monopoly problem. Urban transit, like water and sewerage, is an essential service in urban areas. But management must ensure that they are provided as efficiently and effectively as possible. They will both require subsidies as indicated in *Figures 5.8 and 5.9*. Both a valid and reliable financial rate of return or BEA and an agreement on the necessity for a regulated monopoly governed by a fiscal rule are essential to avoid public sector debt traps. Conversely, the logic of the natural monopoly problem for such services means they cannot be provided profitably in any urban area in the world. If effective services are to be provided to large populations, they cannot do it on a break-even basis without subsidy.

The natural monopoly problem applies to all passenger rail whether national systems in rich or poor countries, or to urban rail and commuter rail. These systems cannot profit because of high-cost operations and pricing limits. Deutsche Bahn (DB), the German state railroad system, has been "profitable" only because of its logistical e-commerce arm, *DB Schenker*, which provides 50% of all DB sales revenues. Otherwise, DB bleeds money, operates currently at a loss, suffers from poor management, bloated bureaucracy, years of underinvestment, and provides low on-time performance (60%) compared to European rail standards.[7] In short, passenger rail (long-distance, urban commuter, light, or heavy rail) is not a commercially viable business unless operated by public natural monopoly authorities and can break-even only through substantial public subsidies.

The consequences of doing a flawed BEA can be serious. For example, in 2011 Harrisburg (PA) declared bankruptcy (unable to pay its bills or insolvent). It borrowed $125m to rebuild its incinerator based on a crude forecast that it would generate enough revenues to break even and make a profit from burning garbage, i.e., producing positive net benefits. The city ended up $288m in debt; it couldn't make debt service payments on existing debt and ended up with the highest trash rates in US! The flawed BEA assumptions on which its financial analysis was performed as part of the city's capital improvement planning process went unchallenged by independent assessments. The financial analysis also ignored risk of failure for a project that would take up half the capital budget and add roughly 40% more to its debt service burden. In short, the Harrisburg fiasco was caused by a flawed affordability analysis that ignored the ratio of this project to total city debt (a standard metric for assessing creditworthiness and ability to repay project or total city debt). These facts were ignored in the face of booster pressure to complete the project.

In Harrisburg, roughly, the normal cost-benefit analysis required of proposed capital projects was replaced by a simple "planning" analysis of costs/estimated net benefit approach, such as used for the Spanish high-speed rail system (AVE) noted above. While the Spanish national government could provide the high subsidies needed to run the system, Harrisburg was a unit of a federal system in which higher layers of government are not normally expected or able to bail out lower levels of government.

Exercise #5.1: Martell Break-Even Problem

The City of Martell Municipal Orchestra incurs $1m in fixed costs/year for its performances. The variable costs for each person attending one of the orchestra's performances are calculated to be $2. The average charge to attend a performance is $60. How many tickets must the Martell Orchestra sell to break even?

The break-even formula for volume, service, and products is the following.

The scenario is what-if demand was only 16k tickets instead of the needed 17,241? The break-even volume must be lowered, that is lowering the volume of service or product outputs required to break even. How can management do this? There are four options without diminishing the quality of their performances:

1 *Refer to flexible budget figures.* Distinguish fixed (salaries, rent, find out what any "other" costs are fixed) and variable costs (supplies, performance-related "other" running costs). If fixed costs do not increase over a range of higher volume (step-fixed), they might be lowered by *outsourcing* (contracting out) some service costs. Transit systems have done this with particular lines or routes. But, as noted, they find that fixed costs often continue and increase. Orchestra management should market more aggressively and solicit more donations. That would add revenue and take some of the pressure off lowering the break-even volume caused by lower patron demand.
2 *Find internal variable cost efficiencies*: Consolidating positions and/ or relying on volunteers can lower variable costs. In schools, the preferred solution here is to consolidate schools and staff positions. Cutting teachers lowers the quality of the service, i.e., learning outcomes or education.
3 *Increase prices or use dynamic pricing*: This is often referred to as variable cost pricing: charging different prices for peak and off-peak performances. Options include matinees, inviting the public to rehearsals, discount sales to multiple performances. As public bus and metro transit services have discovered, off-peak pricing and different kinds of tickets may or may not increase total system revenue.

Table 5.1 New City Subway Flexible Budget

New City Subway Flexible Budget			
Price or Fare	$1.50	$2.00	$2.50
Volume per day (riders)	50,000	40,000	30,000
Revenue per day			
Less fixed cost per day	70,000	70,000	70,000
Less variable cost (x) $0.08 volume			
Surplus/Deficit			
Tickets Sales to Break Even			

Source: Finkler (2001), problem 4–54, and from sources created by the author.

4 *Increase volume via more aggressive marketing to increase revenue.* Orchestras rely heavily on this option to lower break-even volumes. Given the performer salaries, expecting them hold more performances or holding performances in different places is a hard sell. Given the elasticity of demand, where patrons can listen to the radio or watch performances on television or their I-pads, they often end up relying on more public subsidy support to try and break even.

Exercise #5.2: New City Subway (NCS)

New City Subway (NCS) has 40k passengers every day. However, ridership is fairly price sensitive. As indicated in *Table 5.1* if the current fare or ticket price of $2 were to increase to $2.50, it is likely that there would only be 30k passengers each day. Conversely, if the fare were dropped to $1.50, ridership would likely increase to 50k. These figures suggest high price elasticity of passenger demand.

Given

Variable costs are only 8 cents/passenger and fixed costs of operating the subway are $70k/day.

Fill in the four rows and three columns of the flexible budget template in *Table 5.1*. You must calculate and supply the missing data. Thus, prepare a flexible NCS budget for fares of $1.50, $2.00, and $2.50. Based on your new data in the now completed flexible budget:

1 How many passengers are needed to break even at the $2 fare? *Hint*: To get the exact break-even ticket number use the break-even formula *for each fare option*, e.g., the surplus produced by a $2.00 fare for x number of tickets (*Figure 5.10*). In NCS, we have estimated volumes and proposed fares or prices. *Needed are the exact ticket numbers that will maximize surpluses or minimize deficits for each price.*

BE *volume* (e.g., tickets sold) = $\dfrac{\text{Fixed Costs}}{\text{Price or Revenue– Variable Costs}}$

BE *service* (e.g., # pool users/visits) = $\dfrac{FC}{\text{R/user} - \text{VC/user}}$

BE *product* (e.g., # building inspections) = $\dfrac{FC}{\text{R/unit} - \text{VC/unit}}$

Figure 5.10 Break-Even Formula.

Source: Created by the author.

2 What is the optimal fare that will maximize surpluses without substantially diminishing ridership volume? Why? *Hint*: use the break-even volume formula from Martell Orchestra (*Figure 5.11*).

3 Using the given formula, how many subway tickets need to be sold to break even?

4 Explain why higher fares and volumes do not increase NCS profits/surpluses. What happens to the BE volume points with higher or lower fares? *Hint*: cost/unit is always greater than revenues/unit. Management must lower break-even volume.

Fixed cost	-	$1,000,000	total
Variable costs	-	$2	per ticket
Price	-	$60	per ticket

$$ Q \quad - \quad \frac{FC}{P - VC} \quad - \quad \frac{\$1,000,000}{\$60 - \$2} \quad - \quad 17{,}241 \text{ tickets} $$

Therefore, 17,421 tickets must be sold to break even.

Note: The actual calculation yields the result 17,241.349. However, it is important to round out even though the fraction is less than one half. If we sold only 17,200 tickets, the Orchestra would lose money because it would be below its breakeven point.

Scenario: What if the price must be reduced, or variable costs rise? What should the Board do if expected demand is only 16,000 tickets?

Figure 5.11 Break-Even Volume for Martell Orchestra.

Source: Finkler (2010), and from sources created by the author.

Discussion Case #16: Transport Project Procurement, Corruption, and Implementation Management

Procurement is one of the core PFM functions as noted in *Chapter 4*. To get maximum value for money from transport facility use (effectiveness and cyber-security), the projects have to be bid fairly and transparently and awarded contracts must be monitored during implementation to completion. Procurement is also the most lucrative area for big-money corruption! It attracts bribes and payments in almost every country. For road, rail, and other public facilities, projects are typically large (billions of $), complex, and vulnerable to pressure by large engineering and architectural (A&E) firms. They put pressure on bidding systems to try and stack the awards committees and get the contracts for themselves. Rich country officials have trouble resisting such pressures; poorer country procurement officials find it almost impossible.

IFMS systems have tightened fiscal discipline on soliciting, bidding, and awarding processes to prevent and resist political pressures. They have squeezed lots of corruption opportunities out of the systems of taxing, spending, and payments. In contrast with the freewheeling old days, it is difficult to bid and award contracts without clearing the IFMS accounting and procurement controls on registering contract commitments to the annual budget and reconciling those commitments with existing charges on available balances. Overspending is almost impossible with modern real-time IFMSs that link accounting, current, and capital budgeting and treasury payments modules. In poorer countries, threats, personal sectarian, and partisan obligations are overwhelming. There are more buffer institutions and checks that protect public decision-makers from pushback and real threats and intimidation if contracts are not awarded to the right bidders. In addition to IFMSs, independent internal audit institutions exist at all levels of government to review selected procurement contracting transactions for fraud, waste, and abuse.

Watchdog and anti-corruption agencies with investigative and often prosecutorial powers have been created (Guess, 2019:198) globally and nationally. The objective is to reduce or eliminate official corruption. For example, the Extractive Industry Resource Transparency Initiative (EITI) was created in 2003 by the Open Society Institute (Soros Foundation). It has become the global gold standard for reported investment inflows into natural resources, country uses, and capacities to allocate the funds effectively, and outflows of rents and profits subject to taxes or exemptions by host country authorities. It is also a repository of information on investment contract terms and conditions that host countries can learn from to avoid "adhesion" or one-way contract negotiations that deprive them of tax resources. For example, lessons can be learned on what to include in contracts for costs and who should bear responsibilities for such costs as decommissioning and abandonment. EITI also receives information on MNC firm deposits of funds into extra-budgetary funds over which MOFs have little control and often are exempt from taxes or audits. Nevertheless, EITI has been effective at promoting transparency and resource governance, largely in poor countries that receive large investments from mining, oil, and gas projects, such as Guyana noted in **Discussion Case #6**. EITI is a vital global clearing house for primary reported and secondary information on resource extraction firms in largely poorer, resource-rich countries.[8]

At the country level, the Guatemala Anti-Corruption Commission (CICIG) was created with UN backing in 2006. It had effective investigative and prosecutorial powers which were put to immediate use on corrupt officials that took bribes and kickbacks, especially on public contracts. CICIG did an effective job for almost a decade until a political backlash by powerful leaders and interest groups forced its closure and the fleeing to Washington, DC, of supportive judges and CICIG officials. Its problem was that the beneficiaries of its anti-corruption work lacked organization or in-country legitimacy (the UN is an international organization), while its opponents in government were able to use their substantial powers and process knowledge to shut it down. CICIG faced the common constraint of a modern anti-corruption agency operating in a poor corrupt country institutional environment (scoring 24 out of 100 where 0 = corrupt by Transparency International). With similar successes, the HACC was created in 2018 and has so far convicted 65 judges and MPs in just 3½ years. In Ukraine, corruption had been endemic, involving bribes and payments for routine services and for obtaining public contracts. But with years of Western DA, much from USAID, and the enlistment of civil society groups and volunteers, it may be that corruption has moved from a pervasive "system" to merely a treatable "ailment". There are always setbacks—one of HACC's own judges was recently removed by President Zelensky for soliciting bribes on contracts. But public sector transparency has improved there: public procurement details are now online.

In contrast with the first two agencies, the Romanian Anti-Corruption Agency (DNA) has been in operation for more than 20 years. It has been effective and prosecuted and sentenced almost 1k corrupt officials for various crimes; many of which have related to state contracting. DNA was established as a special prosecution office with support from the top of the Romanian government. Romania is a relatively "clean" country scoring 63 out of 100 (where 100 = clean) with relatively strong institutions, especially the judiciary. Public perceptions of corruption over the years have led to establishment of agencies such as DNA and support for prosecution of officials. All three institutions, EITI, CICIG, and DNA, have focused on the honey pot of public monies surrounding bidding and contracting for the acquisition of expensive infrastructure. This context is often opaque and complex with inflows of vast donor and national funds amidst local efforts to control and account for inflows of funds and their expenditure. The expenditures are usually through national budgets but may be through special extra-budgetary accounts which add to fiscal opacity and the blurring of public accountability lines. A lesson of the Guatemalan and Romanian agency experiences is that poorer countries typically have weaker judiciaries that lack independence as a check and balance on executives and parliaments. Wealthier countries such as Romania are better able to establish such institutional checks as DNA and other watchdogs of the public purse.

Even wealthier countries, such as the US and UK, are plagued by corrupt transactions but have been at the forefront of anti-corruption especially surrounding procurement and contracting for more than a century. The US is a federal system that relies on internal controls supervised and reviewed regularly by internal auditors who report to separate often high-level authorities such as state legislatures rather than local officials in the governments they audit. This independence allows them the relative freedom to examine waste, fraud, and abuse more readily. At the federal level, two sets of institutions examine contracts, programs and policies for waste, fraud, and abuse: first, the Comptroller General of the General Accountability Office (GAO) which reviews program and policy performance and provides lessons for future improvements to Congress. In addition to GAO, the Office of Inspectors General (OIG) examines and reviews federal government operations and reports to the US Treasury. Since the 1978 Act, the president appoints inspectors inside 59 government units, 29 of which require congressional approval. These offices attempt to serve as checks and balances to ward off tremendous partisan political pressures as well as intrusions by special interests into contracting. Despite these elaborate checks, interests have often been successful in hollowing out these institutions to suit their purposes which can hide bribery, kickbacks, and phony invoicing.

In the UK, to ensure independence as much as possible, the monarch of the UK appoints the Comptroller and Accountant General (C&AG) to run the NAO. This same institutional structure exists for contracts and value for money and financial auditing for public programs and policies in all Commonwealth countries. The NAO is also the Supreme Audit Institution (SAI) in all Commonwealth countries and reports regularly to Parliament. Despite having legal and constitutional authority and legitimacy, the effectiveness of Commonwealth audit and fiscal watchdog institutions depends on their political support. For instance, in South Africa, its Comptroller General has to deal with kickbacks on local government contracts given to ANC partisan allies outside the municipal areas. That means the contracting process is distorted by partisan influences that also permit local governments to delay or avoid accounting and reporting requirements to the NAO. This distortion also amounts to funds wasted that could be allocated to municipal residents for local jobs.

More visible and actionable problems affect the approval and implementation of contracts for transport infrastructure. These intrusive but largely legal steps are wasteful and contract completions are delayed not by corruption but by a paralytic process that affects most large infrastructure projects in the US and other countries. In some cases, design of the contracts is even more opaque as attempts to bring in the private sector as partners to save money in PPPs often fail to work as planned (Guess, 2008).[9]

Public rail projects (LRT and heavy rail) are complex and costly to build. Procuring railcars is costly because each car is bespoke, or custom made to order and not interchangeable so that a second-hand market does not exist in the US. In Europe, rail cars are pretty standard and thus cheaper. "Buy America" protectionist laws have existed for many decades to benefit labor but have succeeded in driving all real US manufacturers out of business and vastly raising the prices of rail contracts. Purchased cars are mostly from European or Asian firms (German, Spanish, Italian, Taiwanese, Japanese, and Chinese). Winning bidders are forced typically to build factories in the US to satisfy local content and labor laws. Change orders for unexpected costs are frequent in all transit contracts and they have long plagued implementation with higher costs and downstream prices.

PPPs are a form of concession contracts to private firms for the provision of public services. In the PPP, the private firm sells the service to the public authority or other third party with state loan guarantees (World Bank, 2005:145).[10] Private infrastructure firms gain from working with stable governments such as Brazil. Governments expect to gain budget savings and promotion of capital investment which countries like Brazil need as they invest only 2% of GDP on such asset investments (Guess, 2019:15). PPPs are common in Europe but not so much in the US. In Europe, they operate on the margins of EU reporting requirements (World Bank, 2005:137). Budgets are on a cash basis and many payments are off-budget. For instance, "availability payments" which would accrue normally are not accounting or balance sheet liabilities under risk-free Maastricht and ESA 95 criteria (2005:145). This kind of opacity practice is also normal in many US states. For instance, the Virginia PPP Transport Act of 1995 allows off-budget expenditures for projects such as the Metrorail Dulles airport rail project extension and prevents expenditure outlays from adding to fiscal deficits or debts. Such provisions prevent thorough evaluation of financial risks such as cost overruns and expected increases through change orders as well as conflicts of interest, which fail to pro-tect the public trust (Turque, 2007). By contrast, such rail transit projects are part of the normal budgetary accounts in Chile, Argentina, Peru, and Brazil (2005:145). Both EU and US states mask significant and by now obvious fiscal risks.

The PPP method was touted as a cost-saving innovation for the Purple Line LRT project between two counties in the US state of Maryland. It was appraised in 2005 by Maryland MTA as the most cost-effective option for the 16-mile corridor, over bus, BRT, heavy rail, and do-nothing. The US Federal Transit Administration (FTA) financed 50% of the project by capi-tal transfer, leaving the local jurisdictions to find the rest of the funds either by taxes, innovative financing, or General Obligation or GO bonds issued on the basis of transparent market financing and traditional creditworthi-ness and ratings criteria (Guess, 2005:20). The FTA required use of the cost-effectiveness criteria called the "Resource Productivity Approach" (Guess and Farnham, 2011:194) rather than a traditional cost-benefit analysis. This meant that the sensitivity of transit options to costs and benefits with different discount rates and different timing of costs and benefits to break-even points were abbreviated. Moreover, FTA man-dated a 7% discount rate which translated into a preference for invest-ing in the future (Guess and Farnham, 2011:193–194). In short, use of cost-effectiveness rather than cost-benefit or break-even analyses for the Purple Line meant the project's significant financial risks were ignored. Cost-effectiveness analysis can lead to flawed project affordability analysis as here. Cost-effectiveness analysis is simpler to apply than cost-benefit analysis but is limited because it merely compares the estimated monetary costs to produce the primary benefit (here meaning the least $costs for time saved/commuter along the 16-mile route) (Michel, 2001:78).[11]

For the past 17 years of the Purple Line project, as could be predicted, delays from lawsuits by opponents on a variety of rationales, such as fos-sils, squirrel and bird nest destruction, disputes between contractors and the counties over responsibilities for cost overruns, changes of prime con-tractor, and more public complaints about damages to homes, small busi-nesses, golf courses, and country clubs during construction, have driven up the costs of the still to be completed Maryland LRT project (that may be someday tagged in the transit industry as a Purple Elephant!).

Accumulated facts as of March 2023 make it clear that using the stand-ard capital investment technique of market appraisal of creditworthiness and bond financing over PPP would have been far cheaper for everyone. Added to the well-known costs of rail operations and maintenance, the tragi-comic history of attempting to fit this large, complex megaproject in an urban area of a country with a strong litigious culture has diminished the future appeal of any large transit capital projects such as LRT and heavy rail. It is also clear that the appraisal stage needs to ensure thorough due diligence by public sector staff with financial skills and lawyers that can ensure PPP contracts comprehensively protect the public trust from major downstream financial and economic risks that threaten the credit ratings of the county and state governments.[12]

Research into the causes of the frequent costly delays of and cost overruns of megaprojects in OECD countries suggests common but fixable problems. Projects such as the Berlin Brandenburg airport (14 years late from groundbreaking to service), British HS2 high-speed rail (2× estimated costs and 20 years late), Montreal 976 Olympic stadiums (debts paid off 30 years later), and the Boston "Big Dig" (overrun 5× initial budget) all revealed the same two problems. First, they lacked rigorous planning of both procurement and implementation. Projects in all cases faced quagmires of planning rules and legal obstacles. Planning was often hasty, self-serving for the few bidders that compete and failed to anticipate obvious implementation problems. What this suggests is a lack of public sector capacity and salary similarities to private A&E and construction firms bidding to critically review bids and oversee implementation of megaprojects. Second, the more successful projects with fewer cost overruns, construction delays, and attainment of benefits claimed in benefit-cost or cost-effectiveness pre-appraisals featured standardized designs and manufacturing processes from tracks to railcars. US rail transit projects have always included procurement of bespoke or tailor-made products. The Purple Line LRT cars and systems were no different. By contrast, in ten years, the Chinese built the world's largest HSR network with standardized manufacture of everything from viaducts to tracks and railcars. As one would expect rigorous planning and any litigation by civil society and public interest groups, there was not a major obstacle to procurement or implementation management![13]

Questions

Based on the above, why does productivity for public transport projects often stagnate, especially for rail projects? What typically goes wrong at each stage of the project cycle? How can procurement be deregulated to prevent US and other governments from becoming inefficiently clogged by procedural inflexibility? Could deregulation diminish the problem of "coagulated government" in the US? Why does the US fail to learn and apply comparative lessons from overseas transport project planning and implementation experiences such as in China and what have been the consequences? What lessons could be learned? What practices could be avoided?[14] What lessons are known but inapplicable? A major issue at the contract award stage is procurement of passenger rail cars. How could procurement requirements be specified more precisely, and contracts be better managed to provide the greatest value for money (cyber-security and cost effectiveness)?[15]

Discussion Case #17: International and Domestic Constraints to Connectivity in Trade and Commerce

As noted in the introduction to this chapter, ancient sectarian and political animosities continue to prevent sustained transportation and communications linkages across the world. Even in Europe, perhaps the most connected region, petty political rivalries and distrust prevent better and more efficient communication. French railroad crossings warn that one train can conceal another. The same is true of crises impeding focus on macro-level international relations problems. These problems are structural and cannot easily be managed away.

For example, Ukraine's railroad gauges are the same as Russia's (1.52m) because they were once part of the USSR. Now as they attempt to disengage from Russia as it has blockaded their Black Sea ports, they cannot ship goods easily to the east by rail toward Poland since Europe uses a 1.435-m gauge. The Russian-EU rail transport problem has been managed in the past by the time-consuming and inefficient workaround of off-loading grain and steel onto new trains. The long-term and expensive remedy for Ukraine is to rebuild railroads to the EU gauge. The EU and Ukraine have begun new regional cooperation on transportation of energy. Undersea gas pipelines between Poland and Norway with links to Slovakia and Lithuania have already happened. Greece and Bulgaria have forged new links. Croatia opened an LNG terminal in 2011.[16] But as noted, regional efforts to develop even new road links such as the 2006 planned route from Klaipeda (Lithuania) to Thessaloniki (Greece) have been pushed back to 2030, floundering from lack of political solidarity.

Where long-standing problems are actionable and definable, they nevertheless continue to be ignored and overwhelmed by petty local politics. In Africa (SSA), for example, both road and rail capacities as well as ports and pipelines are held back by years of underinvestment and mismanagement. In South Africa, British colonial history collides with modern loss-making SOEs such as Eskom (power) and Transnet (transport). Transnet is responsible for ports, railroads, and pipelines that connect South Africa with the outside world. But Transnet is an ANC party-controlled state firm rife with corruption, patronage, and neglect that serves their own political interests but not the country's transport needs to support economic development. Earlier, colonialists installed narrow gauge tracks to get diamonds and gold out of the country's hinterland as part of their mercantilist policies.[17] Now Transnet engages in sweetheart deals to buy such items as 1,000 overpriced Chinese locomotives for kickbacks. It spends mostly on white-collar salaries and skimps on O&M (which receives about 30% of actual needs). Advised years ago, to concentrate efforts on profitable mainline rail routes that transport coal and iron over unprofitable rural lines that serve many of its voters, it ignored the advice. Bad management has amounted to a major opportunity cost from the gap between what miners could dig and what they could export last year of at least $4.7b as the international price of coal has soared. The "developmental state" has long insisted it needs to own big firms to invest, create jobs, and reduce racial inequality. But utilities and firms need private investment and effective management. They will not be forthcoming as long as they are the plaything of dysfunctional ruling parties like the ANC.

Locally, there are municipal services problems that have been effectively managed even in contexts which are obstructed by fractious and seemingly intractable ethno-religious and nationalist politics. Such topics have been called: "managing services and project implementation in war zones".

Israeli LRT System

Israel, for instance, is traversed by multiple light rail (LRT) lines. The existing and planned routes are often contentious issues, as land tenure and allocations between Palestinians and Israelis are a well-known existential issue and the reason for many violent and unresolved civil conflicts over the years and now. In this volatile context, Israel relies heavily on rail for both passenger travel and freight shipments. The country's rail network of passenger and freight lines is 700 miles which are all owned and managed by the state (Israel Railways Ltd and various city metro authorities such as Tel Aviv Transit Authority, NTA). The Haifa to Tel Aviv heavy rail passenger line is ten years old (2013) and runs 56 miles on a twice-hourly basis. The engines and cars are mostly German (Siemens) and Swedish-Swiss (ABB) with additions from rehabilitated Croatian trains. The heavy rail intercity lines such as this one are standard gauge to match other Middle Eastern systems originally built by the British, such as in Egypt. They also drive on the left like Swiss and Middle Eastern trains planned by the British.

The Tel-Aviv LRT system run by NTA must operate its trains across a city that contains Palestinians and Israelis whose history is violent and volatile. Its trains have been specifically designed to be suicide bomb-proof by Siemens. That means that onboard blasts will no longer impact neighborhoods where the trains happen to be running. NTA managers have to deal with normal transit issues such as train acquisitions, maintenance, rehabilitation, onboard safety and security in its 34 stations over 15 miles (10 below ground, 24 above), signaling, and electrical systems. Current management issues are focused on signaling and safety as trains suddenly brake inside tunnels from software problems. But unlike most urban transit systems, NTA, as noted, has to deal with suicide bombers and terrorists of all stripes. That requires close coordination with city police, fire, and emergency services. Managers must conduct action scenarios constantly as circumstances change. For instance, terrorists employ new methods; police learn that they have made mistakes and need to make course corrections on response times and types of emergency assistance.

Despite these risks and constraints, NTA managers have been remarkably alert, effective, productive, and responsive to normal everyday passenger needs. They must attend to fare structures and fee charging for all types of passengers in several languages. They must ensure that schedules and on-time performances continue to be met. And despite receiving subsidies from the Israeli treasury to make up the difference between operating costs and passenger revenues, the transit system is held to strict fiscal discipline. NTA must find ways to ensure operations and maintenance as well as rehabilitation expenses are well-funded. For marketing and ticketing, NTA needs to ensure that operations are effective and responsive to riders.

What unique constraints face NTA transit managers? How would they compare with urban rail and bus systems that serve poor and rich riders in other jurisdictions, some of them armed, with a history of violence and potentially dangerous to everyday patrons, such as in Chicago, New York, Rio, and Washington? How would you design a training program for current and prospective managers working in such contexts? What topics would be most essential? Referring back to *Discussion Case #10*, what approaches would you recommend to reduce Tel-Aviv's transit security problems?

Discussion Case #18: Japanese Transport Assistance for Vietnam

Japan has demonstrated a unique and effective means of providing green transport infrastructure assistance to Southeast Asian countries. In the face of China's proudly and aggressively touted Belt and Road Initiative (BRI), Japan has quietly taken the lead in investing in such projects in the Southeast Asian region ($259b to $157b). The reason for their success is who the Japanese are and how they provide the assistance.

In Vietnam (GVN), the cases of Hanoi's rapid rail and the HCM transit lines reveal these differences. Japan financed the HCM line and

China the Hanoi line. The differences in designing, procurement, financing, and building projects together with differences in how they managed operations on completion provide explicit technical assistance lessons for overseas transit capital and development assistance. Assistance to the GVN on design of the HCM line and later operations was the responsibility of Tokyo Metro Authority which worked closely with GVN and HCM city transit officials. This was the unique feature of the project in that it put counterpart technicians together between institutions cross-border, contributing to the institution-building of the HCM transit authority that would serve it in operation and design of current and future lines. The Japanese government, through its development assistance agency, JICA, won the contract and arranged the construction consortium led by Sumitomo which arranged for the purchase of Hitachi rail cars for the line.

Financing by the Japanese was through the new Japanese Partnership for Quality Infrastructure (PQI) with additional support from Asian Development Bank (ADB) and Japanese Bank for International Cooperation (JBIC). This consortium approach was in clear contrast with Chinese planning and financing of such projects as the Hanoi line. The Chinese used their SOEs to work with Hanoi authorities and provided most of the labor. The project was part of its BRI. By contrast, Japan used mostly Vietnamese labor where possible, inserting Japanese technicians mainly from Tokyo Metro, a widely respected Metro system and operator. Vietnamese were proud to be teamed with Tokyo Metro and to learn from them. They were also proud to work alongside the Hitachi rail technicians as these are some of the best made and operational cars on the world market. Japan also had a long-standing history and familiarity with and knowledge of Vietnamese market conditions and its political culture context. Japanese firms are closer to Southeast Asian firms and are adept at arranging smooth relations between its government and local firms and governments.

In short, the Vietnamese government trusted these arrangements more than Chinese SOEs and their government's aggressive BRI. The Japanese were viewed as quiet and less heavy handed than the Chinese and easier to work with. Such qualities as proximity and familiarity count a lot in the success of implementing aid contracts and operating such systems as rail transit.[18]

It should be noted that JICA has provided crucial lessons from another program area to Asian countries and now Ukraine: disaster management. Asian countries have been receptive to lessons Japan because of their familiarity with their people and political culture. They also trust the Japanese to share lessons with all countries of the region. While the sector has not been covered in this book, many texts and articles exist on international disaster management. Japan is a critical provider of important technical and managerial lessons, largely because it has suffered: city bombing attacks in WWII, floods, typhoons, nuclear disasters, attacks on their infrastructure, such as subways, as well as to adopt lessons from their frequent and successful responses to earthquakes, tsunamis, and fires. Lessons have been provided so far to Ukraine on: regulations for clearing rubble from earthquakes to be applied to Russian bombs, building underground electrical substations (not to rebuild the old but build a new!), building innovative water pipes and reservoir systems to provide fresh water after disruptions to water supplies from bombing attacks, and building cities that are ready for the worst. JICA taught them to think of innovative responses to Russian attacks as just one of their frequent natural disasters[19]!

What lessons for urban metro infrastructure planning and financing did Japan's JICA provide Vietnam's HCM City? How did these lessons compare with standard technical assistance and financing by donors such as World Bank for other cities?[20]

Discussion Case #19: Bogota's Bus Rapid Transit (BRT) Experience

The case of Bogota's *TransMilenio* (BRT) system is an example of the Dickensian Maxim from *Little Dorrit*[21]: "how it should not be done"! There, Dickens described the frequent tragi-comic absurdity of bureaucratic process run wild—legal "circumlocution" and governmental complexity, waste and incompetence, updated in a 1976 French *Asterix* animated film as "The Place that Sends You Mad". They describe what happens when the imperatives of municipal services delivery and city politics clash: a managerial and planning nightmare!

TransMilenio (TM) was the first BRT line in a large (8m) city built in the late 1990s. The first modern BRT line in the world was built in Curitiba, Brazil (population 2m), in 1974. Since then, hundreds of BRT lines have been built and operate smoothly in every region from a single line in Amman, and Washington, DC, to multiple lines in Guayaquil, and seven in Mexico City (with more planned all linking to its vast metro system). BRTs are popular because they can be built fast and at less than 15% of the cost of heavy rail underground or over ground metros, meaning fares can be far lower. They provide commuters faster trips between two points because the lanes are separated from regular city traffic. The linked buses can travel up to 60 mph. In short, BRT consists of a dedicated two-lane road above and below ground that connects with about 5 stations/mile. Passenger capacity for the electric or diesel articulated buses depends on rapid headway or running trains approximately every 1–2 minutes. To achieve this intense head-way requires that the transit authority procures many of the special articulated buses to keep ahead of passenger demand. Where these sim-ple operational and management rules are followed, they are effective in moving large urban populations rapidly and cheaply to and from destinations.

Bogota TM did not follow these simple managerial rules and soon be-came overcrowded, an easily fixable problem for most transit managers in all regions of the world. But Colombia is a unitary government and issues in major capital cities can become national issues. Candidates for president in Colombia have used Bogota's problems platforms for expensive and often inapplicable solutions, such as the above-ground metros (elevated heavy rail) that were proposed by successive mayors. City buses are run by private companies in Bogota and resented the competitive advantage TM had as a publicly subsidized system. They lobbied for an above-ground metro rail which they perceived correctly was as less of a threat to their ridership given that their bus terminals and stops would always be acces-sible to some of the BRT stations.

TM's single line became overcrowded (2.4m passengers/day) because of mismanagement: *TransMilenio* could not add buses because they had not been procured; electric signaling systems and mechanical breakdowns occurred because TM did not have the funds to prevent the well-known and obvious problems from occurring. Predictably, TM became intensely unpopular leaving the field open for mis-definition of the public transit problem and recommendations of impractical solutions by transit general-ists with dreamy expensive plans. The result was underinvestment in the working existing and practical transit system by successive mayors, in-cluding Bogota Mayor Gustavo Petro now the President of Colombia. His contribution was to cut already low fares 20% more which contributed to more underinvestment in TM which of course made operational prob-lems worse. Meanwhile the Bogota metropolitan area population grew to 11.5m and Petro ordered work to begin on a 14-mile above-ground heavy rail metro. When it became obvious that fares would be exorbitant to sup-port the new metro, and the costs would add to debt service in the national budget, citizen outcries forced Petro to add three more BRT lines to TM and halt work on the heavy-rail metro.

How could better transit management have improved Bogota's *Trans-Milenio* BRT system? How was TM management constrained by the Co-lombian national government? Why did *TransMilenio* lose commuter support after 15 years of successful service? Should the TM's BRT system be expanded or replaced with an above-ground metro system (heavy rail) or light rail (LRT) lines? Was there evidence of a capital improvement pro-cess (CIP) here, that in analysis and ranking of proposed capital projects requires valid data and industry metrics, such as debt affordability, rate of return analyses, and use of weighting and scoring frameworks[22] for any of the options proposed by Bogota mayors? How independent was TM to make key operational and planning decisions, such as ticket pricing, and procuring rolling stock, regarding Bogota transit needs? What other public transit and financing options exist for Bogota urban transit?[23] How have other cities such as Toronto managed their transit system's growing pains?[24]

Notes

1 Debt management is a major problem for aid loans to rebuild war-torn countries such as Ukraine. With bombs falling, it is practically impossible to estimate the funds necessary to rebuild later. A more serious problem is the cost of borrowing. The IMF has just approved a $15.6b emergency loan program that includes the usual cuts in spending for fiscal discipline. But such cuts apply to misbehaving countries and not those under siege for whom spending cuts could mean defeat! In addition, IMF loans to "middle-income" countries require a 3.5% basic rate along with surcharges and fees that make the effective interest burden about 7.5%–8%. That is very expensive but based on the premise that other cheaper donors such as the EU, US, and World Bank will eventually chip in and lower the burden *Economist* "War Economics, Funding Conflict", 4-1-23, p.59.
2 "Green v Green: Blocking Clean-Energy Infrastructure is No Way to Save the Planet", *Economist*, 2-4-23, pp.21–23.
3 Michel (2001), *op. cit.*, pp.15–16.
4 Steven A. Finkler (2010) *Financial Management for Public, Health and Nonprofit Organizations* (Upper Saddle River, NJ: Pearson Education), p.2.
5 Moriah Balingit and Gregory Schneider (2023) "Virginia Erred in Estimating School Funds", *The Washington Post*, 2-1, B1.
6 The term "flexible budget" is used by Steven Finkler (2010) *Financial Management for Public, Health and Nonprofit Organizations* (Upper Saddle River, NJ: Pearson Education).
7 *Economist* (2023) "Trying to Get Back on Track", 5-27, p.54.
8 Additionally, the Financial Action Task Force (FATF) is an international body that battles money-laundering and terrorist-finance with sanctions such as its "grey list". This list dampens investment flows for failure to report suspect banking deposits and loans to corrupt regimes. Like other methods, such as Unexplained Wealth Orders (UWOs) used by the British judiciary to investigate bank transfers, it is a global anti-corruption tool whose sanctions and incentives encourage accountability and transparency.
9 George M. Guess (2008) *Managing and Financing Urban Public Transport Systems, an International Perspective* (Budapest: Open Society Institute, Local Government and Public Service Reform Initiative), pp.14–20.
10 World Bank (2005) *Current Issues in Fiscal Reform in Central Europe and the Baltic States* (Washington, DC: IBRD).
11 R. Gregory Michel (2001) *Decision tools for Budgetary Analysis* (Chicago, IL: Government Finance Officers Association of Canada and the US, GFOA); George M. Guess and Paul G. Farnham (2011) *Cases in Public Policy Analysis (3rd ed)* (Washington, DC: Georgetown University Press), pp.182–183.

12 Debt rating agencies, such as Fitch, S&P, and Moody's use about the same four criteria to assess the fiscal condition of borrowers and their capacity to repay annual debt service, or their creditworthiness. The agencies rate these criteria slightly different accounting for the slightly different grades of risk they are accorded. The criteria are (1) economy—whether growing or contracting, (2) debt, debt history of issuing and repayment; debt burden and high debt service requirements as % of past year revenue, (3) government, degree of managerial professionalism, delays in approving budgets, and budget controls, and (4)financial analysis—trends in revenues and expenditures, adequacy of revenue base; vulnerability to new liabilities such as pensions. John L. Mikesell (2011) *Fiscal Administration, Analysis and Applications for the Public Sector (8th ed)* (Boston, MA: Wadsworth), pp.653–654.

13 *Economist* (2023) "Bartleby: Mega Lowdown", 3-18, p.57.

14 From: "Build Back Under Budget" *Economist* (2021) 5–29, pp.23–24, "Infrastructure Problems".

15 From: "How to Stop a Speeding Train" *Bloomberg Business Week* (October 7, 2019).

16 "Between Three Seas", *Economist*, 1-21-23, p.49

17 "Off the Rails", *Economist*, 1-21-23, pp.44–45.

18 As indicated by its effective aid to urban transit in Vietnam, the Japanese are also providing consensus-building and a strategic diplomatic bridge between the West and the G-7 Indo-Pacific region. While the West, in particular the US, lectures countries in this region about liberal democratic values and pushes for internal rule of law norms (i.e., human rights, democracy-building), Japan and China build actual bridges and roads and push for respect for international rules that respect borders rather than the use of raw power. Japan is especially opposed to the use of raw power or force to border changes, such as Russia is doing in Ukraine and China threatens to do in Taiwan. The takeaway for small countries is that their borders are threatened by power-hungry autocrats immune from the restraining effects of institutional checks and balances in their own much larger countries. *Economist* (2023) "Reviving the G-7", 5-20, pp.31–32.

19 *Economist* (2023) "Banyan: Lessons in Asian Resilience", 6-10, p.34.

20 *Economist* (2021) "A Glimpse into Japan's Understated Financial Heft in Southeast Asia", 8-14.

21 Charles Dickens (1967) *Little Dorrit* (New York: Penguin).

22 George M. Guess (2015) *Government Budgeting, A Practical Guidebook* (Albany, NY: SUNY Press), pp.137–164.

23 *Economist* (2020) "Colombia: Not So Fast", January 4, p.23.

24 See Richard M. Soberman (2008) "Transportation in Toronto" in George M Guess (ed) *Managing and Financing Urban Public Transport Systems, An International Perspective* (Budapest: Local Government Initiative of the Open Society Institute), pp.189–223.

6 Managing International Educational Systems

Context and Problems

Since WWII, educational expenditures have been the fastest growing area of public spending in OECD countries. But educational importance on national agendas is reflected not just in budgetary outlays. The most important values and interests of a society are represented in education policy.[1] Defining such basic interests, managing the competing interests, and reforming the systems that should reflect their needs have been matters of great controversy across the globe. For example, in 2000, representatives from 164 countries met at the World Education Forum in Dakar, Senegal, and pledged six education goals to be achieved by 2015, including expanding early childhood education, increasing access to, and improving the education for all citizens, particularly for girls and the poor, providing equal access to education, improving literacy by 50%, and eliminating education disparities between boys and girls. Two education goals to be accomplished by 2015 also appear among the eight United Nations Development Program[2] (UNDP, 2012) Millennium Development Goals (MDGs). One is the attainment of universal primary education, and the other goal targets the elimination of gender disparity at all levels of education.

This chapter discusses the opportunities and obstacles to educational reforms many of which have been driven largely by the "New Public Management" or NPM literature of the 1980s. This literature urged fiscal and management decentralization for public service organizations and competition between public and private service delivery organizations, supplemented by empirical feedback on actual performance.[3] The reform of educational systems and transfer of applied lessons across countries in the last few decades has been dramatic, with spectacular successes also but some notable failures. This chapter will discuss the problem of how smart educational management can contribute to breaking down cultural segregation, such as in Northern Ireland (NI) now, and as happened in the Netherlands in the 1960s. The Dutch official policy of "pilarization" or

DOI: 10.4324/9781032670959-6

segregation was entrenched through civil society institutions such as unions, religious organizations, schools, sports clubs, and the media which among other negatives, shielded voters from divergent opinions. Educational segregation was broken only by years of sustained educational reform and an increase in the wealth of all classes and ethnicities.

Currently, the US public school system is largely a top-down operation with curricula norms and standards set by the state departments of education and delivery by municipal or county school systems. Funding is by municipal property taxes with a small portion added from federal grants. But most local school officials are constrained in efforts to manage schools by teachers and maintenance unions, parents, and an overall lack of school-level authority to hire and fire as well as to hold staff and teachers accountable for results. Management authority has not been devolved to principals to make the necessary operational decisions and to budget for actual school needs. It is left to US local school principals and teachers to manage politically explosive abstractions like "choice" and "competition" with little authority or incentives to act. Unions, parents, and the public have all taken frozen positions and have become instant classroom experts on educational curricula, teaching methods, and testing. Most other countries rich or poor operate similarly except that the authority to manage schools has been deconcentrated from ministries of education to schools which can be provincial or local units of the national government. The structure of school management in federal or unitary systems is roughly similar to norms, oversight, and accountability standards set by the national or provincial governments.

Consistent with the principles of the NPM literature, which have been widely applied, school reformers and authorities should continue to decentralize discretion and devolve responsibilities and accountability to local principals and teachers in order to improve school performance. To achieve such results, management discretion and accountability have to be devolved along with accountability for educational attainment. School principals and staff would be held to common professional norms and objectives (normative centralization), which they could more feasibly achieve using their added managerial discretion and responsibility for results (operational decentralization). Examples of performance or results targets or metrics include student rates of enrolment, retention, promotion, and graduation. Other important rates are teacher turnover, improvements in student PISA reading, and mathematics scores. In short, the school reforms (mainly in the 1990s in the US but still strong overseas) focused on; and pushed for more spending, competition, data, and accountability. Teacher evaluations and pay should be linked to student outcomes measured by new tests. Poorly attended and otherwise "bad" schools should be shuttered and replaced by charter schools. Charter schools (UK academies) receive public funds but are run independently and compete for students with conventional public schools. Charters are largely unconstrained by union contracts and have been able to invent new ways to engage students.[4]

It should be noted that at about the same time in the 1970s and 1980s, management orthodoxy in the private corporate sector also favored centralization: tight command of local stores and outlets by central headquarters (HQs). Authority was merely "deconcentrated" to local managers as in unitary states, and local managers were still held to centrally set norms, targets, and mandates. Deviations from this orthodoxy were rare in the private sector. Bed Bath and Beyond (BBB) was one firm that shunned the centralized management orthodoxy. As far back as the 1970s, BBB shunned retail orthodoxy and gave store managers wide discretion to stock their shelves. As a result, BBB sales soared as managers responded to local customers near their stores. But HQ executives had another major blind spot: the web. While other retail competitors such as Amazon were moving ahead with an online focus, BBB executives stayed with their bricks and mortar focus. That locked-in strategic incompetence (similar to that of Kodak and other staid, centralized operations seemingly impervious to change and outside advice) brought the store to its present state of bankruptcy.[5]

For public schools, the NPM literature, secondly, would urge the use of management incentives to encourage the setting of objectives and measuring results. These incentives enhance the decentralized discretion, authority, and accountability of line managers. Organizations from militaries and aid agencies to hospitals and schools have applied this incentive theory with positive results. Devolution of fiscal, budget, tax, and personnel authority to line managers increases their discretion to improve service results. In response, fiscal decentralization programs around the world continue to devolve budget, tax, and borrowing authority resulting in more decentralized governance. Management incentives are financial and nonfinancial. For instance, the motivation to reform budget systems formats from inputs to outputs and outcomes focuses on nonfinancial incentives of reducing intrusive and redundant reporting requirements. This removes one of the key obstacles to the use of the budget as a positive management tool and also removes a key cause of goal displacement discussed in *Chapter 5*.

Third, NPM would encourage structural reforms: more pupil choice through competition among schools to offer innovative programs and methods and giving them greater opportunities to attend charter schools (called "academies" in the UK) with stipends or state tuition subsidies and in some places vouchers to attend even privately funded schools.[6] Such structural reforms focus on strengthening both types of schools by incentivizing them to compete in order to attain the learning objectives and norms set by central authorities at the outset.[7] Alternative schools such as charters and academies compete in an educational market to attain excellence on par or greater than public or state schools. To measure and create accountability, both public and charter schools regularly report teacher and student performance data. The NPM premise applied to schools is that devolution of authority and responsibility to schools for their own management will enhance student learning and choice to attend either public or charter schools in order to receive the best available education.

In short, the twofold objective of such reforms is to strengthen the overall educational system at both the strategic policy level that focuses on the design and redesign of the basic norms and policies and provide access options for students that enhance their learning. The reforms begin with building human capital (teachers and principals) that in turn generates more human capital which strengthens the entire system.

Learning Outcomes

1   To review why educational reforms have often been more successful than other aid attempts at capacity-building and institutional-strengthening in particular sectors.
2   To try and apply NPM to education management via critical review of its three tenets. First, do setting goals and measurable objectives together with sufficient incentives to meet them enhance accountability?
3   Second, does the devolution of authority and responsibilities to line officials, public managers, school staff, and elected officials enhance responsiveness to their users, ministries, students and parents, and to their voters?
4   Third, does competition between schools over results attached to funding, enhance student choice of the best schools?
5   To play the role of school principal at Seaview Elementary School in *Discussion Case #20* and face the issue of curriculum development in this Northern Irish community, one divided by a long history of sectarian and racial hatred (refer back to *Discussion Case #4*).
6   To review the lessons for managing urban policing in such places as Chicago and Rio de Janeiro applicable to staffing and managing urban schools.
7   To apply methods of conflict resolution in fractious political cultures such as Belfast, Ulster County, NI, Rio de Janeiro, Brazil, Kano, Nigeria (review *Mr. Johnson's* decision context on the road project there in Kano, northern Nigeria, in *Discussion Case #7*), and Kherson, Ukraine.
8   To examine the four tenets of Michelle Rhee's reforms in Washington, DC, in *Discussion Case #21*.

9   To examine how Rhee focused on the institutional constraints and incentives needed for school, staff, and teacher performance improvements. To review the meaning of school autonomy and the decision to close underperforming and poorly attended schools at the outset to save funds.

10   To review the aftermath and whether reforms have continued subsequently under different mayoral administrations. The question of results and attribution of them to the reforms is still debatable.

11   To understand the severe contexts that school reformers face in African countries such as Liberia in *Discussion Case #22.*

12   To understand what randomized control trials (RCTs) are and how they were used to examine eight different reform proposals in Liberia. To examine their strengths and weaknesses as a policy evaluation tool. Why is the education minister's decision in 2016 considered one of the boldest policy reform experiments in modern African history?

13   To examine the results of the RCT in Liberia after three years.

14   To examine the criteria used in Liberia to select the winning operator and learn why *Rising Academy* was picked over *Street Child.*

15   To examine the potential role of the *Hawthorne Effect* here and how they have affected the results of the proposed reforms.

16   To review the 2018 school reforms in Edo (southern Nigeria) in *Discussion Case #23.* To learn how this reform focused on improvements in teaching and managing classrooms.

17   To review the arguments for and against the *NewGlobe* lesson scripting method. To discuss how the scripts themselves might be revised to improve teaching effectiveness, according to evaluations such as that by *RTI* and your own opinions.

18   To review the need for simple and extreme teaching methods for small children in contexts like Nigeria and Liberia.

Issues and Cases

Discussion Case #20 (Repeated Here from Discussion Case #4)
School Integration in Northern Ireland

Schools are a reflection of the communities and neighborhoods in which they are located. Managing these schools under normal stable conditions is a delicate and challenging balancing act. It is a high-stress job. But if the communities have a history of ethno-racial conflicts, children of these adults will likely bring those prejudices and grudges to school and make the school management job even harder!

Northern Ireland's (NI) first school, Seaview Primary, just left the Catholic educational system run independently of the state to become "integrated", drawing pupils and teachers from both sides of the sectarian divide. Over 50% of integrated schools are new institutions set up by parents who see them as an essential part of a desegregated and more peaceful future. As a measure of the deep social rifts in NI, film start Liam Neeson called the decision by the school "courageous" (!). The decision was one more step in cementing relations healed in 1998 by the Good Friday Agreement after years of civil war. Decades of peace seem to have washed away the legacy of centuries of hatred. As if remaining sectarian tensions were not bad enough, the Brexit referendum was passed requiring a workaround "protocol" for NI to avoid leaving the EU. customs union by the creation of an artificial border in the Irish Sea for trade and commerce between the NI province and mainland Ireland which remains in the EU.

For NI parents and adults generally, the question remains: who should educate NI children and alongside whom? 90% of all pupils go to schools where one religious tradition dominates the intake and atmosphere. 50% go to Catholic system schools; about 43% attend state-run schools that are predominantly Protestant; only 7% attend "integrated" schools like Seaview Primary. Most neighborhoods are still segregated and where supposedly defunct paramilitary forces still hold sway.

Education is a microcosm of the mutual resentment that feeds tribalism. While most young adults claim they are neither Protestant "unionist" nor Catholic "nationalist", in culture and identity they still vote accordingly to protect their turf which means their schools (refer back to the discussion of political culture in *Chapter 2*). A recent parliamentary bill provided that integrated schools would be the default for all new schools. The Democratic Unionist party condemned this as an attack on parental choice. Sein Fein (the party seeking provincial reunion with Ireland and a "united" Ireland) gave lukewarm support for the bill but said it did too little to promote the Irish language, Gaelic music, and sports. A Glenarm school that planned to switch to integrated status found that its Protestant enrollment doubled. But an NI official supporting integrated education said that it will not become the norm anytime soon. As evidence, some Catholic schools are deciding between integration and closure. A school in Derry resists integration saying that it has a long history of promoting social mobility among poorer Catholics and serving their community's culture. The school also has scored some of the highest academic attainments in the province, including the production of two Nobel laureates! The tragic problem is that most NI schools try to maintain the racial and ethnic composition of their student bodies in a context where cross-cultural ignorance allows prejudice to flourish.

Suppose you were the principal of a secondary school in Belfast, Ulster County, Northern Island. Because of the new "troubles" caused by the reaction to Brexit and the hard border issue with Ireland issue, you have been charged with managing student conflicts over curriculum. You have been also encouraged by parents to push for integrated status. You need to find ways to integrate your students amidst tensions between parents, teachers, and community religious and political groups. How would the long history of religious conflict, racial gerrymandering, and socio-political partition be embedded in the NI political culture obstructing conflict resolution? In what ways could you work around this problem and make positive changes at the operational level? What negotiation strategies could you use?[8]

Discussion Case #21: Washington, DC, School Reform[9]

Roger Query was a teacher in a mid-sized high school (HS) in Washington, DC. He had been working for the school system as a teacher for about ten years and hoped to rise someday through the administrative ranks to serve as a principal of his own school. He felt that in order to do so, he should understand more about the position to which he aspired as well as how the central administrative office of the school system functioned. In an effort to learn more about the policy and operations of the DC Public Schools (DCPS), he set up informational interviews with key officials. Over the years, Mr. Query had learned first-hand about the constraints faced by teachers, principals, and support staff by restrictive rules and lack of resources. He also knew about the context of severe poverty in this large urban school district. If he was going to be a principal someday, it was important that he learn whether and how he could overcome some of these constraints to motivate his students, teach better classes, and improve overall student performance.

Background

Despite Mr. Query's optimism, he knew that DCPS had serious problems that had led to severe student academic deficits as well as massive challenges with regard to attendance, safety, and basic operations. The school system had a high teacher and leadership turnover rate. Stakeholders such as the Mayor's office, Board of Education, parent organizations, teacher unions, and the DC City Council did not trust each other on school policy matters or on operations. Institutional power games distracted the schools from their main task of facilitating learning for students. Since the bulk of DCPS students regularly performed poorly, this led many to believe that most students in DC could not learn and that educational reform was nearly impossible. It was well-known that overall DCPS enrollment had been declining for years. While in 1981 DCPS had over 100,000 students, by 2009 actual enrollment had declined to only 45,000. Despite the 55%

drop in enrollment, DCPS still operated and maintained the 143 schools built before 2006. At one point, the number of schools increased to 150. It wasn't that students and their families were leaving Washington, DC. Many of them in fact enrolled in DC independent public charter schools or private schools. By 2009, about 64% or 44,397 of the total 70,044 students were enrolled in traditional public schools and 36% in charter schools. This was an increase in charter school enrollment of 63.6% in only five years (from 15,500 in 2005). The National Assessment of Educational Progress (NAEP) proficiency scores for DCPS were the lowest of any urban district in 2007. Black-white achievement gaps were over 50 percentage points in both reading and math. While DC's $15k spending/pupil was nearly the highest in the US, achievement results were almost the lowest. Apart from a few schools in wealthier DC neighborhoods, low student graduation, attendance, and promotion rates were almost the norm in DCPS. Figures like these reflected obvious systemic problems such as spending inefficiency, high overhead costs, and the fact that available funds were not getting to the students.

Mr. Query knew all this and many of his former classmates who taught at nearby elite county suburban schools (Montgomery County, Maryland, and Fairfax County, Virginia) repeatedly asked him why he stayed on. Yet he persevered and felt that his students needed him there at his school—a "duty" or "service" as he put it. It was enough motivation for him to be told periodically by students and colleagues that he was effective with his students. A pat on the back now and then was just enough to keep him on the job and focused on his tasks.

As luck would have it, one of Mr. Query's professors, Dr. Horst Ritter from UC Berkeley, took a year's leave of absence to study DCPS policy-making and operational results. During Dr. Ritter's stay, in November 2006, Adrian Fenty was elected mayor of Washington, DC, by a large majority. After only two days in office, he submitted legislation to take over the schools from the local Board of Education. Mayor Fenty then appointed Michelle Rhee as Chancellor with a mandate to improve student achievement as soon as possible. While Ms. Rhee had education experience as a former teacher, she was nonetheless a controversial choice since she had never run a school district and had a non-traditional background for the role. This pick was the first in the series of bold reforms and represented the first time in DC history that top-level support existed for institutional reforms (the Board was abolished) and leadership reforms (Ms. Rhee's appointment as Chancellor) to increase student achievement and school performance. Ms. Rhee's young new staff consisted of several ex-classroom teachers who also had Master of Public Policy degrees, such as Liz Smith and Margie Krimmel. Roger Query was soon reunited with his professor and introduced to Ms. Krimmel and Ms. Smith.

The Reform Begins

Mr. Query soon learned from Dr. Ritter that a comprehensive educational reform was about to be implemented. As his field was biology and mathematics, he wasn't terribly interested in politics and knew little about big policy-making or implementation efforts. The last time he had heard those terms was in his introduction to political science class. He had a lot of questions, but for his own edification, he wanted to know first the rationale or operating theory behind their plans.

Dr. Ritter explained that in theory and in the literature, the planned reform was really nothing new. He referred Mr. Query back to the basic readings on the "New Public Management" (NPM) reforms of the 1980s–1990s. Moynihan (citing Allen Schick) summarizes five core NPM concepts: (1) managers have clear goals, (2) managers have the flexibility and discretion to use resources, (3) managers have operational authority, (4) controls focus on outputs and outcomes, and (5) managers are held accountable for resource uses and results (2006:79). To this list he added that it is also critical that managers know the availability and limits of operating and capital funds for the year. Funds should be recognizable and transparent in timely communications from the budget offices. Otherwise, managers could have clear goals, ample discretion, and knowledge of needed outputs and outcomes, and remain unaccountable for performance because of an inability to plan rationally for resource use to achieve goals and objectives. Without funding stability, it is nearly impossible to manage programs or projects.

He added, finally, that the DCPS reform is probably typical in that reformers never start with a clean slate. We faced an established bureaucracy, and for the first 1½ years, most of our efforts were on reforming basic practices and systems in both the central administrative offices and the schools. Thus, the guidance of NPM principles was quite useful as a framework in that we were tackling both public sector governance reforms in general and education reform in particular.

Mr. Query said he knew that these kinds of NPM principles had been applied to health, urban transport, and road maintenance reform programs at the state and local levels. It was part of the "reinventing government" emphasis of the 1980s and early 1990s. In addition, Query was also familiar with the education policy literature.

Which principles would apply here and how? Mr. Query asked.

Dr. Ritter explained that there is a growing body of empirically based educational policy reform literature. School systems have applied all or part of the NPM agenda to improve educational achievement in places as diverse as Singapore, Finland, Chile, Edmonton, the UK, Chicago, New York City, Baltimore, Denver, Austin, Newark, Boston, Little Rock,

Fairfax County (VA), Montgomery County (MD), Prince George's County (MD), and New Orleans. All have taken slightly different approaches based on their local institutional and cultural environment and other special circumstances. For DCPS, we translated the NPM principles into four operational concepts and designed sub-programs around them: (1) choice and competition, (2) decentralization and school autonomy, (3) performance accountability, and (4) financial predictability and sustainability. These were the **four planks** for the reform and were critical to our efforts. Let me explain them to you briefly.

Choice and competition are always high on reformer lists, Dr. Ritter explained. For high-achievers, this means making such alternatives as magnet schools available to cover specialized courses. Not every school even in wealthy districts like Montgomery County next door can afford to offer specialized courses in every school. For districts with limited means, i.e., most urban areas with large minority poor populations like DC's, choice means that parents can be sure that their children are receiving the best available education—a "good" education according to accepted norms and achievement criteria. This requires good teachers, facilities, and supplies. Since those cannot always be guaranteed, parents and students need an alternative. In many cities including Washington, that is provided by religious (often Catholic) and public charter schools. The major alternative to traditional public schools is provided by public charter schools. About 1.2m students attend them in the US. Charter schools are publicly funded schools that are independently managed, usually by a nonprofit entity with a board of directors. Another option is the receipt of government-funded vouchers to allow parents to send their children to any school. The theory is choice maximization will induce competition and force the worst schools to perform better. As voucher proposals are more radical and long-term in effects, they have been defeated many times on ballot referenda but have been imposed by legislatures in several jurisdictions. Vouchers are subsidy coupons worth a portion of tuition costs in either private or public schools of their choosing. In DCPS, voucher grants have been set at $7,500 which covers tuition for its 1,700 voucher students (and impliedly fixed and variable costs of education/student). Only about 100k students receive vouchers in the US, but this number is increasing over time. Since Catholic schools are now having resource problems, the major alternative in practice is really charter schools.

The problem is not just optimizing choice to support some theory. In DCPS, 27 schools have been classified as "failing" by multiple criteria. Overall, 90 of 123 schools are under some form of federal notice to meet US. No Child Left Behind (NCLB) Act standards. The law requires that districts adopt one or more "restructuring" remedies, e.g., bring in private firms to manage the schools (privatization); convert them to charters which are founded and operated by nonprofit organizations; remain in public control but replace principals and teachers; allow the state, or in DC, the US Department of Education, to seize the schools; or devise something else (e.g. lengthen the school day, change curricula).

In Washington, DC, charter schools receive charter status from an independent charter board—the DC Public Charter School Board. This board is not accountable to the local school district but to the state educational agency—specifically to the Office of the State Superintendent of Education (OSSE). Given this model, while charter schools operate in DC, DCPS does not offer charter schools. This administrative and policy arrangement allows relatively efficient establishment and financing of charter schools. With 127 schools and 71k students enrolled, Washington, DC, had 63 charter schools serving about 25k students in 2009. DCPS allocates about $370m/year for charter schools from its 2009 budget of about $760m. A transfer of $8,500/student with facility needs add-ons of between $1,000 and $3,000/student is calculated to cover full educational costs for charter-attending students. By contrast, the NYCPS (NY City Public Schools) system with 1,500 schools and 1.1m students has chartered only 78 schools with 24k enrollment. In short, parents in DC have a choice. The other side of the coin is that if parents exercise the choice to "exit" their children, enrollment in traditional public schools will drop. From 146,000 students in 1960, excluding charter students, DCPS now has only about 45k students. Not all of the enrollment declines can be attributed to dissatisfaction with public school performance. Some of it is pure demographics—people heading for the suburbs. But a lot of the decline is performance-related. Since 2007, the Chancellor has been using choice as a tool of competition—an incentive to improve public school performance. We believe that public school enrollment declines have bottomed out and that overall attendance will increase to 47k in 2010.

Mr. Query listened to this, and it occurred to him that it wasn't as simple as shifting agendas from power to learning through more choice and competition. He said, I went to a school in a poor neighborhood when I was growing up. I recall that those of us who worked hard to learn and avoid being poor like our parents had to deal with bullies and gangs that waited for us after school. They knew us and where we lived and tended to beat us up regularly.

Yes, that's a problem here too, replied Dr. Ritter. Some charter schools have to rely on Metro Transit police to protect their students after class because the DC Police believe their job is to protect only regular public schools and not charter schools (King, 2009b).

Both agreed that the formal or informal rule that produced this enforcement inequity needed to be changed since it constrains competition, choice, and learning.

Another important reform plank is ***decentralization and school autonomy***, explained Dr. Ritter. Here, the premise is that local schools can be more responsive to parents and students than distant central administrative offices. The empirical literature indicates that more principal discretion over human resources (especially teachers and maintenance staff), budget choices, and students leads to better student achievement. Of course, it is not as simple as that. There is a natural tension between the central administration and the local schools. Central administrations need to establish common curricula and performance norms as well as transparent and professional recruitment/promotion criteria; local school staff needs the autonomy and discretion to shift resources in order to attain performance objectives. In some countries such as New Zealand, local managers operate on performance-based, fixed-term, and often multi-year contracts. In exchange for maximum discretion to achieve results in health, education, urban transport, etc., managers can hire/fire as they see fit and shift budget resources to attain the required objectives. With this discretion, managers can then be held almost fully accountable for results. We are using the same model, adapted for local practice. Charter schools in the US often have this greater level of autonomy at the school level, with charters that are authorized and renewed based on performance-based contracts.

All reforms are experiments, and this one is no different. It has been repeatedly documented that the main determinant of student success is the teacher: good teachers lead to more student success. Studies link the achievement gap at DCPS largely to underperforming school staff/teachers. Overall, we find a decades-old culture that still accepts mediocrity and chaos at schools and in the classroom. In order for us to devolve authority to schools, there must be a professional cadre in place in which we can have confidence. We need to have confidence that increasing their discretion will serve the students. Until we have that cadre of high-performing principals and teachers, we cannot decentralize effectively. Consistent with these basic tenets, the strategy has been to develop rigorous educator evaluation systems, replace underperforming principals and teachers, provide performance-based incentive contracts for good teachers to continue, and support better teaching with more supplies, textbooks, and better facilities. All strategies must be paid for. The plan is to finance the replacements, incentive contracts, and improved facilities by closing high-cost under-enrolled schools and obtaining additional private (philanthropic) financing. So far, 23 schools have been closed, more than 100 central staff terminated, and several dozen principals terminated; 150 teachers out of 4,000 have been dismissed; over 11k backlogged maintenance requests have been addressed; and a $2.5b five-year DCPS Capital Improvement

Plan for facilities has been approved (District of Columbia Public Schools [DCPS], 2008).

DCPS also developed a two-tier salary-track incentive system: the red track meant status quo with some modest raises; the green track meant large bonuses in exchange for foregoing tenure. In general, younger teachers would probably select the green path when the contract with the Washington Teachers Union (WTU) is approved. Unfortunately, the WTU forced out the "red-green" plan and strengthened teacher tenure security provisions (Turque, 2009a). In the DCPS-WTU, contract being negotiated principals will have more authority to pick teachers cut from schools that have been closed, consolidated, lost enrollment, lost budget funds, or taken over by an outside organization. They would follow a formula that weights classroom performance highest and seniority lowest (Turque, 2009a). This proposal may also be thrown out in contract negotiations because of WTU opposition.

Some suggest that, consistent with the local autonomy plank, performance-based budget systems should be installed in order to decentralize authority to schools (and in particular to principals). The rationale is that this system would allow principals to allocate resources by educational performance. It would also allow decisions to be made on the basis of unit cost and cost-effectiveness criteria. I'm sure you're aware of the pros and cons of such budget reform systems. We viewed it as a potentially costly distraction at this stage—a danger that we could end up dealing with two reforms at the same time. We found that there are at least two kinds of "structural" level constraints. One stems from the redundancy of the institution itself—time has passed by and there is no more demand—student enrollment drops, and the remaining students are high-risk/high-needs populations, including those at risk for dropping out of the school system, as well as gang-affiliated students. The school is deteriorating and completely lacks the structure and environment needed for the few remaining students to get back on course. This happened with Manual HS in Denver a few years ago (Boo, 2007). Such places should be declared redundant and students/faculty reassigned to better environments. We already have the performance and fiscal data to make those choices without changing the allocation system or calendar. The second kind of structural issue is actually a leadership problem. If better principals and teachers are appointed, often the structural constraints disappear! Either way, you cannot manage yourself out of structural problems through tools such as performance budgeting, management by objectives, or the use of performance management consultants. Personnel changes and solid leadership are needed.

We know that Chicago went the management route in order to target resources more precisely on the basis of school performance. They appeared to be trying to manage their way out of a structural problem. In any case, the new budget system installed with substantial resources of time and money made little difference to results. What they found after installing their "school-based budgeting system" was very little variation in allocations between high- and low-performing schools across the main functions of instruction, instruction support, administration, and operations. There was an important variation in discretionary spending (Stiefel, Rubenstein and Schwartz, 1999). But this was a low proportion of total expenditures and simply underscored a lack of real school autonomy.

In DCPS, a professional cadre of managers, principals, and teachers at the school level is largely missing at this point. We are building the foundation for devolving authority to them. Until that cadre exists, resources should be spent on them, not on accounting and budgeting systems. We already knew that a big problem was the substantial administrative component of some of the highest expenditures/students in the US combined with low achievement. In LA (Los Angeles), they estimate that only $0.60 of every $1 makes it to the classroom. In DCPS, we knew that an even smaller proportion of total expenditures were making it to the classroom. Analysis of the link between teacher salaries, support, maintenance, capital facilities condition, and student performance can tell us a lot of what we need to know now to proceed. Fiscal and physical performance data and solid methods already exist and are being used by us for these purposes. Data is being reported and analyzed at the school level. One of our new incentive programs allows schools with consistently high performance to become autonomous and exempt from many central office regulations.

Dr. Ritter explained that the third plank, *performance accountability*, was tightly linked to the last one. Accountability without discretion is meaningless, he noted. In the decentralization literature, it would be like holding a local mayor accountable for centrally set performance mandates when they often lack the discretion to raise local tax bases or rates. This "earned autonomy" in exchange for accountability was a new concept for DCPS.

We found virtually no emphasis on accountability when we arrived. There was no performance measurement of any kind. It was a low-expectation culture of entitlement to permanent bureaucratic jobs, with their emphasis on the usual inputs of form-filling and frequent meetings. The bureaucracy was fossilized and bloated and students didn't really count to them. A major part of any educational reform is to shift the cultural mindset from inputs to outputs and outcomes. As I've mentioned, budget systems can help—but we already knew what was missing and went directly for the jugular regular reporting on performance metrics for students, teachers, and schools. Logically, DCPS would use this data to classify schools, teachers, and students in order to allocate education funds more rationally.

DCPS would use this system to raise overall expectations and change the culture. That's what a real reform should do. That's why they still call the DCPS office change agents!

I've been a teacher here for ten years and you are right about the lack of interest in performance, Mr. Query noted. But sometimes performance becomes a buzzword and efficiency experts take over. Consultants arrive, measure, and take their knowledge with them. They try to measure everything and require more performance reporting. Under increased time pressure, the staff burns out on reporting data that they feel is often pretty useless. What metrics are you using and how do you know they are the right ones, especially for teachers?

DCPS tracks the usual data at the school level—attendance, drop-out, promotion, and graduation rates for students. With my assistance, we review teacher files to assess their classroom attendance and turnover (transfers to different districts or schools, retirement, disciplinary action, dismissal) and have instructional experts and principals observe and rate their teaching performance. We also track the condition of facilities and the regular availability of supplies (basics like chalk, books, and computers). We found that data and management systems were extremely bad and were damaging the schools, e.g., neglected transcripts preventing graduation, weak attendance data on truancy, and delays in processing textbook orders, purchase orders, and monthly teacher salaries. Those have now been fixed with savings of hundreds of thousands of dollars. Empirically based or data-driven decision-making allows us to target more funds to the classroom and to those areas of highest need. This has allowed us to target $100m in capital expenditures in the summer of 2009 to fix up many of the schools and renovate 10 and refurbish 20 fields and playgrounds.

Teaching evaluations as you know are always a contentious issue. Universities rely on students to provide data that is used for promotion and tenure. At the primary/secondary levels, the reviews almost all have to be external. Observers come in and observe such behavior as whether the students are attentive, the teacher interacts with the students, the teacher is prepared, and either has good classroom support or uses the blackboard effectively. These are admittedly subjective, made worse by the fact that university students evaluate a whole course; primary/secondary evaluators hit only random classes. If announced, the teacher can over-prepare; if unannounced, they may have come on the wrong day for the primary/secondary teacher. Nevertheless, despite these generic methodological limitations, we believe we have identified a lot of very ineffective, poorly performing teachers. Since good teaching is the main determinant of student achievement, we need to have the authority to transfer, dismiss, or sideline and retrain those kinds of teachers.

For principals, the evaluation system is designed to weed out ineffectual staff and reward those who are effective. In both cases, the performance assessment is supposed to be linked to student achievement. While this link has been made with teachers, so far it has not been for principals.

Why not? asked Mr. Query.

It is believed that sufficient school autonomy does not yet exist to hold them accountable. Principals have only minimal staffing authority. If they are dealt a bad hand, they would get the blame. So, the emphasis is now on upgrading data, measuring student performance, and attributing that to teacher performance. At the school level, we have used student achievement data to identify possibilities for institutional synergy. At the outset, the data indicated the need for extreme measures—closing 23 underperforming and under-enrolled high-cost schools. After this *brush-clearing* effort, we concentrated on innovative resource combinations that could increase achievement. I say "could"—remember that this is an experiment like all education reforms. Now in DCPS, special *catalyst* schools act as magnets for particular emphases such as science. We also have *partnership* schools that allow us to outsource students to charter school management organizations. Since charters are often spectacularly successful in generating student results (i.e., reading and mathematics proficiency scores), this increases market competition for the traditional public schools. Finally, our *collaborative* schools are networks of schools that facilitate the transfer of lessons, resources, and skills from high to lower performing schools. They are like mentor relationships. The aim of these new institutional arrangements is to increase student achievement by offering more options and combining resources differently.

You mentioned that *fiscal predictability and sustainability* were basic to the application of NPM reforms to education. What did you mean? asked Mr. Query.

Related to the brush-clearing phase was the effort to upgrade financial management systems. There were two problems. First, principals found it hard to predict flows of funds for capital and operating purposes. That meant that despite their planned and approved budgets, the actual funds didn't materialize in many cases. There was a major variance between planned and actual expenditures. Expenditure planning was made difficult by the existence of 27 different management systems that were not interoperable and did not interface. So, principals and budget officers found it hard to consolidate the budgetary base in terms of overall needs. The procurement system was particularly bad. It did not produce cost-effective bids; the goods often didn't arrive; those that did were often defective or the wrong ones. In some cases, the proper goods arrived, were placed in inventory, and were stolen later. Thus, more predictability was needed for both the flow of funds and for supplies, equipment, and facilities.

The second problem is that lacking performance data and a sound budget system, we could not allocate funds to schools on the basis of targeted needs to produce results. We couldn't distinguish the high from low performers by school, class, or individual student. As I mentioned before, DCPS is doing this reform, not a consulting firm. DCPS will gain the knowledge and experience and its own staff will be able to use it. For this reason, we avoided many of the usual consultant's products like performance or program budgeting. We are now in the position of being able to do almost everything such a system is supposed to do in theory—here in practice. We measure and track outputs by school and individual (*outputs* like improved "proficiency in test scores" and "graduation rates" are even called *outcomes* by some); we know the expenditures and have a good feel for the behavior of fixed and variable costs. This allows us to compare unit costs and cost/result and allocate funds accordingly.

Results

So, are you pleased with your overall results so far? asked Mr. Query.

Let me detail what we've achieved in a little over two years. Most educational reforms take about ten to mature and to be institutionalized. At the structural level, closing 23 schools saved substantial funds, and this has been reprogrammed to the classroom through program support, facility maintenance, and rehabilitation and supplies. Savings from closure enabled DCPS to save program funds and ensure that every student in the system has access to art, music, physical education, and library services. There wasn't enough money to ensure minimum standards for these programs or services before and we learned that much of it was being spent on schools that should have been closed anyway. In addition, 27 more schools have been restructured consistent with the NCLB Act. At the management level, we have installed new systems for personnel (to track employee status and location), treasury (to facilitate faster preparation of purchase orders and ensure on-time payments), and purchasing (to ensure timely arrival of textbook orders and on-time school openings). At the classroom level, we provided 6,300 new computers and connected 103 schools to high-speed broadband networks; improved security within schools and on student trips to and from them; improved facilities by investing $500m for capital modernization, completed 20,000 backlogged work orders; fixed 400 boilers; repaired 2,500 window air-conditioners and overhauled a dozen central cooling systems.

More importantly at the classroom level, more than 40 low-performing principals and 200 teachers have been fired and 150 more instructors have been placed on 90-day probationary programs. More funds have been allocated to instruction and to school leadership. All these activities at the structural, management, and operational levels have raised the expectations of students, parents, and teachers.

Let me show you an example of shifted resources at the school level. Dr. Ritter gave Mr. Query a preliminary 2009 budget for Anacostia HS in which it showed that 76% of the resources would be spent on instruction, 17% on school leadership, and 7% on instructional support. This shows our commitment to reducing administrative expenses and targeting more funds for the classroom.

Mr. Query glanced over the budget. I can't say anything about the totals. But why are classroom supplies and computers considered "instructional" rather than "instructional support"? And why are the principal and assistant principal part of "instructional" expenses when they don't teach? Why would a "business manager" be classified as "school leadership" and not the principal? I only ask these because the classification of these kinds of expenses could raise the percentage tagged as instructional when it is not. That could lead to a claimed reform success that actually might not be. Am I wrong?

Dr. Ritter focused on the budget pages for a moment. No, you are correct. We have to tighten up and rationalize the budget classification system to a greater extent than we have.

So, how are schools and pupils funded? Do they receive what are called "foundation" grants to cover them on a per-pupil basis? Or is it some kind of matching grant?

Dr. Ritter thanked him for his question. We use precisely a foundation grant—a lump sum to schools derived from projected enrollment figures and allocated on the basis of their level and type of school. So, based on a projected enrollment in 2010 of 44k, our budget is $428.3m of which 27.5% will be allocated to grades 9–12. Based on our weighting system, such schools will get $10,173 per pupil while primary school pupils will receive only $8,770 per pupil. This accounts for higher costs at the HS level for a wider variety of academic and elective course offerings as well as expanded extracurricular offerings. The weighting is based on average operating costs for those levels. The system is called the Uniform Per Pupil Funding Formula (UPSFF). As we said, if enrollment doesn't meet our projections, per-pupil funding will drop.

Mr. Query thanked him. It sounds good. But lump sum grants can still be re-allocated within schools and not make it to the classroom. They work best for clients when they are add-ons to per-pupil expenditures that were higher than, for example, the $10,173 for grades 9–12. The grant structure encourages fungibility or shifting funds between line items in the budget. The other problem might be the inability to track funds to the classroom—leakage through the core budget codes. Isn't that so?

As I said, these are real problems not just here but also in other school systems as well...repeated Dr. Ritter.

While it is still too early to tell if the reforms are making a difference, from 2007 to 2009 scores on the DC Comprehensive Assessment System (DC-CAS) tests have increased at the primary level from 38% to 49% in reading and from 29% to 43% in math. At the secondary level, scores have increased from 30% to 42% in reading and 27% to 39% in math (Turque, 2009b). DC-CAS scores revealed that the number of schools with proficiency rates below 20% has been cut from 50 to 29. Since many of these schools are in the poorest neighborhoods, improvements can be attributed largely to the efforts of the reform. This means that DCPS students can achieve when teachers, principals, and parents focus on their achievement. When disincentives for learning are removed by professional leadership and backed up by solid teaching and good facilities, the students respond quickly. This is why we should not short-change them any longer with poorly performing educational institutions.

The only negative is that enrollment in DCPS continues to drop—by 284 for the 2009–2010 year. We hope to turn that around by increasing demand for a better product—supplying the students with more effective public schools. For the first time, DCPS is now operating a student recruitment campaign at selected schools in order to compete with charter schools and other schooling options.

Positive results in DCPS mirror those of other systems that adopted the local autonomy, choice, and school responsibility planks noted above. Since 2002, New York City school-teacher salaries have increased 43% and school funding has gone up 50%. Principals have been given more autonomy and accountability. While in 2002, only 50% of fourth graders met state learning standards, today more than 85% meet or exceed math standards, and 70% meet or exceed English standards. Graduation rates are also increasing (*Economist*, 2009).

Institutional Supports and Constraints

The obvious question then is what constraints have you faced along the way? asked Mr. Query. Reform is about changing minds, generating top-level support, and building institutions that incentivize the right actions to increase achievement. That hasn't been easy in any of the cities you mentioned earlier. What have been the major institutional constraints here?

Let's start from the top, said Dr. Ritter. With the election of a new reformist mayor in 2007, we had the top-level support we needed, which has never existed in Washington, DC. He knew of the reforms being carried out elsewhere and wanted them to begin here from day one. We got another boost from the election of President Obama in 2008. It was clear to DCPS that education reform was a top priority by his selection of Arne Duncan as Secretary of Education. As the Chief of Chicago schools since 2001, he pushed ahead with reform similar to DCPS (attention to data/outcomes, charter schools, serious teacher evaluations and incentives for improvement, etc.) (Glod, 2008).

With this broad political cover, DCPS then started to fix its basic systems, most of which were dilapidated. Financial and performance management systems, as I mentioned, were dysfunctional and could not really be used to manage anything. DCPS was chaotic and tribal; there was no overall system in place or anyone with enough authority to enforce changes at the structural level. So, we began to clear the larger brushes away (e.g., closing schools) and got down to smaller weeds (like books, supplies, and facilities). There was some parental and community resistance to school closure efforts but not as much as experienced in some other cities—once data was presented on enrollments, costs, and poor past results. It was very much a data-driven exercise.

There may be further closures, and some may be re-opened as charter or private schools. But the major stakeholders appear to accept the process of selection and closure—so far.[10] After surplus schools were identified and closures reasonably underway, we moved to governance issues. This has been a much more complex problem—one without clear solutions and categorical data indicating that a preferred governance system should be installed. Thus, governance reforms have been contentious.

In Washington historically, the central educational bureaucracy has always been perceived as a major part of the problem. With the new mayor came a new education office and the dismissal of many of the old guards and deadwood of the past. The elected and dysfunctional local Board of Education was abolished, and its functions were transferred to the mayor. Budget approval and oversight functions now lie with the elected City Council. The central administration (DCPS) is no longer perceived as a meddlesome influence but as a positive force for change and improvement. Of course, the upbeat demeanor and cool, rational tone of the Chancellor backed by the stern expression of the mayor has helped greatly in confronting vocal detractors and in generating support among stakeholders.

Our governance problem boils down to how to energize the roles of teacher and principal. The importance of an excellent educator is hard to overstate. Studies in Tennessee and Dallas showed that if you take students of average ability and give them to teachers deemed to be in the top 20% of their profession, they end up in the top 10% of student performers; if you give them to teachers in the bottom 20%, they end up at the bottom (*Economist*, 2007).

To answer your question then, there are two major institutional constraints. First, there are the teachers' unions that appeal logically to the employment stability of its membership. The legal safeguards provided by unions have been critically important for US labor. But in times of major reform, they become a constraint on management. It is here that our proposals have run up against the mighty teaching union (the WTU), affiliate of the American Federation of Teachers (AFT)) and the effects of vigorous lobbying by older teachers through the City Council—which has reconstituted itself as a de facto school board.

We want the flexibility to replace ineffective teachers and replace them with the highest paid and most effective ones in the system. If teachers opt for our *green* path or "grand bargain", they give up tenure for one year and get large incentive bonuses paid for by foundation funds in exchange (e.g., salaries of over $130k/year). The foundations will only provide the funds for five years if the Chancellor gains authority to (1) recognize and reward teacher performance (merit pay), (2) identify the most and least effective teachers, and (3) remove poorly performing teachers. So far, the WTU has either refused to vote on the proposal or opposed it. The WTU opposes teacher evaluation on the basis of only student scores and wants attendance and other inputs considered for promotion and tenure. The AFT/WTU opposes the abolition of tenure. While the WTU does not explicitly oppose the removal of underperforming teachers, it wants it done in "humane, fair and fast ways". This would include training and support before a final dismissal decision is made (Turque, 2009c). If talks collapse between the Chancellor and the AFT President Randi Weingarten, the decision falls first to the DC Board of Public Employee Relations. If there is still an impasse, it goes to a mediator. If that fails, it goes then to binding arbitration. In short, the major constraint is the fear of many teachers and their AFT representatives that they will be replaced unfairly. The fear of the Chancellor is that AFT will slow up or derail the momentum we have built up to focus on improving teachers. If that stalls, so does our reform. All of us, like you, have been teachers and we want to reward the best ones who will then reward their students.

The second constraint is the political structure and incentive system of the DC City Council—or any city council. The district-based or ward electoral system politicizes the schools, making them just another political resource to get elected and stay in office. This makes policy-making and financing decisions overtly political and subject to pressure politics—more so than technical considerations like student and school performance. The DC School Board was rightly abolished by Mayor Fenty. The need is to maximize what administrative strength the school district has in order to increase educational performance (Bennett, 2009). Failure to do this allows school administrators to play power games at the expense of student achievement—as happened in DC under the school board.

The need is for improved public sector governance of educational reform (Bennett, 2009). Top-level support, together with DCPS efforts to narrow the span of administrative control to focus teachers and administrators on some or all of the four planks outlined above, will strengthen school administration by forcing managers to focus on the mission of educational reform. Chubb and Moe (1990) asserted that outside influences often distract school administrators from their primary tasks. This has been true here, and the need is for structural reform—to change the incentive system—to minimize those distractions. For example, politicizing what should be straight-forward administrative and policy decisions based on existing empirical data and information, is a waste of time and resources. But this is often what happens. The DC City Council has in many ways replaced the previous School Board's functions (more precisely "dysfunctions") and now serves as a new political constraint on the reforms.

The Sequence of Reform

I opted for the green path, so I know what you are up against, said Mr. Query. What about the sequence of the reform? You mentioned that you tried to move from fixing basic failed systems to governance issues. Could you be more specific about the sequence of reform activities?

Dr. Ritter shifted visibly in his chair. In fact, we know very little about the optimal sequencing of school reform—or any other policy really. Some have postulated a three-step sequence in the face of challenges to a reform-minded regime like ours. First, you build top-level support. Then you assess how the severity of the cultural obstacles and long-standing institutional rules. If they are adaptable or changeable, then you move to the third step. Here, you need to come up with a feasible sequence of technical activities to repair and replace broken administrative and policy systems so that reforms are institutionalized (Guess, 2005). In our case, we had top-level support from Mayor Fenty and Chancellor Rhee. We followed the lead of other jurisdictions, such as New York City and Mayor Michael Bloomberg. But in the case of New York City, despite astonishing increases in student performance, teacher salaries, and school funding, the State legislature may re-centralize control to partisan political leadership (*Economist*, 2009). This would fly in the face of both AFT wishes and a major tenet of fiscal federalist theory—that you assign authority and responsibility to the lowest effective level. So, we can't take our victory for granted. We could lose that top-level support and that would severely weaken reform momentum.

For the second challenge, we had to face a decades old culture of mediocrity reinforced by a patronizing school board and make-work unions that knew or cared little about what local students could achieve.

So, instead of moving from step I to III, we started with step I, then moved to step III to repair the systems desiccation at both school and central office levels. This had to include both the teachers and the school systems. Otherwise, the reform would fail, and nothing would have been achieved by the students or us. That meant facing off immediately against the union and the council on restructuring, closing schools, and replacing ineffective teachers.

In short, using the traditional reform sequence as a guide would have suggested spending more time on the second step—changing the culture. Only if the culture (the teachers, the unions, the parents, and the City Council) bought into the reform, would it be safe to go forward to technical sequencing of operational reforms. This is what the textbooks suggested. But unlike, say, a national decentralization reform which really has no time limit, we faced future elections, poorly taught students each day, and enormous stakeholder skepticism at the outset. DCPS had little time and the students were being penalized every day. Given these constraints, we were impatient to increase achievement.

So, we instituted a flurry of pilot programs and policy changes that increased demands on teachers, e.g., Saturday programs to prepare students for DC-CAS standardized tests; a push for serving special education students in regular classes; a new accelerated math program; cash rewards for selected middle schools; and new guidelines for bilingual, arts, and health education (Turque, 2009d). The Chancellor also pledged that teacher job evaluations would now be based not just on standardized test scores but also on students' growth and teachers' pay would be based on what teachers achieved individually and collectively.

In retrospect, overwhelming the teachers and the stakeholders with many new proposals and initiatives by trying to fix everything at once created major resistance problems. DCPS ignored the cultural constraints and the institutional rules. Both had to be changed but DCPS did not spend enough time trying to convince stakeholders the changes would definitely be an improvement. In 2007–2008, teachers learned about restructuring and closing of schools and proposals for declaring the whole system an emergency—as was done in New Orleans (Turque, 2008). This move would pave the way for privatizing the schools, hiring non-union charter and autonomous schools to run the district, and could leave a lot of existing teachers out of a job. There was more talk and lots of rumors about mysterious donors that would pay $100m to finance teachers cooperating with the performance-based reform. Foundation funds are not unusual. But this would be the first time that private foundations would be paying for teacher compensation (King, 2009a). Much of the privatization and emergency talk is off the table now (Turque, 2009e). The Chancellor is now facing the cultural and

institutional variable and learning that if the reform is to persist after this regime leaves, mental habits and supporting rules must be
changed—perhaps more slowly.

Mr. Query thanked Dr. Ritter for his time and said he would mull over
what he had learned and get back to him with more questions. Dr. Ritter
suggested that he talk with representatives of the other institutional actors
first, such as WTU and PTAs (Parent Teacher Associations).

Aftermath

Since Mr. Query's interviews, three events have occurred. First, in 2009
DCPS enrollment was reported as only 37,000 (despite assertions that it
would reach 45k and possibly 47k by 2010). Since the announcement in
August 2009, enrollment has crept up to 39k, and when the numbers are
audited, the figure could reach 44k after all. The latest figures are planned
for 44,681 and an actual 44,397 (Turque, 2009f). Much of the decline in
enrollment so far can be attributed to data systems reporting lag. Second,
WTU forced Chancellor Rhee to modify and water down some of her
boldest reform proposals including the fast-track incentive for pay in exchange for tenure and principal autonomy to hire and fire teachers. This
all speaks to the power of institutions to negatively affect the formulation
and implementation of empirically based and successful policies. Third,
the unanticipated shortfall in budgeted funds for the DC government in
2009–2010 of $43.9m forced the DCPS to propose $40m in cuts, first in
non-personnel categories, then in personnel such as new teachers (Turque,
2009f). In response to the city-wide belt-tightening because of declining
tax revenue on October 2, Chancellor Rhee terminated 266 teachers and
other personnel (Turque, 2009g). Both the WTU and DC City Council
has reacted strongly—charging her everything from age discrimination
on the cuts and illegal reprogramming of budget funds (she can transfer
funds without approval because less money was spent than budgeted—not
more). The institutional constraints to reform mount! Raise your hands if
you want to have the Chancellor's job!

Questions

1 The case mentions other instances of school reform in the United States
   and other countries. Selecting some of them for review, are there comparative lessons that could be applied to the Washington, DC, School
   Reform case?
2 What are the principal lessons for managing school reform from the
   Washington, DC, School Reform case for anticipating and responding
   to the challenges of institutional constraints? Are there lessons that can

be built into the design/appraisal stage of policy-making that would facilitate later implementation? What course corrections, if any, would you recommend to the Chancellor now to facilitate reform success?

3 Would you change any of the four operating principles or planks of the Washington reform? Would you sequence them differently after reading the case?

4 How can reformers change cultures and institutional rules when, for electoral or financial reasons, they don't have a lot of time?

5 What factors led Washington, DC, to be ready for strong reform, and what factors were an impediment to progress? (Guess and Farnham, 2011)[11]

Analysis and Update

By Margie Yeager

In the nearly 15 years since the case described here, there have been extensive developments in the Washington, DC, school reform story, with an overall trajectory of continued success but with many challenges along the way.

A defining feature of many public policy reforms is strong and continued leadership. In this case, Mayor Adrian Fenty was ousted in the 2010 election, in part at least due to his aggressive leadership on education reform and some of the pushback from detractors of his work and that of Chancellor Michelle Rhee. However, unlike in some other jurisdictions, this was not a pivot to a radically different approach, or to a return to the previous dysfunctional model. Instead, the new Mayor Vince Gray opted to appoint Chancellor Rhee's Deputy, Kaya Henderson, as the next Chancellor of DCPS. As Chancellor, Henderson maintained many of the bold reforms that Chancellor Rhee had championed including a rigorous system of educator evaluation with merit pay, a robust system of performance management, and a continued focus on operational effectiveness to support well-aligned resources to student needs.

Although it took several years, confidence in DCPS began to grow, and student enrollment slowly rose, beginning in the 2011–2012 school year. This enrollment increase continued steadily until a slight dip following the Covid-19 pandemic in SY 2020–2021. This was despite continued growth in the public charter sector as well—more families were choosing to enroll their students in public schools in Washington, DC, of all types.

Student achievement continued to increase as well with sustained progress over more than a decade. Data from the NAEP widely considered the strongest comparable measure of student performance across cities and states, Washington, DC, made the largest gains of any city or state in the country. Progress in all student subgroups improved, with faster gains by

Black and Latino students, though very large and troubling achievement gaps remained.

Remarkably, this progress in both enrollment and achievement has survived further leadership transitions as Mayor Muriel Bowser was elected in 2014, and DCPS has had several subsequent Chancellors. While the exact implementation of the reform policies has shifted and adapted over time, the core principles have remained intact and have supported sustained progress. The district has built on its commitment to leveraging data, transparency, and choice by creating clear state-level report cards with comprehensive data on all schools (DCPS and charter) across the city.

Unfortunately, like almost all cities and states in the United States, the Covid-19 pandemic had a devastating impact on education with enormous negative impacts on students. There were dramatic declines in student academic achievement (see *Figure 6.1*) with disproportionately negative impacts for Black and Hispanic students, and students with disabilities. And like many other jurisdictions, politics became very enmeshed in decisions about education. Like most school systems, DCPS shut down in March 2020 with the intention of closing for two weeks. While the Mayor had hoped to reopen schools in the Fall of 2020, there was enormous pushback from the WTU, and schools remained fully virtual for much of the 2020–2021 school year. Many students struggled to learn virtually due to

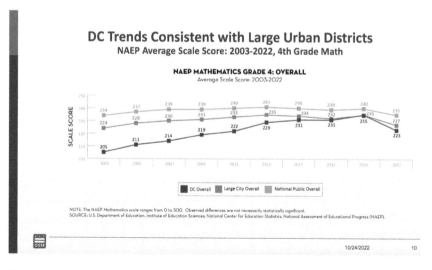

Figure 6.1 DC Fourth Grade Math Score Trends Consistent with Large Urban Districts 2003–2022.

Source: DC OSSE, 2022.

challenges with access to technology, internet, adequate support, food, mental health care, and many other issues that contributed to dramatic declines.

There have been enormous subsequent federal investments in education through the Elementary and Secondary School Emergency Relief (ESSER) Fund as well as substantial local investments in education recovery programming, but it is not clear how long it will take Washington, DC, students to regain the progress they have made over the past 15 years.

Due to the economic impact of Covid-19 which has had a strongly negative impact on the local DC economy (which is heavily reliant on its commercial real estate market and huge population of federal workers to support its downtown corridor), it is also unclear what the capacity will be to fund DCPS at the historically high levels that it has enjoyed in recent years. Additionally, Mayor Bowser is in her third (and possibly final) term, and there are some potential candidates for Mayor who oppose the current system of Mayoral control of schools and might try to return the system to the prior elected School Board model.

So, the Washington, DC, school reform case remains hopeful but incomplete. Since 2007, several cohorts of students have gone through the PK3–12 system under the new model and have demonstrably stronger outcomes to show. But whether this progress can sustain ongoing political and economic challenges is still to be seen.

References

Bennett, Lamar (2009) "Administrative Strength, Reform and School District Performance", Unpublished Ph.D. dissertation (Washington, DC: American University, School of Public Affairs).

Boo, Katherine (2007) "Expectations" *The New Yorker*, pp. 44–57 (January 15).

Chubb, John E., and Terry M. Moe. 1990. *Politics, Markets, and America's Schools* (Washington, DC: Brookings Institution).

District of Columbia Public Schools (2008) *District of Columbia Public Schools Progress Report: 2007-2008 School Year* (Washington, DC: DCPS).

The Economist (2007) "How to be Top" October 20, pp. 80–81.

George M. Guess and Paul G. Farnham (2009) "Political Prisoners: Mayoral Control of Schools in New York" June 20, p. 32.

Glod, Maria (2008) "Chicago School Reform Could be a U.S. Model" *The Washington Post*, December 30, p. A1.

Guess, George M. (2005) "Comparative Decentralization Lessons from Pakistan, Indonesia and the Philippines", *Public Administration Review*, Volume 65, #2, pp. 217–231 (March/April).

_____ and Paul G. Farnham (2011) *Cases in Public Policy Analysis* (Washington, DC: Georgetown University Press).

King, Colbert I (2009a) "The Federal Lab Rat" *The Washington Post*, January 17, p. A25.

_____(2009b) "Trouble Awaits After Class is Dismissed" *The Washington Post*, October 3, 2009, p. A13.

Moynihan, Donald (2006) "Managing for Results in State Governments: Evaluating a Decade of Reform", *Public Administration Review*, 66, #1, pp. 77–89 (January/February).

Stiefel, Leanna, Rubenstein, Ross, and Schwartz, Amy Ellen (1999) "Using Adjusted Performance Measures for Evaluating Resource Use", *Public Budgeting and Finance*, V31, pp. 67–85 (Fall).

Turque, Bill (2008) "Fenty, Rhee Look For Ways Around Union" *The Washington Post*, February 20, p. C1.

_____ (2009a) "Rhee, Union May be Close to Deal" *The Washington Post*, September 11, p. B1.

_____ (2009b) "Two Years of Hard Lessons for D.C. Schools' Agents of Change" *The Washington Post*, June 14, p. A1.

_____(2009c) "Education Heavyweights Prepare for D.C. Contract Fight" *The Washington Post*, February 1, p. A1.

_____(2009d) "Rhee Says Fixes Likely Too Much Too Soon" *The Washington Post*, March 14, p. B1.

_____(2009e) "Takeover Idea Out of Consideration, Rhee Says" *The Washington Post*, February 20, p. C3.

_____(2009f) "D.C. Schools Face Bigger Classes, Layoffs Due to $40m Gap" *The Washington Post*, September 17, p. B1.

_____(2009g) "D.C. Council, Rhee Tensions Grow Over Budget Cuts" *The Washington Post*, October 30, p. A17.

UNDP (2012) Millennium Development Goals and Beyond New York (UN Development Program).

Discussion Case #22: Educational Reform in Liberia

In 2016, George Werner the education minister for Liberia faced one of the most difficult school systems in the world. Liberia was reeling from the effects of grinding poverty, civil war, and the Ebola epidemic in 2014. Many pupils stopped attending school altogether—those who did learn little. Only 25% of girls completing primary school could read. Werner's budget was $50/pupil. Many of his teachers were "ghosts" or paid no-shows.

As education minister, he enacted a drastic policy unmatched in recent African history, outsourcing 93 primary schools with 8.6% of state-school pupils to eight private operators—five charities and three companies. Their performance was monitored in a RCT. In the RCT, a randomized sample of state schools served as the "control group" (or placebos), and the schools exposed to the methods of the eight "measurement" programs competing were evaluated for results achieved. Researchers tracked test scores in the operator's schools and nearby government ones.

After three years of teaching and testing by the schools, researchers found that on average pupils in outsourced schools performed "modestly better" than those in state schools. Private pilot school pupils could read 15 words/minute, while those in state schools could only read 11/minute. This is still far behind the 45–60 words/minute deemed necessary to understand a simple passage and even farther behind the 100+ words that rich country peers can read. Improvements in math skills were similar. School conditions were brutal. Many schools were inaccessible during the rainy season due to bad roads. Electricity in many parts of rural Liberia is spotty. Unlike in US charter schools, staff was mostly recruited from the existing pool of teachers. These people were poorly educated themselves. Operators were unable to fire them or reward good ones.

One advantage the test schools had was funding. With the help of philanthropic funds, the competing operators were able to supplement the state's budget of $50 which was mostly spent on teacher salaries. In the first year, they spent $300 beyond the state contribution. Two years later the figure dropped to $119, suggesting that after start-up costs some of the operators learned to do things more cheaply. The biggest spender was Bridge Academies, a firm that first opened schools in Kenya in 2009 (see *Discussion Case #23* next). Bridge spent $161/pupil after three years and achieved the highest scores (most improved scores). But pupils were also more likely to drop out of schools.

The evaluation design was also advantageous in that it allowed eight different operators with eight different models to compete, allowing policy-makers to decide which worked best and why. The result was that the three-operator approach made no difference to pupil learning as measured by changes in test scores. Five operators did improve student scores. Two of them came away with enhanced reputations, including Rising Academies, which was originally founded in Sierra Leone during the Ebola crisis in 2014. The CEO attributed their success to a willingness to work with the grain of the existing system. For example, it spent more time than the others talking with parents about absenteeism or skipping school. A research paper found that Rising pupils were learning in one year as two years via peer approaches. The other operator was Street Child. They achieved results for $37/pupil (+ state contribution of $50). They described their approach as simple, sustainable, and affordable for countries like Liberia. For example, using their low-tech approach instructors often scratched words in the dirt with sticks.

Nevertheless, Rising Academies was judged to be the best approach. Liberian policy-makers accepted the results. Donors considered the test successful: quick, cheap ($23m), rigorously evaluated (the RCT), and under the control of local politicians (devolved). The GOL gave Rising Academies more schools to operate. It started with 5 and now has 87. Several other African governments are considering such "public-private partnerships" for their schools.[12]

Questions

What was Rising Academy's approach to improved learning in Liberia? Was it more cost-effective than Street Child's simple approach? Why was Rising Academy's approach deemed more successful than those used by the other operators? Could their approach be replicable in other African countries? Could it work in large reformist cities with large Black under-class populations, such as Chicago or New York? As you focus on these questions, consider the following: could some of the student results be attributed to the "Hawthorne Effect" (i.e., effects of simply getting more attention as participants in an experiment)? Are test scores good measures of learning and achievement? Are there other methods of teaching effectiveness relevant to poor countries or poor cities? Were they tried by any of these operators? What are the strengths and weaknesses of the RCT? Is it helpful as a management tool?[13] (Economist, 2023).

Discussion Case #23: Learning from Lesson Scripts in Nigeria

"Good job you!" shouts Pauline Bika, as a group of schoolchildren completes the hokey-cokey. "Good job me!" choruses her class. Ms Bika runs a small government primary school in Edo state, in southern Nigeria. It is reached by a mud track that starts not far outside Benin City, the state capital. Her school has 140 pupils but only three teachers. She seems both pleased and a little embarrassed to offer a visitor a plastic chair.

For all that it lacks, Ms. Bika's school has one advantage. At the start of last year, the state education ministry gave each of her teachers a small tablet with a black-and-white touch screen. Every two weeks they use it to download detailed scripts that guide each lesson they deliver. These scripts tell the teachers what to say, what to write on the blackboard, and even when to walk around the classroom. Ms Bika says this new way of working is saving teachers time that they used to spend scribbling their own lesson plans—and her pupils are reading better, too.

That is sorely needed, for much of the education given in much of the world is strikingly bad. Across the developing world, many schoolchildren learn very little, even when they spend years in class. Less than half of kids in low- and middle-income countries are able to read a short passage by the time they finish primary school, according to the World Bank. Across sub-Saharan Africa, as few as 10% can (see chart). Experiments like those underway in Nigeria mark one attempt to improve things. They also face fierce opposition from critics who are convinced they mark a wrong turn.

The reforms in Edo began in 2018. Godwin Obaseki, the state governor, says that poor schools are one reason youngsters have often left the state for greener pastures (some fall victim to people traffickers promising better lives in Europe). Since then, the government has provided tablets and training to more than 15,000 teachers. They in turn have given the new lessons to more than 300,000 children, most of them in primary schools. On any given day pupils throughout the state receive identical lessons, as dictated by the tablet.

The training and technology are provided by NewGlobe, an education company founded in 2007 by three Americans (Pitchbook, a data firm, valued the company at $250m following a funding round in 2016). NewGlobe developed its approach while running a chain of low-cost private schools, mostly in Kenya, under the brand "Bridge International Academies". A study by academics including Michael Kremer, a development economist at the University of Chicago, found that, over two years, children who attended NewGlobe's primary schools made gains equivalent to almost a whole year of extra schooling, compared with their peers in other schools.

Though Edo was the first state in Nigeria to strike a deal with the firm, NewGlobe's approach has since also been applied in Lagos, the country's biggest city. The firm is starting work in Manipur, a state in north-eastern India, and in Rwanda. Around a million children are now studying in classrooms that use NewGlobe's model—far more than its private schools have ever been able to reach.

Although it seems able to find plenty of clients, the company provokes ferocious arguments among educators. Its private schools have long faced energetic opposition from trade unions and some international NGOs, many of whom hate the idea of profit-seeking companies playing any role in education. Others resent the application of mass production to what they see as a skilled, artisanal profession.

Dennis Sinyolo of Education International, a global group of teachers' unions, says scripted lessons "undermine teaching" and encourage "rote learning and exam drilling". He says good lesson plans are written to match local contexts[14] and the needs of individual students. The freedom to change tack mid-lesson is invaluable if a lesson plan is not working. "There's no one-size-fits-all in teaching", he says.[15]

Visits to schools in Edo provide some perspective on what is going on. There are doubtless many ways to teach a scripted lesson badly. But the idea in Nigeria is that they will tend to make classes more compelling. The scripts enforce instructional practices that are routine in many rich-country classrooms but often neglected in poor ones. These include techniques such as pausing frequently to pose questions to the class, instead of delivering long lectures at the blackboard, or encouraging pupils to try to solve a problem by chatting to the child sitting next to them.[16]

Detailed, prescriptive lesson plans are also supposed to relieve teachers of the burden of having to write their own. That, advocates hope, will leave them more energy for other jobs—such as making sure their charges stay engaged. Teachers in Edo have been trained to lead their classes in short games and songs whenever they think pupils have grown restless (hence the hokey-cokey). Ms Bika says things are better than in the past. Before, bored children would occasionally wander home during the day. Inattention was sometimes punished with the cane.

The changes do more than alter teaching styles. A study published in 2010 estimated that on any given day, around a fifth of Nigeria's primary school teachers were absent from their classrooms. Earlier research suggested as little as one-third of class time is used productively. In Edo, tablets register when teachers arrive. They can tell if a teacher has scrolled through a lesson faster than appropriate, or if they have abandoned one halfway through. Beneath lies a low-tech foundation: a team of officials—about one for every ten schools—that observe lessons and coach teachers, helped by data from the tablets.

The depth of its scripting and the whizziness of its tablets set the work in Edo apart from many other attempts to improve schooling. But the program has things in common with a broader family of reforms burdened with the clunky name of "structured pedagogy", most of which are less controversial. This argues that isolated splurges on goodies such as textbooks often fail to bring benefits. Making big improvements seems to require pulling several levers at once. So the idea is both to give more materials to pupils and better lesson plans to teachers, alongside fresh training and frequent coaching.

In 2020, a panel convened by the World Bank and other bodies concluded that these are some of the best things education reformers can spend money on. In the past few years, the approach has been applied in Gambia, Ghana, Nepal, and Senegal. One program in Kenyan government schools helped push up the number of children reaching the national standard in English by 30 percentage points.

But it is not only in poor countries where tightly structured approaches to schooling are gaining a following. In America, for example, there is growing awareness that schools have been clinging to modish but ineffective "child-led" ways of teaching reading that other developed countries such as Britain have junked. Literacy programs that were dismissed as old-fashioned are coming back into favor.

McGraw Hill, an American publishing company, sells a series of highly scripted courses aimed at primary-school children. Bryan Wickman of the National Institute for Direct Instruction, a charity in Oregon, says that using the simplest, clearest language possible is crucial when teaching the smallest children. He says the idea that lessons based on scripts must inevitably bore children should surprise anyone who enjoys other things that are performed from scripts, such as plays.

Success For All, a program used in some British and American schools, puts much faith in "co-operative learning"—which involves encouraging children to solve problems together in small groups. But much else that goes on in its classrooms is structured and scripted. Such prescriptiveness helps teachers adopt techniques that research suggests work well, says Nancy Madden of Johns Hopkins University, one of Success for All's creators. These include giving pupils quick and frequent feedback and keeping up a rapid pace to keep children interested.

Ms Madden says teachers who have grown familiar with her program's techniques are not expected to keep following scripts to the letter. But when, in the past, her team relied mostly on training workshops to spread their approach, they found that only a fraction of teachers kept up the new practices once they were back in their classrooms.

She admits that teachers sometimes bristle at the constraints that scripts impose: "It is not what they teach you in teacher school". Skeptics often come around, she says, when they see kids making swift progress. Mr. Wickman points out that other expensively trained professionals, such as pilots and surgeons, also have procedures that they must follow to the letter. After some initial complaints (similar to those expressed by dubious teachers), such regimented approaches have become widespread in those fields. They help reduce mistakes and spread better ways of doing things.

Back in Edo, Mr. Obaseki's transformation still has plenty to prove. An analysis published in 2019 by the state government and NewGlobe claims that during the first year of the reforms, children learned as much in a single term as they were previously learning in one year. But the project has yet to undergo a rigorous independent evaluation. Much of the existing evidence that supports scripted schooling relates to basic literacy and numeracy among the youngest children. In Edo, lesson scripts are being used to teach almost every subject and are being applied to teenagers in junior secondary schools.

Whether strict scripting is necessary remains a topic of debate (The World Bank panel, for instance, argued that word-for-word scripts are less effective than simpler guides). In 2018 RTI, an American nonprofit group, analyzed 19 school-reform efforts it had been involved in across 13 countries, including Ethiopia and Uganda. It concluded that programs with slightly less prescriptive guides—a page of notes per day, say, rather than a full-on script—produced better results. Advocates of a more relaxed approach say another advantage is that leaving teachers with a bit of freedom to tinker can help win their support.

Yet Edo's approach appears to have persuaded most local teachers of its worth. Mr. Obaseki, the state governor, says school staff had long felt ignored and unappreciated; he says that providing more training and equipment has brought fresh motivation. He insists that support for the project among unions was crucial to his re-election, in 2020. It has, he says, been "one of my best investments"[17] (Economist, 2023).

1 How much of reform effectiveness depends on sustained top-level official support?
2 What were the key elements of the most successful methods of improving primary school learning?
3 What contextual obstacles to effective classroom management were reduced or eliminated by the new scripted lesson approach?
4 What other developmental obstacles remain untouched by the educational reforms?
5 What modifications would you make to the scripted lesson approach based on this case reading?

Notes

1 Jessica Adolino and Charles H. Blake (2011) *Comparing Public Policies: Issues and Choices in Industrialized Countries* (Washington, DC: CQ/Sage Press), p.321.
2 United Nations (2012) *Millennium Development Goals and Beyond* (New York, UNDP).
3 Michael Barzelay (2001) *The New Public Management: Improving Research and Policy Dialogue* (Berkeley, CA: University of California Press).
4 New wave progressive school reformers argue that focusing on choice, completion, and testing reeks of capitalism and racism; *Economist* (2023) "Reform School", 3-18, p.25.
5 James E. Ellis (2023) "Bed, Bath and Beyond Hope", *Bloomberg Business Week*, 2-13, p.9.
6 Certificates of cash value issued by the state or *vouchers* in exchange for services are viewed as a mechanism to facilitate the choice of services. They are also considered a simplistic panacea to fix public schools and enhance learning but are largely unworkable in serving large city school districts. Similar to privatizing urban transit lines within networks served by natural transport monopoly areas, voucher systems fragment public transit systems while expanding choice for some. In short, vouchers fragment public educational systems and generally make management problems worse.
7 John E. Chubb and Terry M. Moe (1990) *Politics, Markets and America's Schools* (Washington, DC: Brookings Institution).
8 *Economist* (2021) "Northern Ireland: Unhappy Anniversary", 7-31.
9 The Washington, DC, School Reform case was prepared by the author in 2010 who was Scholar in Residence in Public Administration and Policy at American University, Washington, DC, 20016. He wishes to thank Margery Yeager in the Office of the Chancellor at DCPS for her interviews and invaluable guidance in preparing the case. The conclusions are mine and any data errors or inconsistencies are the author's fault.
10 The need for school consolidation for effective school reform in large cities such as Washington, Chicago, and Denver has since become a larger issue. In Chicago, Hirsch HS, for instance, was built for 1,100 students and now has

113 pupils, largely because of neighborhood demographics and the opening of charter schools that compete for the fewer students available. Keeping such schools as Hirsch open is a major fiscal loss as operating costs for heat and maintenance continue to run for almost empty buildings. Money is distributed on a per-pupil basis (capitation) but "equity grants" are available to keep some under-enrolled and staffed schools open. The average per pupil cost is $17k but $42k for under-enrolled schools such as Hirsch HS. In short, schools need to be consolidated but leaders and political candidates are afraid of backlash from the neighborhoods, unions, and parents. *Economist* (2023) "Class Half Empty", 3-18, p.23.

11 Used with permission of Georgetown University Press, from George M. Guess and Paul G. Farnham (2011) *Cases in Public Policy Analysis*; permission conveyed through Copyright Clearance Center, Inc.

12 From: *Economist* (2020) "Lessons from a Radical Education Experiment in Liberia, the Messy Reality of Trying to Improve Schools in a Poor Country", 1-4, p.56.

13 From: *Economist* (2020) "Lessons from a Radical Education Experiment in Liberia, the Messy Reality of Trying to Improve Schools in a Poor Country", 1-4, p.56.

14 The Nigerian teacher's union representative said that lesson plans should be written to match the local "context" meaning nature, village friends, neighbors, families, pets, farm animals, and urban barrio or favela daily dramas. Learning about these elements of the urban or rural "development context" can be encouraged by writing and reflecting upon them. It is a skill that distinguishes educated kids. They can express themselves thoughtfully and succinctly. To do that requires learning about how to write and practicing that under supervision from qualified teachers. Often, the context "to learn how" under qualified supervision in poor rural or urban schools is lacking these supportive elements. The union official was half right: students should write about, reflect, and learn from their surroundings. These may include violence, abuse, family instability, and experiencing larger social prejudices (Northern Irish sectarianism is discussed in **Discussion Case #18**). Schools should be refuges from some of this, a safe place to learn about what they feel and experience and express it on paper or tablet. But the other half beyond reflection from lesson plans based on these surroundings is to learn how to write and to discover experiences beyond the village and one's immediate family. That is where the tablets fit in to serve as foundations from which both the teacher and the student can extrapolate to the larger context.

15 *826dc* is a US educational nonprofit, similar to **NewGlobe**, that provides this kind of experience-based learning and context in multiple US cities: tablets, lessons, exercises, and selected feedback. That is, the nonprofit is offering a management tool for stimulating interest in learning together with writing skills. The nonprofit works with charters and public schools and focuses on student writing skills, and developing student stories, reflections, and essays written from their experiences and surroundings. Best stories are published in book-like compendiums to encourage other students and gain appreciation from their families. The author volunteered for this organization in a DC charter school to learn how it was done. It works spectacularly! But it requires qualified, alert, and energetic teachers to make the learning context work! 826dc has them! So, a "rote" or "canned" approach is important for

foundational structure and as mental frameworks for what students should and avoid in the future—like practice and principles from tennis lessons in order to strengthen one's future play. By contrast, note how important canned or rote approaches are for learning mathematics skills: drilling, regurgitating, working in teams, and grading each other's exercises. Overseas development assistance projects intend to build school and educational systems capacities and to send experts not to do these things in the one to two years that project funding timelines allow. Educational aid workers are there to leave working and tested models of skills that can be used to encourage pupil learning that can continue to be used by local teachers after project termination. Aid projects offer incremental improvements in education, transport, budgeting, and financial management sectors—not total sectoral reforms or improvements in such a short period of time. For that, local government ministries and units need the will to sustain the aid projects' progress.

16 One of the hardest problems for primary teachers (in rich as well as poor countries) is to maintain student attention—their spans are often low, discipline is a serious problem, teachers are often overworked, and reach the limits of their patience. They lose control of their classes. Any technique or method that can help teaching should be welcomed, especially by educational supervisors and evaluators!

17 © The Economist Group Limited, London (1-28-2023). From: "Education in a Can", *The Economist,* pp.54–55. Reprinted with permission.

7 International Environmental Management

Context and Problems

Environmental management will be examined from two perspectives: macro and micro. The macro level views the problems that cross borders and require international remedial solutions: water and air pollution, solid waste deposits from energy generation, factories, and mining. The micro level lens focuses on two main approaches: regulation of emissions and deposits with or without nationalization of the resource. Regulatory regimes work best where countries have strong rules of law and property rights especially for contracts and land tenure. Such rights allow imposition of fines and allocation of incentive payments. But most poor countries lack such clarity and enforceable rules and regulations. Laws can easily be circumvented by corrupt forces that weaken natural resource law enforcement, payments. Countries such as Honduras nationalized their forests to preserve them from foreign investments which are viewed as mercantilism at best and exploitation at the worst. But nationalization rarely works to stem the lawlessness that results in deforestation. State corruption replaces market-driven corruption of laws and rules. State apparatchiks replace wildcat loggers circumventing any laws against damaging the environment by deforestation and pollution. Other countries have taken a market-friendly approach to leverage investments to support their own policies of preservation and production of the resource to stimulate national development. These efforts take the form of landowner tax incentives and locally tailored nature-based debt-nature swaps as in Guyana (see *Discussion Case #6*). Thus, the micro lens focuses on national regulatory and market tools and their applications at the national level (see *Figure 3.4*). Aid managers face the reality of powerful and often dangerous interest groups that oppose reservation of land use for existing tropical forests and indigenous area residents. These problems are largely actionable and amenable to rational solutions, but when local context is factored in, they become messy and ill-structured.

Few air, water, and solid waste pollution problems affect only specific nations, though they may originate from facilities, practices, and sources

DOI: 10.4324/9781032670959-7

at the national level. Development aid can assist in promulgating national policy remedies by transfer of lessons from other comparable jurisdictions. Aid can also assist country policy-makers to leverage funds to fight pollution from existing international pacts such as the reduced emissions from deforestation and forest degradation (REDD) agreement facilitating debt/nature swaps for conservation and preservation and that also incentivizes better natural resource practices.

Environmental policy and management is an extremely fraught sectoral area requiring effective resolution of vicious conflicts between indigenous locals, multinational mining and forestry corporations, ministries of agriculture and natural resources, cattle ranching associations, project staff, forestry NGOs that often have extensive overseas forestry and environmental regulatory experience, and even aid donors with conflicting projects that actually damage the environment! For example, in the mid-1990s a USAID local government strengthening project in Albania included measures to stop the runoff of contaminated water into Lake Ohrid at Pogradec. An obvious source of the contamination there was urban deforestation that loosened the soil by cutting the few remaining hillside trees. Another aid project from EU was planning to cut the trees as part of its road-building agenda. The structural constraint was that in Albania local governments lacked authority to manage and protect their surrounding environments as it was a national or central government function. Our solution was to protest directly to the local EU team and persuade the team that they could build their roads without damaging the lake's water supply by leaving the trees in. The solution was smarter planning and aid coordination. In addition, many agricultural and environmental officials lack actual farming or even gardening experience. They also lack the appetite for taking the risky and bold decisions necessary to manage these brutal conflicts that can erupt into regional or even national civil wars! Poor country states are weak. Many still bear the legacies of misguided colonial attempts at agricultural modernization.[1] And states remain weak because with few exceptions, such as Botswana and Chile, they consist of bureaucracies dominated by political parties that serve primarily their own interests in maintaining power in order to plunder of their national treasuries. Moreover, state budgetary and policy processes that should define, analyze, and manage public problems are reduced to raw power contests between conflicting interests and pressure groups. The annual budgets are a byproduct of such dysfunctional processes in many poor countries which at best produce policies that are rarely implemented in full. Key stakeholders representing public environmental interests should be part of transparent policy and budget processes. But they often must operate below the radar and behind the scenes.

In this international management area, scarce resources and public needs compete for policy solutions and direct expenditures, subsidies, licenses, and concessions. Decentralized federal states typically offer more public mediation and conflict resolution points but also opportunities for systemic leakages through bribery of officials at all levels. More centralized unitary states (such as Albania noted above) are often weak and unable to enforce national norms and standards. Intergovernmental structures may be in fact ethnic federations (such as Ethiopia), encouraging partition, ethno-nationalism, and destructive sectarianism. Budgeting, planning, and approval processes in federations can also suffer from excessive opacity and complexity and exclude many stakeholders. When governments respond with environmental policies and regulatory strictures, they are often ill-suited and counterproductive. Sri Lanka, for instance, banned synthetic chemical fertilizers in order to transition the country to organic farming. Rice and tea production, food, key staples, and export crops suffered dramatically. Unsurprisingly, the result was soaring food inflation and violent protests by farmers, forcing the Sri Lankan government (GOSL) to back-pedal on enforcing the ban.

In a more devastating version of the economic commons tragedy framework used to explain irrational overconsumption of natural resources, a similar tragedy of the "fiscal commons" has taken place in the Brazilian Amazon for many decades. Because of massive annual deforestation, the Brazilian Amazon has been a net carbon emitter since 2016 (releasing out more CO_2 than it absorbs). Here, claimants (mainly loggers, farmers, and cattle ranchers) take more than their fair shares of the carbon commons, leading to excessive fiscal and resource deficits, and destruction of this major carbon sink of global importance to climate stabilization. Populist and demagogic leaders supported by powerful cattle ranching and agro-industrial interests, such as former President Jair Bolsonaro, have made the Amazon deforestation problem far worse.

In the environmental management area, a similar tragedy of the commons (overexploitation of a common pool) occurs when states allow special interests such as domestic cattle, agriculture, palm oil, and foreign investors in oil and mining to destroy, overexploit, and even to gain ownership of local natural resources. They are able to buy off environmental regulators or work around their regulatory regimes under official cover. Individually and collectively, they engage in overexploitation for short-term profit at the expense of the long-term public interest in resource sustainability and mitigating climate change. Massive tropical deforestation and watershed degradation, especially in Latin America, are obvious manifestations of the uncontrolled and opaque processes that are contaminated further by cronyism and special interests that capture state institutions. Overfishing of Lake Victoria in Africa is another example of uncontrolled plundering of a resource commons.

Weak, corrupt, and often illegitimate state regimes use such processes to misallocate budgetary resources. The predictable result is failure to regulate or enforce the legal and regulatory frameworks necessary to prevent the many instances of natural resource commons tragedies. Remedies are available and have worked. For example, pricing to limit demand, control pollution, and conserve resources has been a critical policy tool worldwide (see *Figure 3.4*). At the more micro level, conflicts between particular Costa Rican owners of tropical forests and plantations of agroforests and imported species such as pine and eucalyptus have been successfully managed to satisfy all parties. Other natural resource conflicts over involving water, pastures, different crop types, and oil and minerals have been successfully and sustainably managed. But scaling up of these particular successes to strengthen state natural resource and environmental institutions processes has been more difficult.

Learning Outcomes

1 To practice writing management and policy memos using the structure noted earlier: background context, problem identification, presentation, and analysis of remedial options, rationale for preferred option.

2 To learn of the consequences of weak states in resource-rich poor countries.

3 To understand how, in Latin America, major resource management problems of water, land, energy stem from long-standing failures to manage the tropical and plantation species for development. That is, "why development does not grow on trees" there? To identify instances where failure to plan and manage many primary and secondary industrial forestry projects causes immense opportunity costs for the region.

4 To review innovative techniques for poor country environmental training, management, and regulatory expertise in poor countries. What techniques for effective capacity building were used in Guyana (*Discussion Cases #6 and #23*), i.e., for Nigerian school "management development" as opposed to "development management"?

5 To apply the matched-case comparative methodology (see *Chapter 3*) to the two Indian city water management cases in *Discussion* Case #24 and to explain why Solapur was more successful than Latur.

6 To examine in *Discussion Case #25* whether there are medium-range or intermediate management tools to increase land tenure security incrementally without having to overhaul the entire legal and regulatory structure of African countries. What positive lessons are available from SSA countries in this sectoral policy area?

7 To review successful forestry management systems and practices for indigenous tropical forestry species, such as Ecuadorian balsa in *Discussion Case #26*. Lessons learned on how tropical forestry's boom and bust cycles can be avoided, and from it being the victim of world

market prices for competing commodities such as beef cattle and palm oil and green products such as wind turbines for renewable energy.

8   To review how debt-for-nature swaps (DNS) work in poor countries that are rich in resources, high in debt, and lower in political risk (*Discussion Case #27*). To examine the reasons for successes and failures. To review how much of performance depends on both design and implementation monitoring and contracts enforcement.

9   Focusing on Indonesian forestry in *Discussion Case #28*, to describe what offsets are and what they represent in carbon pricing and cap-and-trade schemes.

10   To explain why the carbon price has fallen and its incentives for tropical forestry management have diminished.

11   To play the role of the environmental minister in deciding what incentives are and are not working for Indonesian farmers.

CASES AND EXERCISES

Discussion Case #24: Unholy Woes: Comparative City Responses to an Indian Water Crisis

"At the dawn of time Lord Vishnu made gods and demons join in churning the milky oceans to extract an elixir of eternal life. After cheating the demons of their share, Vishnu spilled four drops of the precious nectar. Where they fell sprang up sacred rivers whose waters wash away sins, now sites for mass Hindu pilgrimages called Kumbh Mela.

For a lunar month every 12 years it falls to Ujjain, a town in the central Indian state of Madhya Pradesh, to host the Kumbh Mela by the revered Shipra, whose waters meander north into the mighty Ganges and eventually eastward to the Bay of Bengal. By the time the full moon reappears on May 21st tens of millions of bathers, among them thousands of bearded ascetics known as *sadhus* (pictured), will have worshipped on Ujjain's teeming riverbanks.

What few are aware of is that the water is no longer the Shipra's. Urbanisation, rising demand and two years of severe drought have shriveled the sacred river. Its natural state at this time of year, before the monsoon, would be a dismal sequence of puddles dirtied by industrial and human waste. But the government of Madhya Pradesh, determined to preserve the pilgrimage, has built a massive pipeline diverting into the Shipra the abundant waters of the Narmada river, which spills westward into the Arabian Sea. Giant pumps are sucking some 5,000 liters a second from a canal fed by the Narmada, lifting it by 350 meters and carrying it nearly 50 kilometers to pour into the Shipra's headwaters. To ensure clean water for the festival, the Shipra's smaller tributaries have been blocked or diverted, and purifying ozone is being injected into the reconstituted waters in Ujjain itself.

The pilgrims and merchants of Ujjain are happy. But down in the Narmada valley there is little cheer. "They are wasting water on *sadhus*... while our farms go dry," says Rameshwar Sitole, a farmer in the hamlet of Kithud. Since March the canal, which feeds his 2.5 hectares of maize and okra along with the farms of 12 other hamlets, has been bone dry. Mr Sitole's crops have withered and died: a loss, he reckons, of some 50,000 rupees ($750). The government insists the water will return once Ujjain's pilgrimage ends, but he is not so sure. "They turn it on when we protest, and then take it away again," Mr Sitole shrugs. Meanwhile, over the hills, industrial users near Ujjain are lobbying loudly to exploit the fancy new water sources.

Poor monsoons are not unusual, but the back-to-back shortfalls, linked to the El Niño effect, which India has experienced in the past two years are very rare. Ten out of 29 states, with a population of some 330m, have been badly hit, with the worst-affected areas in the centre of the country. India is suffering its gravest water shortage since independence, says Himanshu Thakkar, a water expert in Delhi, the capital. Every day brings news of exhausted rivers and wells, destitute farmers migrating to the cities or even committing suicide, water trains being dispatched to parched regions—and of leopards venturing into towns in search of a drink (*Figure 7.1*).

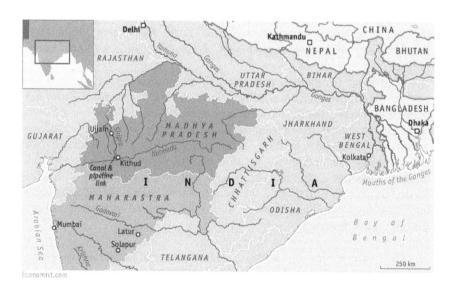

Figure 7.1 Rivers in the Central Indian State of Madhya Pradesh.

Source: The Economist (2016) 5–14, "Unholy Woes", used with permission.

The central government has responded with make-work programmes for afflicted areas, emergency shipments of water, and many promises. In February Narendra Modi, the prime minister, pledged to double farm incomes by 2022. Other ministers speak of massive irrigation projects, and have dusted off an ambitious water-diversion scheme for parched regions that is priced at $165 billion and involves no fewer than 37 links between rivers. Most links would be via canals—some 15,000km of artificial waterways in all.

Hydrologists such as Mr Thakkar are sceptical of big projects, open to massive cronyism, when simpler and environmentally sounder solutions are at hand. India relies not on rivers but on underground aquifers for some two-thirds of its irrigation and for more than three-quarters of its drinking water. With 30m wells and pumps at work, it is hardly surprising that groundwater levels have been dropping. Nearly two-thirds of wells tested in a recent nationwide survey showed levels lower than their ten-year average. Much water is being squandered.

Plenty, Mr Thakkar argues, could be done to conserve groundwater; for instance, by collecting and storing rainwater more effectively, regulating consumption, treating urban sewage properly and providing credit for drip irrigation to replace wasteful flooding techniques. And pricing water properly would be much better than shunting it about at great expense. Despite the severity of the current drought, which will end if meteorologists' predictions of a better-than-average monsoon in June are correct, the real problem is not a lack of water. Per person, India has twice as much of the stuff as water-starved northern China. But India is being hampered by mindless overuse and, in many places, a lack of sensible water-allocation policies".[2]

Recall from *Chapter 5*, that water is a common resource and that a natural monopoly such as a public utility (as seen in *Figures 5.7 and 5.8*) is needed to regulate its use and conservation effectively. The resource whether water or forests should be held to national norms and standards delegated, if necessary, by state or district enforcers. As noted earlier, natural monopoly means individual enforcers and delivery institutions would be cost-ineffective and inefficient. A monopoly public authority or utility is needed to manage and protect the resource in its charge. Multiple competing institutions would collectively allow the resource to be depleted and the commons destroyed.

"The contrast between two districts in a corner of Maharashtra state that is severely afflicted by drought provides a case in point. For the past two months the 400,000 residents of Latur, a city 400km east of Mumbai, have had, at great expense, to rely on tanker lorries and trains coming from the Krishna river 350km away to quench their thirst, while the district's stricken farmers have fled en masse. Nearby Solapur once faced similar problems. Following a bad monsoon in 2012 it had to mobilise more than 650 tanker lorries to get water to needy citizens. This year, under far worse drought conditions, fewer than 20 tankers are operating.

The difference comes down to governance. When Tukaram Mundhe was appointed the main local-government administrator in 2014, he set to work applying laws and policies on groundwater use that had been wilfully ignored in the arid region. "Solapur was not taking any preventive ... measures," he says, "So I took a firm stand. I went directly to the public instead of going through my officers".

Local farmers were encouraged to revive some 5,000 defunct water sources, such as abandoned wells and silted-up ponds, to collect rainwater. Strict regulation was imposed on these and existing sources, with only nearby farms allowed access. Commercial drilling for new wells was restricted. The owners of a water-guzzling sugar factory were fined for polluting nearby water sources. In Latur, by contrast, politically influential owners kept sugar mills running even as the wells dried up.

With the monsoon looming and their storage capacity high, Solapur's farmers appear confident of avoiding future shortages. Mr Mundhe says that all his projects are "scalable and replicable". But he will not have a chance to find out himself. The state government abruptly appointed him last month to a municipal post near Mumbai. Some in Solapur suspect that powerful owners of water-tanker fleets and sugar mills may have had a hand in Mr Mundhe's sudden transfer" (The Economist, 2016).[3]

Questions

In this case, write a memo setting out the problem and its impact, remedial options, constraints and opportunities of each, and preferred policy option for water management. What is the water problem in India? What were the lessons of different responses by Solapur and Latur to their respective crises? How could better water management help Indian states?[4] For other possible management remedies, refer to the works of the NGO *EcoPeace Middle East* in Palestine, Israel, and Jordan.

Exercise 7.1: From Management Development to Development
Management: Upgrading Nigerian School Management and
Building Guyanan Management Capacity of an Oil Windfall
(Discussion Cases 6 and 23)

Does Guyana (*Discussion Case #6*) really have the institutional strength
and regulatory capacity to absorb massive oil and gas revenues and spend
them effectively for its needed development projects? How has environmental management been upgraded there to fill the capacity gaps? What
lessons for management development can be gleaned from the efforts of
Nigerian school reformers in *Case #23?*

Discussion Case #25: Land Tenure Problems in Africa

"Builders are busy outside Louisa Qangiso's house in Khayelitsha,
a township on the outskirts of Cape Town. The 49-year-old is putting up eight studio flats in her backyard that she will rent out for
3,000 rand ($177) per month. This could almost triple the value of
her property, from roughly 570,000 to 1.6m rand. These are life-
changing sums for Ms Qangiso, a grandmother whose warehouse
job pays just 5,000 rand a month. "This is my dream come true," she
says, holding back tears.

The dream is reality because of Ms Qangiso's grit—and because,
unlike most people in the township, she can demonstrate ownership
of her property. Aided by Bitprop, a startup, she proved her claim on
the land, then used the title to raise money for the building works.
Over the next decade she will split the rent with Bitprop, which also
designs the flats, until its share is paid back. Thereafter the takings,
as well as the increase in the asset value, are hers.

Ms Qangiso's story encapsulates the latent power of property
rights. Twenty years ago Hernando de Soto, a Peruvian economist,
published "The Mystery of Capital", in which he argued that, without formal title, the real estate on which billions of poor people live
and work is "dead capital". He estimated these assets to be worth
$9.3trn ($13.5trn in today's money).

Partly inspired by Mr de Soto, over the past two decades there has
been a flurry of attempts to map and parcel land in the developing
world. Between 2004 and 2009 the World Bank committed to 34
land-titling and registration projects worth more than $1bn, com-
pared with three between 1990 and 1994.

Yet the potential of property rights remains largely unrealised,
especially in Africa. Perhaps 90% of rural land in Africa is not formally documented. Just 4% of African countries have mapped and

titled the private land in their capital cities. Well-meaning reformers have often neglected the myriad other factors affecting whether titles are useful or not, such as custom, other laws and the capacity of the state to enforce people's legal property rights. They have also underestimated the ability of vested interests, such as traditional leaders and urban elites, to obstruct reform.

Covid-19 highlights the harm that insecure property rights cause. Evictions and land grabs are rising, as newly jobless tenants cannot pay rent and bigwigs figure they can get away with skulduggery while everyone's attention is on the pandemic. The economic fallout of the coronavirus is so severe that some African countries face a lost decade. So they need growth-boosting reforms more than ever.

As history shows, land reform is hard. Policies in the colonial era varied, but white rulers often designated huge areas *terra nullius* (unoccupied land) and appropriated it for their colonies.[5] Formal property rights were reserved for settlers and European firms. The rest of the agricultural land was given "customary" tenure, meaning it could be used but not owned, and that it was always subject to seizure by the state. Colonists often ruled indirectly, via state-sanctioned "tribal" leaders who exercised control over the land.

After independence most African governments kept bifurcated systems. Urban elites replaced white colonists in state institutions. Customary systems in rural areas endured. Only towards the end of the 20th century did the notion of formalising more of the land take off. By this time the idea that a lack of property rights was a brake on development was commonplace.[6]

Africa has half of the world's usable uncultivated land, and its agricultural productivity is far below its potential. That is a huge drag on growth. Because people in the countryside do not have title to their land they typically cannot rent it out while they are away, and they may fear it may be taken by someone else. This discourages migration to the cities, where wages are higher.

Insecure tenure makes cities poorer, too. Dense urban populations normally make it easier for people to share ideas and find work. But African cities sprawl inefficiently. The World Bank reckons that in some of them 30% of land is not built on, compared with 14% in, say, Paris. Overlapping tenure regimes are one reason why. In Kampala, Uganda, a bewildering mix of freehold, leasehold, customary and "dual ownership" systems gum up formal land markets.

Weak property rights aggravate many other ills. They encourage environmental degradation—if it is not clear who owns the forest it is easier for well-connected businesses to claim it and cut it down. Land disputes are a common cause of conflict. Informal land markets mean governments miss out on taxes. And sexist traditions often make women's property rights especially insecure. According to a survey by Prindex, a research group, nearly half of women in sub-Saharan Africa worry that they would lose land if they were divorced or widowed.

All rich, democratic countries have secure property rights, enabling owners to buy, sell, subdivide and collateralise their assets. Many poor countries have tried to build something similar, usually starting with a formal registry of land ownership. In 2012, for example, Rwanda, completed a programme to map and title all of its land using aerial photography, paid for by Britain's government. Those carrying out the project had to tread carefully. Many of the original occupants of plots had been killed in the genocide in 1994; others had been locked up for their part in it. The team made visits to prisons to help resolve land disputes. The cost per parcel was just $7—much lower than efforts that relied on traditional surveying. Before the project most women were not recognised as landholders; at the end, a woman's name was on 92% of the deeds.

Yet the overall impact of titling initiatives has been disappointing. Most African countries still use paper records. They usually do not know how many titles they have issued or whether more than one person claims ownership; in Khayelitsha, the staff at a local advice centre note that 15% of the titles in the surrounding area are in the names of dead people. The share of Africans who have formal title deeds is therefore unknown, but in some countries it is most likely in the single digits.

Poor administration compounds the problem. On average in Africa it takes 59 days to register a property. Transferring deeds costs 9% of the property's value, more than twice the share in the OECD, a club of mostly rich countries. Land surveyors are scarce and monopolistic. A lack of trust does not help, either. In a different part of Khayelitsha from where Ms Qasingo lives, a group of women meet members of Khaya Lam (My Home), a charitable project that pays for title deeds to be proven. One lady struggles to believe that someone would help her for next to nothing. Waving her title she asks: "Is this for real?" Corruption in South Africa means people are sceptical, says Temba Nolutshungu of the Free Market Foundation, a think-tank. "People are used to being lied to by those with a political agenda."

Technology may help. There is a good deal of enthusiasm around digital platforms such as Cadasta. These help users to prove ownership of their land and resolve disputes, rather than having to go to a bureaucrat's office.

A crucial lesson of the past few decades, however, is that if land reform is treated purely as a top-down technical task, it will not work well. It is not enough simply to map and register a property, as several high-profile efforts show. In Ethiopia, after 20m certificates were issued in the 2000s, land records were rarely updated. In Uganda a project to digitise records has struggled with a lack of data. Even Rwanda's scheme has had teething problems. Though land administration is working well in Rwandan cities, 87% of rural transactions remain informal (mostly because the cost of registering sales is too high).

In sub-Saharan Africa formal title seems to bring less additional security of tenure than it does in other parts of the world. In July Prindex published results of a 140-country survey on how secure people feel in their properties (see map below). It found that there was only a small difference in perceived security between sub-Saharan Africans with formal documentation (70%) and those without (65%). This was the lowest gap anywhere.

The authors suggest this may be further evidence of what researchers call the "Africa effect". Titling also seems to make less difference to productivity in Africa than in Asia or the Americas. A paper co-authored by Steven Lawry of the Centre for International Forestry Research found that agricultural productivity increased by no more than 10% in the African studies they reviewed, compared with 50-100% in the papers from Latin America and Asia—partly because successful efforts in other regions were more efficient and pursued titling alongside other reforms.

Another explanation for the Africa effect is that customary systems offer more security than was previously assumed. These arrangements, which cover perhaps 625m people and 78% of Africa's land, vary hugely in how they combine collective ownership with rights of individuals or families. Yet over the past 30 years there has been what Admos Chimhowu of the University of Manchester calls a "quiet paradigm shift" in customary land laws.

Since 1990, 39 of Africa's 54 countries have passed laws overhauling communal land rights. Most create something of a middle ground between the individualistic freehold systems popular in the West and the colonial customary model where occupants had no formal rights to the land on which they lived and worked. Mr Chimhowu characterises the "old" customary system as one that did not recognise property at all, where power was vested in chiefs and where markets were absent or informal. In the "new" customary tenure, communal rights are recognised as property, local leaders are more accountable and there are greater links with formal markets. This, at least, is the theory.

In reality the potential of new laws, like that of titling efforts, has been undermined by vested interests. Control of land rights is so lucrative that Africa's ruling parties and traditional authorities are reluctant to let it go. "Traditional leaders balk at surrendering what is...colonially encouraged ownership over their citizens' lands," notes Liz Alden Wily, an expert on land and customary law. In countries such as Ghana, Malawi, Namibia and Zambia, chiefs have stymied new laws that would have reduced their power to allocate land.

Since the end of apartheid in South Africa, successive laws have given "traditional" authorities more clout. The 35–40% of people who live in the former "homelands" created under white rule, or other communal areas, are unable to own their land. Black South Africans can now buy property outside the homelands, but inside them they remain, in effect, subjects.

Several studies have found that chiefs, in cahoots with politicians, use their powers to sell land to mining or other firms without the say-so of their people. In 2016 South Africa's public protector, a legal ombudsman, found that the leaders of the Bapo ba Mogale people of North West province, who live on platinum-rich land, had somehow lost 800m rand that was supposed to belong to their people. Activists who raised the issue were beaten up.

A process that was meant to correct some of the injustices of apartheid has instead been hijacked by corrupt elites. Land restitution schemes are "captured" by those who have access to money and connections, according to a study of 62 land projects by the Institute for Poverty, Land and Agrarian Studies, an academic group.

Another way in which African bigwigs exert power over land, to the detriment of ordinary citizens, is what Ms Wily calls "state landlordism". This can take several forms. Some bigwigs abuse the process of mapping communities to grab the choicest surrounding land for agri-businesses, as in Tanzania. Some take an expansive interpretation of the state's power to seize land in the "public interest". In Kenya a law passed in 2012 was supposed to reduce the political power of the ministry of lands by setting up an apolitical land commission. But vested interests have eroded its authority and land grabs have increased over the past eight years. The designation of dozens of protected forests has frequently served to deprive indigenous people of their land.

State landlordism is an urban problem, too, especially as cities have grown to encompass erstwhile farmland. A report published in 2019 by enact, a research group funded by the EU, suggested that drug-traffickers are small fry compared with criminal land-lords. "Land allocation, real estate and property development", it wrote, "may be the largest type of organised criminal activity in Africa".

In Kibera, a slum in Nairobi, more than 90% of residents rent their homes from absentee landlords. enact cites a survey estimating that 42% of these landlords "reputedly had associations with state and political actors", while 41% were government officials and 16% were politicians. In Ghana there is a similar pattern, where urban land ownership is dominated by state bodies, political leaders and chiefs.

Those who benefit from a murky status quo can also take advantage of archaic planning laws. In former British colonies many cities are governed by laws influenced by the UK Town and Country Planning Act of 1947, which was not designed for dense Kenyan slums. This is one reason why English-speaking cities have more sprawl than French-speaking ones. French planners were generally keener on compact, dense cities, while English-speaking cities have 50% more patches of built-upon land with no surrounding developments.

Despite state landlordism, promising reforms continue. Land-rights lawyers are campaigning for governments to obey their own laws. Rwanda is trying to reverse the slide into informalisation. In Ethiopia several states are issuing certificates that allow people to formally rent out their land and to borrow against it.

The pandemic has made everything harder. Titling has slowed in Ethiopia. It is hard to gather around a map or a smartphone if you are meant to be social distancing. Courts that are not sitting cannot resolve disputes. Elsewhere covid-19 has underlined the fragility of many Africans' land rights. Women are at risk, especially those whose husbands or fathers have died. There is some evidence that in Kenya widows were thrown out of their homes by their in-laws during lockdown, as they are seen as a burden.

Back in Khayelitsha, a few miles from Ms Qasingo's house, is a reminder of how the pandemic and a lack of property rights combine to make people's lives insecure. On the same day your correspondent met Ms Qasingo, scores of people left destitute by the pandemic set up shacks on state-owned land. Many had been evicted from their previous abodes; their jobs gone because of covid-19. Their new homes could be bulldozed at the click of an official's fingers. It would be tragic if one legacy of a pandemic that forced billions to stay in their homes was that it made it harder for others to keep theirs" (The Economist, 2020).[7]

As noted above, land titling reform efforts in Asia have been more effective since they are often pursued together with other reforms. In India, for example, urban slums are pervasive, and basic municipal services, such as clean running water, toilets, sewers, street lighting, and public transit are scarce. The Modi administration has invested billions of dollars in an attempt to build infrastructure for the medium and smaller sized cities where a lot of growth will happen. As part of the effort, land titles have been distributed to slum dwellers in "fourth tier" cities such as Odisha (250k titles) and larger cities such as Punjab (1.4m titles). The titling reform includes greater involvement of slum resident associations in decisions that affect them. But a major constraint is that the constitution allocates powers to federal and state levels but not local governments. Mayors are indirectly elected and have short terms and few powers over such basics as planning and sanitation. Future reforms should focus on strengthening the autonomy of mayors and local governments (the third tier in the federal system) rather than a fourth tier of slums. Successful decentralization requires strong local autonomy and a strong central government to enforce fiscal discipline and to remove corrupt leaders who abuse their powers.[8]

Questions

Write a *management memo* stating: (1) the land tenure problems in representative African states, (2) their impacts on development, (3) remedial options, (4) constraints and opportunities of each option, and (5) preferred policies for improved land management.

1 How have customs and vested interests affected land tenure reform in Africa? Have these constraints to tenure security been a serious opportunity cost to African agricultural productivity?
2 How has land tenure insecurity led to increased deforestation and environmental degradation in Africa?
3 What has been the "Africa effect" on land titling and productivity?
4 Land mapping, titling, and tax valuation are typically local functions. But most African states are unitary, and local governments lack public legitimacy and authority to strengthen property rights in land.
5 What efforts have been tried to strengthen tenure rights under these conditions? Which have been successful? Have efforts to strengthen urban property rights been any more successful than rural land reforms?

Discussion Case #26: Balsa Deforestation Exercise for Ecuador

Resource-rich poor countries often face overlapping crises and inter-related problems at the same time. It seems that their governments constantly face mutually reinforcing political, economic, and environmental crises. Their problems need to be defined, prioritized, and acted upon. But managing these crises and problems requires strong, legitimate institutions which countries like Ecuador lack.

"In late 2019 loggers started arriving in Ewegono, a village of nine indigenous Waorani families on the Curaray river in the Ecuadorean Amazon. They were looking for balsa, a fast-growing species of tree whose wood is used in blades for wind-power turbines. There was a global shortage. At first, villagers "grabbed chainsaws, axes and machetes to cut it down", says Saúl Nihua, Ewegono's leader. The pay could be $150 a day, a fortune in a region where most people have no jobs.

Soon the harvest became a free-for-all. Some loggers got permits with the help of the Waorani, but others forged them and invaded the indigenous reserve. Many took truckloads of wood without paying their workers. People from less remote places cut all the balsa they could find, stacking it along the road to Arajuno, the nearest town, says Mr Nihua. Buyers in trucks paid as little as $1.50 per tree. Uncontrolled logging degraded the forest. "They've killed off vegetation tremendously...without respecting legal limits," says Mr Nihua, who partly blames himself. He encouraged his fellow Waorani to earn money from the coveted timber. The influx of cash and liquor fuelled family violence.

The origin of the crisis lies oceans away, in growing demand for wind power from the world's largest economies. Thanks to ambitious targets to reduce the use of fossil fuels and technology that is bringing down turbine prices, global wind-power capacity has been increasing by 9% a year over the past decade. In 2020 new installed capacity surged by 24% to a record 78gw. Wind farms in China and the United States, which made up 60% of that demand, were rushing to install them before tax credits and subsidies expired. "It was like the end of a gold rush," says a China-based representative of a Western turbine maker.

Unlike gold, wind turbines benefit the whole world, not just their owners. They are an indispensable technology for phasing out fossil fuels. But "the sudden surge in demand put enormous strain on the entire wind-industry supply chain," says Shashi Barla of Wood Mackenzie, a consultancy. Wind fever caused the biggest problems in Ecuador, which provides more than 75% of the world's balsa. The word is Spanish for "raft".

A stiff, light wood that is also used in model aeroplanes and real aircraft, balsa goes into the core of a blade, where it is sandwiched between two fibreglass "skins" to add strength. Windmills built in the 1980s had 15-metre (49-foot) blades and could generate 0.05mw of electricity. Now, an offshore wind turbine with blades more than 100 metres long generates up to 14mw. Bigger blades require more balsa. Engineers at the National Renewable Energy Laboratory in the United States have calculated that a 100-metre blade requires 150 cubic metres (5,300 cubic feet) of balsa wood, or several tonnes.

Balsa trees reach optimal density in just five to seven years, which has helped suppliers cope with rising demand. Leading turbine manufacturers like Vestas in Denmark and Siemens Gamesa, in Spain, get most of their wood (along with foam, a less popular substitute) from three core-materials suppliers. 3a Composites, a Swiss firm, has more than 10,000 hectares (25,000 acres) of balsa plantations in Ecuador's coastal lowlands. Gurit (also Swiss) and Diab (Swedish) depend on independent suppliers and farmers growing balsa along with other crops, to whom they give seeds and training.

It is harder to predict demand for balsa than for, say, Christmas trees. As a result, says Ray Lewis of Diab, "there has always been a bit of a balsa crisis." Rising demand in the mid-2000s led to new plantations. But in 2011 turbine installations slowed sharply due in part to tighter regulations and a slower economy in China. Balsa prices plummeted. Growers planted less of it in Ecuador.

The most recent crisis was different. Demand, which revived in 2018, outstripped the supply of plantation-grown balsa by a lot, not a little. The price doubled from mid-2019 to mid-2020. In 2019 Ecuador exported $219m-worth of balsa wood, 30% more than the previous record in 2015 (see chart). In the first 11 months of 2020, it exported balsa worth $784m. Diab sold balsa for $1,800 per cubic metre in 2020, three times what it had in 2018.

The main source of new demand was China, which has built more turbines than any other country. In 2006 it had just 2.6gw of installed capacity, compared with 21gw in Germany and 12gw in the United States. By 2019, when Germany had 61gw and the United States had 105gw, China had blown past both, to 236gw. At the end of last year China's president, Xi Jinping, announced plans to reach 1,200gw of wind and solar capacity by 2030.

Chinese turbine manufacturers such as Goldwind and Envision, founded in 1998 and 2007 respectively, now have nearly 30% of global market share. They have erected turbines in dozens of countries. At first they used the same handful of Western blademakers and core-material suppliers as their competitors, but before long Chinese firms had edged into all levels of the supply chain. Sino Composite bought a stake in Cobalsa, a long-established Ecuadorean balsa firm.

The rising price of balsa also lured middlemen "like bees to a honeypot", says Mr Lewis. A 40-year veteran of the wind industry, he got emails from companies he had never heard of offering to sell him truckloads of balsa. He ignored them. Chinese firms, though, were aggressive buyers. Some set up roadside sawmills. More than 75% of Ecuador's balsa exports in the first 11 months of 2020 ended up in China. Despite having one of its best years ever, Plantabal, 3a's Ecuadorean subsidiary, saw its share of balsa exports drop from 20-25% to 8%, while Diab's fell from 15% to 5–6%.

The balsa boom, and the bust that has now followed, recall the rush to exploit rubber in the Amazon at the beginning of the 20th century. Rubber-tappers employed in slave-like conditions supplied industrialising Europe and the United States until production shifted to Asia, leaving them even more wretched. Indigenous Ecuadoreans have more protections, but are still vulnerable to exploitation. Like miners and oil-drillers before them, *balseros* "took advantage" of indigenous poverty and naivety, says Mr Nihua. The Waorani have been in contact with society only since the 1950s.

Often payment from loggers was partly in the form of liquor or marijuana; that encouraged drug abuse and violence, which were already big problems. Gilberto Nenquimo, the president of the Waorani Nation of Ecuador (nawe), says that his brother-in-law was murdered with a chainsaw in a dispute over balsa.

Overlogging was another result. Balsa trees get less regulatory protection than older, rarer trees. Fast-growing "pioneer species" can be chopped down almost anywhere, including in the rainforest, using simplified "collection permits". Balsa taken illegally—without legitimate permits or from protected areas like Yasuní National Park, which is home to uncontacted tribes—can be "laundered" by mixing it with other wood, says a customs agent. At the height of the frenzy, loggers extracted trees too young to be suitable for blademaking or shipped balsa to China without drying it, which meant it rotted on the way. The environment ministry boasts that it checked 1.4m cubic metres of balsa in 2020, twice as much as in 2019, and confiscated four times as much. But the total amount seized was less than 4,000 cubic metres.

Balsa is not an important store of carbon like bigger trees in the Amazon, but unregulated logging encourages traffic, hunting and extraction of species besides balsa. Denuded riverfronts raise the risk of flooding. The Global Forest Watch, an online platform that uses satellite data to track deforestation, recorded an "unusually high" number of "tree-cover loss alerts" in Ecuador in the second half of

2020, concentrated in the Amazon region. Land is Life, an NGO, says that extraction of balsa is partly to blame.

After several assemblies, the Waorani decided in October to kick out the loggers. The Wampís, another indigenous group that lives on a 1.3m-hectare territory on the border of Ecuador and Peru, made the same decision. When their guests refused to leave, the tribe seized seven boatloads of wood. The loggers retaliated by holding 19 Wampís hostage at a river crossing on December 2nd. They were released later that day, after Peruvian authorities persuaded the tribe to hand over the wood.

To get to Ewegono from Puyo, you zigzag down a narrow road to Arajuno, past two large sawmills. (One, called Hessental, was built in 2018 by a Chinese businessman, corporate records show.) Then, from a tiny port on the Curaray river where all that remains of a logging camp are mounds of sawdust and rubbish, you board a *peke-peke*, a wooden canoe with a trolling motor. Loggers left Ewegono just before *The Economist* arrived in December, but signs of the balsa boom were still visible: a new social hall, a satellite dish and sawdust outlining a football pitch.

The bust had clearly begun. Piles of balsa were stacked messily near the river. The price of balsa had fallen by half because Chinese turbine companies halted their work until after Chinese new year in February. Villagers were collecting donations for a man who had burned himself in a drunken domestic dispute. On a scrubby river island stripped of most trees, locals were growing maize. "Three years ago, this was full of balsa," said Johnny Tocari, of nawe. A few scrawny balsa stalks, identifiable by their heart-shaped leaves, had started to reclaim the banks.

There is a chance that last year's balsa boom will be the last. The shortage accelerated a shift to blade cores made partly or completely of pet, a synthetic foam that is cheaper but was long considered inferior. After Vestas, the world's largest turbine-maker, introduced the first all-pet blade designs, others began to adopt them. In 2020, "all the CEOs had to do a second bill of materials" that excluded balsa, says Mr Lewis. "Now their success depends on their ability to switch."

Wood Mackenzie forecasts that the share of pet will increase from 20% in 2018 to more than 55% by 2023, with demand for balsa staying stable. Chinese blademakers will continue to use it in the short term, since they have yet to make pet price-competitive, says the China-based representative. Balsa's long-term future as a blade component depends in part on whether the problems Ecuador has experienced over the past couple of years can be solved.

Ecuadorean officials and indigenous folk hope so. In November, after news reports about social and environmental damage from the balsa boom, the environment ministry excluded balsa from the list of the fast-growing species that can be logged with simplified permits. It is drafting stricter rules for how it can be harvested from forests.

The Waorani plan to start a co-operative to harvest balsa sustainably and sell it at fair prices to a lumber plant in Guayaquil. Similar initiatives are springing up across the region, some funded by NGOs like the Nature Conservancy, others by balsa exporters like Plantabal. They hope that consumers of green energy will care enough to insist on high social and environmental standards. "Would a person in Stockholm charging an electric car with energy generated from wood bought illegally in the Amazon feel right about that?" wonders Ramón del Pino, Plantabal's CEO. The answer is probably no. The question is whether drivers in Beijing will feel the same" (The Economist, 2021).[9]

For this case exercise, write a *management memo* identifying the scope of the forestry problem, the primary or proximate cause, the secondary or indirect causes, feasible options for mitigation, and your preferred remedy for management of this problem. Must poor country resources go through a boom-bust cycle and attendant destruction for the social and physical environment before management solutions can be applied? Ecuadorian tropical deforestation and attempts at forestry resource management (excluding balsa) have been recognized for many decades. Why did the Ecuadorian environmental and forestry ministries wait until the balsa market boomed before they acted? What tools are available to assist management in deciding between energy (wind energy) and environmental (forestry) opportunity costs where preserving one resource could damage another?

Discussion Case #27: Debt-for-Nature Swaps: Win-Win Solution or Environmental Imperialism?

Debt-for-nature swaps (DNSs) allow debtor nations to pay off some of their debt stock by promising to preserve a non-renewable natural resource within their borders. DNRs are seemingly win-win for all parties: the poor country, the resource beneficiary, the international donor organization, and the private creditor agency. Otherwise, the benefits of conservation accrue to a thin slice of world's population. By contrast, the benefits of deforestation go in large lucrative chunks to the men wielding the chainsaws—the "rule of saw" instead of the rule of law. Poor country local communities often resist the forces of law and order because they see more benefits from deforestation than conservation—they support illegal loggers and miners and often profit from them backed in rural areas by lawless militias. In the middle of this, DNSs try in theory fix the market failure by utilizing the world's governments to pay rainforest custodians to somehow not chop them down.

But a rational legal solution to this problem requires strong property rights and clear titles to demonstrate land ownership. In countries with strong legal institutions, it would be straight-forward to pay owners to conserve them. With clear deeds to their land, poor farmers sell carbon credits for preserving their forests to buyers who pollute and want offsets. Farmers gain offset payments to preserve their forests. Where property rights are muddled and rule of law is weak, whom do you pay and how do you know he or someone else won't chop down the forest anyway?[10] Unfortunately, most tropical rainforests are in the countries with weaker property rights as noted previously in *Figure 3.4*. Despite this constraint on performance, since the first DNS in Brazil in the late 1970s (Lovejoy, 1984), there have been over 100 DNSs, 50 trilateral swaps, and 90 bilateral swaps generating billions of dollars in private investment capital. They are considered "green" or "nature-based" development financing tools.[11]

How do DNSs work and what have they achieved in reducing or preventing tropical deforestation (i.e., averted deforestation)? Highly indebted countries with valuable natural resources such as forests and barrier reefs can gain debt reduction (savings of debt service payments), by preserving their resources, thereby contributing to the global reduction of carbon. Generally, creditor countries work with NGOs and banks to sell and cancel debts, in effect giving grants to debtor countries in exchange for their resource protection obligations. Grants instead of low-interest loans remove performance incentives and raise moral hazard issues. The renewed destruction of Brazilian tropical forests by past President Bolsonaro's constituent agro-industrial farmers in the Amazon, facilitated by his hollowing out Brazilian environmental institutions, damaged both the forests and increased the risks of future DNS investments by investors.

A newer DNS version was negotiated in 2022 in Belize which relies on loans instead of grants. The US Development Finance Corporation (DFC), which "invests" in poor countries using low-interest loans that are treated like grants rather than equity capital, guaranteed "Blue Bonds" issued by The Nature Conservancy. (This treatment by US federal budget rules lowers investor risk.) DFC would buy back discounted Belizean external commercial debt in exchange for GOB obligations to protect its barrier coral reef (the second longest in the world) and coastal mangrove forests from environmental degradation. Mangroves sequester carbon, protect against storm surges that flood coasts, and help provide fishermen make a living. Mangrove protection is one of many adaptation and resilience measures such as higher sea walls, better electricity grids, and greater electricity generation capacity to deal with climate change. But the Belizean DNS was more complicated than the earlier DNS grants but was more effective in that they required some continuing loan payments by the debtor government. Their commercial debts (30% GDP) were purchased via "superbond" revenues, resulted in fiscal savings and increased debt sustainability. With TNC oversight to promote sustainable development and build country resilience to natural disasters, the new DNS mechanism should generate greater environmental and development benefits to Belize.[12]

The swap mechanism is a popular conflict resolution tool. In this case, resources were exchanged to solve a seemingly intractable problem: how to incentivize a poor, resource-rich country to protect its resource? The swap is also a standard contractual tool for successful negotiation: compromise to solve a problem with material consideration—cash savings and grant payments exchanged for an enforceable obligation. Fundamentally, the question is what price or how much money is it worth our country's while and your environmental convictions to protect our natural resource? The process of back-and-forth disagreement and adjustment between local country officials and the sellers of the DNS method is what makes a market: sellers need buyers. That determines the discounted bond price and ultimately how much the resource-rich poor country gains financially. It also can determine what a farmer in such countries as Indonesia can earn by keeping his land in forest or selling the timber (see next *Discussion Case #27*).

The DNS is one remedy for two global commons problems—natural resource depletion and a potentially devastating country external debt load. Both are examples of Hardin's (1968) commons tragedy where precious resources are open to use by all but effectively controlled by no one. That some types of resource use within individual countries can be viewed as everybody's business raises questions of sovereignty. The claim to be acting to protect and mitigate damages to vital global resources is based on international morality, justice, and community. Such actions by international organizations raise local sovereignty questions, as is evident now where populist leaders such as Brazil's Bolsonaro can claim that whether their precious Amazon carbon sink should be protected is a matter of their internal choice. In addition, there is an international obligation to try and mitigate global poor country debt burdens and prevent the catastrophic defaults that would have adverse effects on the global financial community. Swap methods such as DNSs are used to try and incentivize proper management of resources in the name of protecting the commons as applied to debt crises.

As indicated, the DNS requires three institutional participants with varying degrees of participation on a case-by-case basis. The organizing donor for many swaps has been the World Bank. The Bank knows the candidate

Debt-Nature Swap (DNS)

Requisite Problems: Deforestation and High-Country Debt (e.g., Bolivia, Costa Rica)

1. ***Willing Donor:*** World Bank (etc.) put deals together; can offer credit enhancements for banks selling bonds; role is to raise capital to purchase country debt.

2. ***Debtor Government with valuable NR*** + Local Bank Participation: NGOS (e.g., WWF, Nature Conservancy), indigenous groups; Central bank may want to exit market and have discounted amount recovered for investment.

3. ***Participating Creditor Bank:*** Sell country debt to Conversation Bond buyers at ***discount***. Bond valued by $ pricing: P & Y inverse: less than 100 face or par value (discount) = more Yield for leveraged purchase power/cash for country.

Figure 7.2 Mechanics of the DNS.

Source: From sources created by author.

countries well and has worked intimately with the main environmental NGOs. It is trusted by all parties. An NGO is often responsible for overseeing and implementing the swap. The participating creditor bank raises cash by selling country debt at a discount or less than par value. As bond prices move inversely to yield, lower bond prices mean yields are higher and thus more palatable for investors in their search for yields. And that dynamic generates more cash for the country's treasuries. The bond market selling discounted bonds means that the funds raised usually become grants to the country rather than low-interest loans (*Figure 7.2*).

Questions

What DNS implementation problems have occurred? Most of the countries with DNS contracts are at lower political risk, meaning their institutional strength is stronger. Strong legal and regulatory frameworks are required for successful results, that is, actual results aligned with planned objectives. Nevertheless, in some DNS cases, it has often been a mystery what institution actually monitored the use of funds raised through discounted bond sales. In countries such as Brazil and Bolivia,[13] they were evidently spent for non-environmental purposes. There is also the problem that in a DNS the country is offered debt relief in exchange for environmental protection or climate change pledges. The mechanism is inefficient in that it subsidizes the creditors who do not actually take part in the swap. Creditors benefit from borrowers with more resources to repay them, but does the resource actually benefit from this arrangement? The latter point is the DNS criticism that it is "environmental imperialism". That is, it locks the country into the capitalist financial system in which the benefits primarily accrue to the creditors and only indirectly to the borrower country.

Unfortunately, these problems and systemic flaws occur for all poor high political risk countries selling sovereign debt, such as those in SSA where high yields are on offer for purchasers. In such cases, funds raised through debt were either stolen or spent for higher salaries and other current items. That leakage led to more debt, more crises, and greater potential need for more IMF bail-outs or other donor loans. In short, to restate the above point, DNSs become a tool of the environmental imperialism structural dynamic whereby debt relief generates more oppressive debt.

Discussion Case #28: Managing Forest Carbon Emissions for Development via Nature-Based Offsets in Indonesia

Context

The loamy soils and dense jungle of the Sumatran rainforest in Indonesia can store an average of 282/tons of CO_2/hectare. If a couple of climate conscious airline passengers were to find a hectare of such forest at risk of being cut down for palm oil and were able to stop that from happening, they would offset the amount of greenhouse gases emitted by 175 passengers flying economy class from NY—London and back.

Companies that have nothing to do directly with rainforests, such as airlines and power-generation firms, buy carbon credits from forest-rich countries that allow such firms to "offset" their emissions by doing good elsewhere. A popular option is to pay for others to avert deforestation.[14] Demand for such carbon offsets is forecast to rocket over the next two decades as businesses attempt to make good on their promises to reach net zero carbon emissions. Most offsets promise to subsidize renewables or pay for carbon sinks such as forests to be restored or preserved. For example, Brazil makes money by selling carbon credits based on its Amazon rainforest.[15] Other nature-based offsets have included protecting wetlands in Colombia or even restoring peatland in Scotland.

But the market is not working. The price of a carbon offset is far too low. The opportunity cost of leaving land uncultivated is rising. A hectare of Sumatran rainforest, for instance, could produce around 2.5 tons of palm oil/year, and palm oil prices have risen to $1520/ton from around $1k a year ago. But the price of nature-based offsets has fallen this year to around $10/ton of CO_2 according to contracts traded on the Chicago Mercantile Exchange. Under these conditions, set by world market prices for palm oil and traded carbon offsets, it is economically rational to deforest. While palm oil still captures around 170 tons/hectare, leaving the land uncultivated only offsets 112 tons/hectare.

Why has the market for offsets fallen? Some cap-and-trade schemes in which companies must buy permits for their emissions allow for a certain amount of emissions to be offset. By and large, however, offsets are not required by regulation. Firms and individuals that seek to reduce their carbon footprints choose to buy them, meaning that the demand for offsets is largely driven by ethical or public relations imperatives. As the war in Ukraine began and attention turned away from climate change, offset prices declined.

The incentive-based regulatory approach was created as a tax alternative to the regulatory approach for reducing greenhouse gas emissions. Regulations limiting timber removal are circumvented regularly by such means as forged concessions and cutting permits, phony title deeds, landgrabbers with chainsaws, high salaries for poor unemployed rural laborers, lack of institutional and political will, and, as indicated, the low opportunity costs of deforestation. The Kyoto conference established the clean development mechanism (CDM) to reduce emissions by creating certified credits for each ton of CO_2 avoided. The emissions trading system (ETS) was added as an annex to the CDM and allowed the purchase and sale of credits for emitters, thus creating a global market—selling credits to reduce pollution or pollute and buying spare permits from more efficient firms and investing in mitigation technologies. But as noted, the carbon price has been too low to encourage investment and reduce emissions from Q2 to Q1 in *Figure 7.3*. There are too many emission permits on the market (5× more than demand!). Hence the current (2023) $10/ton price....

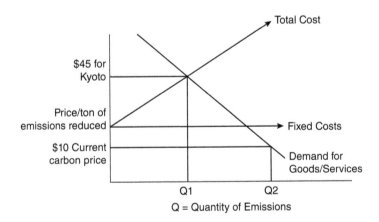

Figure 7.3 Economics of the Emissions Trading System (ETS).

Source: Created by the author.

Calculating the Scope of the Problem

Suppose as the Indonesian environmental minister you had to decide whether to continue subsidizing renewables via the voluntary carbon market using "offsets" or tradable units that prevent destruction of the carbon sink (i.e., tropical forests) and further air pollution? The idea is that efficient farmers or ones with valuable asset such as tropical hardwood forests on their land could offset or sell credits on the market and make a profit on reducing pollution by preserving his piece of forest if the market price was high enough. What should she do and why?

The minister has the following facts: the Sumatran rainforest can store 282 tons of CO_2/hectare. As noted, the current price of a nature-based offset is $10/hectare on the Chicago Mercantile Exchange. The carbon tax and ETS currently price carbon at $10/hectare even though $40/ton is the minimum social cost of carbon—a measure of the damage done to global welfare by increasing emissions. She knows also that the Sumatran Island tropical forest is also the home for famous Indonesian songbirds that are fast becoming extinct elsewhere. On the other hand, a hectare of rainforest could produce around 2.5 tons of palm oil/year. Palm oil sells for $1520/ton. A palm oil plantation captures about 170 tons of CO_2/hectare. But leaving the land uncultivated offsets only 112 tons.

Questions

She needs to answer these five questions: (1) how much income could a farmer of uncultivated land make from selling offsets? (2) How much income would a farmer lose from selling offsets instead of growing palm oil on that same land? That is, what is the opportunity cost for a farmer claiming offsets on his land vs. growing palm oil? (3) Would it be economically rational to preserve the forest at these prices? (4) What offset price is needed to make forest preservation more rational than cattle ranching? Why? (5) What other legal, tax, fiscal, and regulatory options exist for reducing deforestation and encouraging forestry development in Indonesia?[16]

Here are the answers: explain how you arrived at them.[17]

Notes

1 In the last 20 years of Belgian rule over Zaire, they tried and failed to develop modern agriculture with larger farms and machineries, such as tractors. But Naipaul claimed (1981: pp.199–200) that "an organized bush was an illogicality". The way of the bush was to burn, cultivate, and abandon.

This is the shifting cultivation pattern which still exists and can be a problem in many poor countries with forest resources. The Belgians were "too theoretical and removed from the peasants whom they considered 'ignorant' and 'irrational'". In the 19th century, the Belgians and Ottomans (that practiced slavery at the time) ruled in the eastern Congo. Colonialists also thought flogging was an effective means of improving industrial agriculture!

2　*Economist (2016)* "Unholy Woes: India's Water Shortages Owes More to Bad Management than Drought". 5-14, pp.29–30.

3　© The Economist Group Limited, London (5-14-2016). From "Unholy Woes: India's Water Shortage Owes More to Bad Management Than Drought", pp.29–30. Reprinted with permission.

4　From the *Economist* (2016) 5-14, pp.29–30, "Unholy Woes: India's Water Shortages Owes More to Bad Management than Drought".

5　British colonies, such as Borneo, Barbados, and Malay (Federated Malay States or FMS), were called "Crown Colonies".

6　For effective land tenure reform in Africa, policies must avoid deconstruction of Black land ownership as evidenced by the US South during Civil War Reconstruction programs and during the New Deal experiments in rural land reform that actually weakened Black ownership thru partition sales of their existing tenancies in common. By weakening secure land tenure, the programs undermined Black political independence by keeping them out of the credit markets for mortgages and bank accounts. They weakened the very targets of the rural agrarian reform. Lester M Salamon (1979) "The Time Dimension in Policy Evaluation: The Case of the New Deal Land Reform Experiments", *Public Policy*, Volume 27, Number 2, pp.159–183.

7　© The Economist Group Limited, London (9-12-2020). From "Property Rights: Parcels, Plots and Power", pp.37–39.

8　*Economist* (2024) "Urban Development, Dirty Old Towns", 8-19, 30-31.

9　© The Economist Group Limited, London (1-30-2021). From "Wind Power Boom Sets Off Scramble for Balsa in Ecuador", pp.25–27. Reprinted with permission.

10　*Economist* (2023) "The Rule of Saw", 3-4, pp.52–54.

11　Chamon, Marcos et al. (2022) *Debt-for-Climate Swaps Analysis: Design and Implementation* (Washington, DC: IMF Working Paper), August.

12　Analisa Bala et al. (2022) "Meeting the Future" *Finance and Development* Volume 3, Number 22, pp.38–40.

13　Vicki Golich and Terry Young (1993) "Debt-for Nature Swaps. Win-Win Solution or Environmental Imperialism in Bolivia?" Washington DC. Pew/GU IDS case #454.

14　*Economist* (2023) "Rule of Saw", *op.cit.*, p.54.

15　World Bank estimates that the value of the Brazilian rainforest merely as a carbon store or sink is $317b/year. Most of the benefits accrue to the rest of the world. That is three to seven times more than the estimated value which could be made from farming, mining, or logging in the area. *Economist* (2023) "Brazil's Green Agenda, Unsustainable" 6-17, p.21. As in Indonesia, the core constraints to preserving sufficient value for all parties are controlling, logging, and maintaining a high enough carbon price to lower the opportunity cost of keeping rainforests intact.

16　From: *Economist* (2022) "Climate Finance: Carbon Sinks" 5-21, pp.70–71.

17 *Nature-Based Offsets (Indonesian Case #20 answers):*

1 Revenue from uncultivated land: 112 tons × $10/hectare offset price + $1120. Offset revenue.

2 Opportunity cost for not cultivating palm oil: $1520 palm oil (P.O.) price/ton × 2.5 tones/hectare for palm oil = $3800 market price.

3 No, it would not be rational.

4 An offset price of at least $20 is needed to incentivize forest preservation and discourage cattle ranching: palm oil (PO) captures about 170 tons of CO_2/hectare × $20 = $3400 which is roughly equivalent to the $3800 market price for P.O.

5 Options are tax credits for agroforestry, sustained-yield tropical forestry management, regulatory enforcement, and payments under REDD for forest carbon removal or sequestration.

8 Summary and Conclusions

This book attempted to focus on management of international development. To do this, I used eclectic sources from a wide variety of rich and poor countries and from multiple regions and cultures. The sectors were selected partially from my familiarity with them and from the ready availability of good sources. Sectors are like industries and have their own norms, systems, and objectives. The health sector, public or private, is not the K–12 sector, nor the urban transport sector. Still, general techniques for personnel management of teams and individuals are similar—people are employed by development organizations and must be managed! For example, budgeting techniques are similar—break-even analysis, flexible budgeting, and enterprise cost accounting methods can be useful and easily applied to all three sectors and others such as energy, election administration, and environmental management.

I wrote it largely because I was unable to find one book that combined the theories and practices of international development and management. I always admired the short book *Development Projects Observed* by Albert O. Hirschman (Brookings, 1965)[1] while in graduate school and thought that it should be a model for a larger text that focused on management in varied cultures and institutional systems. Such a book should provide tips on basic reading lists by development issues and deal with the practicalities of overcoming obstacles to success. It would be a book for graduate-level students with international interests and some overseas experience. I hoped it would be something like this one....

Very often graduate students have built-in overseas experiences being "from over there" or from US experiences such as teaching in blighted urban areas what have been called variously poor pupils from the underclass. Often students have done some of this but claim they have no international experience. Or they may have worked as a restaurant waitress or hotel clerk in a rural area of the US and still claim they have no field experience. In fact, they do as the cultural puzzles, ambiguities, institutional desiccation, and absence of sufficient resources or any institutional support

DOI: 10.4324/9781032670959-8

put them in the difficult place of outstation employees teaching, working, and relating to entirely different contexts from what they were used to. Several students from the International Management course I taught at GMU for the past ten years have entered international work for NGOs, State Department, USAID, Peace Corps, UN agencies, such as UNDP or UNHCR, from their experiences in the US education sector. K–12 education everywhere faces many of the same constraints, and its study provides transferable management and policy lessons across countries and cultures. I hope that is clear from *Chapter 7*.

We conclude with a review of five important constraints on effective international development management and how to deal with them.

Cross-Cultural Management

International managers need to act and set goals for their teams, motivate them with incentives or penalties, and monitor and evaluate their work. To act and make such decisions, they need to fit into the culture. The culture may demand that they often do not act! From picking up cues before arrival and learning more nuances when in-country, they will quickly learn what to do and not to do in particular social contexts. Often, the pace is much slower in transitional and developing contexts, and the manager must avoid pushing people at their homeland pace. Managers are often surprised that word travels fast on their style and degree of empathy. The wrong pace can lead to distrust which can destroy needed political capital for future initiatives with the team and institutions involved in a development project.

This was the dilemma for project team leader Moses in *Mission in the Oriente* and the Resident in *Outstation in Mongolia* (*Cases #1 and #2*, respectively). Warburton in Mongolia had to deal with a conflict between him and his assistant Cooper, initially driven by class status and later by the assistant's treatment of the local servant "boys". These carried over into violent interpersonal confrontations. The trigger was the cruel and tyrannical mismanagement of prisoner work teams by the assistant and the inability of the Resident to de-escalate conflict. It is also useful to recognize that locals often behave differently toward each other than when being supervised or talked to by outsiders. Political culture was once defined as how people behave when no one is watching.... It is worth bearing in mind as one works out exactly what is going on! In any case, the characters in the Mongolia outstation were typical of personnel in isolation for long periods of time getting on each other's nerves, a very modern and common situation in military and civilian settings.

Koehn and Rosenau (2010:8–9), as noted, provide a useful "transnational competence" framework for international development managers (IDMs) who are planning to go abroad or to use as a reminder of what needs to be done for competence in the field. The five essential competence areas are analytic, emotional, creative/imaginative, communicative, and functional. Analytic means ability to understand paradoxes of cultural counterparts (clearly missing from Cooper!). Emotional means motivation and ability to open oneself up continuously to divergent cultural influences and experiences. This is harder to do in some places than others! Creative/imaginative means the ability to foresee the synergistic potential of diverse group perspectives for collective problem-solving. Communicative means proficiency in understanding and using appropriate nonverbal cues and codes. Functional means building and maintaining positive interpersonal relations.[2]

Corruption

The issues with this constraint are gauging the degree and frequency of corrupt transactions and deciding what to do about them, i.e., the degree of abuse of power for private purposes. As someone noted about Haiti, if corruption explains everything, it explains nothing. Doing nothing about clear instances of bribery, theft, and misuse of funds may actually be the best course in certain contexts to keep tensions down. The infraction may be unimportant, and it is often best to treat it as such. Some country systems, such as public sector contracting approvals, invite corruption by their requirements of endless process steps which fail to control anything substantial and are merely access points for bribery and kickbacks. Often the approvals are manual and not even parts of a GFMIS which obscures what has really happened. Such crude and archaic systems delay state transactions for licenses and permits as well as further diminishing the efficacy of development aid. Approvals are a way of ensuring formal accountability in Civil Law systems where permission must be granted to act. Common Law legal accountability frameworks focus on post audits and punishments after the fact, i.e., asking for forgiveness rather than permission. That is, to prevent clogging up bureaucratic processes in lengthy time-wasting approvals, they incentivize forgiveness rather than permission. In poor countries, the legal distinction may be without a real difference in practice.

Computerized financial management and treasury systems have beefed up internal accounting controls and eliminated many of the standard methods for funds diversion and budgetary leakage, especially in procurement and contracting. But if expense transactions are not actually entered in journals, they can often avoid passing through general ledger systems altogether! Internal audit units are often hamstrung by Civil Law legal systems that focus on formal rather than actual practices that divert funds and weaken program performance. Political cultures have been defined as like-minded communities of values that influence what rules are made and how strictly they are enforced. The Nigerian Road project in *Mr. Johnson* was implemented in the context of multiple cultures and parallel institutions that all worked against accountability but intended to get the job done despite formal British accounting, reporting, and auditing practices. International managers must deal with the fact that often Western norms against corruption violate local norms of empathy or "mirroring" others in contexts where that is often accepted local practice. Locals often try to deal with rigidly codified laws and tight regulations by shortcuts and workarounds that follow the well-known practice of obeying but not complying, known as *jeitinho* in Brazil.

"Corruption" largely explains why development projects often fail to lead to accumulated development in poor countries. Corruption is often a synonym for "lawlessness" where too many irrelevant and unenforceable laws are on the books. The Haitian secretary of state in Graham Greene's *Comedians* noted that there is always money for "projectors" as long as the projects are not actually begun (108). That refers to the many ghost hospitals, schools, employees, and roads that one finds in poor countries.[3] So, it is best to steal the donor's money before project completion. But if completed, then projects are often not maintained or staffed adequately and simply allowed to rot in the jungle and deteriorate. Other projects may be only half completed where budgeted funds run out or someone didn't receive their cut. But such problems are more visible and easily detectable, meaning potential legal and criminal liabilities. The paradox of development is that project money is often available to poor countries but clogged in process and not spent by sectoral ministries, misspent, or stolen due to lack of fiscal accountability in cultures that excuse or accept the "mirroring" behavior just noted. "Lawlessness" may consist in bribes to speed things along to get the contracted work finished. In poor countries, the levels of corrupt transactions often have to be "managed" properly to pay off the few insider participants at expense of the many poor intended project beneficiaries. Another way of viewing the problem is to distinguish the *opaque* corruption (ways of local life) that exists in poor contexts, such as bribes and inspection points to obtain licenses and permits vs. more *transparent* corruption in rich countries caused by redundant bureaucratic processes, such as fees and documents approvals that keep people employed and waste the public's time. The latter has been largely replaced by online processes and computerized signatures. Some call that "efficient corruption"!

Institutions and Norms

Fred Riggs (1964)[4] once described the "prismatic" local institutions that performed multiple functions normally not associated with that institution. Aid workers in poor countries confronted formal institutions from their organizational charts and remits. But they saw its administrative systems through prisms which diffracted light into separate beams producing surprising results for accountability and control. What the organizations actually did (or did not do) was a real puzzle! In poor and uncertain contexts, Western accountability and control norms and standard systems such as recruitment, procurement, and budgeting were "diffracted" and put to different and puzzling uses. In such contexts, aid managers need to be aware of the many cases where metrics are turned into targets. That violates Goodhart's Law which states that metrics turned into targets distort purposes and lead to both perverse incentives such as goal displacement where process becomes more important than results. Goal displacement becomes the operating norm! Performance targets create problems when evaluators and internal audit institutions waste management time by constant interruptions of real work simply to meet their own targets, such as attainment of maximum numbers of inspections. In the worst cases, intrusive inspections are driven by the constant quest for bribes—solicited to stop them from conducing more intrusive inspections!

Weak Incentives for Smarter Development Management

It is critical for the future success of aid that incentives be changed and strengthened both for the donor and host country. Host country recipients need more buy-in to ensure successful results. That means they need to administer country aid allocations and be responsible and accountable for program and project results. Currently, the US-aid system is top-down with allocations, monitoring, and evaluations arranged by the donor at headquarters. Aid firms are fixated with performance accountability to Congress that is largely clueless about both metrics and their actual meaning. Decentralization and devolutions of responsibilities can improve management performance, strengthen host country government personnel, and enhance civil services. To achieve these results, management discretion and accountability should be devolved to host countries along with accountability for aid results. Managers can be held accountable for attainment of donor norms and objectives (normative centralization) and for field results given their added discretion and responsibility (operational decentralization).

There are at least three precedents for such changes:

First, many multilateral and several bilateral donors decentralize their aid allocations to country ministries of finance where they are distributed to sectoral ministries to spend. This allows the aid to be apportioned to areas of real need rather than donor priorities. Roughly 96% of USAID (DA) is centrally allocated. By contrast, the UK devolves 53% of its aid to country PFM systems (World Bank 36% and Norway 56%). The US utilizes host country procurement systems for only 15% of its aid vs. 51% for the UK and 56% for Norway. There is evidence that more devolved aid increases country stakes and improves returns from projects and programs.[5]

Second, the New Public Administration (NPM) literature of the 1980s urged use of management incentives to set objectives and report on performance accurately. Such incentives focused on decentralized discretion, authority, and accountability to line managers. The new approach to administration was based on distaste for rigid hierarchies and devolution of decision-making. Organizations would be less hierarchical and more responsive to public needs. Organizations from state railways, militaries, and aid agencies to hospitals and schools have applied this approach with positive results. Devolution of fiscal, budget, tax, and personnel authority to line managers increased discretion and improved results. It also reduced corruption, reducing it from a system or culture of self-inflicted pain to an ailment that could be treated by beefing up institutions such as internal audit units and independent anti-corruption agencies and units. Transparency and responsiveness were increased with the help of automated FMIS systems that made tracking transactions and payments much easier. Most importantly for IDM, aid would be run through country accounting and reporting systems. Currently, most foreign and domestic financing systems are separated and disconnected from country accounting and treasury systems. That leads to perpetuation of PFM institutional weaknesses. Aid management units (AMUs) within ministries (typically for larger grant and loan-financed aid projects), for instance, try to satisfy individual donor reporting requirements and are unable to record third-party payment transactions from donor accounts as part of local fiscal accounts. At present AMUs do not, which weakens fiscal accountability and makes budgets and finances harder to manage.[6]

DA from USAID is one of the more centralized aid systems in the world. Devolution of aid fiscal and program management to country systems would also be consistent with ongoing country policies to devolve their own finances to local governments. Fiscal decentralization programs around the world have devolved budget and tax authority to local governments resulting in more decentralized governance. The only rich country exception is Britain where only 6% of tax revenue is collected by local governments. The rest is collected and allocated by Whitehall. For centuries, that problem has diminished overall productivity and prevented management from exercising real authority and accountability for performance of essential local services.

Third, aid agencies from USAID and DFID to World Bank decentralized financial administration and operational authority to regions and countries with positive results, such as increased host country stakes in design and implementation of aid programs and projects. The critical factor of positive results was increased internal and external audit capacity to oversee implementation and to guard against the many forms of corruption that impede aid program progress. The USAID risk assessment framework (RAF) exercise performed analyses of country fiscal capacity to undertake aid program responsibilities in more than 50 countries. The results from application of this reporting framework and corresponding analysis have been improved country program performance and greater stakes in results by host countries (Guess and Husted, 2011).

Decentralization of aid programmatic and financial management discretion and authority has taken place in DA as well as humanitarian aid. USAID, UN agencies, and international NGOs have all done this. Thus, their aid is smarter and more effective. After the earthquakes in Turkey, Syria, and on the front lines and remoter parts of Ukraine, local volunteer networks stayed and delivered life-saving help, whereas many international agencies withdrew or never ventured in. Including local networks and organizations as all or part of the delivery apparatus has never been a part of the standard operating model of humanitarian aid. In most cases, international NGOs and donors have sidelined local organizations rather than reinforced them. In some cases, international humanitarian NGOs or donors contract them in to DA projects that do not adequately cover their overheads or simply poach their staff. In the past decade, humanitarian crisis aid has been provided in the form of more cash directly to the victims. To deliver smarter as well as more effective aid, donors and NGOs should now focus more on localized aid through local groups and networks to get the job done. The Carter Center, for example, has been effectively engaging with local leaders and networks in Sudan and other highly unstable countries. Their volunteer networks have served as first responders and service providers to distribute humanitarian aid and evacuate victims of natural and man-made disasters. Since 2020, the Center has supported a Youth Citizen Observer Network to promote civilian voices in monitoring ceasefires and apportioning aid to local populations.[7]

It should not be forgotten, however, that effective local networks and organizations may be hard to find and that if given grants directly to perform emergency assistance will likely have to pay their host governments a "rent" or share of the donor funds. The reality is that even local networks and organizations work at the pleasure of host governments and provide them with licenses and certificates to operate. But count that as a cost of doing needed [8]business....

A different approach to induce smarter IDM is to strengthen the cohesion of aid project teams through training and solidarity rituals. The theory is that stronger team chemistry and solidarity can improve productivity, as cohesion and solidarity can improve baseball team performance. As we learned from the efforts and failures of Moses, Cooper, Warburton, and Rudbeck, the problem is how to create the solidarity in the first place. Organizations use a variety of team-building methods. For example, retreats are used to get away from the organizational environment to learn about each member through shared stories that are intended to build trust between members and with the team leader. Their rationale is that by dis-connecting employees from their daily routine, organizations, public or private, can build camaraderie and foster creativity. Additionally, in an era of remote work, without the thousands of micro-interactions that happen in the office, team-building has gained an important structural role in good management.

I've participated in several, and they do build team solidarity in the short term. For IDMs, "failure fairs" are organized regularly at the World Bank or sometimes online by ICT4 *to reveal management failures on aid projects in the field. Individual or team "sinners"* share stories of screw ups that are intended to induce honest vulnerability before peers. Peers respond in turn by sharing their stories in a confessional atmosphere where one dares to be humiliated and show weaknesses before peers. The lesson is "we all do these things" and need to admit and atone for them in a safe environment. The confessionals are followed by uplifting shows of group forgiveness, inclusive clapping of hands, and "aren't we all laughter". Rituals such as these are intended to build a sense of community. The atmosphere is occasionally that of a tent revival where sinners confess publicly, atone, and repent, and are saved by the group.

One might question the efficacy of team-building rituals such as these. Failure fairs often cover familiar, small bore, and almost safe problems such as design and implementation of IT systems. Participants swoon over personal stories (confessions) that project designers for a multi-million-dollar project forgot that electricity is often intermittent in the African bush! Rarely do confessions reveal a bad manager or bully in action. The confession and forgiveness of such oversights is hardly a life-changing experience. Few confessionals reveal tense interpersonal relations and what to do about them. The experience of dealing with a difficult counterpart or team member is typically not covered. But the food, open bar, and posh setting are worth it!

Capacity-Building for IDM

Finally, development management is constrained by a lack of experienced training personnel and practical materials. As noted in the introduction, rich country in-service and pre-service education of IDMs in the US is primarily the remit of university graduate programs in multiple areas such as MPAs, MPPs, Master of International Affairs, Non-Profit Management, and International Development. Professional certificates are also offered in each of these areas for completion of a selected sequence of courses and work experiences. Training, which differs from education in its practical focus on systems and skills for particular jobs, such as PFM, is largely left to the public sector institutions themselves. Government ministries and departments also offer their own certificate programs for their staff, in such areas as financial and personnel management.

Levels of government in both federations and unitary states typically have their own training and education centers, such as the Federal Executive Institute (FEI) and the now-defunct French national school of administration (ENA). Local governments often have their own training institutions for particular technical specialties, such as International City Management Association (ICMA) and Government Finance Officers Association of the US and Canada (GFOA). Many public sector training institutes are attached to universities, such as the International Management Development Institute (IMDI) at University of Pittsburgh,[9] the Maxwell School at Syracuse University, and the Carl Vinson Institute of Government at University of Georgia. These institutes provide training modules and materials for both international managers and state and local government officials. Cases and materials are often first rate and may also be used in formal graduate courses such as in MPAs and MPPs.

Poorer countries are typically the beneficiaries of Western ODA Paris Club training programs. (Paris Club aid means no loan collateral is required of borrowers, in contrast with Chinese loans that require such asset collateral.) ODA training aid targets both the weak institutions and their often poorly trained staff. Such countries, mainly in Africa and Latin America, have few training institutions of their own, reflecting the diminished status of public sectors as providers of minimal and bad services such as health care or urban transport to the citizens of their countries. Civil servants are viewed as insular sinecures hidden inside vast closed bureaucracies from the complaints of citizens outside. Governments are generally viewed as closed systems, unresponsive to citizen needs in poor countries, unless one has contacts or relatives inside these "castles". The average public perception of government services and officials is that they are corrupt and often exchange basic services for financial and nonfinancial bribes. Citizens view all this as double taxation and definitely not fair value for money.

These dysfunctions may be viewed as both causes and consequences of insufficient in-country supplies of training courses, tools, and modules. In cases of technical specialties such as accounting and finance, reliance is on university degree programs consistent with state licensing requirements to distinguish levels of experience. As noted in **Discussion Case #16,** the Japanese aid agency (JICA) provides technical assistance to specific sectors, such as the urban transport sector. In Vietnam, the JICA-led consortium assisted the construction of its metro line in Ho Chi Minh City (HCM) by twinning its expertise from the Tokyo Metro with HCM city transit officials very effectively for design, construction, signaling systems, maintenance facilities, and control systems. The technical assistance amounted to on-the-job training that remained with HCM officials after the JICA project ended, which was precisely how capacity-building should work.

For more advanced and prestigious fiscal and tax administration training, poor country officials know that the IMF Institute and World Bank Institute (formerly Economic Development Institute) are the places to be selected for both training and fast tracks to further their careers. Other practitioner funding for training courses includes the Open Society Institute's (OSI's) Local Government and Public Service Reform Institute (LGI) formerly in Budapest. LGI often provided onsite modules for visiting officials as well as materials and books for in-country training.[10]

USAID has been providing training courses and materials for many decades. An example is USAID's extensive provision of training materials, courses, modules, and institution-building assistance to Bulgaria. There, aid teams composed of contractors from US public sector associations such as ICMA and GFOA provided courses and materials in generic subjects such as financing of capital programs and treasury management as well as generic management of personnel and municipal services such as water, sewer, heat, and electricity. USAID also funded a grant program to city officials for production of action-forcing cases and technical exercise development based on local issues with which they were familiar, such as housing, sanitation, public transit, and road maintenance. The officials received nonfinancial incentives and awards such as extra vacation days and other benefits for producing the best materials. Thus, demand for training was created as well as the supply of modules and materials.

It is important that IDM capacity-building employs methods of experiential learning to engage locals in shared transfer of methods, systems, and skills between them and instructors. Often training is mechanical, rote, and focused on box-checking skills. The goal should be to build transnational competence (TC) for both instructors and trainees/students.

The Future of IDM

What is the future of international development management? For several decades the country shares of ODA have been declining relative to the shares of trade and investment. This is as it should be. Investors should be attracted by increased financial, economic, and political stability, and trade should increase between regional neighbors as well as with countries in other regions. Trade and investment leads to economic growth with development as an important byproduct. But not every poor country can claim that they are essential targets for FDI and trade to stimulate their political economies. Not every country grows in a linear path consistent with W.W. Rostow's five-stage "takeoff theory" of development (1960) onward and upward and stays there. Poor and developing countries may suffer multiple crises and not have the policy and management capacities or luck to be able to respond to them. They may reverse course and head downward toward unexpected places and unexpected landings. And whether developing or "transitional", ODA won't directly lead these countries to growth. Trade and investment are needed to stimulate sustained growth. ODA sustains them when poverty, fiscal mismanagement, external shocks, and wars put their macro- and micro-economic stability at risk. ODA is then an indirect stabilizer, a temporary expedient until local institutional capacities and human capital are strong enough to sustain the political economy.

Development, in terms of increasing country income and employment opportunities, will always be a needed objective. Whether Chinese BRI or World Bank sectoral aid programs achieve this is less important than how efficient and effective those programs are and whether they are more responsive to country needs than simply donor objectives. Whatever the development topics, they need to focus on strengthening states to deliver needed service to their residents for the long term.

Managers with poor country instability experience and in multiple types of political cultures will be in great demand by commercial and public sector organizations working in overseas contexts. Nuances in political cultures can often be revealed in market preferences that are a product of histories and geography. Denton (2019) noted this for the seven different markets and associated political institutions and behavioral patterns for Central America. That is, IDMs working in particular countries could do worse than read regional and country marketing books for cultural insights into what to expect from their new political environments. Moreover, countries grow and develop, but many have often backtracked into wars, pandemics, external shocks from commodity export reliance and face renewed poverty and weakened public services. The Russian war in Ukraine will require major reconstruction efforts and financing contributions.[11] Social assistance development and financing programs and projects need to be designed, financed, and managed to restore facilities and services as they did during the FSU/CEE "transition" in early 1990s.[12]

Development assistance loans and grants from ADB, DFID, EU, USAID, and World Bank financed these programs and projects then and armed with that lengthy and invaluable experiences could easily do so again. Much of the needed current funding will be targeted to rebuilding social service facilities such as rehabilitation centers and nursing homes and to recruiting, training, and paying more staff. Resolving that conflict and reconstructing infrastructure and services will be a major task requiring experienced people, many of whom have been or will be development managers. Effective conflict management skills are needed at the international, national, local, and team levels. Responding effectively to major crises, such as in health care, energy, and environmental resilience and restoration, breakdowns in educational institutions and fixing dilapidated urban transport require technical and management skills. Ukraine will obviously be a large source of reconstruction aid work. Since such problems occur with regularity around the world, they will require experienced development managers who have worked in donor aid programs, private firms, and NGOs. Programs and institutions will always have to recruit and motivate staff from in-country and abroad toward achievement of precise objectives and evaluate their performance.

Such people may just as well have MBAs as well as MPAs and speak several languages and have experience in both commercial and public sector organizations, nationally and internationally. They may have experience from work and/or universities in managing budgets in finance departments, ensuring operational efficiencies, and monitoring systems to make certain transit, education, and health services are delivered effectively. Thus, such "developmental" experience will always be in demand whether financed by aid organizations, international trade partners, or investing commercial firms.

In short, demand for public sector and state enterprise managers at all levels will be growing fast, especially in the soft sectors such as health, education, social assistance, international aid, rural and urban economic development, transport, disaster responses, and election management. Staffing needs will be greatest at state, local, and international levels. After many years of flat employment and hollowing out in the wake of leaders who denigrated government service and public sector management, the need for professionally designed and delivered public services, programs, and projects has never been greater.

Specifically, public budgeting, costing, auditing, accounting, capital financing, debt management, public infrastructure investment analysis, and project implementation skills will be more critical than ever. In addition to World Bank and regional development banks such as Inter-American Development Bank (IDB) and Asian Development Bank (ADB) in Manila, check for openings with USAID, nonprofit organizations (501c3) such as World Vision, private international firms, such as Development Alternative Inc (DAI) (in Bethesda, MD), Abt Associates (Bethesda and Cambridge, MA),

Chemonics International (in D.C.), Nathan Associates (in Arlington), and the newly created International Development Finance Corporation (www. dfc.gov) formed in 2019 by merger of OPIC and USAID's Development Credit Authority. For specific interests, such as public financial management, you should network with professionals in that area. For PFM, attend the monthly luncheon meetings in DC sponsored by the International Consortium on Government Financial Management (ICGFM).

Notes

1 Albert O. Hirschman (1965) *Development Projects Observed* (Washington, DC: Brookings Institute).
2 Koehn and Rosenau (2010), *op.cit.*, pp.8–9. As I prepared to spend two years in Costa Rica writing my doctoral thesis years ago, my thesis advisor told me that many of my predecessors had married or become permanent partners of locals and stayed in their respective topic countries, while others had gone local and never finished their theses! They had met most of the thesis criteria and were likely happy and had new lives but never finished their intended work and that of their funders and sponsors!
3 The term "bloated" states and civil services usually refer to formal positions and not actual payroll outlays. The states are bloated with workers who are not actually there doing any work. That is, monthly payroll wage bill can be much larger than organizational chart positions because of "ghost" workers or paid no-shows. This is why the formal establishment roster must be periodically reconciled by management with the payroll to maintain control of the civil service and wage bill. IFMSs facilitate this by ensuring that treasury outlays for wages are for actual working employees.
4 Fred A. Riggs (1964) *Administration in Developing Countries: The Theory of Prismatic Society* (Boston, MA: Houghton-Mifflin).
5 Guess (2019), *op.cit.*, pp.118–119.
6 William Allan A. (2013) "Managing Foreign Aid Through Country Systems" in Richard Allan, Richard Hemming, and Barry Potter (eds) *The International Handbook of Public Financial Management* (New York: Palgrave Macmillan), pp.546–548.
7 Paige Alexander (2023) "Sudan's Peace Process" *Economist* 6-14, p.14 (letter).
8 Howard Mollett (2023) "Promoting Local Aid" *Economist* (letter), p.15.
9 IMDI was established at Pitt in the 1970s as unit of GSPIA. It was unique in IDM capacity-building as it provided training in African countries through local universities, NGOs, and sponsored academic exchanges and degree programs with GSPIA financed mostly by USAID. Director David Gould perished in Pan Am F103 flying back with a group of Pitt students who had been interning at local institutions for the year.
10 See, for example, George M. Guess (2006) *Training of Trainers for Local Government Financial Management* (Budapest: Local Government Institute of the Open Society Institute), 53pp.
11 Lawrence Summers, Philip Zelikow, and Robert Zoellick (2023) "There's Justice in Giving Ukraine $300b in Russian Assets", *The Washington Post*, 3-22, p.A24.
12 The author provided technical assistance to the city administrations in two Kyrgyzstani oblasts, Osh and Jalal-Abad, to plan and budget for rehabilitation

or maintenance of several social assistance rehabilitation and nursing homes, clinics, hospitals, and even several schools in Kyrgyzstan in the late 1990s. The competitively-bid Asian Development Bank (ADB) financed project was a hybrid loan and grant to the government for two years. The project contract was won by a consortium led by Development Alternatives, Inc. (DAI) in Bethesda, MD with sub-contractor Abt Associates also of Bethesda. The first year of the project concentrated on strengthening the planning and budgeting system for multiple social services. It was followed in the second year by a loan to finance capital needs for reconstruction of the targeted facilities, using the multi-year budgeting system installed by the project.

References

A

Adolino, Jessica and Charles H. Blake (2011) *Comparing Public Policies: Issues and Choices in Industrialized Countries* (Washington, DC: CQ/Sage Press), p. 321.

Albert van Hall (2004) "Case Study: The Inter-Ethnic Project in Gostivar", in Nenad Dimitrijevic and Petra Kovacs (eds) Managing Hatred and Distrust: Prognosis for Post-Conflict Settlement in Multiethnic Communities in Former Yugoslavia (Budapest: Local Government and Public Service Reform Initiative of the Open Society Institute)

Alexander, Paige (2023) "Sudan's Peace Process", *Economist*, 6-14, p. 14 (letter).

Allan, William A. (2013) "Managing Foreign Aid through Country Systems", in Richard Allan, Richard Hemming, and Barry Potter (eds) *The International Handbook of Public Financial Management* (New York: Palgrave Macmillan), pp. 546–548.

Almond, Gabriel and Sidney Verba (1963) *The Civic Culture or The Civic Culture: Political Attitudes and Democracy in Five Nations* (Princeton University Press)

Apocalypse Now (1979) Directed by Francis Ford Coppola, Omni Zoetrope.

Ardó, Zsuzsanna (2000) *Culture Shock Hungary: A Guide to Customs and Etiquette* (London: Kuperard).

B

Bala, Analisa *et al.* (2022) "Meeting the Future", *Finance and Development*, Volume 3, #22, pp. 38–40.

Balingit, Moriah and Gregory Schneider (2023) "Virginia Erred in Estimating School Funds", *The Washington Post*, 2-1, p. B1.

Barzelay, Michael (2001) *The New Public Management: Improving Research and Policy Dialogue* (Berkeley, CA: University of California Press).

Bird, Kai and Martin J. Sherwin (2006) *American Prometheus: The Triumph and Tragedy of J. Robert Oppenheimer.*

Bird, Richard (1992) "Public Finance in Developing Countries", *Public Budgeting and Finance Journal*

Bloomberg Businessweek (2019) "How to Stop a Speeding Train", 10-7.

_____ (2021) "Austerity Backfires in Colombia", 5-17, pp. 38–39.

_____ (2022) "Guyana Petrostate", 11-21, pp. 35–41.

_____ (2023) "Can Nigeria Get Back on Track?", 1-16, p. 16.

Boehm, Christopher (2007) "Political Primates" Greater Good Magazine https://greatergood.berkeley.edu/article/item/political_primates

Boswell, Thomas (2023) "These Nationals Are Fun and Scrappy and They Seem To Be on Their Way Back", *The Washington Post*, 5-12, p. D1.

Braybrooke, David and Charles Lindblom (1970) *A Strategy of Decision* (New York: Free Press).

Brown, Brené (2015) *How the Courage To Be Vulnerable Transforms the Way We Live, Love, Parent and Lead* (New York: Avery).

Bykove, Yury (2014) *Durak (The Fool)* (Locarno: 67th Annual Festival del Locarno).

C

Caiden, Naomi and Aaron Wildavsky (1974) *Planning and Budgeting in Poor Countries* (New York: Wiley).

Cary, Joyce (1939) *Mr. Johnson* (London: Thistle Press).

Ceux Qui Travaillent (2018) *Those Who Work* directed By Antoine Russbach (Locarno: 71st International Film Festival), 8-1-11, p. 130.

Chamon, Marcos *et al.* (2022) *Debt-for-Climate Swaps Analysis: Design and Implementation* (Washington, DC: IMF Working Paper), August.

Chubb, John E. and Terry M. Moe (1990) *Politics, Markets and America's Schools* (Washington, DC: Brookings Institution).

Conrad, Joseph (1950) *Heart of Darkness (1899)* (New York: Signet Classics).

_____ (1964) *Under Western Eyes* (London: Penguin).

_____ (1965) *Nostromo* (New York: Dell Paperbacks), p. 228.

_____ (2019) *Outpost of Progress (1897)* (Mineola, NY: Dover Thrift), p. 13.

Corning, Gregory (2011) *"Managing the Asian Meltdown: IMF and South Korea*, Case #235 (Washington, DC: GUISD Pew Case Study Center).

D

Delderfield, Ronald Frederick (2009) *To Serve Them All My Days* (New York: Sourcebooks Landmark).

Dener, Cem, Johanna Watkins and William Dorotinsky (2011) *Financial Management Information Systems: 25 Years of World Bank Experience on What Works and What Doesn't* (Washington, DC: IBRD).

Denton, Mark (2019) *The Efficiency Trap: Maximizing Business Growth in Central America by Embracing Diversity and Avoiding the Pitfalls of Over-Standardization* (San Jose: San Jose, Costa Rica: Pacifico Press).

De Soto, Hernando (2003) *The Mystery of Capital: Why Capitalism Triumphs in the West and Fails Everywhere Else* (New York: Basic Books).

Dickens, Charles (1967) *Little Dorrit* (New York: Penguin).

Diggins, Simon (2023) "Reforming the Police", *Economist*, 2–4, p. 14 (letter).

Downs, Anthony (1967) *Inside Bureaucracy* (Boston, MA: Little, Brown).

Downs, Charles (1988) "Negotiating Development Assistance: USAID and the Choice between Public and Private Implementation in Haiti" (#117) (Pew Case Study/Institute for Study of Diplomacy, Georgetown University).

Drucker, Peter (1954) *The Practice of Management on MBO* (London: Heinemann).

Dunn, William (2007) *Public Policy Analysis: An Introduction* 4th Edition (Upper saddle river, New Jersey: Pearson).

E

Economist (2015) "A March Around the Institutions" and "Unhappy Anniversary", 1-17, p. 14 and pp. 35–36.

_____ (2016) "Unholy Woes: India's Water Shortages Owes More to Bad Management than Drought", 5–14, pp. 29–30.

_____ (2017a) "Namibia's Economy", 4-22. http://www.economist.com/news/middle-east-and-africa/21720932-such-policies-did-not-work-out-well-zimbabwe-namibias-president-flirting

_____ (2017b) "A Time to Sow", pp. 6–10.

_____ (2018) "Corporate Graft in Europe: Cleaner Living", 7-18, p. 46.

_____ (2020a) "Bartleby, Digital Taylorism", 8-8, p. 54.

_____ (2020b) "Bartleby: Why We Need to Laugh at Work", 10-3, p. 57.

_____ (2020c) "Colombia: Not So Fast", 1-4, p. 23.

_____ (2020d) "Lessons from a Radical Education Experiment in Liberia, the Messy Reality of Trying to Improve Schools in a Poor Country", 1-4, p. 56.

_____ (2020e) "Property Rights: Parcels, Plots and Power", 9-12, pp. 37–39.

_____ (2020f) "©The Economist Group Limited", London (9-12-2020). "Property Rights: Parcels, Plots and Power", pp.37–39.

_____ (2021a) "Ecuador, a Worrying Windfall", 1-30, pp. 25–27.

_____ (2021b) "Whatever It Took?", 4-15, p. 48.

_____ (2021c) "Northern Ireland: Unhappy Anniversary", 4-21, pp. 23–24.

_____ (2021d) "Down to the Wire", 4-3, pp. 17–19.

_____ (2021e) From: "Railway Lines Once Connected the Middle East", pp. 12–18.

_____ (2021f) "One City Two Worlds", 8-14.

_____ (2021g) "Protests in Colombia: Taxing Times", 5-8, pp. 35–36.

_____ (2021h) "No Longer the Top of the Class: Costa Rica is Struggling to Maintain Its Welfare State", 4–15.

_____ (2021i) "Build Back under Budget", 5-29, pp. 23–24.

_____ (2021j) "A Glimpse into Japan's Understated Financial Heft in Southeast Asia", 8-14, pp. 56–57.

_____ (2021k) "Northern Ireland: Unhappy Anniversary", 7-31, pp. 14–16.

_____ (2021l) "© The Economist Group Limited", London (1-30-2021). From "Wind Power Boom Sets Off Scramble for Balsa in Ecuador", pp. 25–27. Reprinted with permission.

_____ (2022a) "The 2 Brazilian Booms that Bookmark the History of the Car", 12-24, p. 11.

_____ (2022b) "Climate Finance: Carbon Sinks", 5-21, pp. 70–71.

_____ (2022c) "Bartleby: Purpose and the Employee", 1-29, p. 52.

_____ (2022) "Special Report, Italy Spreadeagled", 5-27.

_____ (2022) "Briefing "The War in Ukraine: The Cult of War"", 3-26, pp. 17–18.

_____ (2022) "A Bitter Life for All", pp. 39–40.

_____ (2022) "Xi Jinping's Covid Retreat", 12-17, p. 38.

_____ (2022) "Aiding and Abetting, Foreign Aid Has Done Little to Help Haiti", 7-24, pp. 2–5.

_____ (2022) "Making a Success of Failure", 5-8, p. 44.

_____ (2022) "The Paradox of Untapped Riches", 5-7, p. 42.

_____ (2022) "Argentina, Blood on the Dance Floor: IMF Cannot Solve Argentina's Dysfunction", 1-29.

_____ (2023) "Thinking for Themselves", 8-12, p. 47.

_____ (2023) "China and Latin America, Comrades across Continents", 6-17, pp. 22–23.

_____ (2023) "Banyan, Race to the Bottom", 8-22, p. 30.

_____ (2023) "Brazil's Green Agenda, Unsustainable", 6-17, p. 21.

_____ (2023) "Dodging the Resource Curse, Diamond Geyser", 6-10, p. 12.

_____ (2023) "The World Ahead 2023, It's Time to 'Rephrase' How Companies Work", 1-23, p. 120.

_____ (2023) "Bartleby: The Bottleneck Bane", 5-20, p. 60.

_____ (2023) "Why Economics Does Not Understand Business", 4-8, p. 6.

_____ (2023) "How to Prevent World War III, a Conversation with Henry Kissinger", 5-20, p. 17.

_____ (2023) "Genomics, 20 Years Later", 4-15, pp. 68–69.

_____ (2023) "Bartleby, Dominic Raab, Bully or Victim?", 4-29, p. 58.

_____ (2023) "Professional Services: The Too-Big Four", 4-22, p. 54.

_____ (2023) "Accounting, Why EY?", 4-8. p. 57.

_____ (2023) "A Land of Frustrated Workers", 6-10, pp. 27–28.

_____ (2023) "Militarizing Russia, the Home Front", 2-25, pp. 23–26.

_____ (2023) "Russian Art in Wartime: Culture in the Time of Z", 2-18, pp. 75–76.

_____ (2023) "El Chapo: The Sequel", 1-28, p. 28.

_____ (2023) "The Incentives War", 2-25, pp. 29–30.

_____ (2023) "Bartleby, the Bottleneck Bane", 5-20, p. 60.

_____ (2023) "Climate Change, Water Works", 5-27, p. 69.

_____ (2023) "Changing Cash Flows", 2-25, pp. 73–74.

_____ (2023) "Helping the Poor, Cautious Pioneers", 4-22, p. 63.

_____ (2023) "The World's Toughest In-Tray", 2-18, pp. 41–42.

_____ (2023) "A New Source of Sustenance: *World Ahead 2023*", 1-23, pp. 65–66, and "A Suffering Sluggish Giant", p. 67.

_____ (2023) "*World Ahead 2023*: Middle East", 1-23, p. 62.

_____ (2023) "Bartleby: Faulty Reasoning, Why Pointing Fingers Is Unhelpful, and Why Bosses Do It More Than Anyone", 1-21, p. 56.

_____ (2023) "Africa's State Owned Firms, Arresting Development", 1-21, pp. 11–12.

_____ (2023) "Arab Bureaucracies: The Incredible Shrinking State", 3-11, pp. 33–34.

_____ (2023) "The NHS, Dr. No Go", 1-14, pp. 48–50.

_____ (2023) "The Debt-Relief Duet", 5-20, p. 10.

_____ (2023) "Bye-Bye to Bungs", 6-10, p. 41.

_____ (2023) "Egypt, Debt on the Nile", 1-28-23, p. 14.

_____ (2023) "It's Still the Economy Stupid", 6-24, pp. 23–24.

_____ (2023) "War Economics, Funding Conflict", 4-1, p. 59.

_____ (2023) "Green v Green: Blocking Clean-Energy Infrastructure Is No Way to Save the Planet", 2-4, pp. 21–23.

_____ (2023) "Trying to Get Back on Track", 5-27, p. 54.

_____ (2023) "Bartleby: Mega Lowdown", 3-18, p. 57.

_____ (2023) "Between Three Seas", 1-21, p. 49.

_____ (2023) "Off the Rails", 1-21, pp. 44–45.

_____ (2023) "Reviving the G-7", 5-20, pp. 31–32.

_____ (2023) "Banyan: Lessons in Asian Resilience", 6-10, p. 34.

_____ (2023) "Reform School", 3-18, p. 25.

_____ (2023) "Class Half Empty", 3-18, p. 23.

_____ (2023) "Education in a Can", 1-28, pp. 54–55.

_____ (2023) "Putin's Time of Troubles", 7-1, pp. 39–40.

_____ (2023) "The Rule of Saw", 3-4, pp. 52–54.

_____ (2024) "Urban Development, Dirty Old Towns", 8-19, pp. 30–31.

Ellis, James E. (2023) "Bed, Bath and Beyond Hope", *Bloomberg Business Week*, 2-13, p. 9.

F

Farnham, Paul (2010) *Economics for Managers, 2nd edition* (Upper Saddle River, NJ: Prentice-Hall).

Finkler, Steven A. (2001) *Financial Management for Public, Health and Not-for-Profit Organizations, 1st edition* (Upper Saddle River, NJ: Pearson).

_____ (2005) *Financial Management for Public, Health and Not-for-Profit Organizations, 2nd edition* (Upper Saddle River, NJ: Pearson).

_____ (2010) *Financial Management for Public, Health and Nonprofit Organizations, 3rd edition* (Upper Saddle River, NJ: Prentice-Hall).

Fukuyama, Francis (2014) *Political Order and Political Decay* (New York: Farrar, Straus and Giroux).

G

Golich, Vicki and Terry Young (1993) *Debt-for Nature Swaps: Win-Win Solution or Environmental Imperialism in Bolivia?* (Washington, DC: Pew/GU IDS case #454).

Gosselin, Tania (2004) "Info-Klub: Creating a Common Public Sphere for Citizens of Vukovar", in Dimitrijevic Nenad and Kovacs Petra (2004), *op.cit.*, pp. 68–69.

Grosse, Robert E. (2023) *People Are People—A New View of Cross-Cultural People Management* (New York: Routledge).

Grupo Propuesta Ciudadana (2006) *Seminario Internacional: Democracia, Descentralizacion and Reforma Fiscal en America Latina y Europa del Este* (Lima: GPC).

Guerard, Albert (1904) "Introduction" (Joseph Conrad's Nostromo, *1904*).

Guess, George M. (1982) "Institution-Building for Development Forestry in Latin America", *Public Administration and Development*, Volume 2, #4, pp. 309–324.

_____ (1985) "Role Conflict in Capital Project Implementation: The Case of Dade County Metrorail", *Public Administration Review*, Vol. 45, # 5, pp. 576–585.

_____ (1987) *The Politics of United States Foreign Aid* (New York: St. Martin's), p. 1 (Republished by Routledge Development Library Edition, Volume 7, 2011).

_____ (1992) "Centralization of Expenditure Controls in Latin America", *Public Administration Quarterly*, Volume XVI, #3, pp. 376–394.

_____ (2001) "Decentralization and Municipal Budgeting in Four Balkan States", *Journal of Public Budgeting, Accounting and Financial Management*, Volume 13, #3 (Fall), pp. 397–436.

_____ (2005) *The Dogs of Bucharest.* (London: Athena Press).

_____ (2007) *Fast Track: Municipal Fiscal Reform in Central and Eastern Europe and the Former Soviet Union* (Budapest: Local Government and Public Service Reform Initiative of the Open Society Institute), pp. 4–8.

_____ (2007) *Training of Trainers for Local Government Public Financial Management* (Budapest: Local Government Initiative of the Open Society Institute).

_____ (2008) *Managing and Financing Urban Public Transport Systems, an International Perspective* (Budapest: Open Society Institute, Local Government and Public Service Reform Initiative).

_____ (2014) "Close Shaves in Ukraine: The Well-Groomed Autocrat", in *The American Interest*, March 30 (Review of *Stalin's Barber*) New York: Taylor Trade Publishing), p. 378).

_____ (2015) *Government Budgeting, A Practical Guidebook* (Albany, NY: SUNY Press).

_____ (2019) *Building Democracy and International Governance* (New York: Routledge).

_____ (2019) and Dennis DeSantis, in Guess (2019), *op.cit., Appendix A.*

_____ (2020) *Dogs of Catherine Town* (Charleston, South Carolina: Palmetto Publishing).

_____ (2022) "A Hallmark of Tyranny", *Letter to the Editor: The Washington Post*, 9-3, p. A20.

_____ and James Savage (2021) *Comparative Public Budgeting Global Perspectives on Taxing and Spending* (New York: Cambridge University Press)

_____ and Ma, Jun (2015) "The Risks of Chinese Subnational Debt for Public Financial Management", *Public Administration and Development*, Volume 35, pp. 129–139.

_____ and Paul G. Farnham (2011) *Cases in Public Policy Analysis, 3rd edition* (Washington, DC: Georgetown University Press), Chapters 4 and 6.

_____ and Thomas Husted (2011) "Fiscal Incentives for Decentralized Aid Management", paper presented at American Society for Public Administration (ASPA) conference, Baltimore.

_____ and Thomas Husted (2017) *International Public Policy Analysis* (New York: Routledge).

_____ and Jun Ma (2015) "The Risks of Chinese Subnational Debt for Public Financial Management", *Public Administration and Development*, Volume 35, pp. 129–139.

_____ and James D. Savage (2022) *Comparative Public Budgeting: Global Perspectives on Taxing and Spending, 2nd edition* (Cambridge: Cambridge University Press).

_____ and Stoigniew J. Sitko (2004) "Planning, Budgeting and Health Care Performance in Ukraine", *International Journal of Public Administration*, Volume 27, #10, pp. 767–798.

_____, William Loehr and Jorge Martinez-Vazquez (1997) *Fiscal Decentralization: A Methodology for Case Studies*, CAER Discussion Paper #3 (Cambridge, MA: Harvard Institute for International Development).

H

Hammerich, Kai and Richard P. Lewis (2013) *Fish Can't See Water: How National Culture and Can Make or Break Your Corporate Strategy* (New York: Wiley).

Hancock, Tom (2023) "Taxing China", *Bloomberg BusinessWeek*, 6-19, p. 26.

Haskel, Jonathan and Stian Westlake (2022) *Restarting the Future, How to Fix the Intangible Economy* (Princeton, N.J.: Princeton University Press).

Harrison, Lawrence E. (1985) *Underdevelopment as a State of Mind: The Latin American Case* (Lanham, MD: Center for International Affairs).

Heritage Foundation (2022) "Tax Revenue % GDP by Country".

Hill, Matthew and Borges Nhamirre (2023) "Reviving Dreams of Gas Riches", *Bloomberg Businessweek*, 6-12, pp. 30–31.

Hilton, James (2021) *Goodbye Mr. Chips* (London: Sanage Publishing).

Hirschman, Albert O. (1964) *The Strategy of Economic Development* (New Haven, CT: Yale University Press).

_____ (1965) "Obstacles to Development: A Classification and a Quasi-Vanishing Act" in AOH (1971) *op.cit.*

_____ (1965) *Development Projects Observed* (Washington, DC: Brookings Institute).

_____ (1971) *A Bias for Hope: Essays on Development and Latin America* (New Haven, CT: Yale University Press).

Hirschman, Albert O. and Richard Bird (1971) "Foreign Aid: A Critique and a Proposal", in Albert O. Hirschman (eds) *A Bias for Hope: Essays on Development and Latin America* (New Haven, CT: Yale University Press).

Hockstader, Lee (2023) "Europe Has a Monuments Problem of Its Own", *The Washington Post*, 2–9.

"Hometown Heroes", (2023: www.ukraineaid.group – Dennis DeSantis 9215 Jeffery Road Great Falls, VA 22066 703-759-0165, June.

Hughes, Thomas (2008) *Tom Brown's Schooldays* (London: Oxford University Press).

I

Inglehart, Ronald (1988) "The Renaissance of Political Culture", *American Political Science Review*, Volume 82, pp. 1203–1230.

International Center for Human Development (ICHD) (2006) *Citizen's Participation in Local Government Budget Policy Development: A Case Study on Involving Citizen's Voice into the Policy-Making Process* (Yerevan: ICHD; Budapest: Local Government and Public Services Reform Initiative).

K

Kai Hammerich and Richard P. Lewis (2013) *Fish Can't See Water: How National Culture and Can make or Break Your Corporate Strategy* (New York: Wiley).

Kaplan, Seth (2017) "Risk Cascades and How to Manage Them", *The American Interest*, Volume XII, #4 (March/April), p. 109.

Kennicott, Philip (2022) "Putin's Brutality against Ukraine Complicates Our Appreciation of Russian Culture", *The Washington Post*, 12-18, pp. E2–E3.

Kligaard, Robert (2020) *Bold and Humble, How to Lead Public-Private Citizen Collaboration with 5 Success Stories* (Bhutan: Royal Institute for Strategic Studies).

Klitgaard, Robert E. (2022) *Bold and Humble, How to Lead Public-Private Citizen Collboration, with Five Success Stories* (Bhutan: Royal Institute for Governance and Strategic Studies).

Koehn, Peter H. and James N. Rosenau (2010) *Transnational Competence: Empowering Professional Curricula for Horizon-Rising Challenges* (Boulder, CO: Paradigm Publishers).

L

Levy, Brian (2014) *Working with the Grain, Integrating Governance and Growth in Development Strategies* (New York: Oxford university Press).

Lovejoy, Thomas (1984) "Aid Debtor Nation's Ecology", *The New York Times* Opinion https://www.nytimes.com/1984/10/04/opinion/aid-debtor-nations-ecology.html

M

Markey, Daniel (2016) "Subcontinental Drift", *The American Interest*, Volume XII, #1, pp. 88–90.

Maugham, W. Somerset (1963) "The Outstation", in *Collected Short Stories*, Volume 4, (London: Penguin), pp. 338–366.

Meier, Gerald and James E. Rauch (eds) (2005) *Leading Issues in Economic Development, 8th edition* (New York: Oxford University Press).

Michel, R. Gregory (2001) *Decision Tools for Budgetary Analysis* (Chicago, IL: Government Finance Officers Association of Canada and the US, GFOA), pp. 59, 77.

Mikesell, John L. (2011) *Fiscal Administration, Analysis and Applications for the Public Sector, 8th edition* (Boston, MA: Wadsworth), pp. 653–654.

Mokyr, J. (2018) *A Culture of Growth: The Origins of the Modern Economy* (Princeton, N.J.: Princeton University Press).

Mollett, Howard (2023) "Promoting Local Aid", *Economist* (letter), June 23, p. 15.

Morwitz, Scott (2023) "AT&T New Job Plan My Bring Job Cuts", *Bloomberg BusinessWeek*, 6-19, p. 14.

Mummolo, Jonathan (2023) "Don't Give Up on Diversifying the Police", *The Washington Post*, 2-5, p. A23.

Mundell, Robert (1961) "A Theory of Optimum Currency Union Areas", *American Economic Review*, Volume 51, #4, pp. 665–675.

N

Naipaul, Vidiadhar (1967) *The Mimic Men* (London: Penguin) (this one is already in the reference list) Downs, Anthony, Inside Bureaucracy (Boston: Little Brown).

_____ (1969) *The Mimic Men* (London: Penguin), p. 103.

_____ (1981) *The Return of Eva Peron and the Killings in Trinidad* (New York: Vintage).

Nemtsova, Anna (2023) "Ukraine Reveals Its Secret Weapon: Self Scrutiny", *The Washington Post*, 8-19-23, p. A19.

North, Douglass C. (1990). *Institutions, Institutional Change and Economic Performance* (New York: Cambridge University Press).

North, Douglass C., John Wallis and Barry R. Weingast (2009) *Violence and Social Orders: A Conceptual Framework for Interpreting Recorded Human History* (New York: Cambridge University Press).

_____ and Stephen Webb (eds) (2013) *In the Shadow of Violence: The Problems of Development in Limited Access Order Societies* (New York: Cambridge University Press).

Norton, Brian (2019) "Past Tension: Why We Should Read Works That Offend Us", *New York Times*, Volume 1, #13, p. A15.

O

"*Oppenheimer*" (1980) 7-part BBC TV mini-series.

P

Petersen, John E. and Wesley C. Hough (1983) *Creative Capital Financing for State and Local Governments* (Chicago, IL: Government Finance Officers Association of Canada and the U.S), p. 83.

Pilcher, W. William (1972) *The Portland Longshoremen: A Dispersed Urban Community* (New York: Holt, Rhinehart and Winston).

Pressman, Jeffrey and Wildavsky, Aaron (1984) *Implementation 3rd Edition Revised and Expanded* (Berkeley: University of California Press).

Pushkin, Alexander (2007) *Boris Godunov and Other Dramatic Works* (London: Oxford World's Classics).

Putnam, Robert D. (1993) *Making Democracy Work, Civic Traditions in Modern Italy* (Princeton, N.J.: Princeton University Press), pp. 156–157.

_____, Robert Leonardi and Raffaella Y. Nonetti (1993) *Making Democracy Work: Civic Traditions in Modern Italy* (Princeton, N.J.: Princeton University Press).

Pye, Lucian W. and Sidney Verba (1965) *Political Culture and Political Development* (Princeton, NJ: Princeton University Press, republished 2105 by Princeton Legacy Library).

R

Rainey, Melissa (2023) "I'm Leavin' It", *Bloomberg Businessweek*, 1-9, pp. 35–41.

Raudla, R. (2013) "Estonian Budgetary Policy during the Crisis: How Explain the Outlier?", *Public Administration*, Volume 91, #1, pp. 32–50.

_____, Aleksandrs Cepilovs, Vytautas Kuokštis, and Rainer Kattel (2018) "Fiscal Policy Learning from Crisis: Comparative Analysis of the Baltic Countries." *Journal of Comparative Policy Analysis*, Volume 20, #3, pp. 288–303.

Reynolds, Justin (2017) "Training Wreck", *The American Interest*, Volume XII, #4 (March/April), p. 95.

Riggs, Fred A. (1964) *Administration in Developing Countries: The Theory of Prismatic Society* (Boston, MA: Houghton-Mifflin).

Rodik, Dani (2009) "Diagnostics before Prescription", *Journal of Economic Perspectives*, Volume 24, #3, pp. 33–44.

S

Sayre, Wallace (1958) "Public and Private Management: Are They Alike in All Unimportant Aspects?", *Public Administration Review*, Volume 18, #2, pp. 102–105.

Sen, Amartya (1999) *Development as Freedom* (New York: Anchor).

Shell in Nigeria: CSR and the Organi Crisis, Pew Foundation, Georgetown University Institute for Development Studies GUISD Case # 267, 1995.

Snyder, Timothy (2022) "By Denying a Ukrainian Culture, Putin Flattens His Own", *The Washington Post*, 4-10, p. B1.

Soberman, Richard M. (2008) "Transportation in Toronto", in George M Guess (ed) *op. cit., Managing and Financing Urban Public Transport Systems, an International Perspective* (Budapest: Local Government Initiative of the Open Society Institute), pp. 189–223.

Staronova, Katarina (ed) (2007) *Training in Difficult Choices: Five Public Policy Cases from Slovakia* (Bratislava: Institute of Public Policy).

Stendhal (2004) *The Red and the Black* (1830) (New York: Modern Library), p. 254.

Strindberg (August, 1985) *Miss Julie and Other Plays* (New York: Oxford University Press), *Preface*, p. 58.

Summers, Lawrence, Philip Zelikow and Robert Zoellick (2023) "There's Justice in Giving Ukraine $300b in Russian Assets", *The Washington Post*, 3-22, p. A24.

Sweeney, Paul and Dean McFarlin (2011) International Management: Strategic Opportunities and Cultural Challenges (Routledge)

T

Taylor, Frederick Winslow (1911) The Principles of Scientific Management.

Tertz, Abram (Andrey Sinyavskiy) (1965) *The Trial Begins* and *On Socialist Realism* (New York: Vintage).

Turque, Bill and Alexis MacGillis (2007) "A Barrelful of Evidence for a Tunnel Through Tysons" *The Washington Post*. https://www.washingtonpost.com/archive/local/2007/02/01/a-barrelful-of-evidence-for-a-tunnel-through-tysons/2b9d6948-f229-4007-bc1b-794d4a253b6d/

U

United Nations (2012) *Millennium Development Goals and Beyond* (New York: UNDP).

V

van Hall, Albert, (2004) "Case Study: The Inter-Ethnic Project in Gostivar", in Nenad Dimitrijevic and Petra Kovacs (eds) (2004) *Managing Hatred and Distrust: Prognosis for Post-Conflict Settlement in Multiethnic Communities in Former Yugoslavia* (Budapest: Local Government and Public Service Reform Initiative of the Open Society Institute), pp. 187–205.

Velu, Chandler *et al.* (2023) *Economist* "The Business of Economics" (letter), p. 14.

W

Washington Post Editorial Board Opinion (2023) "21st-Century Editors Should Keep Their Hands Off of 20th-Century Books", 6-14, p. A22.

Watts, Cedric (1987) "Introduction" to James Joyce (1987)", in *Ulysses* (London: Wordsworth), p. xxxii.

Webne, Ted (2019) "Reducing the Population of Stray Dogs in Ukraine" Capstone Paper, Schar School of Policy and Government (Fairfax, VA: George Mason University).

Weick, Karl E. (1979) *The Social Psychology of Organizing* (Reading, MA: Addison-Wesley).

Williamson, Oliver E. (1981) "The Economics of Organization: The Transaction Cost Approach", *American Journal of Sociology*, Volume 87, #3, pp. 548–577.

World Bank (2005) ***Current Issues in Fiscal Reform in Central Europe and the Baltic States*** (Washington, DC: IBRD).

X

Xavier, J. (1998) "Budget Reform in Malaysia and Australia Compared", ***Public Budgeting and Finance***, Volume 18, #1, pp. 99–118.

Z

Zimbardo, Philip and Ebbson Ebbe (1970) ***Influencing Attitudes and Changing Behavior*** (Reading, MA: Addison- Wesley).

Index

For Product Safety Concerns and Information please contact our EU
representative GPSR@taylorandfrancis.com
Taylor & Francis Verlag GmbH, Kaufingerstraße 24, 80331 München, Germany

www.ingramcontent.com/pod-product-compliance
Ingram Content Group UK Ltd.
Pitfield, Milton Keynes, MK11 3LW, UK
UKHW020933180425
457613UK00013B/337